Innovative Finance for Technological Progress

Innovative businesses and startups contribute to job creation, economic growth, and technological advancement in most countries. Finance helps nurture innovative firms like startups. Unfortunately, most startups and innovative projects cannot secure finance through the usual and conventional methods.

This book goes beyond traditional financing to explore innovative ways to help finance startups and novel businesses. The book covers institutional innovation, innovation in products and processes, and the recent progress in financial innovations in various countries through empirical and case studies. It gives an in-depth look at regulatory, policy frameworks, and risk assessments for financial innovations. It also assesses the role of various innovations, including Fintech, machine learning, big data, scoring models, credit databases, digital platforms, credit guarantees in funding startups, and novel technologies.

This book offers valuable insights into how policymakers can nurture a more conducive ecosystem for startups and technologies through innovative finance.

Farhad Taghizadeh-Hesary is an associate professor of economics at Tokai University in Japan. In addition, he is a vice-president and co-founder of the International Society for Energy Transition Studies (ISETS). He is a recipient of the Excellent Young Researcher status from the Ministry of Education of Japan (MEXT). He is also a visiting professor at Keio University (Japan), the Technology Studies Institute (Iran), Chiang Mai University (Thailand), and a distinguished research fellow at the University of Economics Ho Chi Minh City (Vietnam). Currently, he serves as the editor-in-chief of the *Journal of Environmental Assessment Policy and Management* and as an associate editor/board member of several scholarly journals. His research credits include authoring more than 250 academic journal papers and book chapters and editing 15 books published by Springer Nature, Routledge, World Scientific, and Asian Development Bank Institute. Dr. Taghizadeh-Hesary holds a PhD in economics from Keio University with a scholarship from the government of Japan (MEXT).

Roohallah Aboojafari is an assistant professor of science and technology policy and director of the knowledge-based economy department at the Technology Studies Institute of Presidency in Iran. He is also an advisor on knowledge-based economy to the Minister of Economic Affairs and Finance of Iran. He has taught as an assistant professor at various universities in Iran, including Amirkabir University and Imam Sadiq University. His research area includes innovation economics, financing innovation, and science and technology policy. He is a referee of several journals in Iran, including *Innovation Management* (ISC) and *Technology Development Management* (ISC). He has authored more than 30 peer-reviewed academic journal papers and book chapters published by academic publishers, including Routledge and Asian Development Bank Institute. Dr. Aboojafari is the founder of Etemad Co., a knowledge-based credit rating company in Iran as well as a vice-chairman of the board of a fintech company under Iran's stock exchange regulations. Dr. Aboojafari holds a PhD in sciences and technology from Tarbiat Modares University in Iran.

Naoyuki Yoshino is professor emeritus of Keio University in Tokyo, Japan, and Director of the Financial Research Center (FSA Institute, Government of Japan). He obtained a PhD from Johns Hopkins University in 1979, where his thesis supervisor was Sir Alan Walters (United Kingdom Prime Minister Margaret Thatcher's economic adviser). He worked as an assistant professor at the State University of New York at Buffalo, visiting scholar at the Massachusetts Institute of Technology (United States), visiting scholar at the Central Bank of Japan, and visiting professor at the University of New South Wales (Australia) and Fondation Nationale des Sciences Politiques (France). He was the dean and CEO of the Asian Development Bank Institute in Tokyo (2014–2020). Dr. Yoshino received honorary doctorates from the University of Gothenburg (Sweden) and Martin Luther University of Halle-Wittenberg (Germany). He was also conferred the Fukuzawa award from Keio University for his contribution to research.

Banking, Money and International Finance

28. **The Digital Disruption of Financial Services**
International Perspectives
Edited by Ewa Lechman and Adam Marszk

29. **The Economics and Finance of Commodity Price Shocks**
Mikidadu Mohammed

30. **Artificial Intelligence and Big Data for Financial Risk Management**
Intelligent Applications
Edited by Noura Metawa, M. Kabir Hassan and Saad Metawa

31. **The Role of Crises in Shaping Financial Systems**
From the Global Financial Crisis to COVID-19
Małgorzata Iwanicz-Drozdowska, Elżbieta Malinowska-Misiąg, Piotr Mielus, Paweł Smaga, and Bartosz Witkowski

32. **Insurance Market Integration in the European Union**
Slawomir Ireneusz Bukowski and Marzanna Barbara Lament

33. **The Economics of Financial Services in Emerging Markets**
Measuring the Output of the Banking and Insurance Industries
Bhagirath Prakash Baria

34. **Innovative Finance for Technological Progress**
Roles of Fintech, Financial Instruments, and Institutions
Edited by Farhad Taghizadeh-Hesary, Roohallah Aboojafari and Naoyuki Yoshino

35. **Understanding the Polish Capital Market**
From Emerging to Developed
Edited by Marek Dietl and Dariusz Zarzecki

For more information about this series, please visit: www.routledge.com/series/BMIF

Innovative Finance for Technological Progress

Roles of Fintech, Financial Instruments, and Institutions

Edited by
Farhad Taghizadeh-Hesary, Roohallah Aboojafari, and Naoyuki Yoshino

Routledge
Taylor & Francis Group
LONDON AND NEW YORK

First published 2023
by Routledge
4 Park Square, Milton Park, Abingdon, Oxon OX14 4RN

and by Routledge
605 Third Avenue, New York, NY 10158

Routledge is an imprint of the Taylor & Francis Group, an informa business

British Library Cataloguing-in-Publication Data
A catalogue record for this book is available from the British Library

ISBN: 9781032115115 (hbk)
ISBN: 9781032115122 (pbk)
ISBN: 9781003220220 (ebk)

DOI: 10.4324/9781003220220

Typeset in Galliard
by codeMantra

Contents

Figures

Tables

Contributors

Roohallah Aboojafari is an assistant professor of science and technology policy and director of the Knowledge-Based Economy Department at the Technology Studies Institute of Presidency in Iran. He is also an advisor on the knowledge-based economy to the Minister of Economic Affairs and Finance in Iran.

Parisa Alizadeh is an assistant professor of technology management and the head of the Economics and Science, Technology and Innovation Financing research group at the National Research Institute for Science Policy (NRISP) in Iran.

Sakib Bin Amin is an associate professor of economics at the School of Business and Economics (SBE), North South University (NSU) in Bangladesh.

Nguyen Ba Binh is an associate professor of law and dean of the faculty of international trade & business law at Hanoi Law University in Vietnam. He is also an arbitrator of the Vietnam International Arbitration Centre (VIAC) in Vietnam.

Phadet Charoensivakorn is a senior executive vice president of National Credit Bureau Co., Ltd, in Thailand.

Lee Chin is an associate professor of economics at the School of Business and Economics, Universiti Putra Malaysia in Malaysia.

Esra Alp Coskun is a post-doctoral researcher at the Department of Economics of Middle East Technical University in Turkey.

Yener Coskun is an associate professor in finance at the Capital Markets Board of Turkey and visiting lecturer at TED University in Turkey.

Mahsa Darehshiri is a PhD student of business administration with a specialization in finance at the American University of Sharjah in UAE.

Dharish David is an associate faculty at the SIM-GE University in Singapore. He teaches courses relating to political economy.

Mahdi Dehghani is a researcher at the Technology Studies Institute of Presidency in Iran.

Kiarash Fartash is an assistant professor of science and technology policy at Shahid Beheshti University in Tehran, Iran. He is an advisor to government agencies on foresight, science, and technology (S&T) monitoring and evaluation, as well as S&T indicators and statistics.

Vajhollah Ghorbanizadeh is an associate professor of public administration and head of the department of management and accounting at Allameh Tabataba'i University in Iran.

Zamon Haldarov is the first deputy director at the Institute of Forecasting and Macroeconomic Research in Uzbekistan.

Juhi Jannat is an economics graduate from the School of Business and Economics (SBE), North South University (NSU) in Bangladesh.

Takhaui Kamzabek is a PhD candidate at The University of Sydney Business School in Australia.

Ikboljon Kasimov is the head of the foreign economic activities research department at the Institute of Forecasting and Macroeconomic Research in Uzbekistan. He is also lecturing econometrics at Tashkent State University of Economics in Uzbekistan. He is a PhD candidate at Zhejiang University in China.

Farhan Khan is a graduate economics student at the School of Business and Economics (SBE), North South University (NSU) in Bangladesh.

Mahatab Kabir Khandaker is an economics student at the School of Business and Economics (SBE), North South University (NSU) in Bangladesh.

Seyed Ali Fatemi Khorasgani is a PhD in technology management from Allameh Tabataba'i University in Iran.

Ali Nazemi is an assistant professor of economics at Kharazmi University in Iran and Chief Investment Officer (CIO) of the Iranian National Innovation Fund (INIF).

Lan H. Nguyen is deputy director of the international department of Credit Risk Database (CRD) Association and CRD Business Support Ltd. Her main experience is in credit risk modeling, machine learning for alternative data, and financial data analysis.

Vali Parsaie is an investment analyst at the Iranian National Innovation Fund (INIF) and a member of the investment committee at Pishraft venture capital fund.

Mohsen Rahmati graduated from the University of Tehran in finance management and is a board member of Iran Farabourse and the Central Securities Depository of Iran.

Cedric Rimaud is an expert in climate finance and green bonds. He has been consulting for Climate Bonds Initiative, the Asian Development Bank, the United Nations, and other non-for-profits, in addition to his current role as a fund manager in Singapore.

Megumi Sagara is a director of the international department of CRD Association and CRD Business Support Ltd. She has about 15 years of work experience in building credit scoring models and internal rating models for financial institutions.

Hayot Berk Saydaliev is the head of the macroeconomics department at the Institute for Forecasting and Macroeconomic Research under the Ministry of Economic Development and Poverty Reduction of Uzbekistan and an affiliated research fellow at Tashkent State University of Economics in Uzbekistan.

M. Subramanian is a senior advisor, independent consultant, and visiting faculty at Bharathiar University in India.

Seyed Habibollah Tabatabaeian is an associate professor of technology management at the School of Management and Accounting of Allameh Tabataba'i University and the head of the Technology Studies Institute of Presidency in Iran.

Farhad Taghizadeh-Hesary is an associate professor of economics at the School of Global Studies and a member of the TOKAI Research Institute for Environment and Sustainability (TRIES) of Tokai University in Japan. He is a vice president and co-founder of the International Society for Energy Transition Studies (ISETS) in Australia.

Andrew Terry is a professor of business regulation at the University of Sydney Business School and an Emeritus Professor at the University of New South Wales in Australia.

Sanjana Bernadette Williams is a project research associate at the Economic Research Institute of ASEAN and East Asia (ERIA) in Indonesia.

Pornchai Wisuttisak is an associate professor of economic law at the faculty of law and is an assistant to the president of Chiang Mai University in Thailand.

Naoyuki Yoshino is a professor emeritus of Keio University in Japan and director of the Financial Research Center (FSA Institute, Government of Japan). He was the dean and CEO of the Asian Development Bank Institute in Tokyo (2014–2020).

Acknowledgments

We are grateful to the Iran National Innovation Fund (INIF), especially to the president and chairman of INIF, Dr. Ali Vahdat, for his support of this book project. We also thank Professor Naoto Yoshikawa (Tokai University, Japan); Dr. Siavash Malekifar (INIF, Iran); Dr. Mehran Mahramian Moallem (Central Bank of Iran); and all the participants of the workshop titled *Innovative Finance for Technological Progress: Roles of Fintech, Financial Instruments, and Institutions* hosted by Tokai University, Technology Studies Institute, and INIF on July 5, 2021, for their comments on the presented papers. We also thank Ms Yong Ling Lam and Ms Payal Bharti of Routledge: Taylor and Francis for their help in publishing this book. We are exceedingly grateful to all contributors, without whose valuable contributions we would not have been able to finalize this book.

Introduction

Farhad Taghizadeh-Hesary, Roohallah Aboojafari, and Naoyuki Yoshino

Innovative businesses and startups play a significant role in job creation, economic growth, and technological progress in most countries. Finance is a critical constraint on the development of innovative firms like startups, most of which have difficulties accessing financing, because they lack a business credit history, which impedes lenders' assessments of their risk, and do not own valuable tangible assets to pledge as loan collateral (Taghizadeh-Hesary et al., 2021). Moreover, they are in the early stages of development and face a very high possibility of failure, which significantly raises financing and investment risk. As a result, innovative projects usually fail to access financing through conventional methods. Alternatively, venture capital is a common form of financing, used mainly in the US and several other western economies, to absorb private investment into tech-based startups. However, venture capital is not well accepted in Asia and other developing regions because of their bank-oriented financial markets. This means that Western institutions and financing solutions might not work in other regions. Bruton and Ahlstrom (2003) found that China's institutional environment for financing has significant differences from that of the West.

Startup businesses fail more often than larger enterprises; therefore, bank loans are not suitable for financing startups, as the Basel Capital Accord prevents financial institutions from lending to risky sectors. Banks need to hold more capital against assets with higher risks. Therefore, it is essential to look for innovative financing methods to ease these enterprises' access to stable and cheap financing, which will have a significant role in technological advancement, especially in developing countries.

Fintech can play an essential role in filling the funding gap of tech-based startups and other innovative firms (Muganyi et al., 2022) and be instrumental in promoting financial and social inclusion in developing countries by reducing inefficiencies in resource allocation within the banking sector and creating economic opportunities that increase financial access, social development, and technological progress (Salampasis and Mention, 2018). Fintech can also provide access to financial services for market segments that do not meet the financing threshold of large commercial banks (Makina, 2019). By leveraging advanced technologies such as big data, artificial intelligence, biometrics, and blockchains, fintech companies aim to provide financial services that are more

DOI: 10.4324/9781003220220-1

personalized, convenient, and consumer-centric than what traditional providers offer (Christensen, 2016; Drasch et al., 2018). The rapid rise of fintech has expedited the digitalization of traditional banks. By working with fintech companies, traditional banks can offer greater convenience to their consumers (Drummer et al., 2016). Traditional banks have widely adopted fintech technologies, such as biometrics, for customer authentication to enhance efficiency and security (Goode, 2018). This trend of investing in fintech is expected to make traditional banks more appealing to modern, tech-savvy consumers (PWC, 2019).

Innovative Finance for Technological Progress: Roles of Fintech, Financial Instruments, and Institutions is a book that provides 14 chapters of empirical (quantitative and qualitative) and case studies on financial innovations that facilitate innovative firms' and startups' access to funding and investment. The chapters consider three dimensions: institutional innovation, innovation in products, and processes.

The book comprises three sections. Section 1 concerns opportunities, challenges, and solutions and consists of four chapters.

In Chapter 1, Cedric Rimaud answers the question "What Are the Risks Associated with Innovative Finance and How to Cope with Them?" The recent COVID-19 crisis has been addressed through a large stimulus package, which will need to be financed by issuing new government debt. Corporations must adapt to new regulations which attempt to tackle the many challenges linked to the environment or to social inequality across the world. However, the utilization of non-financial parameters alongside more traditional financial characteristics brings new types of risks to practitioners. This chapter identifies and explores ways of coping with the risks of innovative finance.

In Chapter 2, Hayot Berk Saydaliev et al. test whether financial innovations may help construct an inclusive financial system that would eventually lead to macroeconomic stability at macroeconomic and the micro-bank levels in Kazakhstan. The estimates produced by the Generalized Method of Moments (GMM) and Dynamic Panel Threshold Model (DPT) reveal a heterogeneous effect of financial inclusion on macroeconomic stability in Kazakhstan. The first type of innovation, i.e., disruptive financial technologies that make financial services affordable and accessible, affects macroeconomic stability positively. Furthermore, inclusion tends to lead vulnerable portions of the population to mainstream financial institutions, which results in instability. Second, efficiency innovation makes financial services affordable; however, it pressures stability by shrinking the labor market. Third, sustaining innovation seems to be insignificant.

In Chapter 3, Kiarash Fartash and Mahsa Darehshiri provide an analytical comparison of incentives and supports concerning financing innovation in startups by specialized innovation financing agencies in eight countries. They also explore the variations and similarities between countries' financial support for startups and how each national innovation agency assists them. The chapter's findings demonstrate the joint attention of innovation agencies to several issues, such as supporting technological collaboration and promoting commercialization. Some agencies adopt a more comprehensive approach, while others have a less broad view of innovation in the design and implementation of financial support. The intensity and proportion of attention to supporting innovation's demand and supply sides vary. The chapter suggests that co-investment models and funding innovative projects as an investor are the notable aspects that innovation financing agencies should consider.

In Chapter 4, Ali Nazemi and Vali Parsaei assess the barriers and issues concerning implementation of intervention strategies in the venture capital markets of developing ecosystems. This chapter investigates the challenges and impediments confronting the government in developing a sustainable venture capital market. The authors present information about the current programs and practices of venture capital investments and financing offered by the Iranian National Innovation Fund (INIF) as a case study. The chapter further provides policy recommendations for enhancing the effectiveness of financing programs.

Section 2 comprises three chapters on the regulatory and policy frameworks.

In Chapter 5, Pornchai Wisuttisak et al. review the nature and operation of crowdfunding, and they examine and compare the regulatory frameworks for startup crowdfunding in selected ASEAN countries, namely Singapore, Thailand, and Vietnam. They conclude that the exciting potential that crowdfunding offers is unlikely to be fully realized without the development of an appropriate regulatory framework that facilitates its use by a startup business while offering appropriate protection to the crowd investing in it.

In Chapter 6, Sakib Bin Amin et al. discuss the essence of institutional and regulatory requirements given the current status of fintech development in Bangladesh. This chapter indicates that fintech development in Bangladesh has been skewed mostly toward mobile financial services (MFS), and other advanced fintech methods, such as peer-to-peer (P2P) lending, distributed ledger technology (DLT), crowdfunding, cloud computing, credit rating firms for startups or other innovative firms, partner financing, blockchains, etc., have not been adequately considered. The chapter reveals that such an outcome persists due to the prevailing regulatory and institutional drawbacks. By explaining the importance of institutional and regulatory requirements, the chapter proposes a framework for fintech market development in Bangladesh and other emerging economies.

In Chapter 7, Yener Coskun and Esra Alp Coskun investigate the role of government in the development of innovation. As a case study analysis, the chapter considers Turkish gaming and technology startups. The experimental analysis shows that emerging market tech startups may quickly reach global venture capital investors and increase their market value. The Turkish experience could be inspiring for other emerging market startup ecosystems, because local entrepreneurship and startup ecosystems may go global despite the lack of sound institutional support from the state.

Section 3 focuses on innovations in institutions, products, and processes: best practices and policies, and it consists of seven chapters.

In Chapter 8, Megumi Sagara and Lan H. Nguyen stress the role of the database of financial statements as a financial infrastructure to assess the creditworthiness of micro-, small-, and medium-sized enterprises (MSMEs). They introduce the application of machine learning to the credit scoring model to achieve a high-performing credit scoring tool based on a large amount of complex deposit data while complementarily evaluating traditional financial statements. The chapter discusses how to improve the model's accuracy by revising model building by applying new AI technology and alternative data.

In Chapter 9, Phadet Charoensivakorn presents the role of the National Credit Bureau (NCB) in supporting the credit decision process for financial institutions to help SMEs in Thailand access funding. In Thailand, member financial institutions use credit information from the NCB to understand the ability and willingness of SMEs to repay their debts so as to calculate appropriate credit limits for SMEs. The chapter illustrates many aspects of operations of a credit bureau, such as its support of financial institutions, the implications of credit information in its credit decision-making process, and the technology used in boosting SME financing. The study also brings up the issue of pain points and solutions to them.

In Chapter 10, Seyed Ali Fatemi Khorasgani et al. identify the role of credit guarantee schemes in funding technology-based firms in Iran. The limited efficiency of conventional methods, such as direct government financing and venture capital, has placed the focus on credit guarantee instruments in recent decades. In Iran, despite the prevalent use of credit guarantees, the total capacity of this tool is still not used. This chapter analyzes the main challenges of this system and provides policy recommendations for utilizing the role of credit guarantee schemes in filling the finance gap of tech-based SMEs and startups in developing countries.

In Chapter 11, Parisa Alizadeh and Mohsen Rahmati present an assessment of the role of the capital market in innovation finance. In recent years, the capital market has been considered a complementary source of funding for technology-based SMEs and fast-growing startups through equities, debt instruments, and collective investment vehicles. Innovative SMEs generally do not use debt instruments because of the lack of market liquidity, transparency, and sufficient rating coverage. To use the capacity of the capital market in innovation finance, an integrated mix of policies for enhancing the demand-side (SMEs), expanding the supply-side (the investor base), and improving market infrastructure to make SMEs a broader and deeper capital market are required.

In Chapter 12, Dharish David and Sanjana Bernadette Williams take a look at major trends in financial inclusion in The Middle East and North Africa (MENA) region and how fintechs play a crucial role in the remittance market. Fintechs largely depend on particular technologies that provide low-cost and scalable solutions, such as covering remittance services in the MENA region, where cross-border financial transactions are among the largest requirements for migrants who need to send back money to their families and countries of origin. Because this is an emerging area, this chapter covers several case studies of fintech working in technologies such as e-remittances, digital identification solutions, insuretech, and mobile payment solutions to provide financial inclusion to migrant workers.

In Chapter 13, M. Subramaniam explores the impact of the COVID-19 pandemic on innovative fintechs in India. In meeting the objective, the study looks back on the emergence, growth, and development of innovative fintechs, financial inclusion issues, and the impact of COVID-19 in India. This study highlights some key areas from recent research trends and focuses on the author's professional expertise in the field. The policy recommendations for fintech's future possibilities provide researchers, economists, policymakers, and financial experts with a better understanding of innovative funding and fintech in India.

In Chapter 14, Roohallah Aboojafari and Mahdi Dehghani develop a conceptual model to assess the credit risk of knowledge-based companies using quantitative and qualitative variables by employing a statistical analysis technique, namely principal component analysis (PCA). PCA results demonstrate that financial and non-financial variables are required to assess credit risk, the evaluation of which should be based on different components, including total equities, total revenues, and company age and type. Collecting financial and non-financial information and making big data aids in assessing the credit risk with higher probability.

This book is a valuable resource for researchers and policymakers of finance, technology management, technology policy, and economics. The policy recommendations are essential to accelerating the development of innovative institutions, products, and processes for filling the finance gap of new technologies.

References

Bruton GD, Ahlstrom D (2003) An institutional view of China's venture capital industry: explaining the differences between China and the West. *J Bus Ventur* 18(2):233–259. doi: 10.1016/S0883-9026(02)00079-4

Christensen CM (2016) *The innovator's dilemma: when new technologies cause great firms to fail.* Harvard Business Review Press, Brighton

Drasch BJ, Schweizer A, Urbach N (2018) Integrating the 'Troublemakers': a taxonomy for cooperation between banks and fintechs. *J Bus Econ* 100:26–42. doi:10.1016/j.jeconbus.2018.04.002

Drummer D, Jerenz A, Siebelt P, Thaten M (2016) *Fintech—challenges and opportunities. How digitization is transforming the financial sector.* McKinsey & Company, Chicago

Goode A (2018) Biometrics for banking best practices and barriers to adoption. *Biom Technol Today* 2018(10):5–7. doi:10.1016/S0969-4765(18)30156-5

Makina D (2019) The potential of FinTech in enabling financial inclusion. In: Makina D (ed) *Extending financial inclusion in Africa.* Academic Press, Cambridge, pp 299–318. doi:10.1016/B978-0-12-814164-9.00014-1

Muganyi T, Yan L, Yin Y, Sun H, Gong X, Taghizadeh-Hesary F (2022) Fintech, regtech and financial development: evidence from China. *Fin Innov* 8(29):1–20. doi:10.1186/s40854-021-00313-6

PWC (2019) *How Fintech is shaping China's financial services?* PricewaterhouseCoopers, China, Chengdu

Salampasis D, Mention AL (2018) FinTech: harnessing innovation for financial inclusion. In: Chuen DL, Deng RH (eds) *Handbook of blockchain, digital finance, and inclusion*, vol 2. Academic Press, Cambridge, pp 451–461. doi:10.1016/B978-0-12–812282-2.00018-8

Taghizadeh-Hesary F, Yoshino N, Kim CJ, Morgan PJ, Yoon D (2021) Introduction. In: Taghizadeh-Hesary F, Yoshino N, Kim CJ, Morgan PJ, Yoon D (eds) *Investment in startups and small business financing*. World Scientific, Singapore. doi:10.1142/12246

Section 1

Opportunities, challenges, and solutions

1 What are the risks associated with innovative finance and how to cope with them?

Cedric Rimaud

1 Introduction

In 2002, the International Conference on Financing for Development introduced the concept of "innovative financing for development." Building on eight international development goals established following the Millennium Summit of the United Nations in 2000, the Sustainable Development Goals (SDGs) were created. Among these goals were the eradication of hunger, universal primary education, gender equality, the reduction of child mortality, better maternal health, the fight against diseases, environmental sustainability, and global partnerships for development. These goals have now increased to 17 Sustainable Development Goals, or SDGs.

In parallel, the Paris Accord was signed on December 12, 2015, adopted by 196 parties at COP21, entered into force on November 4, 2016, and is a legally binding international treaty on climate change. While aiming to limit global warming to well below 2 degrees Celsius (preferably 1.5) compared to pre-industrial levels, it encourages climate financing that is needed for mitigation and adaptation purposes against climate change. The COVID-19 pandemic, while not strictly attributable to climate change, is thought to originate from the increased impact that humanity is having on natural habitats. This has resulted in a rapid growth of thematic financial instruments which seek an outcome beyond the traditional financial return. Bonds and loans, including green, blue, social, sustainability, pandemic, climate-aligned, ESG- and SDG-linked types have emerged as new types of financial instruments that respond to the challenges of making our world a more climate change-resilient, and beyond that, a more socially balanced place.

Any advance in the field of finance brings benefits to economic ecosystems but also new types of risks. Innovative finance holds the promise of channeling much-needed funds from developed countries to less endowed and more vulnerable communities. It also endeavors to channel finances parked in pension funds and other institutional portfolios toward projects with a positive impact on the environment to combat climate change.

Recently, the emergence of innovative finance has given birth to new financial instruments with explicit non-financial parameters. Yet, little research has been

DOI: 10.4324/9781003220220-3

conducted in this field. Market practitioners have embraced these innovations, hoping to create a new segment that responds to the objectives of their clients, themselves increasingly subject to new regulations to address environment, social, and governance (ESG) criteria, which are becoming ever more potent. Yet these instruments also give rise to new types of risks that could undermine the stability of the financial markets, which is the topic of this chapter. While regulators can establish rules to create some boundaries to these new advances, investors, financial intermediaries, and issuers must remain aware of these new types of risks, which have never before been studied.

2 The growth of thematic finance brings new types of risks

The growth of green, social, sustainability and sustainability-linked bonds and loans demonstrates a very large interest from the investor community. The Climate Bonds Initiative counted $1.7 trillion of sustainable debt issued as of the end of 2020 (Fatin, 2021). This growth has been underpinned by several market standards, which ensure that there are clear boundaries and definitions on what these instruments are financing. Investors demand that these innovative instruments be accompanied by the strictest criteria, backed by scientific evidence, to ensure that the identified projects are truly aligned with the Paris Agreement. Yet the potential for "greenwashing", defined as branding "green" an investment that is not beneficial to the environment, or "socialwashing", defined as branding "social" or "sustainable" an investment that is not beneficial to the target populations, is real, as well as the risk of abuse of such financial transfers, which often include very substantial sums.

Green, social, sustainability and sustainability-linked bonds or loans being debt instruments, it is also important that the borrowers are correctly assessed to be able to support such debt. Putting on unnecessary debt onto a weak borrower, in order to achieve some green or social objectives, is counterproductive. Contrary to foreign technical assistance, which generally does not need to be repaid, a borrowing is the promise to repay the borrowed principal. Amounts of capital available in a bond or loan format are multiple times larger than those obtainable through inter-governmental support programs. Leaving poor nations indebted as a result of this transition would be the worst possible outcome.

This chapter focuses on all the risks that innovative financial instruments bring for investees, investors, the wider economy, and the global order. It seeks to identify all areas of risk that innovative finance brings to the various stakeholders. After identifying these risks, solutions that can be used to cope with these risks are presented. The objective of this research is in no way to reduce the importance of these financial transfers, but rather, to ensure that the strong momentum in the demand for non-financial returns remains anchored in the highest possible standards of transparency, adequacy, and compliance so as to ensure that the trends will continue at a solid pace for the benefit of the world and the people who live in it.

Using desk-based research, we have built on the existing body of knowledge available. Using the most reputable sources of analysis, we first review the existing academic literature about the risks of innovative financial instruments. In a second phase, we allocate into categories these various risk types to which innovative financial instruments are subject. Third, we identify and analyze the various safeguards that exist to prevent the risks associated with innovative financial instruments. In the fourth phase, we recommend new policy tools that ought to be developed to further reduce the various types of risks that have as yet been left unaddressed. In the fifth and final part, we make recommendations, using a stakeholder mapping exercise, on which members of society must be engaged to respond to the various safeguards needed.

Financing development has become an important field of study, and several conceptual frameworks can be used to analyze the various types of techniques available to finance development: (i) the principal-agent model from the economic literature, with a principal extending financing and an agent receiving it; (ii) the governance model; (iii) the contractual framework; (iv) hybrid frameworks (Davis, 2008).

The issuance of thematic bonds has grown very quickly since 2014, when the International Capital Markets Association (ICMA) first released its "Green Bond Principles." According to the Climate Bonds Initiative (CBI, 2021),

> total volumes for the labeled sustainable debt market – including labeled green, social, and sustainability (GSS) bonds, sustainability-linked bonds (SLB), and transition bonds – reached nearly half a trillion (USD496.1bn) in the first half of 2021. This amount represents 59% year-on-year growth from the equivalent period in 2020.

This brought the cumulative total labeled issuance to USD2.1 trillion at the end of June 2021, including USD1.3 trillion of green bonds (Climate Bonds Initiative, 2021).

In a speech she gave during her tenure as Vice President and Treasurer of the World Bank (Oteh, 2018), Arunma Oteh justified innovative finance as "achieving the sustainable development goals (SDGs) by 2030 will require $3.9 trillion to be invested in developing countries each year." She went on to explain that the issuance of innovative finance instruments will benefit from the fact that, "Investors like these products because they are able to maximize social good and at the same time maximize financial returns." Yet, the field has not yet totally defined of what should be included and what should be excluded. Reporting on non-financial parameters is inherently complex (Baret and Helfrich, 2019). Regulators, in particular, will be interested to put boundaries on what innovative finance must cover. The regulation of innovative finance is a major question that can foster or hamper its development. The strong growth of sectors in many underdeveloped economies is a testament to the fact that loose regulation is conducive to greater innovation. When governments try to regulate, they often create unfair competition and work against the sustainability of microfinance institutions (Lin and Sung, 2017).

3 New types of risks associated with innovative finance

Many types of risks are associated with new innovative finance instruments. Investors often cite credit risk as their primary concern when deciding whether to deploy capital. Liquidity risk can be higher for these new types of instruments, as they are often placed among holders with extra-financial objectives. Finding similarly minded investors is not always easy. A risk of undervaluation also exists, as the transfer price can differ significantly from the reference valuation because of the specific nature of the underlying assets. Currency risk remains a key driver of international investment. Very often, the green, social and sustainable capital is sourced from developed economies and channeled toward emerging ones with foreign exchange risk a key concern. Interest rate risk, similarly, is to be considered. Volatility risks can be high as well, as vulnerable emerging economies are more often prone to bouts of volatility, affecting their currency and interest rate. Low levels of compliance create an additional level of risk for investors, as the target investees often lack the required reporting systems and data management processes to correctly comply with all levels of disclosure, to which international investors are accustomed.

Climate change's impacts are being felt by the poorest nations of Africa, Southeast Asia, the Pacific, and Latin America. It is often the nations the less capable of mitigating the harm and adapting to change that are the most badly hit by severe heat waves, rising sea levels, high winds, the melting of glaciers, insect plagues, etc. Sustainable finance can bring vital sources of capital to create more resilient societies. Yet the promise of new sources of financing for climate-resilience projects in the developing world could also be abused. To be mobilized at scale, financial flows need the highest environmental, social, and governance (ESG) standards to convince global investors that the non-financial objectives can truly be met.

Traditionally, financial instruments are evaluated in terms of well-known associated risks, such as liquidity, interest rate, currency, volatility, and valuation. Innovative finance has introduced new parameters, most of which are non-financial in nature. In so doing, it has created new externalities, which we propose to review in the following sections.

3.1 New advances in innovative finance require further conceptual frameworks

By mobilizing the trillions of US dollars currently parked in low-yielding financial instruments, financing development appears to be an attractive proposition. Yet traditional conceptual frameworks do not always apply to the objectives of innovative finance. Existing frameworks need to be adapted, and development is highly context-specific (Davis, 2008).

In the principal-agent model, the relationship between the privileged party (in the traditional framework, the principal) and the agent (the borrower) is reversed for innovative finance. As Davis observes, "In the development context, though, it is not so clear that the interest of financiers deserves to be privileged over those of recipients" (Davis, 2008). There is a need to carefully evaluate how these interests align, and how the legal claims made by each party (e.g., to be repaid for the lender versus to protect fundamental rights of decent living conditions for the borrower) can be treated.

In a governance framework, innovative finance creates a need to establish new rules between institutions providing development financing and organizations, often not-for-profit, providing outcomes that are only loosely related to financing (Davis, 2008). For example, microfinance is often administered outside the traditional boundaries of consumer lending regulations, while being financed by investors that are themselves regulated. Attempts to establish limits on interest rates or subsidize regulated entities that compete with microfinance lenders often prevent microfinance from becoming self-sustainable (Lin and Sung, 2017).

The need for solid contracts highlights the risks associated with both principal-agent and governance models. A number of such examples can be listed (Davis, 2008): the enforceability of donors' pledges or the resolution of disputes in foreign courts, public policy or breach of authority, the applicability of special interpretations in case of ambiguity, and to protect weaker parties. As Davis explains, however, because of contractual agreements, "events that precede or follow the life of any agreement and actors who are not parties to any agreement become peripheral." Innovative finance seeks to encompass a holistic set of outcomes which often go beyond contractual terms.

3.2 Risks associated with non-financial parameters

All over the world, regulators have started to implement new rules to force listed firms to report on non-financial parameters. For example, the Securities and Exchange Board of India (SEBI) issued in May 2021 a circular to force the top 1,000 listed companies by market capitalization to report on new sustainability-related items. The Securities and Exchange Commission requires company boards to publish a sustainability report that meets domestic and international standards in Thailand. The Singapore Stock Exchange (SGX) has recently announced plans to make the Task Force on Climate-Related Financial Disclosure (TCFD) mandatory for SGX-listed companies (Janssen, 2021). Although more disclosure is generally considered a good thing, allowing investors to better assess the performance of their investments, this creates new areas of concern.

Stolowy and Paugam (2018) investigated the definition of non-financial reporting and its recent growth and found a significant increase in non-financial reporting between the early 2000s and 2015–2016 in South Africa, the United States, and Europe. They noted that there was a variety of underlying concepts and a large number of channels used for reporting non-financial information. They found that firms sometimes reported in their annual report, in a separate 'sustainability' report, as CSR, or integrated reports. They also found evidence that firms changed the title of their reports over time. This variability of reporting can create confusion and makes it difficult for investors to correctly assess the information that is made available to them. A report by the Financial Reporting Faculty in 2013 (ICAEW, 2013) had already pointed to "widespread complaints of information overload in financial reporting." The addition of non-financial to existing financial reporting can add an additional "overload" in the information made available to market participants. More than 100 ESG standards have emerged over the last two decades, which can also create too many options for users.

Finding the right balance between too much and not enough information is difficult. In an article published in the Harvard Business Review, Simon MacMahon (2020), Head of ESG Research at Sustainalytics (an ESG and corporate governance research consultancy), acknowledged that "creating the [ESG] ratings is challenging work. There are no uniform requirements for reporting ESG information, and many environmental and social impacts are hard to measure." For every company in each of 138 industries, a list of relevant environmental, social, and governance risks is drawn. From this, the researchers try to evaluate "how well a company is managing its risk exposure. This involves looking at types of programs, policies, and management practices." Mr MacMahon is recognizing that this work, based mostly on survey questionnaires sent to the management of these firms, often complain of "survey fatigue." The risk is that an analyst, whose role it is to assess how strong these "programs, policies, and management practices" actually are, may not be able to correctly evaluate them. This assessment is very different from an accounting standard, which auditors can use to assess the financial accuracy of items in financial reporting such as revenues, costs, and inventories.

In a paper titled "Fixing ESG: are mandatory ESG Disclosures the Solution to Misleading Ratings?" (El-Hage, 2021) J. El-Hague describes instances where inconsistent methodologies can find different results for the same company, while current disclosures can mislead the market. Research from Florian Berg, cited by Mr El-Hague (Nauman, 2019), shows that ESG ratings from different sources are aligned in only about six out of ten cases compared to creditworthiness ratings, which match 99% of the time.

Furthermore, most ESG disclosures are not audited, unlike financial reporting. There is likely to be a strong incentive by companies reporting on ESG scores to portray favorably their policies and programs to achieve a higher ESG rating. Some biases have also been reported: by size (larger companies have better ESG ratings than smaller ones), by geography (European companies rank higher than North American ones), and by industry, and tend to fail to identify risks, such as the Volkswagen deception of using tools to beat official emissions-testing software, while maintaining a higher ESG rating than its peer average (ESG, 2018).

3.3 Risks associated with regulatory oversight

In April 2021, the Securities and Exchange Commission (SEC) of the United States issued a risk alert on "The Division of Examinations' Review of ESG Investing" (ESG, 2021). Noting the growth in investment products and financial services with ESG factors, the SEC noted the proliferation of references to ESG factors by practitioners looking to "enhance performance and manage investment risks" as well as "provide higher returns or result in better ESG-related outcomes." In its review, the SEC noted some weaknesses in internal controls for investment advisors and funds. Of particular concern was whether market participants are accurate in their description of ESG products and in their use of ESG-related terminology. The SEC points out in a footnote that Advisers Act Section 206 "imposes a fiduciary duty on investment advisers to provide full and fair disclosure of all material facts relating to the advisory relationship and to provide advice that is in the best interest of the client." Similarly, the SEC examines regulatory filings, websites, reports to sponsors, client presentations, responses to due diligence questionnaires, requests for proposal, and client/investor-facing documents including marketing materials with respect to any claims of ESG characteristics. This also included any commitment to follow any framework, such as the Principles for Responsible Investment ("UNPRI") or the Sustainable Development Goals ("UN SDGs"). The SEC also reviews the written policies and procedures, compliance rules, and ESG practices and disclosures.

In its risk alert, the SEC warned that its staff identified some "potentially misleading statements regarding ESG investing processes and representations regarding the adherence to global ESG frameworks." In particular, it found that there were some "compliance programs that did not appear to be reasonably designed to guard against inaccurate ESG-related disclosures and marketing materials." A very closely watched example is that of Deutsche Bank's asset manager DWS which, in August 2021, came under the investigation of both the US SEC and the Justice Department for allegedly giving a false representation of its ESG credentials, when it claimed that half of its assets under management ($900 billion in size) were subject to ESG criteria.

Among the most important risks identified by the SEC are: (i) portfolio management practices inconsistent with disclosures about ESG approaches; (ii) inadequate controls to maintain, monitor, and update clients' ESG-related investing guidelines, mandates, and restrictions; (iii) proxy voting inconsistent with advisers' stated approaches; (iv) unsubstantiated or otherwise potentially misleading claims regarding ESG approaches; (v) inadequate controls to ensure that ESG-related disclosures and marketing are consistent with the firm's practices; (vi) inadequate compliance programs; and (vii) limited knowledge of compliance personnel.

Nowhere more than in the European Union have new advances in regulatory oversight focused on extra-financial criteria. The Non-Financial Reporting Directive (Directive EU, 2010) updated an earlier accounting directive (Hertog, 2015) to review the rules on disclosure of non-financial and diversity information by an estimated 11,700 companies with more than 500 employees on matters such as (i) environmental matters, (ii) social matters and the treatment of employees, (iii) the respect of human rights, (iv) anti-corruption and bribery, and (v) diversity on company boards in terms of age, gender, educational and professional backgrounds. Additional guidelines by the European Commission

(Financial Stability, 2019) added more rules for disclosure of environmental and social as well as climate-related information. It was further complemented by the adoption in April 2021 of a proposal for a corporate sustainability reporting directive (CSRD) (Financial Stability, 2021) and the proposed adoption in 2022 of new EU sustainability reporting standards. The Taxonomy Regulation was published in June 2020 and entered into force in July 2020 to establish the basis for EU taxonomy with six environmental objectives: (i) climate change mitigation, (ii) climate change adaptation, (iii) the sustainable use and protection of water and marine resources, (iv) the transition to a circular economy, (v) pollution prevention and control, and (vi) the protection and restoration of biodiversity and ecosystems. The Sustainable Finance Disclosure Regulation (European Union, 2019) came into effect in 2021 to guide the disclosure requirements of financial products and services offered in the European Union. The Shareholders Rights Directive II that came into force in June 2017 focuses on additional disclosure requirements on directors' remuneration, shareholders, related party transactions, intermediaries' obligations, and transparency. The review of MiFID and UCITS/AIFMD also supplements the various pieces of legislation that add to the mix of rules related to non-financial parameters.

The Securities and Markets Stakeholder Group of ESMA along with the European Securities and Markets Authority released in September 2020 a statement (SMSG, 2020) warning of the risks associated with ESG disclosures. It noted that new pieces of legislation have contributed to the increased sustainability of the European Union economy, but it warns that "neither the timings nor the concepts of these different pieces of legislation are fully synchronized or aligned with one another." For example, it noted that "the social indicators (…) are underdeveloped compared to the environmental indicators."

3.4 Risks associated with conflicts of interest

In a report published by IOSCO (2020) in September 2020, its members pointed to several areas where conflicts may arise between the intermediary and its issuer clients and between the intermediary and its investor clients, such as: (i) the pricing of debt securities, (ii) related risk management transactions, (iii) the quality of information to investors, and (iv) the allocation of debt securities. The report identified four key risks and potential harms in the debt capital raising process: pricing, risk management transactions, quality of information, and allocations.

Regarding pricing, an arranger may have an incentive to price a transaction in a way that benefits its interests rather than those of the issuer or the investor, resulting in the under- or over-pricing of the security. Thematic instruments are currently priced at levels that sometimes differ from that of similar instruments, despite having similar characteristics. The business of issuing fixed income securities for corporate clients is a major source of revenue for investment banks. The Climate Bonds Initiative reported (GBULT, 2020) in H1 2020 that four banks (BofA, Citi, JP Morgan, and BNP Paribas) helped issue more than USD4bn green bonds in the first six months of 2020, while another six banks contributed to more than USD3bn each over the same period (Morgan Stanley, Credit Agricole, Barclays, ING, Société Générale, and HSBC). In a study (Joffe, 2015) on the costs of issuing municipal bonds, Marc Joffe found that the average issuance cost of a municipal bond varies between 1.23% (for issues larger than $10m) and 2.71% (for issues lower than $10m). The incentives to portray thematic bonds in a favorable light are likely to be high to convince issuers to go to market.

Regarding risk management transactions, IOSCO indicates that "conflicts of interest could potentially arise from risk management transactions (RMTs), causing idiosyncratic movements in reference rates, which could, in turn, compromise the integrity and efficiency of both the reference rates and the pricing of new debt instruments." For example, the German government issued identical securities on September 3, 2020, one labeled "green" and another, identical security labeled conventional. The order book for the green security received EUR33bn in demand and was priced one basis point lower than its "conventional" twin (Ravindirane, 2020). In a paper (Green Bond Pricing, 2021), the Climate Bonds Initiative noted that "the German green Bund priced with a "greenium" maintained a lower yield in the secondary market, and exhibited lower volatility compared to its vanilla twin." It is possible, using short-selling practices, to benefit from this pricing difference. According to the ICMA (ERCC Publications, 2022), short-selling is an essential function performed in the financial market by market-makers, hedgers, and traders. By selling the expensive Bund and buying the cheaper one, a trader can derive a riskless profit. The market for euro-denominated repurchase agreements (or "repos") was estimated at EUR8,285bn on December 9, 2020, by ICMA (2021). The use of automatic trading systems (27.1% of the total trading in December 2020) allows these transactions to be easily executed, and 18% of the transactions are said to be executed on an anonymous basis. If a large number of traders were to execute similar transactions, however, the price difference would correct over time and the riskless arbitrage opportunity would disappear. The persistence of the pricing difference, as noted by the Climate Bonds Initiative, is a sign that there are other factors at play. Some investors may hold these thematic instruments for their non-financial charactderistics, rather than for the financial objective. One could argue that the hypothesis of perfect markets, in this case, would not be satisfied.

Regarding the quality of information, innovative finance includes additional disclosures for the process of issuing securities that have non-financial features embedded in them. For example, green bonds, if they are aligned with the Green Bond Principles published by the International Capital Markets Association (ICMA), are required to have a so-called "green bond framework" which lists the types of capital expenditures that the issuer will fund with the capital it has raised. This green bond framework is reviewed by a third party called the "verifier," which will issue a second-party opinion report, an assurance report, or a verification report, as the case may be. In some instances, the verification report can lead to certification against the Climate Bond Standard run by the Climate Bonds Initiative (CBI) using specific, publicly available criteria of its taxonomy.

The issuance may be followed by an additional "post-issuance" report (in the case of the certification scheme run by the CBI). Each year until maturity, the issuer of the green bond must report on the use of proceeds, in particular on how it has allocated the proceeds to the planned investments. Through this process, more information is made available to investors, and transparency is increased.

IOSCO highlights the quality of information as a potential risk for a security issued with insufficient information. In the case of innovative financing, the information made available to investors has been greatly expanded. For example, in "use of proceeds" instruments, a list of assets to be financed is specified. Only for these assets will investors be explained exactly how their capital will be deployed. For "Sustainability-Linked" instruments, certain performance targets are a condition for some financial rewards. The risk with these new instruments is that investors rely on the opinion provided by second-party opinion providers with the false confidence that the "green" proceeds are a sound investment. These providers, however, only give an opinion on whether the assets being financed are "green," and not whether they are a good economic value or whether their cash flows will allow the repayment of the debt. Arguably, these instruments are a debt obligation of the issuer, and their creditworthiness is analyzed by the rating agency through the credit rating process. As investors appear to demand more of such instruments, there is a risk that they may choose innovative instruments for their non-financial rather than financial characteristics.

As IOSCO points out, there is sometimes insufficient time to consider disclosures and evaluate the information provided to investors. A bond issuance may sometimes be announced in the morning and priced in the afternoon, leaving relatively little time for a thorough review of the extra disclosure provided by the issuer. This is a fair concern, as the alignment of green or social securities with economic objectives is a new field that remains unexplored, and it is likely that investors will have little understanding of how a labeled security may align with economic and return objectives. They will rely on arranging banks to disclose sufficient information to make an educated opinion on these non-financial parameters.

Another area of concern regarding the quality of the information is the risk of connected research, where some conflicts of interest may exist, as there is pressure to portray research in a favorable light to support the issuance of thematic bonds. In particular, there is an increasing focus on the so-called "transition to net-zero carbon emissions" for issuers. As thematic instruments have become very popular with investors, there is a risk that arrangers publish supporting research that sets a transition strategy for an issuer that does not correctly reflect the true path that the issuer is likely to take. The industry has also seen the emergence of new consultancies, for example, the so-called "verifiers," who attest to the alignment of capital expenditures with green bond standards without a proven expertise in the technologies that they are reviewing. There is a risk that, in pursuit of business, these verifiers may publish opinions that are favorable to the issuer. IOSCO noted in its analysis that "the conflict of interest risk may be amplified when investment decisions are typically taken very quickly, particularly on transactions involving a frequent issuer" (IOSC, 2020). Thematic issuance is currently going at a very strong pace. Many maiden green, social, or sustainability bonds are issued by issuers that already have issued bonds in the markets. While a thematic bond may be considered a bond that is similar to other bonds issued by the issuer, to win a mandate, arrangers may rush through the process and take shortcuts. For example, the first sustainability-linked bond issued in Singapore by Surbana Jurong in February 2021 (Jurong, 2021) did not provide investors with the usual second-party opinion that investors have come to expect for such thematic issuance. Strictly speaking, the sustainability-linked bond principles (SLBP, 2020) do not require such a report, but it has been a good practice to accompany a thematic bond with such a review. The consulting firm PwC provided an assurance report, but this was rather succinct.

IOSCO also points to the risk that information on a specific issuance may be provided selectively to investors, who are often invited to a roadshow by invitation only. In the case of thematic securities, arrangers may have an incentive to direct the information on non-financial characteristics to investors that have a mandate to allocate more of their investments to such themes, while disclosing less to more traditional investors. As a result, the information provided to investors may be biased with non-financial disclosure being biased toward investors who have a tilt toward non-financial objectives.

Regarding allocations, IOSCO points to the risks that the bond issuance process may give higher allocations to specific investors based on their relationship with the intermediary. Investors who are more actively trading in the secondary markets may be preferred. Investors connected to the financial intermediary or who have contributed to the price discovery process may be given advantageous access. In the case of innovative finance instruments, there is a risk that arrangers may give a higher allocation to investors that have a declared strategy to invest in thematic instruments. These investors may be consulted early in the process for the arranger to better understand how to structure the thematic bond issuance so that it aligns with the green, social, or sustainability objectives of such investors. The strong demand from investors appears to be skewing the issuance process toward what practitioners have been calling a "greenium" or "socium," i.e., a lower yield than conventional securities, because of their non-financial characteristics. Issuers will judge arrangers in their ability to drive this pricing advantage, as it reduces the cost of debt for the borrower. An incentive exists for the arranger to allocate more of the proposed thematic securities to investors who will accept a lower yield in exchange for specific non-financial characteristics. The arranger will be able to better judge which investors are more likely to accept a lower than usual yield during the price discovery process, when they discuss with the investors what types of non-financial characteristics they would be looking for.

IOSCO also points to the likelihood of such conflicts of interest being mitigated by documented allocations policies, the disclosure of relationships between the arranger and its clients, the oversight by a control function, a regular review of allocation decisions, or a limit on fees. Thematic securities represent only 1%–2% of the total size of bonds issued globally, yet the total size is already approaching $2trn. While it is likely that the issuance of thematic bonds will appear small, within the total book of business of a global investment bank, the control functions may be less effective in ensuring that these particular securities are not subject to the conflicts highlighted above. The market is very young, having become a significant business over the last three to five years. Whether all control functions are aware of all the risks associated with them in the large and the less large investment banks remains to be seen.

3.5 Risks associated with strong demands by investors

In a recent article, the Bank of International Settlements (BIS) noted that "the pre-GFC [Great Financial Crisis] growth and size of the private label MBS [Mortgage-Backed Securities] market are comparable with those recently observed for ESG mutual funds and ETFs." They support their observations with examples from the financial markets themselves: high price-to-earnings ratios of clean energy companies, rich valuations in credit markets, and lower premiums for financial instruments supporting environmental (greenium) or social (socium) objectives. Researchers at Amundi (Bennani et al., 2018), a large asset manager, have looked at ESG data over the period from January 2010 to December 2017 and found that the evidence is mixed. Between 2010 and 2013, "Introducing ESG scores in stock picking strategies would have led to neutral or negative results" and "from a risk management perspective, we observe a negative impact of ESG screening on drawdowns in the Eurozone and a neutral impact in North America." However, they also found that between 2014 and 2017, "most indicators turned positive," particularly regarding governance.

In an article on strategic asset allocation (Bekkers et al., 2009), the authors distinguish ten different investment categories to determine the optimal investment portfolio, building on early papers from Markowitz (1952), who started the Modern Portfolio Theory. They compute a market portfolio across these ten asset classes based on a mean-variance model. However, innovative finance is pushing investors into areas that are adding selection criteria outside of a mean-variance model. The issuance of green, social, and sustainability bonds began, for the most part, within the last five years. The timeframe is insufficient to compute reliable variance numbers on the prices of such securities, as there is insufficient data for deriving such measures. When investors build their portfolios, giving an increased weight to non-financial parameters, they are forced to make allocation decisions that deviate from the mean-variance model. In its publication on the pricing of green bonds, the Climate Bonds Initiative indicated that green bonds tend to exhibit lower volatility than conventional instruments. There may be some deviations from historical correlations because of the strong demand by investors for ESG-themed investments. The correlation calculation must usually be made on a long period to correct trending biases in the underlying data sets. Given that innovative finance is relatively new, having emerged as a meaningful market segment over the last five years, any correlation calculation with other asset classes is likely to be inaccurate. The research team at Amundi Asset Management also noted that "by imposing a too strong ESG excess score, the optimized portfolio is increasingly constrained, implying that the diversification decreases." Investors with a thematic bias will be exposed to a reduced investment universe, which may distort their ability to build an optimal investment portfolio.

4 Expected policy implications

Policy formulation can help develop safeguards to counteract the negative side effects caused by the rapid rise in innovative financial instruments. The growth of innovative finance needs to be accompanied by specific policies to correct any biases that may arise because of the strong growth currently seen in the markets. Security regulators have released specific policies to guide market participants in shaping the markets. For example, the International Capital Markets Association has released a number of guidelines for green (GBP, 2021), social (SBP, 2021), and sustainability (SBG, 2021), as well as sustainability-linked (SLBP, 2020) bonds along with a Handbook for Climate Transition Finance (ICMA, 2020). The European Union has been advancing its regulations through its EU Taxonomy for Sustainable Activities (2022). China has developed a series of regulations, including a Green Bond Catalogue (Green Finance Platform, 2020). Beyond the existing policies that have already been deployed throughout the world to organize the market for thematic instruments, a number of additional areas could be further developed. The same regulations are needed for what constitute acceptable outcomes for social and governance-related objectives.

4.1 New conceptual frameworks

It is necessary to develop new research areas to correctly assess the relationships between all parties when it comes to innovative finance. Links must be established between the objectives of a profit-driven investor and a series of non-financial outcomes embedded in innovative financial transactions. Academics can use existing frameworks and further develop new considerations for ESG products to expand the body of knowledge that will drive more robust financial markets going forward. The Anthropocene Fixed Income Institute (www.anthropocenefii.org), launched in July 2020, is a non-profit research institute that takes a markets-based approach to bring more transparency to the thematic bond market. Some of its research focuses on using new pricing techniques that measure the price of the embedded options in sustainability-linked instruments.

4.2 Addressing the ESG measurement dilemma

The field of ESG research is relatively new, and the abundance of methodologies calls for efforts to converge toward a few market standards which have been tested and found to be more robust. This is not so different from the methodologies of credit rating agencies, which do include not only financial but also non-financial evaluations to form a view on the creditworthiness of a borrower. By making ESG reporting mandatory across firms (for example, for those listed on an exchange), regulators can also steer the market toward specific methodologies, thus forcing market practitioners to adopt similar evaluation tools. Over time, the defaults in the methodologies will be tested by events and will converge toward a stronger set of rules.

4.3 *Addressing the complexity of extra-financial reporting*

The report by the ICAEW (2013) proposed to reform the process for setting disclosure requirements. Among others, it suggested: (i) Disclosure requirements should be structured to reflect a balancing of interests; (ii) they should allow firms to differentiate between the various needs of different users, with mainstream information provided in a concise format; (iii) unnecessary disclosure should be weeded out; (iv) firms should be encouraged to minimize the quantity of immaterial disclosures; (v) auditors should encourage firms to omit immaterial disclosures; (vi) enforcement agencies and auditors should reform their approach to materiality; and (vii) there should be more communication between preparers and users regarding voluntary public disclosure of information rather than relying on market-wide standards for new disclosure requirements.

4.4 *How to address the complexity of regulatory oversight*

The plethora of standards that have emerged over the years to address concerns over non-financial criteria has resulted in a complex playing field for participants in the financial markets. Some attempts are underway to create harmony among regulatory approaches. For example, China and the European Union have worked together to find a common ground for setting the standard for financial markets and their approach to climate finance through a taskforce on sustainable finance taxonomies (Azizuddin, 2020). Such efforts should be encouraged to minimize the disparity of various standards.

4.5 *How to address conflicts of interest*

To protect investors, new policies should be designed to ensure that investors are assessing investment opportunities with careful consideration of financial and non-financial criteria. New ways to evaluate the interaction between non-financial criteria must be developed. Rating agencies, in particular, should update their methodologies to reflect the impact that "net zero carbon" strategies designed by borrowers are included in the credit risk evaluation process that support credit ratings. ESG consultancies, particularly those selling ESG data to investors, must ensure that they develop high integrity levels in the ratings they design. Any conflict of interest must be rooted out. The ESG ratings must be tested over time to ensure that they correctly reflect actual strategies and that any biases are identified early on.

4.6 *Addressing risks associated with strong demands from investors*

Many financial innovations have been met with strong demands, which can sometimes result in excesses, bubbles, and market crashes. One such example of the recent past was the emergence of credit derivatives as a powerful tool to distribute credit risks among a larger universe of investors. The emergence of such instruments may have been the cause of the Great Financial Crisis. The very large interest from global investors for ESG instruments carries similar risks that could lead to another "bubble," as the BIS recently warned (Behrmann, 2021). To address these risks, constant monitoring of strong and easy-to-read reporting standards is needed. Investors must carefully apply ESG factors in their investment selection process to ensure that they make their decisions independently and correct for any reliance on third-party data.

4.7 *How to address risks associated with a reduced investable universe*

The market must continue to grow and diversify to allow investors a large choice of investment opportunities. As the market expands, the share of instruments that have ESG features will increase, improving the universe of ESG investable assets. Researchers and risk managers must be encouraged to develop new sets of data series (mean variance, correlations, etc.) to allow investors to create a portfolio that optimizes risk and return consistently. Regular back-testing must be performed to ensure that risk managers have the tools needed to identify risk areas.

5 Conclusion and policy recommendations

We have reviewed the various risks that are emerging out of the rapid rise of innovative finance as a new segment of the financial industry. From the need for new conceptual frameworks to new safeguards to ensure that ESG data is correctly measured, with a layer of complexity that comes from extra-financial reporting and the need for regulatory oversight, it is necessary to develop new ways to ensure that potential conflicts of interest are minimized, while the strong upswing in investors' demand for innovation may lead to incorrect valuations and a reduction of the investable universe. Future research areas must include the analysis of new frameworks, the methodologies to evaluate ESG outcomes, the design of economic policies that ensure a sound growth for the market, and new ways of incorporating ESG parameters in portfolio construction. Using new approaches, a careful approach in the design of regulatory frameworks and constant monitoring of potential excesses, the market will be able to capitalize on these new advances and build on the strong foundations already laid down.

References

Azizuddin K (2020) Available at: https://www.responsible-investor.com/articles/eu-and-china-to-co-chair-international-taskforce-on-sustainable-finance-taxonomies

Baret P, Helfrich V (2019) The "trilemma" of non-financial reporting and its pitfalls. *J Manag Gov* 23(2):485–511. doi:10.1007/s10997-018-9430-z

Behrmann N (2021) Available at: https://www.businesstimes.com.sg/banking-finance/bank-for-international-settlements-warns-of-green-asset-bubble-risk (Accessed on Aug 26, 2022)

Bekkers N, Doeswijk R, Lam T (2009) Strategic asset allocation: determining the optimal portfolio with ten asset classes. *J Wealth Manag* 12(3):61–77. doi:10.3905/jwm.2009.12.3.061

Bennani L, Le Guenedal T, Lepetit F, Ly L, Mortier V, Roncalli T, Sekine T (2018) How ESG investing has impacted the asset pricing in the equity market. *Amundi Asset Manag*. doi:10.2139/ssrn.3316862

CBI (Climate Bonds Initiative) (2021) Sustainable Debt Market Summary H1 2021. Available at: https://www.climatebonds.net/files/reports/cbi_susdebtsum_h12021_02b.pdf (Accessed on Aug 26, 2022)

Davis KE (2008) 'Financing development' as a field of practice, study and innovation. *NYU Law and Econ Res Paper*, 08–61:08–65. doi:10.2139/ssrn.1341291

Directive EU (2010) 63/EU of the European Parliament and of the Council of 22 September 2010 on the protection of animals used for scientific purposes. *Off. J. Eur. Union*, 276:33–79. Available at: https://ec.europa.eu/info/business-economy-euro/company-reporting-and-auditing/company-reporting/corporate-sustainability-reporting_en#overview

El-Hage J (2021) Fixing ESG: are mandatory ESG disclosures the solution to misleading ESG Ratings? *Fordham J Corp Fin L* 26:359

ERCC Publications (2022) Available at: https://www.icmagroup.org/Regulatory-Policy-and-Market-Practice/repo-and-collateral-markets/icma-ercc-publications/frequently-asked-questions-on-repo/30-what-is-short-selling-and-what-is-the-role-of-repo/ (Accessed on Aug 26, 2022)

ESG (2018) How VW Paid $25 Billion for "Dieselgate"—and Got Off Easy, Propublica, February 2018. Available at: https://www.propublica.org/article/how-vw-paid-25-billion-for-dieselgate-and-got-off-easy (Accessed on Aug 26, 2022)

ESG (2021) The division of examinations' review of ESG investing. Available at: https://www.sec.gov/files/esg-risk-alert.pdf (Accessed on Aug 26, 2022)

EU Taxonomy for Sustainable Activities (2022) Available at: https://ec.europa.eu/info/business-economy-euro/banking-and-finance/sustainable-finance/eu-taxonomy-sustainable-activities_en (Accessed on Aug 26, 2022)

European Union (2019) Regulation (EU) 2019/2088 of the European Parliament and of the Council of 27 November 2019 on sustainability-related disclosures in the financial services sector. *OJEU*, 1–114, http://data.europa.eu/eli/reg/2019/2088/oj (Accessed on Aug 26, 2022)

Fatin L (2021) Climate bonds initiative, sustainable debt: global state of the market 2020. Availableathttps://www.climatebonds.net/resources/reports/sustainable-debt-global-state-market-2020

Financial Stability (2019) Financial Services and Capital Markets Union. Available at: https://ec.europa.eu/info/publications/non-financial-reporting-guidelines_en (Accessed on Aug 26, 2022)

Financial Stability (2021) Financial Services and Capital Markets Union. Available at: https://ec.europa.eu/info/publications/210421-sustainable-finance-communication_en#csrd

GBP (The Green Bond Principles) (2021) Available at: https://www.icmagroup.org/sustainable-finance/the-principles-guidelines-and-handbooks/green-bond-principles-gbp/ (Accessed on Aug 26, 2022)

GBULT (Green Bonds Underwriters League Table) (2020) Available at: https://www.climatebonds.net/resources/league-table (Accessed on Aug 26, 2022)

Green Bond Pricing in the Primary Market H2, Climate Bonds Initiative (2021) Available at: https://www.climatebonds.net/resources/press-releases/2021/03/climate-bonds-releases-green-bond-pricing-report-h2-2020-greenium (Accessed on Aug 26, 2022)

Green Finance Platform (2020) Available at: https://www.greenfinanceplatform.org/policies-and-regulations/peoples-bank-china-green-bond-endorsed-project-catalogue-2020-edition

Hertog E (2015) Directive 2010/64/EU of the European Parliament and of the Council on the Right to Interpretation and Translation in Criminal Proceedings: transposition strategies with regard to interpretation and traduction

ICAEW (2013) Financial reporting disclosures: market and regulatory failures, ICAEW financial reporting faculty, financial reporting faculty. Available at: https://www.icaew.com/-/media/corporate/files/technical/financial-reporting/information-for-better-markets/frd-final.ashx (Accessed on Aug 26, 2022)

ICMA (International Capital Market Association) (2020) Climate transition finance handbook. Available at: https://www.icmagroup.org/sustainable-finance/the-principles-guidelines-and-handbooks/climate-transition-finance-handbook/ (Accessed on Aug 26, 2022)

ICMA (2021) European repo market survey. Available at: https://www.icmagroup.org/News/news-in-brief/icma-publishes-landmark-40th-survey-of-the-european-repo-market/ (Accessed on Aug 26, 2022)

IOSC (2020) Conflicts of interest and associated conduct risks during the debt capital raising process, International Organization of Securities Commissions, FR08/2020. Available at: https://www.iosco.org/library/pubdocs/pdf/IOSCOPD661.pdf (Accessed on Aug 26, 2022)

Janssen P (2021) South-east Asia catches the sustainability bug. Available at: https://www.thebanker.com/Sustainability/South-east-Asia-catches-the-sustainability-bug (Accessed on Aug 26, 2022)

Joffe M (2015) Doubly bound: the costs of issuing municipal bonds. UC Berkeley: Othering & Belonging Institute. Available at: https://escholarship.org/uc/item/0qh2n6n3 (Accessed on Aug 26, 2022)

Jurong S (2021) Available at: https://surbanajurong.com/sjconnects/surbana-jurong-breaks-new-ground-with-public-sustainability-linked-bond-issuance/ (Accessed on Aug 26, 2022)

Lin J, Sung J (2017) Comparative study of the regulatory framework on microfinance. *J Basic Appl Res Biomed* 3(2):53–58

MacMahon S (2020) The challenge of rating ESG performance. *Harvard Business Review*. Available at: https://hbr.org/2020/09/the-challenge-of-rating-esg-performance (Accessed on Aug 26, 2022)

Markowitz HM (1952) Porfolio selection. *J Finance* 7(1) 77–91. doi:10.12987/9780300191677

Nauman B (2019) Credit rating agencies join battle for ESG supremacy. *Financial Times*. Available at: https://www.ft.com/content/59f60306-d671-11e9–8367-807ebd53ab77 (Accessed on Aug 26, 2022)

Oteh A (2018) Leveraging innovative finance for realizing the sustainable development goals, World Bank. Available at: https://www.worldbank.org/en/news/speech/2018/05/15/leveraging-innovative-finance-for-realizing-the-sustainable-development-goals (Accessed on Aug 26, 2022)

Ravindirane J (2020) German sovereign innovates with its Bund's inaugural green twins, Natixis, Sep 2020. Available at: https://gsh.cib.natixis.com/our-center-of-expertise/articles/german-sovereign-innovates-with-its-bund-s-inaugural-green-twins (Accessed on Aug 26, 2022)

SBG (2021) (The Sustainability Bond Guidelines) Available at: https://www.icmagroup.org/sustainable-finance/the-principles-guidelines-and-handbooks/sustainability-bond-guidelines-sbg/ (Accessed on Aug 26, 2022)

SBP (2021) (The Social Bond Principles) Available at: https://www.icmagroup.org/sustainable-finance/the-principles-guidelines-and-handbooks/social-bond-principles-sbp/ (Accessed on Aug 26, 2022)

SEBI (2021) Business responsibility and sustainability reporting by listed entities. Available at: https://www.sebi.gov.in/legal/circulars/may-2021/business-responsibility-and-sustainability-reporting-by-listed-entities_50096.html (Accessed on Aug 26, 2022)

SLBP (2020) (The Sustainability-Linked Bond Principles) International Capital Market Association. Available at: https://www.icmagroup.org/sustainable-finance/the-principles-guidelines-and-handbooks/sustainability-linked-bond-principles-slbp/

SMSG (2020) Advice on ESG disclosure, September, Ref. ESMA22–106–2858. Available at: https://www.esma.europa.eu/sites/default/files/library/esma22-106-2858_smsg_advice_on_esg_disclosure.pdf (Accessed on Aug 26, 2022)

Stolowy H, Paugam L (2018) The expansion of non-financial reporting: an exploratory study. *Account Bus Res* 48(5):525–548

2 Financial inclusion, financial innovation, and macroeconomic stability

Hayot Berk Saydaliev, Takhaui Kamzabek, Ikboljon Kasimov, Lee Chin, and Zamon Haldarov

1 Introduction

A systemic crisis in a financial market has a substantial adverse effect on macroeconomic stability and economic growth. Specifically, financial instability has had dramatic consequences, such as high unemployment and inflation, volatility in exchange rates, and unsustainable debt levels, jeopardizing progress toward the MDGs (Cotter and Suurlaht, 2019; Danisman and Demirel, 2019). Numerous initiatives, such as the implementation of financial inclusion and the formation of the Financial Stability Board, were prioritized to increase the financial system's stability (Casu et al., 2014; Čihák et al., 2016). Financial inclusion has been promoted through different international institutions, including the World Bank, under the objective of universal financial access, the United Nations' Sustainable Development Goals, the Global Partnership for Financial Inclusion, and the Maya Declaration (Čihák et al., 2016; Klapper et al., 2016). With a goal of "Build resilient infrastructure, promote inclusive and sustainable industrialization, and foster innovation," the SDG 9 are targeted to "increase the access of small-scale industrial and other enterprises, particularly in developing countries, to financial services, including affordable credit, and their integration into value chains and markets." Academics and policymakers have paid special interest to financial inclusion, as it could be an essential driver of macroeconomic stability. Financial inclusion translates into providing access to affordable financial products and services to different population segments, especially for vulnerable sections such as low-income groups, by official financial intermediaries. It intends to integrate financially excluded populations into the financial system and facilitate the access and use of financial services. These services include transfers to credit, insurance, savings, and payments (Hannig and Jansen, 2010). Maintaining financial inclusion, therefore, is a prerequisite for macroeconomic stability.

The literature on financial inclusion has put forward three main channels through which financial inclusion can affect macroeconomic stability. First, by extending existing loans and increasing credit supply, financial expansion deteriorates the loan portfolio quality, undermining banking system stability in countries with weak financial sector supervision (Khan, 2011; Sahay et al., 2015). Second, financial inclusion tends to improve banking system stability through

DOI: 10.4324/9781003220220-4

loan diversification, as more individuals and businesses help mitigate the financial risks (Khan, 2011; Le et al., 2019; Morgan and Pontines, 2014). The third view advocates that the expansion of financial inclusion (through financial innovations) might bolster credit supply coupled with the velocity of money, balancing the supply and demand for finance during the rapid fixed investment growth that follows the displacement. However, the rapid growth of demand for credit may lead to rising interest rates and source "financial instability" (Fisher, 1933; Kindleberger, 1978; Minsky, 1977).

Overlooking the financial inclusion and macroeconomic stability relationship may result in financial exclusion and systemic crises (Čihák et al., 2016). The importance of increasing empirical estimations on the financial inclusion and macroeconomic stability nexus has been highlighted in numerous studies, such as Morgan and Pontines (2014). Likewise, Demirguc et al. (2017) emphasized the need for improving our understanding of the advantages of financial inclusion as well as the significance of tailored financial products and services. Still, the existing literature lacks a comprehensive theoretical explanation of whether financial inclusion results in financial system stability and the drawback of the imbalance in financial innovations.

This chapter aims to bridge this gap by examining the effects of financial inclusion on macroeconomic stability. It is argued that financial inclusion is tightly linked to financial innovation sources utilized by banking systems; hence, it depends on which financial innovation is spread over financial institutions and the economy. Even though innovation has been comprehensively studied in an organizational and industrial context, it still has an implicit role in macroeconomics studies. This paper is rooted in the findings of (Christensen et al., 2019), where fundamentally, three types of innovations are at play. First, *disruptive innovation* (or *new market)* is the new business model innovation that makes unavailable products affordable and accessible, so many more people can access them. The second type is *sustaining* (or *incremental) innovation,* which denotes incremental modifications in traditional business models which have a limited effect on job creation. The third type is *efficiency innovation,* which implies making products affordable and accessible by eliminating assets through automation and operational excellence. For those reasons, we argue that prominent institutions and robust contract enforcement factors are significant for accessing and using various financial institution services and investigating the impact of remittances and institutional quality on financial inclusion.

This chapter has both theoretical and methodological contributions. Theoretically, the prior literature does not take the nonlinear relationship between financial inclusion and macroeconomic stability into account. Considering the types of innovation, the current study makes the following contributions: First, the study links the innovations in banking systems with macroeconomics stability by stating that the accessibility of financial services does not necessarily mean financial stability. It deploys the term innovations from organizational contexts to a much broader macroeconomic system, whereby macroeconomic stability depends not on quantity invested in financial innovations but on a balance of proposed innovations. To do so, this study reveals some significant findings. The first type of innovation, disruptive financial technologies that make financial services affordable and accessible, has a positive effect on stability. Furthermore, inclusion tends to trigger the enrollment of vulnerable population segments in mainstream financial products and services, leading to instability. Second, efficiency innovation makes financial services affordable; however, it pressures stability by shrinking the labor market. Third, sustaining innovation seems to be insignificant. Another contribution is using the GMM and DPT estimation methods to explain the interplay of those financial technologies.

The remainder of the chapter is structured as follows. Section 2 provides a review of the related literature. Section 3 reports the methodology, description of data, and empirical models. The empirical findings and discussions are presented in Section 4, and Section 5 concludes the chapter with policy recommendations.

2 Literature review

The stability of monetary and financial systems is an essential element with a crucial role in the effective functioning of the market economy, because macroeconomic stability provides an avenue for rational decision-making concerning timely real resources allocation, enhancing savings, and the investments environment. Instability in the financial system, however, creates uncertainties that may give way to resources being misallocated and the readiness to participate in intertemporal contracts being reduced. A financial system is considered stable when the markets and institutions that make up the said system are functioning smoothly. If a market is stable but institutions are unstable, the financial system's stability may still be threatened. Achieving monetary and financial stability is among the essential features of a well-functioning market economy, which helps shape the decision-making mechanism related to timely real resources allocation, promoting a suitable environment for savings and investments. Theoretically, the opportunity to deal with the financial sector's risk depends on the financial systems' specific properties, particularly on the financial system's structure. The economic-financial structure affects the competition between financial markets and banks, which establishes various inducements and opportunities for risk management (Crockett, 1996). The performance of the banking system and the probability of crises may also depend on the degree and structure of the development of financial systems, which is one of the principal concerns of financial inclusion. This relationship based on comparative financial systems theory is described as financial competition, which corrodes the chances to be involved in inter-temporal risk activities (Allen and Gale, 2004).

Most of the research on financial stability focused on the causes and significances of financial instability. These two views contemplate what caused opposing financial instability in Minsky (1977) and Kindleberger (1978) systems. Based on their assertion that cyclical excess leads to crash, it is argued that the process commonly begins when promising events start bidding up asset prices. They argue that rises in prices stimulate people to purchase more assets (bandwagon effects), and the expected profits influence speculators to finance more purchases on margin. Finally, when the prices reach overvalued stage or some external shocks occur that affect market confidence and lead to a deterioration of prices, then the portfolios of borrowing based on financial intermediaries are affected. Monetarists, such as Friedman and Schwartz (2008), believed that financial instability occurs because of distractions created by the inappropriate mechanism of money supply; therefore, in the monetarist's view, financial instability is related to the effectiveness of the monetary phenomenon. The improper implementation of monetary policy could lead to instability, causing minor distractions in the financial system. It was discussed that financial intermediaries gradually eliminate agency friction and transaction costs through their distinct functions and aid in eliminating market failure (García and José, 2016). In the same study, the authors pointed out that financial inclusion does not necessarily reduce the screening and monitoring that cause financial instability, but rather it eliminates market imperfections (such as new lending technologies reducing transaction costs or improving the identification of borrower and diminishing information costs) by enhancing monetary supply. Later, the scholars empirically tested and found support for the significant association between financial inclusion and macroeconomic stability (Danisman and Tarazi, 2020; García and José, 2016; Le et al., 2019; López and Winkler, 2019) as well as between economic growth (Chuc et al., 2021; Huang et al., 2021). For example, lending to SMEs reduced non-performing loans (NPLs) as well as the default probability by financial institutions (Morgan and Pontines, 2014). Moreover, other factors, such as financial remittances, positively impacted the economic growth of low-income countries through effective financial inclusion (Chuc et al., 2021; Huang et al., 2021). As the population can retain those remittances deposited in banks, more people interact with financial institutions, enhancing the availability of credit and savings products (Chuc et al., 2021). Thus, inclusive money leads to a less pronounced drop in credit growth in economic downturns by mitigating credit boom-bust cycles (López and Winkler, 2019). Even though rapid financial inclusion (e.g., credit growth) raises the concerns of financial unsettlement or irregularity, the diversification of risks through financial inclusion aids in creating a resilient financial system (García and José, 2016), especially during financial turbulence (López and Winkler, 2019).

Nevertheless, another group of scholars found financial inclusion had a mixed effect. Evidence shows an inverted U-shaped relationship, meaning that inclusion positively affects stability under a certain threshold, and above that threshold, it is reversed (Vo et al., 2019). Thus, the scholars do not rule out the reverse effect of inclusion, wherein the studies of Koong et al. (2017) and Kouki et al. (2020) found that the expansion of business (and household) credit leads to tightening financial conditions, which further leads to instability. Kouki et al. (2020) preliminary findings, however, indicated that financial inclusion may indeed enhance stability through competition among banking services. Hence, competition contributes to higher deposit penetration (García and José, 2016), and advancements in digital payments in banking products stabilize the system.

The same authors suggested that the regulatory frameworks for banking innovations in low-income segments (young, uneducated, unemployed, disadvantaged adults living in rural areas) improve stability. Those financial service developments aid the enhancement of financial instruments and institutions, gradually encouraging financial innovativeness in the financial system in both the long- and short-run (Qamruzzaman and Wei, 2019). The emerging financial innovations introduced in the form of crowdfunding, blockchain, ICO (initial coin offering), new trading and digital advisory systems, mobile payment, artificial intelligence (A.I.), machine learning, and robot-advisor started to take central academic attention (Cai, 2018; Philippon, 2016); however, scholars debate the economic outcomes of those technologies. Initially, the Schumpeterian school distinguished innovation as a core of economic growth by arguing that individual innovation per se is sufficiently important to affect the entire economy. The main idea was that innovations result from prospects of monopoly rent, and economic growth requires creative destruction (Aghion et al., 2015; Aghion and Howitt, 1990). Recently, a group of scholars found that fintech technologies provide low-leverage solutions and require heavy equity to deploy (Anagnostopoulos, 2018; Philippon, 2016), which in turn has very similar characteristics to the theory of disruptive innovations by Christensen (Christensen, 2013; Christensen and Bower, 1996). According to Christensen, innovative products are introduced to the unserved population, and if heavy capital is invested in these innovations, economic growth will ensue (Christensen et al., 2019). Acemoglu and Autor (2011) discussed that creative task innovations per se result in increased wages, employment, and labor share. Recent data has shown that fintech technologies have led to the emergence of shadow banking organizations, which have begun to replace traditional financial intermediaries (Cai, 2018; Thakor, 2020). The share of shadow banks almost doubled between 2007 and 2015 by meeting high demand in low income, minority, and FHA borrowers in mortgages (Buchak et al., 2018) as well as SMEs (Mills and McCarthy, 2016). Also discussed was that high interest rates are another indicator of the growing popularity of these new affordable banking services (Buchak et al., 2018). Though they don't necessarily eliminate the need for traditional banks, blockchain technologies, for example, seem to reduce the intermediation layers to advance the payment process (Cai, 2018; Thakor, 2020). As the boundaries have shifted, the industry has come under siege: Fintech is not a sector of ordinary financial office occupants, and the regulator is (or should be) no longer concerned with the financial system (Anagnostopoulos, 2018).

In organizational studies, the competition between financial organizations fostered the democratization of many products or services. The literature states that organizations often face innovation ambidexterity, where there are two choices of investments. First is the investments in expansion or development of their current product portfolio, and second is searching for entirely new sources of profit (Andriopoulos and Lewis, 2009). In other words, a dilemma exists between continuing the mainstream business and looking for new customers by making products affordable and accessible (Christensen, 2013). Most organizations and individuals have been faulted for opting for the first path, which eventually led to a fall in economic growth due to a lack of new market innovation (Christensen et al., 2019; Gordon, 2017), hence falling in productivity. Gordon (2017) and Clark (2016) empirically illustrated the decrease in total factor productivity, labor productivity, and diminished impact of innovation after the 1970s. This stream demonstrated that new technologies replace human labor, which contradicted the logic of disruptive technologies. Acemoglu and Restrepo (2018a) demonstrated the interplay between the speed of automation and reinstatement. Their evidence showed that the new technologies made further automation cheaper and struggled to generate new labor-intensive tasks. The speed of automation has increased more than the technologies that create tasks. This type of technology helps financial sectors or others embody more productive (or cheap) capital, which has a substitution effect on labor. The idea findings were consistent with the notion of "efficiency innovation" from (Christensen et al., 2019), wherein firms typically maximizing efficiency tend to decrease assets and increase cash flow. The main commonality between "disruptive innovation" and "efficiency innovation" is that both offer affordable and accessible products, while the former creates jobs, but the latter eliminates them (Christensen et al., 2019). It was discussed that a stable balance exists in growth when two types of innovation move concurrently (Acemoglu and Restrepo, 2018b); however, inequality may induce instability.

In the later stage of rapid diffusion of any innovations, organizational operations tend to move incrementally and usually remain the same product as at its inception (Acemoglu et al., 2022; Hanusch and Pyka, 2007). Nevertheless, most financial institutions continue serving traditional products and rarely face dramatic changes such as mortgages. Research conceptualizes it as sustaining innovations. Evidence shows that while sustaining innovations contribute to productivity growth (Acemoglu and Restrepo, 2019), their effect is not sizeable (Christensen et al., 2019). Both authors have arrived at an analogous conclusion that new market innovations are indeed the drivers of economic growth. Sustaining innovations tend to experience diminishing returns from this previous technology (Acemoglu and Restrepo, 2019). The authors modeled this under the assumption that the extra productivity improvements produced by innovation decrease in the number of prior sustaining innovations within a previous technology cluster.

The technologies above seem to increase financial inclusion, especially reaching unserved (due to regulatory restrictions) previous borrowers, increasing the total loans. However, the outcomes of each innovation may have a heterogeneous nature. In particular, shadow banks and new business models of traditional banks usually have few regulations (Buchak et al., 2018), because regulations tend to be established based on an *ex-post* approach in detecting possible risks, and technology-led business models may foster systemic risks (Anagnostopoulos, 2018). Simultaneously, the conventional banking system operates under complex regulations and usually prefers to go incrementally or deploy efficiency innovations. As the nature of incremental innovation is predictable, the main concern touches on the interplay between efficiency and disruptive innovations.

Following the literature on efficiency and automatization, we assumed that efficiency innovation eliminates jobs, even though it makes the product accessible, which may weaken stability. Disruptive innovations may cause instability because of high credit potential, undermining loan-to-value (LTV) caps, and thus increasing the risks associated with credit (Braggion et al., 2018). In addition, disruptive technologies might cause instability because of the exponential growth of money market fund mismatches and unexpected demand deposit withdrawals (Aggarwal and Stein, 2016). Capital requirements are also rapidly becoming no longer relevant or appropriate. The algorithms may contain critical errors, as they are highly effective in quick typical decision generation when managing multiplex decision-making burdens (Anagnostopoulos, 2018).

Furthermore, we hypothesize that disruptive financial innovation that makes financial services affordable and accessible strengthens macroeconomic stability, while efficient innovations have a negative effect on it. Additionally, inclusion tends to trigger the enrollment of vulnerable population segments to the mainstream financial system, leading to instability.

3 Methodology and data analysis

3.1 Data

Data from 28 banks from 2014 to 2020 was obtained from the World Bank, the Statistics Committee, and the National Bank of Kazakhstan. The list of selected banks is provided in Table A2.1 in Appendix.

Following previous studies, such as Vo et al. (2019), our dependent variable is macroeconomic stability (M.S.); non-performing loans, stock market index, money supply, spread of Kazakh Government Treasury bills for one and ten years, money market rate spread, net international reserves, real effective exchange rate, domestic credit to private sector, crude oil price, and house price index were selected to create the macroeconomic stability index. Then, the predictive capacity of the new stability index was tested against the business cycle in Kazakhstan and employed to investigate the influence of financial inclusion on macroeconomic stability in the country. Based on the prior literature, financial inclusion, financial innovation, bank size, loan size, management quality, return on asset, and compliance are included as explanatory variables.

The primary regressor is financial inclusion (FI), which measures the inclusive financial sector of the country. FI was constructed based on the methodology used in previous studies, such as Wang and Guan (2017). Banking system penetration is used in estimations, as commercial banks have the essential leading role in providing financial services. Banking system usage is measured by bank customers' frequency and regularity of using financial services. This index was created using the number of borrowers and the number of depositors from commercial banks per 1000 adults in line with previous studies. Brue and Grant (2012) have highlighted Francois Quesnay's statement that "society was analogous to the physical organism. The circulation of wealth and goods in the economy was like blood circulation in the body. Both conformed to the natural order and both could be understood through thoughtful analysis" (p. 39). Equally, an efficient and productive financial system affordable and accessible to all population segments indicates financial stability using socially productive investment opportunities.

However, an inefficient financial system may cause financial instability because of the improper allocation of scarce resources. Studies on the association between financial inclusion and macroeconomic stability have found equivocal effects. Anzoategui et al. (2014), for example, found financial inclusion to have the capacity to boost stability by fostering savings. Exploring bank services, Pagano and Pica (2014) found positive and significant association between financial development and employment for developing economies. On the contrary, Brown et al. (2014) found financial inclusion to have a negative impact on macroeconomic stability, fostering credit supply and/or money circulation velocity and balancing financial supply and demand during fixed investment growth.

Nonetheless, rapid increases in credit demand mean that interest rates eventually rise, leading to "financial fragility." This implies that financial inclusion may not ultimately lead to macroeconomic stability. Furthermore, financial inclusion could increase credit demand and even have a dampening effect on credit markets. Hence, the inconclusive findings of the mentioned studies have motivated us to test whether or not a nonlinear relationship exists between the two indicators of financial inclusion and macroeconomic stability.

Technology innovation (fintech) is the second explanatory variable and measures innovation in terms of disruptive innovation (the number of bank products), sustain innovation, and efficient innovation (net income to employee). Prior studies, such as Anagnostopoulos (2018), reveal that technological innovations have contributed to financial development and macroeconomic stability in developing economies. For that reason, fintech is hypothesized to have a positive effect on macroeconomic stability, as it is positively associated with financial development over the long term.

To estimate the effects of fintech innovations on financial innovations for the macroeconomic stability in Kazakh banks, this study also incorporated the interaction between financial inclusion and financial innovations (FI*fintech). This is, in fact, a bullet point of this research. The necessity to address the influence of financial innovations on how financial inclusion is channeled toward macroeconomic stability was motivated by a number of previous studies, such as Stanley and Fleming (2019). They revealed that access is higher in urban locations than in rural areas, and other authors found distance to bank branches to have a negative impact on bank inclusiveness (Bouoiyour and Miftah, 2015, 2016; Bucheli et al., 2018). Access to banking services through official channels directly impacts financial inclusion and indirectly economic growth, or macroeconomic stability, by increasing earnings and consumption. This study predicted that financial inclusion along with strong financial innovations would strengthen the macroeconomic environment; therefore, the interaction term was expected to produce a positive coefficient.

This study used five control variables: (i) loan size (LSit) is the logarithm of total loans. Ideally, bigger banks have a more stable environment, as large economies of scale and capacity to invest in technology helps to achieve efficiency. Nevertheless, to the extent that the size of a bank is symptomatic of market share in deposits and loans, a positive association between bank size and macroeconomic stability is not surprising. The logarithm of total bank assets is used to proxy for (ii) bank size (BSit). Larger banks are typically linked with lower interest rate spreads, owing to economies of scale and the opportunity to invest in efficiency-improving technologies. However, a favorable association between macroeconomic stability and bank size is not surprising, given that bank size denotes market control in the deposit and lending markets. Next, (iii) management quality (MQ) is estimated as the ratio of operating income to operating expenses (management quality). Under the "bad management" hypothesis, low-cost efficiency tends to be positively associated with better macroeconomic stability in the future. Bad management is arguably linked with poor skills, especially in evaluating pledged collaterals, credit scoring, and monitoring borrowers. ROA is the return on assets (iv) and proxied by the ratio of net income to total assets. Typically, this measure is regarded as a good measure for evaluating and comparing profitability on assets between companies across the same industry. Thus, we hypothesize a positive relationship with interest rate spreads. Bank's liquid-assets-to-total-assets ratio, (v), is used to measure liquidity (LQDR). It determines the differences in vulnerability-to-liquidity risk among banks. Because of a lower liquidity premium on loans, a bank with stronger liquidity has less liquidity risk and is, therefore, more likely to be associated with lower spreads. Banks exposed to significant risk incur a high cost of borrowing emergency funds, resulting in higher liquidity premiums and spreads (Ahokpossi, 2013). Table 2.1 presents the sources of the data and expected signs of the variables. Based on extant research findings, the signs for remittances, social infrastructure, government spending on education, income, institutional quality, and the interaction term between remittances and social infrastructure were predicted to be positive.

Table 2.1 Sources of Data and Expected Signs of Variables

Dependent Variable	*Proxy*	*Source*	
Macroeconomic Stability	Created Index	Computed by authors	
Explanatory Variable	Proxy	Source	Expected sign
Financial Inclusion	Claim to loans	National Bank Kazakhstan	+/−
Financial Innovations	Fintech usage	Computed by authors	+
Bank Size	Bank Size	Kazakhstan Stock Exchange	+
Loan Size	Log of total loans	Kazakhstan Stock Exchange	−
Liquidity	Liquid assets to total assets ratio of the bank	Kazakhstan Stock Exchange	+
Return on asset	Net income to total assets	Kazakhstan Stock Exchange	+
Management Quality	Operating income to operating expenses	Statistic Committee	+
Interaction term	F.I.*FinTech	Computed by authors	+

Source: Authors' compilation.

3.2 Empirical specification

The current study uses the dynamic panel threshold method introduced by Kremer et al. (2013), built on the original panel threshold estimation technique and the cross-sectional instrumental variable (IV) threshold model of Hansen (1999) and Caner and Hansen (2004), respectively. The relationship between macroeconomic stability and financial inclusion is empirically examined using the benchmark Equation (1), where the theoretical underpinning is adapted from Merkl and Stolz (2009). Given the notion of technology innovation and macroeconomic stability from Demetriades and Law (2006) and Esanov and Kuralbayeva (2011), they conclude that innovation – disruptive financial technologies that make financial services affordable and accessible – has a positive effect on stability. Furthermore, inclusion tends to trigger the enrollment of vulnerable population segments to the mainstream financial system, leading to instability innovation; disruptive financial technologies that make financial services affordable and accessible positively affect stability. Moreover, inclusion can lead to instability because of the vulnerable portion of the population's contact with mainstream financial institutions. This view motivated us to assess the nonlinear effect of financial inclusion on macroeconomic stability and test whether more inclusive financial system leads to a more stable macroeconomic environment. The dynamic threshold model is used with a twist to the threshold variable:

$$\begin{aligned} MS_{i,t} &= \beta_0 + \beta_1 MS_{i,t-1} + \beta_2 FI_{i,t} + \beta_3 FinTech_{i,t} + \beta_4 BS_{i,t} + \beta_5 LS_t + \beta_6 MQ_t \\ &+\beta_7 ROA_t + \beta_8 LQDR_t + \beta_9 FI_{i,t} * FinTech_{i,t} + \delta(FI_t - \gamma)1\{FI_t \geq \gamma\} \\ &+\alpha_i + \varepsilon_{i,t}, \end{aligned}$$

where FI_{it} represents both the threshold and the regime-dependent variable. The macroeconomic stability (MS) is measured using unemployment and interest rates. Overdue loans are used to proxy for macroeconomic stability for bank-specific level (MS), innovation technology (fintech), bank size (BS), loan size (LS), management quality (MQ), and liquidity (LQDR) signify partially endogenous control variables with slope coefficients predicted to be regime-independent. In line with Bick (2010), discrepancies in the regime intercept, δ, were allowed, and p lags $log(MS_{it-1}), log(MS_{it-2}),\dots, log(MS_{it-p})$ are considered dependent variables, as in Arellano and Bover (1995). β_5 and $\beta_5 + \delta$ denote the regime-dependent slopes for the threshold FI_t, where FI_t is below and above the threshold γ, respectively. The linear regression model is recovered when delta = 0 and can be construed as having no threshold effect. $1\{FI_t \geq \gamma\}$ signifies that financial inclusion is a regime and threshold variable. We take the first difference of the model given above to eliminate the bank-specific effect α_i and obtain the following:

$$\begin{aligned} \Delta MS_{i,t} &= \Delta\beta_1 MS_{i,t-1} + \Delta\beta_2 FI_{i,t} + \Delta\beta_3 I_{i,t} + \Delta\beta_4 BS_{i,t} + \Delta\beta_5 LS_t + \Delta\beta_6 MQ_t \\ &+\Delta\beta_7 ROA_t + \Delta\beta_8 LQDR_t + \Delta\beta_9 FI_{i,t} * FinTech_{i,t} + \delta(FI_t - \gamma)1 \\ &\{FI_t \geq \gamma\} - \delta(FI_{t-1} - \gamma)1\{FI_{t-1} \geq \gamma\} + \Delta\varepsilon_{i,t}. \end{aligned}$$

Before employing a dynamic panel threshold method, the nonlinear relationship between FI and MS was tested using the test of linearity as in Hansen (1999) and Kremer et al. (2013). The Panel Unit Root and Hansen diagnostics tests were also conducted to assess the reliability and efficiency in the long-run of the estimated parameters of interest, where the results of the dynamic panel threshold are valid when the *p*-values of these tests are not significant.

Table 2.2 provides the panel unit root test results using Im et al. (2003). The estimates present that the null hypothesis of the unit root for all variables is rejected at the 1 and 5% significance level for all variables taken in level. Table 2.3 reports the linearity test results and reveals that the hypothesis of model linearity is rejected at the 1 and 10% significance levels. These findings indicate a nonlinear relationship between financial inclusion and macroeconomic stability. The estimates reported in Table 2.3 show the stationarity of all variables included in the model, demonstrating that the dynamic panel threshold method used is a suitable estimator with valid empirical results to make statistical inferences.

Furthermore, the Wald and Fisher tests affirmed the robustness of our model. The coefficients for Lagrange multiplier and Fisher tests show the rejection of the null hypothesis at the 5 and 1% significance levels, respectively. Overall, the estimates reported in Tables 2.2 and 2.3 indicate that the estimated models are well-specified.

Table 2.2 Panel Unit Root Test

Series	*Coef.*	*P-value*
Macroeconomic Stability	0.9991	0.0000***
Financial Inclusion	0.5095	0.000***
Bank Size	0.4656	0.0002***
Loan Size	0.0281	0.000***
Management Quality	0.0713	0.000***
Return on asset	0.0652	0.000***
Liquidity	0.0148	0.0024**

Note: The standard errors are reported in parentheses. ***, **, * denote $p < 0.01$, $p < 0.05$, and $p < 0.1$, respectively.

Table 2.3 Linearity Test

Series	*Coef.*	*P-value*
The Lagrange Multiplier (LM)	-0.2	0.000943**
The Fisher Test (Lm)	0.0051	0.0000279***
The Likelihood-ratio Test (LR)	2.58	0.00001***
95% Confidence interval, Fieller method		[-8.3: -0.77]

Note: The standard errors are reported in parentheses. ***, **, * denote $p < 0.01$, $p < 0.05$, and $p < 0.1$, respectively.

4 Results and discussion

The threshold estimates for financial inclusion are presented in Table 2.4. The coefficient for the L.M. test for no threshold is not significant, whereas the threshold level estimate for the financial inclusion is 700 and significant at the 1% level. Table 2.5 provides the regression results for the impact of financial inclusion on macroeconomic stability. The estimates demonstrate that the relationship between macroeconomic stability and its determinants is consistent with our expectations. The coefficient for the one-year lagged dependent variable,

Table 2.4 Threshold Estimates of Financial Inclusion

Threshold Estimates	*Sample*
The L.M. test for no threshold	1.896
	(0.259)
The Bootstrap p-value	0.00207***
	(0.000637)
The Threshold estimate	700.20***
	(1.927)

Note: The standard errors are reported in parentheses. ***, **, * denote $p < 0.01$, $p < 0.05$, and $p < 0.1$, respectively.

Table 2.5 Macroeconomic Stability: Regression Results Using Financial Inclusion as a Threshold Variable

VARIABLES	*(1)*	*(2)*	*(2)*
	Disruptive	*Efficient*	*Sustain*
Macroeconomic stability (–1)	0.195***	0.196***	0.193***
	(0.273)	(0.273)	(0.273)
Financial Inclusion	0.404***	0.381***	0.414***
	(0.235)	(0.235)	(0.235)
FinTech	0.71***	0.81***	0.73***
	(1.127)	(1.127)	(1.127)
Bank Size	0.0857	0.00853	0.00863
	(0.009148)	(0.00892)	(0.00812)
Loan Size	-0.00115**	-0.00231**	-0.00326**
	(0.00144)	(0.00144)	(0.00144)
Management Quality	0.00139**	0.000571**	0.000463**
	(0.000291)	(0.000291)	(0.000291)
ROA	0.0366*	0.0178*	0.0291*
	(0.0220)	(0.0220)	(0.0220)
Liquidity	0.0274	0.0212	0.0183
	(0.0168)	(0.0168)	(0.0168)
FI*FinTech	0.0206*	-0.0181*	0.0012
	(0.0119)	(0.001)	(0.349)
R-square	0.12	0.12	0.12
Heteroscedasticity test	0.37	0.37	0.37
No. of banks	25	25	25

Note: ***, **, * denote $p < 0.01$, $p < 0.05$, and $p < 0.1$, respectively.

macroeconomic stability, is positive and significant in all cases. The inference can thus be made that MSs tend to multiply when they have grown in the previous period (month). This may be due to write-offs that did not occur very often in Kazakhstan and that the volume of MSs has remained relatively unstable and high since 2014.

The regression results for control variables indicate that all macroeconomic variables have statistically significant coefficients with the expected signs. Loan size increases the likelihood of macroeconomic instability at the 5% significance level. The coefficients for bank size, management quality, return on asset, and liquidity are positive and significant, as expected, and aligned with the theory. Furthermore, capital liquidity has a significant, positive impact, implying that higher liquidity is associated with more macroeconomic stability.

The threshold panel regression estimations in Columns (1), (2), and (3) confirm our hypothesis. The single threshold model is presented in the first column for disruptive innovation. The estimated first stage coefficient is $(\beta = 0.404)$ at the 1% significance level, where financial inclusion is below the estimated threshold of 700 out of 1000 people. This indicates a strong positive link between use of financial services and macroeconomic stability. The results thus far imply that financial inclusion negatively influences stability and suggests that increasing financial inclusion up to 700 can lead to diversification of risks by serving more clients, whereas extending it beyond the threshold of 700 people may increase macroeconomic instability because of increased involvement of the vulnerable population segment. Furthermore, greater access to mainstream financial services triggers economic activity, thereby improving bank performance and reducing unemployment. This reduces instability and subsequently enhances the country's macroeconomic stability. These results are consistent with other findings, implying that financial inclusion can lead to macroeconomic stability (IMF, 2015; Khandelwal et al., 2016).

The coefficients for fintech $(\beta = 0.71)$ and management quality $(\beta = 0.00139)$ are positive and significant at the 1 and 5% levels, indicating that developing financial technologies can lead to better banking stability. Correspondingly, increased management quality can lead to more stable banking operations. Banks with larger loans, however, are associated with greater risks compared to banks with relatively smaller loan portfolios. Hence, the coefficient for loan size $(\beta = -0.00115)$ is negative and significant at the 5% level. The estimate for return on assets $(\beta = 0.0366)$ signifies the importance of the net income-to-assets ratio, as higher returns are associated with higher profitability and stability. Lower liquidity exposes banks to increased liquidity risk; the coefficient for liquidity is positive but statistically not significant in our estimations.

The coefficient for the interaction term between financial inclusion and financial innovations $(\beta = 0.0206)$ is positive and statistically significant at the 10% level, suggesting that financial inclusion coupled with disruptive innovations can lead to higher macroeconomic stability.

Consequently, this study concludes that the nonlinear impact of financial inclusion on macroeconomic stability should be measured. Estimations in the second and third columns for efficient and sustained innovations, respectively, exhibit that financial inclusion is above the threshold of 700 out of 1000 people. The coefficients for financial inclusion were ($\beta = 0.381$) and ($\beta = 0.414$) for efficient and sustained innovation estimations, respectively. Financial inclusion has a significant negative effect on macroeconomic stability at the 1% significance level. This finding implies that financial inclusion has a negative effect on macroeconomic stability after financial inclusion (use of bank services) that exceeds the threshold estimate of 700 per 1000 people. As mentioned above, this negative effect can be explained by increasing risks associated with the involvement of financially the vulnerable segment of the population in mainstream financial services in the country.

5 Conclusion and policy recommendations

This research examined the impact of financial inclusion on the macroeconomic stability of 28 banks in Kazakhstan banks between 2014 and 2020. The dynamic panel threshold estimation method was employed to estimate the impact of financial inclusion, financial innovation, bank size, loan size, return on asset, liquidity, and management quality on macroeconomic stability. In contrast to previous literature, where financial inclusion is positively and linearly associated with macroeconomic stability, this study demonstrates the existence of a negative nonlinear association. The findings demonstrate that the degree to which vulnerable individuals have access to formal financial services has a major effect on banking stability, highlighting the need for the establishment of an inclusive financial system. An inclusive financial system will enable banks to capitalize on the untapped potential of clients with a lack of or no access to banking products and services, thereby strengthening their balance sheets and making them more robust against possible future risks. Because improving access to financial products and services is critical for financial development initiatives, deliberate and persistent efforts of mainstream financial institutions to deploy resources in more productive economic sectors can lead to higher profits. The first type of innovation, i.e., disruptive financial technologies that make financial services affordable and accessible, has a positive effect on stability. Furthermore, financial inclusion can cause vulnerable population segments to engage with the mainstream financial system, thus leading to instability. Second, efficiency innovation makes financial services affordable; however, it pressures stability by shrinking the labor market. Third, sustaining innovation seems to be insignificant. As such, this study concludes that optimal borrowing and lending should be actively monitored to mitigate potential liquidity problems of banks. Accordingly, the findings of this research have significant implications for policymakers. First, our results highlight the necessity for adopting macro-prudential policies to ensure the financial stability of banks in the face of potentially vulnerable clients enrolling in the system. Hence, additional policies should focus on ensuring access for all excluded citizens with the ability to repay debts and obligations to the financial services used through financial innovation. Effective macro-prudential tools can also help minimize credit boom incidences along with their possible unfavorable endings (Dell'Ariccia et al., 2012). This would lessen the vulnerability of banks to undesirable financial expansion. However, because experienced borrowers have lower default risks, financial institutions can also consider providing repeat loans to existing clients with positive credit histories. The use of digital technology, especially fintech, can also help enhance macroeconomic stability by reducing the short-term volatility of economic activities and prices. However, this may give rise to new risks and increase existing ones, notably when regulation lags behind innovation. Furthermore, the advantageous effects of financial inclusion on bank stability are contingent on the type of financial innovation, such as disruptive, efficient, or sustained innovations. Therefore, increasing access while ignoring the possible negative effects of innovation on financial stability is undesirable, because financial innovation is believed to be beneficial to extending financial access but detrimental to banking stability. Given that, regulators and policymakers should maintain a balance between financial inclusion and innovation types to avoid financial instability. The access-stability nexus can be complemented by establishing an innovative environment.

References

Acemoglu D, Akcigit U, Celik MA (2022) Radical and incremental innovation: The roles of firms, managers and innovators. *AEJ Macroecon.* 14(3):199–249

Acemoglu D, Autor D (2011) Skills, tasks and technologies: Implications for employment and earnings. *Handbook of labor economics*: D Card and O Ashenfelter (Eds). Elsevier: Amsterdam

Acemoglu D, Restrepo P (2018a) Modeling automation. Paper presented at the AEA Papers and Proceedings

Acemoglu D, Restrepo P (2018b) The race between man and machine: Implications of technology for growth, factor shares, and employment. *Am Econ Rev* 108(6): 1488–1542

Acemoglu D, Restrepo P (2019) Automation and new tasks: How technology displaces and reinstates labor. *J Econ Perspect* 33(2):3–30

Aggarwal R, Stein P (2016) The complex regulatory landscape for Fintech: An uncertain future for small and medium-sized enterprise lending. Paper presented at the World Economic Forum White Paper

Aghion P, Akcigit U, Howitt P (2015) Lessons from Schumpeterian growth theory. *Am Econ Rev* 105(5):94–99

Aghion P, Howitt, P (1990) *A model of growth through creative destruction.* Cambridge, MA: National Bureau of Economic Research

Ahokpossi MC (2013) *Determinants of bank interest margins in Sub-Saharan Africa.* Washington DC: International Monetary Fund

Allen F, Gale D (2004) Competition and financial stability. *J Money Credit Bank.* 36(3):453–480

Anagnostopoulos I (2018) Fintech and regtech: Impact on regulators and banks. *J Econ Bus* 100:7–25

Andriopoulos C, Lewis MW (2009) Exploitation-exploration tensions and organizational ambidexterity: Managing paradoxes of innovation. *Organ Sci* 20(4):696–717

Anzoategui D, Demirgüç-Kunt, A, Pería, MSM (2014) Remittances and financial inclusion: Evidence from El Salvador. *World Dev* 54:338–349

Arellano M, Bover O (1995) Another look at the instrumental variable estimation of error-components models. *J Econom* 68(1):29–51

Bick A (2010) Threshold effects of inflation on economic growth in developing countries. *Econ Lett* 108(2):126–129

Bouoiyour J, Miftah A (2015) The impact of migrant workers' remittances on the living standards of families in Morocco: A propensity score matching approach. *Migr Lett* 12(1):13

Bouoiyour J, Miftah A (2016) The impact of remittances on children's human capital accumulation: Evidence from Morocco. *J Int Dev* 28(2):266–280

Braggion F, Manconi A, Zhu H (2018) Can technology undermine macroprudential regulation? Evidence from peer-to-peer credit in China. CEPR Discussion Papers 12668, C.E.P.R. Discussion Papers. Washington DC: Center for Economic and Policy Research

Brown M, Kirschenmann K, Ongena S (2014) Bank funding, securitization, and loan terms: Evidence from foreign currency lending. *J Money Credit Bank* 46(7), 1501–1534

Brue S, Grant R (2012) *The evolution of economic thought.* Boston: Cengage learning

Buchak G, Matvos G, Piskorski T, Seru A (2018) Fintech, regulatory arbitrage, and the rise of shadow banks. *J Financ Econ* 130(3):453–483

Bucheli JR, Bohara AK, Fontenla M (2018) Mixed effects of remittances on child education. *IZA J Dev Migr* 8(1):1–18

Cai CW (2018) Disruption of financial intermediation by FinTech: A review on crowdfunding and blockchain. *Account Finance* 58(4):965–992

Caner M, Hansen BE (2004) Instrumental variable estimation of a threshold model. *Econ Theory* 20(5):813–843

Casu B, Fabbri D, Wilson JO (2014) *Emerging issues in financial institutions and markets*: Taylor & Francis

Christensen CM (2013) *The innovator's dilemma: When new technologies cause great firms to fail.* Massachusetts: Harvard Business Review Press

Christensen CM, Bower JL (1996) Customer power, strategic investment, and the failure of leading firms. *Strateg Manag J* 17(3):197–218

Christensen CM, Ojomo E, Dillon K (2019) *The prosperity paradox: How innovation can lift nations out of poverty.* New York: HarperCollins

Chuc AT, Li W, Phi NTM, Le QT, Yoshino N, Taghizadeh-Hesary F (2021) The necessity of financial inclusion for enhancing the economic impacts of remittances. *Borsa Istanb Rev* 22(1):47–56. doi:10.1016/j.bir.2020.12.007

Čihák M, Mare DS, Melecky M (2016) The nexus of financial inclusion and financial stability: A study of trade-offs and synergies. World Bank Policy Research Working Paper (7722)

Clark G (2016) Winter is coming: Robert Gordon and the future of economic growth. *Am Econ Rev* 106(5):68–71

Cotter J, Suurlaht A (2019) Spillovers in risk of financial institutions. *Eur J Finance* 25(17):1765–1792

Crockett A (1996) The theory and practice of financial stability. *Economist* 144(4):531–568

Danisman GO, Demirel P (2019) Bank risk-taking in developed countries: The influence of market power and bank regulations. *J Int Financ Mark Inst Money* 59:202–217

Danisman GO, Tarazi A (2020) Financial inclusion and bank stability: Evidence from Europe. *Eur J Finance* 26(18):1842–1855

Dell'Ariccia G, Igan, D, Laeven, L. U (2012) Credit booms and lending standards: Evidence from the subprime mortgage market. *J Money Credit Bank* 44(2-3):367–384

Demetriades P, Law SH (2006) Finance, institutions and economic development. *Int J Finance Econ* 11(3):245–260

Demirguc-Kunt A, Klapper L, Singer D, Ansar S, Hess J (2017) *The global findex database: Measuring financial inclusion and the fintech revolution*: World Bank Group

Esanov A, Kuralbayeva K (2011) Public saving and private spending. *Plundered nations? Successes and failures in natural resource extraction*: P Collier and T Venables (Eds). Palgrave Macmillan: London

Fisher I (1933) The debt-deflation theory of great depressions. *Econometrica: J Economet Soc* 337–357. doi:10.2307/1907327

Friedman M, Schwartz AJ (2008) *A monetary history of the United States, 1867–1960* (Vol. 14): New Jersey: Princeton University Press

García MJR, José M (2016) Can financial inclusion and financial stability go hand in hand. *J Econ Issues* 21(2):81–103

Gordon RJ (2017) *The rise and fall of American growth*. Princeton: Princeton University Press

Hannig A, Jansen S (2010) Financial inclusion and financial stability: Current policy issues. ADBI Working Paper No. 259. doi:10.2139/ssrn.1729122

Hansen BE (1999) Threshold effects in non-dynamic panels: Estimation, testing, and inference. *J Econom* 93(2):345–368

Hanusch H, Pyka A (2007) *Elgar companion to neo-Schumpeterian economics*. Cheltenham: Edward Elgar Publishing

Huang R, Kale S, Paramati SR, Taghizadeh-Hesary F (2021) The nexus between financial inclusion and economic development: Comparison of old and new EU member countries. *Econ Anal Policy* 69:1–15

Im KS, Pesaran MH, Shin Y (2003) Testing for unit roots in heterogeneous panels. *J Econom* 115(1):53–74

IMF (2015) Where are we headed? Perspectives on potential output, Ch. 3. In: *World economic outlook. Uneven growth: short- and long- term factors*. Washington DC: International Monetary Fund

Khan H (2011) Financial inclusion and financial stability: Are they two sides of the same coin. Address by Shri HR Khan, Deputy Governor of the Reserve Bank of India, at BANCON, 1–12

Khandelwal P, Miyajima, MK, Santos MAO (2016) *The impact of oil prices on the banking system in the GCC*. Washington DC: International Monetary Fund

Kindleberger M (1978) *Manias, panics, and crashes: A history of financial crises*. New York: Basic Books

Klapper L, El-Zoghbi, M, Hess, J (2016) Achieving the sustainable development goals. *The Role of Financial Inclusion* 23(5):2016. Available online: http://www.ccgap.org

Koong SS, Law SH, Ibrahim MH (2017) Credit expansion and financial stability in Malaysia. *Econ Model* 61:339–350

Kouki I, Abid I, Guesmi K, Goutte S (2020) Does Financial inclusion affect the African banking stability? *Econ Bull* 40(1):863–879

Kremer S, Bick A, Nautz D (2013) Inflation and growth: New evidence from a dynamic panel threshold analysis. *Empir Econ* 44(2):861–878

Le TH, Chuc AT, Taghizadeh-Hesary F (2019) Financial inclusion and its impact on financial efficiency and sustainability: Empirical evidence from Asia. *Borsa Istanb Rev* 19(4):310–322

López T, Winkler A (2019) Does financial inclusion mitigate credit boom-bust cycles? *J Financial Stab* 43:116–129

Merkl C, Stolz S (2009) Banks' regulatory buffers, liquidity networks and monetary policy transmission. *Appl Econ* 41(16), 2013–2024

Mills K, McCarthy B (2016) The state of small business lending: Innovation and technology and the implications for regulation. Harvard Business School Entrepreneurial Management Working Paper 17-042:17–042

Minsky HP (1977) The financial instability hypothesis: An interpretation of Keynes and an alternative to "standard" theory. *Challenge* 20(1):20–27

Morgan P, Pontines V (2014) Financial stability and financial inclusion. ADBI Working Paper 488. doi:10.2139/ssrn.2464018

Pagano M, Pica G (2014) Finance and employment. *Economic Policy* 27(69):5–55. doi:10.1111/j.1468-0327.2011.00276.x

Philippon T (2016) The fintech opportunity (No. w22476). National Bureau of Economic Research. doi:10.3386/w22476

Qamruzzaman M, Wei J (2019) Financial innovation and financial inclusion nexus in South Asian countries: Evidence from symmetric and asymmetric panel investigation. *Int J Financ Stud* 7(4):61

Sahay MR, Cihak M, N'Diaye MP, Barajas MA, Mitra MS, Kyobe MA, Yousefi MR (2015) *Financial inclusion: Can it meet multiple macroeconomic goals?* International Monetary Fund. doi:10.5089/9781513585154.006

Stanley D, Fleming, N (2019) The impact of foreign and domestic remittance types and senders on education outcomes. *Econ Notes: Rev Bank Financ Monetary Econ* 48(3):e12140

Thakor AV (2020) Fintech and banking: What do we know? *J Financ Intermediation* 41:e100833

Vo AT, Van LTH, Vo DH, McAleer M (2019) Financial inclusion and macroeconomic stability in emerging and frontier markets. *Ann Financ Econ* 14(02):e1950008

Wang X, Guan J (2017) Financial inclusion: Measurement, spatial effects and influencing factors. *Appl Econ* 49(18):1751–1762

Appendix

Table A2.1 List of Banks Used in the Analysis

No	*Bank Name*
1	Subsidiary JSC Bank VTB (Kazakhstan)
2	JSC "Shinhan Bank Kazakhstan"
3	JSC "Housing Construction Savings Bank of Kazakhstan"
4	JSC "National Bank of Pakistan in Kazakhstan"
5	JSC "Zaman-Bank"
6	JSC "TsesnaBank"
7	JSC "TengriBank"
8	JSC "Nurbank"
9	JSC "ATFBank"
10	JSC "Eurasian Bank"
11	SJSB "Alfa-bank"
12	JSC "Commercial and Industrial Bank of China in Almaty "
13	JSC Subsidiary Bank JSC "First Heartland Bank" (Kazakhstan)
14	SJSB "SB Sberbank of Russia JSC"
15	SJSB "Bank of China in Kazakhstan"
16	JSC "Home Credit Bank"
17	JSC "Bank CenterCredit"
18	SJSB Citibank Kazakhstan JSC
19	JSC RBK
20	SJSB "Capital Bank Kazakhstan"
21	JSC "JB "AsiaCreditBank"
22	JSC "KASPI BANK"
23	JSC "Halyk Bank Kazakhstan"
24	Bank Kassa Nova
25	Al-Hilal Islamic Bank
26	Altyn Bank
27	SB Kazakhstan-Ziraat International Bank,
28	JSC ForteBank

3 Role of national innovation financing agencies in promoting startups

A comparative study

Kiarash Fartash and Mahsa Darehshiri

1 Introduction

The innovation challenge is not new; the issue is that innovation is a moving target. This implies that not only are the actors in this game competing, but the enormous space in which the game is played is also continuously altering (Tidd et al., 2020). Successful innovation depends not only on a favorable business environment but also on supporting policies and initiatives, particularly in innovation financing. Startups and their high rate of innovation output attract increased attention because of their significance and relevance in economic development and national welfare (Hsu et al., 2017). While science and technology (S&T), creativity, and flexibility serve as the primary foundation for the success of startups and innovative businesses, without adequate funding, they will probably fail. In other words, fiscal, tax, and financial policies are used as policy instruments by governments to create an innovation-friendly environment or to encourage innovation. In contrast, economic and industrial policies have a direct effect on encouraging innovation. Achieving a desirable objective in terms of greater competitiveness, national security, environmental sustainability, and/or social welfare is the ultimate goal of all innovation policy components, regardless of their category (Liu et al., 2011; Wisuttisak, 2021).

Why innovation fails has long been a source of contention among researchers. After several years of investigation and observation, the key factors identified as being responsible for the failure of startups include lack of an innovation-friendly culture; lack of a thorough procedure for innovation; inadequate resource allocation for this process; failure to devote sufficient time and attention to resolving organizational ambiguities; failure to foster diversity in processes (differing and competing viewpoints); inadequate creation of instruments and measurements for progress measurement; and a scarcity of skilled coaches on innovation teams (Roed, 2016). Innovation financing is either partially or fully the root cause of many of these factors, making it more instrumental. Various governments across the globe have enacted legislation to offer financial and intellectual assistance to projects, innovators, and businesses engaged in innovation. Some hurdles regarding innovation funding, however, complicate the situation for investors and innovators because of the high risk and uncertainty inherent in investments in

DOI: 10.4324/9781003220220-5

innovation. Limited information is also a barrier to innovation investment (Lee et al., 2015). Limited collateral for small- and medium-sized enterprises (SMEs) and startups, which leads to higher interest rates on loans, is another barrier to funding innovative firms (Yoshino and Taghizadeh-Hesary, 2019).

This chapter attempts to summarize the experiences of countries around the world with government funding agencies. This study contributes to our understanding of startup funding by comparing national innovation financing agencies for startups and innovative firms. After a short overview of several key terms linked to innovation and its significance for a country's development, the critical role of startups and innovative businesses, and financing innovation in Sections 2 and 3, we present a brief history of public innovation agencies in section 4, which also contains an in-depth examination of the national agencies of eight countries. In Section 5, we undertake a comparative assessment of the financial instruments available to national innovation agencies to assist startups as drawn from the literature in Section 4. The final section presents conclusions and some policy recommendations based on the preceding section's findings.

2 Why financing startups matters

2.1 The importance of innovation for a country's development

Innovation contributes to enhancing productivity and results in improved resource efficiency (Edquist and Zabala-Iturriagagoitia, 2020). In today's dynamic business environment, innovation is critical to a firm's profitability and performance, and possessing the skill of innovation is critical to a firm's competitiveness and success. Innovation is one of the essential instruments that small- and medium-sized businesses may use to boost the economic dynamism of any industry. Choosing and adhering to appropriate policies lead to innovation. For small- and medium-sized businesses to develop and remain creative, government or national agencies must implement an innovation-driven policy.

Innovation is critical for both developed and emerging countries to achieve economic development and income growth in the long run. Startups play a vital role in the development and diffusion of technologies and in creating quality new jobs. Nonetheless, they are often in dire need of financial resources to continue innovating and growing (Bellavitis et al., 2017). Funding innovative processes is essential in the creation and distribution of economically viable products and services across the innovation system (Borrás and Edquist, 2019). Information asymmetry and a lack of collateral limit startups' and entrepreneurs' access to funding is a timely problem, particularly in emerging nations where startups contribute to the economy (Taghizadeh-Hesary et al., 2021).

Financing a startup entails a substantial amount of risk-taking. Techno-Economic Feasibility Study Methods (TEFS) provide adequate evidence to investors and stakeholders that a startup initiative is feasible and worthwhile for investing. TEFS is a financial and economic feasibility study used to determine whether a new business venture has the potential to be financially and economically prosperous. For entrepreneurs and financial institutions alike, the TEFS technique may assist in making investment choices based on a project's technical and financial viability. It further highlights a project's risks and the steps needed to mitigate them (Subramanian and Taghizadeh-Hesary, 2021).

Because startups and SMEs do not have traditional and acceptable collateral or guarantees to seek funding from mainstream financial institutions, they usually experience difficulty in acquiring funding for innovation. Startups, especially those that are more innovative, face a "funding gap" that arises when they are limited on internal and external financial sources for their innovative initiatives (Mazzucato and Penna, 2016). Inadequate access to funding impedes the growth and development of startups (Wisuttisak, 2021). This fact has become more apparent since the advent of the Covid-19 pandemic and its impact on the global economy (Kuckertz et al., 2020) and is likely to resurface in the future if not resolved.

2.2 Traditional financing systems impede startups' innovative efforts and growth

The term "policy tools" refers to the tactics and strategies used by governments to promote, influence, or prevent social change. To be effective, tools must be adapted to the objectives of a government, the country's condition, and cultural norms (Bemelmans-Videc et al., 2011). Government policy tools can be classified into four broad categories based on the type of intervention: "direct assistance," "indirect (tax) support," "catalytic financial support," and "macroeconomic reform and infrastructure development policies" (Ghazinoory and Ghazinoori, 2014). *Direct assistance* refers to cases in which public funds are used to promote research and technology, including subsidies, networking, financing public sector research, and providing information and assisting with mediation (Bemelmans-Videc et al., 2011). *Indirect* or *tax supports* are intended to influence a company's investment behavior in research and development. They include three subcategories: "offering tax incentives to businesses (tax exemptions, tax credits, and accelerated depreciation)"; "providing incentives in the form of tax deductions on research and development personnel salaries and social security costs"; and "offering tax advantages to individuals (entrepreneurs)" (Bemelmans-Videc et al., 2011; Liu et al., 2011).

Catalytic supports channel to innovation processes as catalysts and stimulate a specific process but are expected to cover the whole process. Some of the most popular kinds of such assistance include supporting venture capitalists and business angels, providing loans and stocks, establishing a new stock market, and making small loans. Eventually, macroeconomic reforms and infrastructure development policies focus on competitive policy (such as eliminating monopolies), the country's intellectual property (IPR) system, legislative and regulatory frameworks, and other infrastructure and environmental factors. Additionally, they focus on promoting an entrepreneurial culture in universities and human resource development (Allman et al., 2011).

Credit assessments of startups have prevented many businesses from receiving financial aid. Banks and financing agencies consider certain factors when assessing, i.e., due diligence, a startup, or a business for loans and aids (Lee et al., 2015). Credit scores are calculated based on various items, including a firm's credit history, legal judgments, and the profiles of their owners and directors, in which startups fail to get a high score (Lee et al., 2015). In Russia, the Russian Venture Capital (RVC) agency uses a meaningful structure to assess an innovative project for financing. It evaluates the team, product, or technology being used, growth potential, expected financial returns, the project's competitiveness, shareholder structure, and legal aspects (RVC, 2019). However, as financial institutions, especially traditional banks, lack professional accounting and due diligence systems, they prefer to lend to big corporations rather than SMEs and startups, whose financial statements are rarely audited and often unclear (Yoshino and Taghizadeh-Hesary, 2019).

3 Governments as the champion of startup's innovation financing

Financing innovation often requires risk-taking and has a longer payback time between investment and return than conventional types of investment. When an investment is directed toward funding a startup, the picture becomes hazier (Brown et al., 2020; Ferrando et al., 2019). Therefore, governments should take the risk of investing in innovation in favor of national economic development (Mazzucato and Penna, 2015). Historically, and even now, financing innovation is a significant structural barrier for countries. Hence, governments are responsible for providing financing resources for innovation (Lee et al., 2015).

Innovation funding agencies are expected to provide innovation funding to promote growth, which will eventually yield myriads of benefits for society (Mazzucato and Penna, 2016). It is a short-sighted approach, arguing that private innovation funding agencies have no role in tackling societal challenges by their support. To develop a financially sound system for supporting innovation, public banking and private funding must be utilized symbiotically (Mazzucato and Penna, 2016).

Public innovation agencies are expected to address innovation policy issues that private players cannot or are not willing to confront. In the early phases of innovation, which are characterized by risk and a long payoff period, public agencies come forward to promote innovation. In some sectors, such as pharmaceuticals and biotechnology, a long temporal period is needed to realize the results of innovation, which is not acceptable for private investors. Therefore, public financing will promote innovation in such instances without impeding or crowding out the private sector, i.e., crowding in. If private capital is available, there is no need for government funding, and the private sector could be crowded out. In other words, a public innovation financing agency should avoid competing "unfairly" with private organizations using public funds (Borrás and Edquist, 2019).

Governments establish specialized financing intermediaries who contribute to the development and diffusion of innovation. They are tasked with filling the existing innovation finance gap (Agogué et al., 2017). Consequently, several dedicated national agencies, i.e., national funds, banks, state investment banks (SIBs), and other types of institutions, are available to finance the innovative activities of startups. These agencies play four main roles: market and system fixers, industry builders, mission drivers, and system optimizers. They engage in either one or a combination of these functions and finance innovation through various mechanisms, such as grants, investments, subsidies, skills development, creating demand, regulation, standards for innovation, and leveraging governments' demand by public procurements for innovation (PPI) (Edquist and Zabala-Iturriagagoitia, 2012, 2020; Glennie and Bound, 2016).

3.1 The governments' mechanisms to provide financial support for startups

In the literature on government-led innovation financing, several studies focused on SIBs and their roles in funding innovation through various types of investment (de Luna-Martinez and Vicente, 2012). In their review, Mazzucato and Penna (2016) classify the roles of innovation financing agencies into four categories: (a) countercyclical role, which is concerned primarily with averting financial collapse during recessions and breaking the lock-in caused by financial crises; (b) capital development (or developmental) role that funds long-term projects or national industrialization; (c) new venture support (or "venture capitalist") in which the private sector assumingly accepts a significant risk of loss related to investments in innovative startups and lengthy innovation processes; (d) challenge-led role to direct investments toward complex societal issues such as climate change (Mazzucato and Penna, 2016).

Hochstetler and Montero (2013) emphasized three distinct innovation financing policies to encourage SMEs and startups to engage in innovation, i.e., (a) direct financial support and loans to businesses to invest in their innovation programs, research and development, or to accelerate the internationalization of their expertise and standards; (b) providing easy and favorable loans to underserved areas; and (c) collaborative financing efforts with other national or worldwide innovation organizations to ease knowledge transfer and boost exports and internationalization (Hochstetler and Montero, 2013). Recent research by Janeway et al. (2021) explains three catalyzing roles of the government's investment in innovation to support startups and SMEs: (a) funding "mission-driven initiatives" to assist in developing new high-tech ideas and entrepreneurial businesses; (b) customer role of the government through procurement and R&D; (c) defining ownership and property rights, with a particular emphasis on encouraging an equal playing field and innovation in startups (Janeway et al., 2021).

Innovation agencies are also efficient in providing flexible, patient, and accessible funding for startups in contradiction with the strict requirements of traditional financing programs of commercial banks and even private VCs (Raimi, 2020). Innovation agencies use a diverse range of financing mechanisms to finance innovation, and several classifications of these supports exist. For example, the OECD offers a list of funding mechanisms for startups and SMEs based on risk and reward levels in four categories: (a) debt-based financing, (b) financing through government interventions, (c) asset-based financing, and (d) alternative debt-based financing (OECD, 2015). Drawing on the literature on innovation financing tools, we propose a typology of startups innovation financing mechanisms, which comprises four main categories.

(1) General financial incentives to facilitate startups operations through direct public investment – the most frequent mechanism innovation agencies adopt to invest in startups and innovative firms. Tax incentives are another common form of general financial incentives that include tax credits on investments in new or small businesses, gains from venture capital investments, and tax deductions or even exemptions for new innovative businesses (Borrás and Edquist, 2019). Support for selling or buying intellectual property rights (IPR) is also considered in this category (Liu et al., 2011).
(2) Export- and production-based financing. This type covers legal arrangements and processes that encourage foreign investment, which can help startups and SMEs benefit from technology transfer options and strengthen their link to the global market. Additionally, innovation events help startups connect with investors and showcase their capabilities to secure future investments (Borrás and Edquist, 2019). The provision of export credit insurance is another mechanism for helping startups expand their market to the global level (Liu et al., 2011).
(3) Loans, grants, procurements, and co-investment. Public procurement is a transformational tool, as it fosters creativity and develops, spreads, and incorporates new ideas to respond to government needs (Edquist and Zabala-Iturriagagoitia, 2020). Co-investment (fund-in-fund), or public-private collaboration on investment, is another mechanism of funding innovation in startups. Buy-out options, soft loans, and loan and credit guarantees are efficient options where innovation agencies intend to support startups and venture capitals (Borrás and Edquist, 2019; Liu et al., 2011).
(4) Societal and mission-oriented financing. As global challenges become more prevalent and destructive, new technologies are being replaced with existing ones. Thus, long-term commitments by both public and private financing agencies are in demand. These societal challenges include aging/demographic crisis, inequality, and youth unemployment; driving technologies behind military and energy complexes like climate change and in various fields such as health and agriculture (Mazzucato and Penna, 2015). Green and low-carbon investment plans, particularly in European countries, include innovation agencies' financial support to startups on green technologies, which is getting momentum and has raised attention (D'Orazio and Löwenstein, 2020).

Table 3.1 summarizes the funding instruments that can promote the innovative efforts of entrepreneurs and startups and provides a holistic perspective on financial tools that innovation agencies can offer to startups. We categorize instruments in three thematic areas: general financial incentives; export- and production-based financing; and loans, grants, procurement, and co-investment. The fourth category entails societal and mission-oriented financing, which has become more and more pertinent given the current situation of global pandemics, climate, and environmental challenges.

Table 3.1 National Innovation Agencies' Financial Tools (Author's Conclusion)

Category	*Tools*	*References*
1) General financial incentives to empower and facilitate startups operations	• Consulting services and Commercialization • Direct investment • Tax incentives • Knowledge development • Developing 'national champions' capable of competing in global marketplaces • Supporting IPRs	(Borrás and Edquist, 2019; Liu et al., 2011; Mazzucato and Penna, 2015)
2) Export- and production-based financing	• Infrastructure financing • Licensing • Communication and Networking • Angel networks • Encourage strategic trade (e.g., import substitution and material security) and financial leverage • Facilitating foreign capital investment • Export credit insurance	(Borrás and Edquist, 2019; Liu et al., 2011; Mazzucato and Penna, 2015)
3) Loans, grants, procurement, and co-investment	• Investment priority in emerging S&T areas • Co-investment (fund-in-fund) • Lower interest rates on loans • Credit guarantees and Collateral • R&D and military procurement • Public procurement/ Public procurement for innovation • Grants, subsidies (including tax credits), innovation prizes and other non-reimbursable public funds for basic research and innovation development	(Borrás and Edquist, 2019; D'Orazio and Löwenstein, 2020; Edquist and Zabala-Iturriagagoitia, 2020; Liu et al., 2011; Mazzucato and Penna, 2015)
4) Societal and mission-oriented financing	• Dedicate easy and patient finance to • Environmental issues and sustainability • Societal challenges • National strategic technology areas and priorities	(Edquist and Zabala-Iturriagagoitia, 2020; Mazzucato and Penna, 2015)

4 The emergence of financing innovation agencies

Financing agencies are specialized institutions responsible for financing startups and SMEs to foster innovation. Their history dates back to the initiation of state investment banks that were primarily in charge of financing and supporting construction and industrialization. At the end of World War II, the construction plan in Europe was initiated due to the 1944 Bretton Woods monetary agreement. The first founded financing agency was the International Bank for Reconstruction and Development (IBRD) – now called the World Bank. The IBRD was tasked with providing a continuous supply of funds to rebuild destruction from the war. In principle, it was a means to assist with post-World War II economic stabilization and avoid long-term negative consequences of speculative, pro-cyclical, private banks (Mazzucato and Penna, 2016). Several national development banks, e.g., Canada's Industrial Development Bank (1944) and Germany's Kreditanstalt für Wiederaufbau (KfW – meaning "reconstruction credit institute") (1948), were established around the same time. They all aimed at channeling international and domestic funds toward long-term growth, infrastructure development, and economic progress (Schröder et al., 2011).

In the 1980s and early 1990s, several policy tools and initiatives were designed. They reflected a new view of innovation, including mechanisms of technology transfer, assisting the formation of new technology-based firms (NTBFs), and university spin-off businesses. Funding intermediaries for supporting innovation were also taken into account (Ghazinoory and Ghazinoori, 2014). The importance of innovation and its impact on the economy and society became more and more critical when the term competitive advantage played a crucial role in the strategic plans of countries. Dedicated agencies were responsible for financing innovation and startups in various forms like banks, national funds, etc.

4.1 National innovation agencies in selected countries

Considering the importance of national agencies to inspire innovation for startups, a comparative study on government-run innovation funding agencies at a national level is provided. This chapter sets to dive into financial support to startups and innovative ideas provided by national innovation agencies. This section will analyze the role of government's central national bodies in financing innovation and fostering an innovative startup environment. The authors have classified financing tools to promote startup innovation in eight countries. The selected countries are a balanced combination of national innovation agencies in developing and developed countries, including Iran (INIF), China (Innofund), Russia (RVC), South Africa (TIA), France (Bpifrance), Germany (KFW), Japan (DBJ), and South Korea (KOTEC/ KIBO). We select our cases to reflect a variety of financing options for startups and innovative firms from a balanced sample of perspectives from both developed and developing countries. France, Germany, Japan, and South Korea are high-income countries that leverage these supports to foster innovation and prosperity within their nations. China, Russia, South Africa, and Iran, however, are upper-middle-income countries that aim to benefit from innovation financing to enhance creativity and create new economic opportunities. Our comparative study of the agencies, as mentioned earlier, provides a more comprehensive account of the financial supports for innovation and, particularly, startups.

4.1.1 Iran: National Innovation Fund

The Iran National Innovation Fund (INIF) was established in 2011 to provide support and facilities to aid in the commercialization of innovations and inventions as well as the development and diffusion of technological knowledge. These supports are provided mainly to businesses and knowledge-based entities. In the Iranian business context, knowledge-based firms (KBFs) are startups, innovative technology-based firms, and small businesses. The INIF's primary operating areas are providing financial facilities and guarantees to knowledge-based businesses, strengthening the capacity of knowledge-based businesses to commercialize products, and venture capital.

The INIF's supports under the first category of financial tools (Table 3.1) include consulting and strategy development for new businesses, providing various financing services, managing intellectual property, commercialization, participating in domestic and international exhibitions, and providing loans and guarantees to support the country's innovation development. The INIF's ultimate aim as a development organization is to enhance the knowledge-based economy by contributing to the country's economic prosperity through the areas of knowledge-based and high-tech innovations (INIF, 2019).

The INIF has five different methods for developing innovation ecosystems, each of which has distinct and functional features based on particular requirements and circumstances. In the approach of marketing and helping to shape the domestic market, the INIF works on both the supply and demand sides to shape the market for knowledge-based products. On the supply side, it assists knowledge-based companies that sell knowledge-based products by providing industrial production facilities, empowerment services, warranty, or working capital. On the demand side, by providing leasing services, the INIF enables purchasers to make purchases consistent with their demands in the market for KBF products. These supports fall under the category of "Loans, grants, procurement, and co-investment."

The INIF's second approach to the innovation ecosystem is "knowledge-based export development." Measures such as offering export packages (facilities, empowerment services, etc.), providing support for companies' participation in international exhibitions, sending and accepting trade delegations, and, in other cases, assisting knowledge-based businesses in obtaining certificates, standards, and export approvals are implemented in line with this approach. The INIF also helps develop and form intermediary organizations, in particular, export and market brokers, to shape national and international markets of Iranian-made knowledge-based goods and services. These tools encompass almost all four categories of financial instruments mentioned in Table 3.1.

The INIF's third focal strategy is the "value chain development and knowledge-based supply network," which acts as an intermediary and facilitator between supply and demand by hosting events to present industrial needs to knowledge-based businesses. INIF's role in this regard conforms to providing leasing, procuring, and meeting buyers' needs; it also provides services such as accelerator facilities, warranty, industrial production facilities, and empowerment services on behalf of service and product providers. This strategy is pertinent to the second and third categories of financial tools.

The fourth approach is "active participation in the development of new and emerging technologies," including support of specialized accelerators in emerging technological areas. "Resolving national and strategic problems and challenges" is mostly problem- or future-oriented. Examples of support in this regard are funding solar energy, desalination, and water extraction projects regarding societal and mission-oriented financing (INIF, 2021).

The INIF recently introduced new empowerment approaches which include a focus on expanding KBFs export potential, developing new services tailored to the needs and sizes of firms in various fields of industry and technology, collaborating with professional brokers, and developing local empowerment services (empowerment hubs). The INIF provided numerous supports and services with the advent of Covid-19 pandemics. While the lack of Covid-19 detection kits harmed Iran, the INIF aided Pishtazteb Zaman, a healthcare knowledge-based firm, by providing empowerment services and funding a state-of-the-art Covid-19 detection kits manufacturing line. Additionally, INIF assisted Pishtazteb Zaman in acquiring world-class licenses that strengthened its export potential (INIF, 2020).

4.1.2 China: innofund

The Innovation Fund for Small Technology-based Firms, or Innofund, established in 1999, is a specialized government agency assisting small businesses' innovative activities, especially in the early stages of research and development, and the transfer of research accomplishments through diverse funding mechanisms. Part of the 1990s revolutionization of state-owned companies (SOEs), it is affiliated with the Chinese Ministry of Science and Technology and the Ministry of Finance, mandated with promoting economic development and enhancing the employment situation in China (Cong et al., 2021; Xin et al., 2016).

Innofund actively engages in innovation and research financing for small technology-based firms (STFs). Additionally, it seeks to draw investment from all sectors within the economy. Innofund has challenged about US$3.1 billion to 30,537 projects from 1999 to 2011 (Innovation Fund for Small Technology-based Firms, 2022).

Innofund assists startups and firms with three categories of financial tools. The first is appropriation, to assist entrepreneurs in establishing their businesses, especially those researchers that create small businesses to commercialize innovative solutions that have not yet matured enough to qualify for commercial financing by venture capital or bank loans. Additionally, it subsidizes a portion of the expenses associated with creating new products and pilot projects for small technology-based businesses (Xin et al., 2016).

The second approach is loan interest subsidy that covers a portion or all of the commercial banks' lending interest that small technology-driven businesses need to grow their innovative products.

The third approach used by Innofund is an equity investment in a limited number of high-tech projects with a promising industrial market. Typically, Innofund's investments do not exceed 20% of the company's registered capital, and according to legislation, these shares will eventually be transferred and the allocated funding withdrawn (Guo et al., 2016). These supports belong to the "Loans, grants, procurement, and co-investment" category. Priority is given to projects with technological innovation, high value-added intellectual property undertaken by researchers (university professors), and students studying abroad who have returned to China, a systematic effort pertinent to societal and mission-oriented financing (Xin et al., 2016).

Additionally, Innofund supports the creative ideas of both startups and leading high-tech companies like Zhongxingwei and Huawei (Guo et al., 2016). Moreover, approximately one-third of the companies listed on the Small and Medium Board of China are Innofund's award winners (Wang et al., 2017). Firms and startups eligible for Innofund's support must have less than 500 employees, of which 30% must possess a tertiary degree. The firm's annual R&D expenditures should also exceed 3% of total sales, and the number of R&D staff needs to be higher than 10% of total employees (Cong et al., 2021). According to Innofund's estimate, it generated over 450,000 jobs in its first decade of operation (Wang et al., 2017).

4.1.3 Russia: Russian Venture Company

The Russian Venture Company (RVC) is a government venture capital fund and development agency founded in 2006. RVC aims to develop a mature capital market through the integration and development of the resources, competencies, and initiatives of investors, investment portfolio managers, and entrepreneurs. This is a part of RVC's ambitions to help Russia become a worldwide technological leader by promoting new products and technologies. RVC's strategy is to support Russian high-tech entrepreneurs in successfully transforming technical and scientific achievements into innovations, products, and services (RVC, 2019, 2021).

Since 2015, RVC has implemented the National Technology Initiative (NTI). It attracts domestic and international private investments in key areas of the Russian economy and encourages new investment in the innovation ecosystem. These initiatives are pursued through funds established by public-private partnerships – common venture capital funds, young managers fund, venture capital funds in the stage of business maturity, venture capital funds in the early stages of business, corporate funds, and finally, foreign funds. RVC is particularly interested in knowledge-incentive industries with low levels of private equity, which are critical to establishing a balanced innovation system (RVC, 2021).

The success story of the SOVA platform, an open-source platform for the creation of chatbots and voice assistants, indicates the importance of funding in the early stages. SOVA received 300 million rubles to develop the platform in 2018 by NTI. NTI has four main supports, including NTI infrastructure (funding infrastructure initiatives that help businesses with a global market perspective grow, e.g., test facilities, R&D centers, or business accelerators), NTI technological breakthrough (create practical prototypes of ground-breaking innovative products that outperform competitors on international markets), NTI spin-off (for new technology-based businesses), and NTI export (for the latter phases of development and commercialization of technical goods, or those whose TRL are above 6) (RVC, 2019).

4.1.4 South Africa: Technology Innovation Agency (TIA)

The Technology Innovation Agency (TIA) is a governmental agency that serves as a binding institution between educational institutions, scientific institutes, government agencies, and the business sector, and as a bridge to commercialization. It was established by the Technology Innovation Act (Act No. 26 of 2008), which authorizes the TIA to encourage the development and exploitation of public interest in discoveries, inventions, innovations, and advancements. As a governmental agency, The TIA's mission is to promote and accelerate technological innovation to enhance economic growth and quality of life for all South Africans (TIA, 2021). To bridge the divide between scientific research, which generates technological or scientific concepts, and starting a business, TIA provides both financial and non-financial services. Financing is intended to assist in creating new or improved innovations or innovative technologies (including products, services, and processes) with the goal of commercialization. The non-financial programs of the TIA includes Seed Fund Program, Youth Technology Innovation, Innovation Skills Development, Technology Stations Program, Technology Platforms, Technology Innovation Cluster Program, and Global Cleantech Innovation Program. The TIA created the Seed Fund, the Technology Development Fund, and the Commercialization Support Fund. TIA offers both pre-and post-investment incentives. Non-financial assistance for projects continues to be strengthened through the TIA Innovation Skills Growth Center, which focuses on company development and entrepreneurship (TIA, 2021).

TIA has six strategic responsibilities and has supplied services and facilities following these tasks. As a "connector," it facilitates cooperation between small and medium-sized businesses, industries, institutions, and academics to create a conducive environment for innovation and global competitiveness. The role of "Thought Leader" supports intellectual capital required to develop technological innovation. This has strengthened the agency's capacity to offer information and counsel on policy problems, frameworks, and procedures for technological innovation advancement. These two roles are aligned with the "societal and mission-oriented financing" national innovation agencies' financing tools.

As an "active funder," the TIA undertakes risk and assists inventors in advancing ideas to market and commercialization. As an "enabler," it pioneers the development of new ideas through various methods, including previously unexplored ones, such as the open innovation process. These two roles support the "General financial incentives to empower and facilitate startups operations" tool. The "facilitator" function also includes attracting and assisting the last stage of financing (businesses, industries, venture capital firms, and development financial agencies) for the commercialization of ready-to-enter innovations and technologies. It also lowers obstacles to obtaining the most expensive skills and equipment for innovators by shifting the location of technology stations and platforms in the form of a service provider. In this scenario, the TIA's unique function is to fund and assist host institutions in providing the necessary services. These two roles link both financing tools of "Loans, grants, procurement and co-investment" and "Export- and production-based financing" (TIA, 2020).

FiberPoynt is a promising startup funded by TIA which provides cheaper and stronger Internet access by a new technology that is highly efficient and cost-effective, and rapid rollout is provided for high-speed broadband deployments in regions that were previously considered too challenging to perform. By benefitting from TIA support, FiberPoynt commercialized its solution with broad socioeconomic outcomes (South African Government DSI, 2021).

4.1.5 France: Bpifrance

Bpifrance is a public investment agency formed in 2012 by the merger of several French public funds and organizations. It is defined as a public body dedicated to funding and empowering businesses while pursuing state and regional government objectives. While serving several roles, Bpifrance primarily fulfills its obligations as an investment bank, an innovation agency, a sovereign fund, and a credit agency for the promotion of exports. There are two specified general interest missions with which Bpifrance is charged, i.e., actively promoting and supporting innovation and contributing to and encouraging the growth and financing of small- and medium-sized companies. It is also tasked with boosting sustainable growth in creating new jobs (Bpifrance, 2020; Mazzucato et al., 2018).

Bpifrance offers a variety of financial mechanisms, of which investment in funding long-term projects and assisting in the stabilization of share ownership in competitive, high-growth, high-impact companies that benefit the French economy are worth noting. Instruments are related to the "Societal and mission-oriented financing," including adherence to female-owned small- and medium-sized companies; transition to digital technologies and a socially responsible economy; and encouraging the adoption of ecologically and energy-conscious transition measures (Mazzucato et al., 2018). Overall, Bpi provides five categories of support for innovative businesses and startups:

1) Loan Plans, including various sub-plans for firms' cash-flow empowerment, loans for specific industrial activities, no-need guarantee loans, leasing, export credit, regional loans, and long-term loans.
2) Investment Plans, including subjective investment plans, co-investment plans, public investment plans, and venture capital plans.
3) Guarantee and Insurance Plans, containing multiple sub-plans like currency rate insurance during the contract, international investment insurance, international prosperity insurance, international credit insurance, bank guarantees, bond guarantees, and international pre-financing.
4) Grant Plans, including but not limited to plans to support innovative businesses, plans for cooperative innovation projects, innovation licenses, and innovation awards.
5) Accompanying Plans, which includes networking, consultancy, partnership, and university projects and plans.

FAN is an early-stage startup financing fund affiliated with Bpifrance. It helps fast-growing French digital technology startups dominate global marketplaces. It offers series A and B rounds of financing ranging from €2m to €25m in Deep Tech, SaaS, and digital consumer services. The Internet-connected consumer electronics company Netatmo helps customers make their homes smarter. FAN invested in the seed round of Netatmo in May 2013 and helped find industrial partners. As a consequence of FAN's support, Netatmo partnered with Legrand, a worldwide leader in electrical and digital building infrastructures, in 2015. Eventually, Legrand acquired Netatmo in November 2018 (Bpifrance, 2018).

4.1.6 Germany: KfW

The KfW (Kreditanstalt für Wiederaufbau in German, meaning Credit Institute for Reconstruction) is a state-owned investment and development bank headquartered in Frankfurt since 1948. The original goal of the KfW was to contribute to postwar reconstruction. After a couple of rounds of revisions in its mandate, KfW now promotes small- and medium-sized businesses, facilitates exports, preserves the environment, encourages innovation, and contributes to global development (Mazzucato et al., 2018). The KfW comprises a mother company KfW and five affiliated companies (KfW Group, 2019). It provides myriad financial supports and services, addressing challenging issues in the world, including climate change and the environment, globalization, social change, digitization and innovation, and SMEs. Its activities are funded by local and international financial and capital markets. KfW IPEX-Bank fulfills KfW's primary operations by promoting export and project funding in developing and emerging countries and pursuing renewable energy technology development (KfW Group, 2020).

Considering the introduced financial tools' classification for innovation agencies, KfW's instruments in "General financial incentives to empower and facilitate startups operations" consist of startup financing, financing of general corporate investments, holding arrangements for the Federal Republic of Germany, education financing, and promotional activities (KfW Group, 2020).

In the "Loans, grants, procurement and co-investment" category of financial policy tools, KfW offers services such as customized corporate financing with equity and debt capital, customized financing of banks and promotional institutions of the federal states, investments in German and European venture capital and venture debt funds, securities and money market investments, central interest rate and currency management, and strategic equity investments (KfW Group, 2020). Furthermore, KfW supports export by financing projects and investments of interest to Germany and Europe, supporting projects co-financed by the European Investment Bank or similar European financing institutions (KfW Group, 2020; Law Concerning KfW, 2020).

KfW also pays attention to "Societal and mission-oriented financing" which differentiates it from other national innovation agencies, at least those elaborated in this chapter. According to Germany's adherence to a green environment, KfW supports green-technology-based firms on the supply side. Moreover, it has a dedicated line of financing for solar and wind energies (Mazzucato et al., 2018). In other words, sustainability plays an instrumental role in KfW's business strategy (KfW Group, 2020).

With the emergence of Covid-19, KfW announced coronavirus aid, and 97% of funds went to small- and medium-sized companies and startups. By the end of 2020, KfW had provided more than 100,000 loans totaling roughly EUR 46 billion. KfW has dedicated itself to place digitalization, sustainability, alleviating poverty, the mitigation of crises and causes of displacement, and Africa at the heart of its efforts (KfW Group, 2020).

The biotech company MYR is a German unicorn that developed the drug Hepcludex, the first active component for treating chronic hepatitis D in the world.is The High-Tech Startup Fund (HTGF), a plan presented by KfW Capital (a subsidiary of KfW), invested in MYR during its challenging early stages. The funding enabled the active ingredient to be further developed and tested in healthy volunteers for the first time as part of clinical phase I. HTGF also supported MYR in other aspects, including strategic consultancy and networking (KfW Stories, 2021).

4.1.7 Japan: DBJ and JFC

In 2008, the Development Bank of Japan Inc. (DBJ) was transformed into a joint-stock company from a special government agency. DBJ is affiliated with Japan's Finance Ministry and provides a range of financial market services as a government-affiliated financial institution. Long-term loans, equity, mezzanine finance, and other forms of risk capital as well as M&A consulting services are some examples of DBJ's diversified supports. DBJ's top three priorities are (1)

Rebuilding and reinforcement of infrastructure, (2) Creation, conversion, and growth in the industry, and (3) Self-reliance and revitalization of local economies (Development Bank of Japan Inc., 2020).

The JFC (Japan Finance Corporation), a government-affiliated financial institution, was established in October 2008 to complement the financing activities of private financing institutions by supporting small businesses and individuals (Kuroda, 2019). The JFC provided approximately $2.21 billion (255,997 million Yen) in loans in 2019 (JFC, 2022). It has three major lines of operations having a synergic effect on each other.

Its first support stream relates to Micro-Business and Individual Unit that includes various types of loans (educational loans, small loans, loans secured by government pensions, etc.), support for startups and business succession. The second support line is SME Unit, providing long-term business financing. Furthermore, the JFC aids in insuring credit guarantee corporations (CGCs). It also assists in resolving business challenges, such as networking. The last stream of JFC's support falls under the Agriculture, Forestry, Fisheries, and Food Business Unit. This unit offers loans to the aforementioned areas. Additionally, it offers management support services such as consulting and matchmaking (JFC, 2021).

The DBJ has played various roles since its conception. In 1951, the Japan Development Bank (JDB) was established to develop major industries, forming the backbone of economic and industrial development after World War II in a phase called "economic recovery." In the rapid growth phase, the Hokkaido Development Finance Public Corporation was founded to expand and reinforce industrial bases, develop domestic technologies by high-growth infrastructure development, and strengthen international competitiveness. A case worth mentioning for promoting technological capability through commercialization in this period is Sony's Trinitron color television factory. From the 1970s to 1980s, JDB funds helped improve the quality of life and transform industrial infrastructures.

The post-bubble economy phase was mainly about developing innovative financial products focused on sources of corporate values. At the end of this phase, regional revitalization was revealed through the cooperation of regional financial institutions by financial solutions that support communities, the environment, and technology. JDB aimed to support business regeneration in their recovery toward revitalization of the Japanese economy in the 1990s. DBJ was founded in 2008 – amid the Global Financial Crisis in 2008 and The Great East Japan Earthquake in 2011 – following the promulgation of Act No.85 of 2007, JDB ceased to exist and all of its rights and responsibilities were transferred to DBJ. During the early 2000s, DBJ responded to innovation and financial crises by persistently revising its supports and facilities. In 2015, DBJ extended its support for Japanese businesses' competitiveness by establishing the Special Investments Operations (Development Bank of Japan Inc., 2017). DBJ, JFC, and other agencies specialized in supporting the commercialization of Japanese firms and startups, included social and environmental challenges in their facilities. With the advent of the Covid-19 pandemic, DBJ and JFC actively supported firms to mitigate pandemic-related challenges and offered many financial facilities to startups damaged by the pandemic as well as those working on Covid-19-related solutions and goods (JFC, 2021).

DBJ's facilities cover all four categories of national innovation agencies financial tools (Table 3.1), including crisis response operations, providing risk capital through integrated investment and loan services, sharing risks with financial institutions, offering asset management opportunities and strengthening them, building a stable investment portfolio, offering collaborative funds, commercializing new technologies, consultancy in business restructuring, overseas business development, and offering supports in line with environmental and societal challenges (globalization, climate change, etc.; Development Bank of Japan Inc., 2017).

4.1.8 South Korea: KOTEC

The Republic of Korea has a variety of legal bodies and legislative frameworks in place to promote startups and SMEs. Supporting frameworks for startups and SMEs are geared toward facilitating transition to an innovation-based economy. In this regard, the government has developed legislative tools and policy incentives for funding startups and SMEs (Wisuttisak, 2021).

Korea Finance Technology Corporation, or KOTEC (with the abbreviation in Korean called KIBO), is a non-profit government-affiliated agency under the Ministry of SMEs & Startups established in 1989 to support SMEs by easing their access to funding for technology and innovation development. KOTEC addresses the funding gap faced by technologically capable but credit-constrained SMEs. It provides a variety of services to support startups and new businesses, including credit guarantee, technology appraisal, guarantee-linked equity investment, technology transfer, and protection. KOTEC, in particular, has been a pioneer in promoting technology transfers by developing a financing framework for technology appraisal. Other key programs offered by KOTEC include helping universities and research institutes match and transfer technologies to small businesses as well as protecting IP and supporting high-tech innovative businesses (KIBO, 2020).

KOTEC's incentives fall into two main categories, i.e., core services and supplementary services. Credit guarantee enables technologically viable but collateral-constrained SMEs to receive funding for technology innovation or business operations. Technology appraisal estimates the future value of the technologies of SMEs by evaluating their technical competency, marketability, and commercial viability. KOTEC's equity investment provides direct equity investment for early-stage, commercially viable technology startups. It also provides IP registration incentives for Korean SMEs.

To support commercialization of R&D results, KOTEC acts as a technology transfer office, facilitating the transfer of IP rights from universities and research institutions to SMEs. Its supplementary services encompass consulting and certification assistance. Business consultancies are provided to empower managerial skills and knowledge at SMEs. It also consults SMEs on whether they meet the requirements for different government-sponsored certification programs, such as Venture Businesses and INNO-Biz (KIBO, 2022). KOTEC facilities cover all four types of financial instruments offered by national innovation agencies, as shown in Table 3.1.

5 Comparative discussion of innovation financing mechanisms for startups

Considering all eight studied national innovation financing agencies discussed in this chapter, this section provides a brief comparative analysis of their services and assistance to startups and new businesses. First, we compare their financial resources and their affiliated funds. Then, we present a summary of financing tools adopted by these agencies according to categories of financing tools (c.f., Table 3.1). Table 3.2 presents the aggregated amount of funding and affiliated structure of the eight studied agencies in this chapter.

Table 3.3 compares the financial instruments used by the eight innovation financing agencies profiled in this chapter. Based on the facilities and incentives mentioned in the annual reports and websites of each innovation agency, we specify whether a financial tool, in line with the categories and tools stated in Table 3.1, is being utilized.

As Table 3.3 indicates, all innovation funding agencies have a common goal: to promote innovation and wealth creation in society as a whole. This is reflected clearly in the general funding methods and their approaches for supporting innovation by encouraging collaboration between universities, research institutes, startups, and firms. Additionally, they offer consulting services in the early phases of innovation and assist in commercialization in the later stages. However, in line with issues such as climate change, globalization, Covid-19, and digitalization, all of which impact startups, innovation agencies are developing new services to counteract the harmful effects of such issues on startups. Nevertheless, it is a work in progress, and it is too early to draw any conclusions. The current depth and breadth of innovation agencies' support regarding the prevalent socio-economic challenges are as of yet neither sufficient nor effective.

Given the investment banking background of KfW and DBJ, their support is broader in scope and riskier in nature than those of other agencies. For instance, they offer infrastructure and renovation services as well as assistance through public procurement and reduced interest rates on startup and business loans. However, KOTEC also offers infrastructure services, particularly for smart manufacturing and other technology-related infrastructure. China's Innofund services are comparable in scope and amount to Germany and Japan's, with relatively more domestic emphasis and job creation than export and international partnerships; as China has delegated these functions to other specialized agencies, Innofund has focused on local development.

RVC supports are notable in attracting foreign resources to promote innovation and technology development in innovative startups and high-tech companies in Russia, which is also the case in TIA. Although INIF has increased its

Table 3.2 Overview of Innovation Agencies in Terms of Amounts of Funding and Structure

Innovation Agency (Establishment)/ Country	*Approximate Amount of Aggregated Funding and Facilities in 2020/2021*	*Number of Subsidiary Funds or Associated Organizations*
INIF (2011)/ Iran	4000 billion (IR Rials)/$948 million USD	9 partner organizations, 12 partner banks and 60 partner research and technology funds
Innofund (1999)/ China	$672 billion USD	NA
RVC (2006)/ Russia	30 billion (Rubles)/$388 million USD	Subsidiary Funds. 4 RVC Infrafund, 2 Funds in Foreign Jurisdictions, 3 funds established in the form of Closed-End Venture Funds (CEVF), 2 Funds established in the form of Investment Partnership Agreement (IPA), 22 partner Regional Venture Capital Funds
TIA (2008)/ South Africa	440.9 million (South African Rand)/$31 million USD	3 funds and 9 partner organizations
Bpifrance (2012)/France	€94.3 billion	Bpifrance Financement, Bpifrance Investissement, Bpifrance Assurance Export
KfW (1948)/ Germany	€107 billion	KfW Development Bank, DEG – Deutsche Investitions- und Entwicklungsgesellschaft mbH, Domestic business, KfW Capital, KfW Stiftung
DBJ (2008)/ Japan	13.7 trillion Yen/$125 billion USD	10 branch offices, 8 representative offices and 4 overseas subsidiaries
KOTEC (1989) South Korea	195.5 billion KRW direct investment/$163 million USD Direct Investment and 25.7 trillion KRW ($ 2.145 billion USD) guarantees for SMEs	9 regional headquarters, 62 technology appraisal centers, 8 technology innovation centers, 4 cultural content finance centers, venture investment center, social venture valuation center, 1 patent mutual aid operation center, institute of future innovation, central technology appraisal institute

Sources: Author's conclusion based on agencies annual reports and websites (Development Bank of Japan Inc., 2020; INIF, 2021; KfW, 2021; KIBO, 2020; KOTEC, 2022; Luong et al., 2021; RVC, 2021; TIA, 2020).

Note 1: The year in parentheses represents the establishment date of each innovation agency.

Note 2: The amount of funding and facilities are the most recent information available as of February 2022.

financial and service support for innovative businesses within the last five years, there is a considerable gap between its support scale and those of leading agencies such as Bpifrance and Innofund. Bpifrance mostly targets issues and challenges related to startups and businesses in the French market. In other words,

Table 3.3 Financial Tools Adopted by Innovation Agencies

Country/ Agency		*Iran*	*China*	*Russia*	*South Africa*	*France*	*Germany*	*Japan*	*Korea*
Category	Tools	INIF	Innofund	RVC	TIA	Bpi	KfW	DBJ	KOTEC
1 General financial incentives to empower and facilitate startups operations	Consulting services and Commercialization	•	•	•	•	•	•	•	•
	Direct investment	•	•	•	•	•	•	•	•
	Tax incentives	•				•			•
	Knowledge development	•	•	•	•	•	•	•	•
	Developing 'national champions' capable of competing in global marketplaces	•		•		•	•	•	•
	Supporting IPRs								
2 Export- and production-based financing	Infrastructure financing		•				•	•	•
	Licensing				•	•			•
	Communication and Networking	•	•	•	•	•	•	•	•
	Angel networks				•	•			•
	Encourage strategic trade (e.g., import substitution and material security) and financial leverage	•		•	•	•	•	•	•
	Facilitating foreign capital investment	•		•	•		•	•	
	Export credit insurance					•	•		•
3 Loans, grants, procurement and co-investment	Investment priority in emerging S&T areas	•	•	•	•	•	•	•	
	Co-investment (fund-in-fund)	•	•	•	•	•	•	•	•
	Lower interest rates on loans		•				•	•	•
	Credit guarantees and Collateral	•	•			•	•	•	•
	R&D and military procurement			•		•			•
	Public procurement/ Public procurement for innovation	•		•		•	•	•	
	Grants, subsidies (including tax credits), innovation prizes and other non-reimbursable public funds for basic research and innovation	•	•	•	•	•	•	•	•
4 Societal and mission-oriented financing	• Environmental issues and sustainability • Societal challenges • National strategic technology areas and priorities	•	•	•	•	•	•	•	•

Sources: Author's conclusion based on agencies annual reports and websites (Development Bank of Japan Inc., 2020; INIF, 2021; KfW, 2021; KIBO, 2020; Luong, et al., 2021; RVC, 2021; TIA, 2020; Authors' compilation).

Bpifrance's services are tailor-made to the French context, which is also considered to some extent by other agencies. Overall, despite myriad supports provided by these agencies, some key societal considerations need to be addressed by them.

6 Conclusion and policy recommendations

6.1 Policy recommendations

This chapter explained national innovation finance startups and innovative firms and compared similarities and variations of supports. Our results reflect variations and existing neglections in funding. Herein, we present policy suggestions for governments and innovation institutions. It should be noted that our findings are drawn based on the reports and websites of the studied innovation agencies in this chapter.

6.1.1 Avoiding crowding-out by innovation funding agencies

There is concern that the private sector is being crowded out by governmental innovation agencies. While this is not true in most cases, the primary function of innovation funding organizations is to assist the private sector and work alongside it symbiotically. Thus, innovation agencies need to define their functions so that they do not restrict the efforts and assistance of the private sector. These positions should supplement the private sector's riskier ventures to limit risk and encourage startups when the private sector lacks the means or inclination to support startups alone (Borrás and Edquist, 2019).

6.1.2 Enhancing transparency and simplicity in the credit assessment process of startups and SMEs

A frequent challenge confronted by SMEs and startups is the traditional loan evaluation and credit assessment process. This complicates the situation for startups for obtaining loans and financial facilities. To address this inadequacy, it is necessary to create a customized credit information infrastructure for startups and to apply credit-rating approaches to them. It is worth mentioning that establishing a long-term loan guarantee program to empower startups and SMEs without conventional collateral requirements is critical for startup funding schemes in national innovation financing agencies (Yoshino and Taghizadeh-Hesary, 2019).

6.1.3 Promoting business evaluation by using standard metrics

Considering the due diligence assessment, innovation agencies should tailor the assessment process to promoting startups with the potential for future development in their incentives and financing plans.

6.1.4 Covering the key risks and obstacles that startups face realistically

Helping startups resolve their bankruptcy situation caused by failed innovation efforts is a much-needed support that is ignored by innovation agencies ignore, at least by those studied in this chapter. Financial initiatives based on the very challenges startups face should cover the whole innovation process, from idea to concept development, growth, bankruptcy, and M&A. Similarly, innovation agencies are expected to use a diverse range of financial instruments that are suited for different stages of a startup's life cycle. Innofund in China is an interesting agency that focuses on early-stage R&D funding, whereas other national funds overlook it. Startups need early-stage assistance and education. These services include a range of mentoring, financing, and connections (Cong et al., 2021).

6.1.5 Addressing societal and mission-oriented approach in funding programs

Problem- and mission-oriented approaches in the design of financial instruments and the structuring support programs would be a leap forward in enhancing the effectiveness of these agencies. Global problems relating to sustainability, health, and the environment, such as climate change, pandemics, air pollution, and water shortages, call for innovation agencies to play an active role in financing schemes to direct innovation efforts of startups toward these challenges now more than ever. Although this is a trend apparent in all studied agencies in this chapter, the amount and diversity of support in this regard are not balanced enough to meet the growing challenges we face.

6.1.6 Setting a systematic evaluation system at national innovation agencies

Another recommendation for innovation financing agencies is to scrutinize examples of their successful and failed support. The latter is usually neglected, even though it is an instrumental source of learning for future funding efforts. A systematic evaluation system would specify which instruments are more suited to target startups, which instruments are associated with a higher degree of success in achieving their predefined goals, unexpected outcomes, and byproducts of each instrument. This approach will provide agencies with pragmatic insight into future initiatives and allow them to adapt their services to the industry and country's specific conditions.

6.2 Conclusion

This chapter conducts comparative analyses of national innovation finance institutions for startups and SMEs in eight countries. We have provided recommendations for improving the effectiveness of technology and innovation funding to promote startups and SMEs. Noting that the literature on startup financing is still not mature, hence, this chapter may fill some of the existing gap through its comparative analysis of recognized innovation funding institutions. Lastly, we must acknowledge that national innovation financing agencies have more significant responsibilities than just providing funding for startups and innovation; they are the ones who can shift society's view on innovation and financing. This may be accomplished through a symbiotic collaboration with the private sector on creative risk-taking initiatives, empowering services, social responsibilities. Working with policymakers and central banks to customize financial and banking regulations considering startups' limitations to get funding from mainstream banking and the financial sector is also an essential duty of national innovation agencies beyond their daily role in financing startups.

References

Agogué M, Berthet E, Fredberg T, Le Masson P, Segrestin B, Stoetzel M, Wiener M, Yström A (2017) Explicating the role of innovation intermediaries in the "unknown": A contingency approach. *J Strategy Manag* 10(1):19–39

Allman K, Edler J, Georghiou L, Jones B, Miles I, Omidvar O, Ramlogan R, Rigby F (2011) Measuring wider framework conditions for successful innovation. A system's review of UK and international data, Report published by Nesta, January 2011, UK. https://media.nesta.org.uk/documents/measuring_wider_framework.pdf

Bellavitis C, Filatotchev I, Kamuriwo DS, Vanacker T (2017) *Entrepreneurial finance: New frontiers of research and practice: Editorial for the special issue Embracing entrepreneurial funding innovations*, Venture Capital. *Int J Entrepreneurial Behav Res* 19(1–2): 1–16

Bemelmans-Videc ML, Rist RC, Vedung EO (2011) *Carrots, sticks, and sermons: Policy instruments and their evaluation*. New York, United States: Transactions Publisher

Borrás S, Edquist C (2019) *Holistic innovation policy: Theoretical foundations, policy problems, and instrument choices*. First ed. Oxford: Oxford University Press

Bpifrance (2018) FAN fund. [Online] Available at: https://www.bpifrance.com/private-equity/direct-investment/venture-capital/fan-fund [Accessed 2021]

Bpifrance (2020) Bpifrance 2020 Universal Registration Document, AMF

Brown R, Rocha A, Cowling M (2020) Financing entrepreneurship in times of crisis: Exploring the impact of COVID-19 on the market for entrepreneurial finance in the United Kingdom. *Int Small Bus J* 38(5):380–390

Cong LW, Lee CMC, Qu Y, Shen T (2021) Financing entrepreneurship and innovation in China. [Online] Available at: https://arxiv.org/abs/2108.10982

de Luna-Martinez J, Vicente CL (2012) Global survey of development banks. World Bank Policy Research Working Paper, p 5969

Development Bank of Japan Inc (2017) Fourth medium-term management plan, Tokyo: Development Bank of Japan Inc. (DBJ)

Development Bank of Japan Inc (2020) Integrated report 2020, Tokyo: Development Bank of Japan (DBJ)

D'Orazio P, Löwenstein P (2020) Mobilising investments in renewable energy in Germany: Which role for public investment banks? *J Sustain Finance Invest* 12(2):451–474. doi:10.1080/20430795.2020.1777062

Edquist C, Zabala-Iturriagagoitia JM (2012) Public procurement for innovation as mission-oriented innovation policy. *Res Policy* 41(10):1757–1769

Edquist C, Zabala-Iturriagagoitia JM (2020) Functional procurement for innovation, welfare, and the environment. *Sci Public Policy* 47(5):595–603

Ferrando A, Pal R, Durante E (2019) Financing and obstacles for high growth enterprises: The European case. EIB Working Paper 2019/03, March

Ghazinoory S, Ghazinoori S (2014) *An introduction to science, technology and innovation policy making.* Second ed. Tehran: Tarbiat Modarres University

Glennie A, Bound K (2016) How innovation agencies work: International lessons to inspire and inform national strategies. [Online] Available at: https://www.nesta.org.uk/report/how-innovation-agencies-work [Accessed June 2021]

Guo D, Guo Y, Jiang K (2016) Government-subsidized R&D and firm innovation: Evidence from China. *Res Policy* 45(6):1129–1144

Hochstetler K, Montero AP (2013) The renewed developmental state: The national development bank and the Brazil model. *J Dev Stud* 49(11):1484–1499

Hsu CH, Chang AY, Luo W (2017) Identifying key performance factors for sustainability development of SMEs–integrating QFD and fuzzy MADM methods. *J Clean Prod* (161):629–645

INIF (2019) Iran National Innovation Fund, Tehran: Presidency of the Islamic Republic of Iran

INIF (2020) A review of the Iran Innovation National Fund's activities and accomplishments in assisting knowledge- and technology-based businesses in developing products and services to tackle Corona, Tehran: Iran National Innovation Fund

INIF (2021) Amount of facilities granted. [Online] Available at: https://www.inif.ir/web/guest/amount-facility [Accessed 12 09 2021]

Innovation Fund for Small Technology-based Firms (2022) Innovation Fund for Technology Based Firms. [Online] Available at: http://innofund.chinatorch.gov.cn/english2/xhtml/02_fund_nature.htm [Accessed 12 02 2022]

Janeway WH, Nanda R, Rhodes-Kropf M (2021) Venture Capital Booms and Startup Financing. Harvard Business School Entrepreneurial Management Working Paper

JFC (2021) Japan Finance Corporation Annual Report, Tokyo: Public Relations Department, Japan Finance Corporation

JFC (2022) Japan Finance Corporation. [Online] Available at: https://www.jfc.go.jp/n/english/mbis/performance.html [Accessed 12 02 2022]

KfW (2021) KfW – Responsible banking. [Online] Available at: https://www.kfw.de/KfW-Group/ [Accessed 12 02 2022]

KfW Group (2019) KfW financial report 2019, Frankfurt: KfW Group in accordance with IFRS

KfW Group (2020) KfW financial report 2020, Frankfurt: KfW Group in accordance with IFRS

KfW Stories (2021) The billion-euro drug. [Online] Available at: https://www.kfw.de/stories/myr-2.html [Accessed 2021]

KIBO (2020) 2020 KOTEC Annual Report, Busan: CCA

KIBO (2022) Korea Technology Finance Corporation. [Online] Available at: https://www.kibo.or.kr/english/about/about010400.do [Accessed 12 02 2022]

KOTEC (2022) Korean Technology Finance Corporation. [Online] Available at: https://www.kibo.or.kr/english/about/about010100.do [Accessed 12 02 2022]

Kuckertz A, Brändle L, Gaudig A, Hinderer S, Reyes CA, Prochotta A, Steinbrink KM, Berger ES (2020) Startups in times of crisis – A rapid response to the COVID-19 pandemic. *J Bus Ventur Insights* 13(e00169)

Kuroda A (2019) Credit supplementation system for unlocking SME and startup access to finance: The case of Japan. In: Yoshino N, Taghizadeh-Hesary F, eds. *Unlocking SME finance in Asia: Roles of credit rating and credit guarantee schemes.* First ed., London: Routledge, pp 247–268

Law Concerning KfW (2020) Law Concerning Kreditanstalt für Wiederaufbau, Frankfurt: KfW Group

Lee N, Sameen H, Cowling M (2015) Access to finance for innovative SMEs since the financial crisis. *Res Policy* 44(2):370–380

Liu FC, Simon DF, Sun YT, Cao C (2011. China's innovation policies: Evolution, institutional structure, and trajectory. *Res Policy* 40(7):917–931

Luong N, Arnold Z, Murphy B (2021) Understanding Chinese government guidance funds - an analysis of Chinese-language sources. [Online] Available at: https://cset.georgetown.edu/publication/understanding-chinese-government-guidance-funds/ [Accessed 12 09 2021]

Mazzucato M, Macfarlane L, Penna C, Ryan-Collins J (2018) The role of patient finance in mission-oriented innovation: The market shaping role of state investment banks. The European Union Horizon 2020 Research and Innovation action

Mazzucato M, Penna CC (2015a) *Mission-oriented finance for innovation: New ideas for investment-led growth.* London: Rowman & Littlefield International, Ltd

Mazzucato M, Penna CC (2015b) The rise of mission-oriented state investment banks: The cases of Germany's KfW and Brazil's BNDES. The Rise of Mission-Oriented State Investment Banks: The Cases of German SWPS 2015–26

Mazzucato M, Penna CC (2016) Beyond market failures: The market creating and shaping roles of state investment banks. *J Econ Policy Reform* 19(4):305–326

OECD (2015) *New approaches to SME and entrepreneurship financing: Broadening the range of instruments*, Paris, France: OECD

Raimi L (2020) Breaking the formal financing barriers facing entrepreneurs: Crowdfunding as an alternative financing for enterprise development in Nigeria in the Digital Era. In: Efosa CI, ed. *Handbook of research on social and organizational dynamics in the digital era.* United States: IGI Global, pp 218–234

Roed I (2016) Disentangling the family firm's innovation process: A systematic review. *J Fam Bus Strategy* 7(3):185–201

RVC (2019) RVC 2019 Annual Report, Moscow: Russian Venture Capital (RVC)

RVC (2021) Investment approach. [Online] Available at: https://rvc.ru/en/about/ [Accessed 12 02 2022]

RVC (2021) RVC — About the company. [Online] Available at: https://www.rvc.ru/en/about/ [Accessed 10 September 2021]

Schröder M, Ekins P, Power A, Zulauf M, Lowe R (2011) *The KFW experience in the reduction of energy use in and CO2 emissions from buildings: Operation, impacts and lessons for the UK*, London: London School of Economics

South African Goverment (2021) Science and innovation funds the development of affordable internet. [Online] Available at: https://www.gov.za/speeches/science-and-innovation-funds-development-affordable-internet-5-may-2021-0000 [Accessed 30 August 2021]

Subramanian M, Taghizadeh-Hesary F (2021) Techno-Economic Feasibility Study Methods in Startup Financing. In: Taghizadeh-Hesary F, et al. eds. *Investment in startups and small business financing*, Singapore: World Scientific Publishing Co. Pte. Ltd, pp 107–136

Taghizadeh-Hesary F, Yoshino N, Fukuda L, Rasoulinezhad E (2021) A model for calculating optimal credit guarantee fee for small and medium-sized enterprises. *Econ Model* 95: 361–373

TIA (2020) Technology Innovation Agency Annual Report 2019/20, Technology Innovation Agency

TIA (2021) About technology innovation agency, technology innovation agency. [Online] Available at: https://www.tia.org.za/about-us/ [Accessed 20 August 2021]

Tidd J, Bessant JR, Pavitt K (2020) *Managing innovation: Integrating technological, market and organizational change*. Third ed., United States: John Wiley & Sons

Wang Y, Li J, Furman JL (2017) Firm performance and state innovation funding: Evidence from China's Innofund program. *Res Policy* 46(6):1142–1161

Wisuttisak P (2021) Comparative study on regulatory frameworks for promotion of startup businesses and SMEs in Japan, Republic of Korea, Malaysia, and Thailand. In: Taghizadeh-Hesary F, et al. eds. *Investment in startups and small business financing*, Singapore: World Scientific Publishing Co. Pte. Ltd, pp 3–22

Xin F, Chen Z, Du X (2016) Do the types of subsidies and firms' heterogeneity affect the effectiveness of public R&D subsidies? Evidence from China's Innofund programme. *Asian J Technol Innov* 24(3):317–337

Yoshino N, Taghizadeh-Hesary F (2019) Role of SMEs in Asia and the financing challenges they face. In: Yoshino N, Taghizadeh-Hesary F, eds. *Unlocking SME Finance in Asia*, Abingdon: Routledge, pp 3–22

4 Innovation financing challenges from the perspective of structural barriers and business environment of Iran

Case of the Iran national innovation fund

Ali Nazemi and Vali Parsaei

1 Introduction

Numerous scholars have shown that venture capital activities are essential for the creation and growth of high-tech and innovative businesses (Denis, 2004; Gompers and Lerner, 2001). The success of venture-backed businesses in the United States resulted in the employment of thousands of people in a few years. However, the United States and the United Kingdom are outliers in having established important venture capital (VC) and PE industries as early as the 1960s. Singapore, Taiwan, and China are examples of Asian countries that have successfully developed a notable venture capital market. The venture capital industry in Singapore began in the 1980s with the establishment of the first Singapore Science Park (1980) and the rise of the first venture capital fund (1983) (Bartzokas and Mani, 2004). From 1985 to 1990, the venture capital pool in Singapore reached one billion Singapore dollars (Bartzokas and Mani, 2004). The 1990s was a period of expansion in the VC industry of Singapore, when the venture capital pool of the country grew over tenfold, from S$822 million to over S$9,197 million in 2000. In 2021, the yearly venture capital and private equity deals were valued at S$16.54 billion (Statista, 2021a). The Singapore Economic Development Board (EDB), a governmental body, acts as a catalyst and facilitator to support and encourage entrepreneurship in the country and has played an important role in the development of the VC industry in Singapore. EBD initiated its first venture capital fund in 1985 with the committed capital of S$100 million, and from 1986 to 1990 it invested in seven other VC funds and ten venture businesses, comprising a total portfolio of more than S$33 million (Buchanan, 1989). In addition to direct investment, the EDB also initiated various strategic programs to support venture capital activities, including establishing the Venture Capital Club of Singapore, forming the Strategic Business Unit, and sponsoring Capital Assistance Scheme loans

DOI: 10.4324/9781003220220-6

(Bartzokas and Mani, 2004). Moreover, the government started the Stock Exchange of Singapore Dealing and Automated Quotation system (SESDAQ) in 1987 to facilitate the public offering of high-tech enterprises in the Singaporean capital market. SESDAQ was eventually replaced with a sponsored-based market in 2008 named CATALIST that is more friendly for fast-growing businesses (SGX, 2021). The success of the VC industry in Taiwan is mainly due to policies learned from the United States and Japan. Upon Taiwan's removal from the United Nations, the country had to face growing pressure to attract international capital. In 1981, Kwoh-Ting Li, who came to be known as the "Father of Taiwan's Economic Miracle," started a research journey to Silicon Valley, Boston's Route 128, and Japan. With the lessons and experiences learned from different policy models, he adopted two main policies: first, the 20% tax credit which was previously implemented to support growing ICT activities; and second, a specified local company structure for venture capital funds to empower nervous local investors to take control of their investment decisions (Klingler-Vidra et al., 2016). The subsidy tax policies encouraged foreign VC firms to invest in new industries in Taiwan, which eventually resulted in a dynamic VC environment. In fact, the birth of the VC industry in Taiwan happened outside its borders; according to the Asian Venture Capital Journal, until the 2000s, every important Taiwanese venture capital fund had an office in the United States and invested 20 to 30 of its resources outside Taiwan (Asian Venture Capital Journal, 2001). China's VC industry is a result of political, economic, and institutional changes, particularly its transition from a central communist planning system to a more market-based ecosystem (Bartzokas and Mani, 2004). In 1984, the National Research Center of Science and Technology for the Development of China first suggested to the governments to establish a venture capital system to promote high technology. In response, the Chinese Communist Party approved in 1985 the use of venture capital to support high-technology areas, which led to the first limited corporation focused on VC investments (China New Technology Venture Investment Corp.). In 1986, 863 high-technology programs started to invest over RMB10 billion in research and development activities. The first Chinese incubator was started in 1987. By the late 1980s, China's first Sino-foreign joint venture in venture capital was established. In 1991, many Chinese institutions were allowed to initiate VC funds in high-technology zones. With the new regulation in 1993, Chinese ventures were allowed to list on foreign exchanges, and international investors were permitted to establish VC companies in China. In 1994, three American venture capital firms established offices in China. Over the next two years, more than 20 venture capital firms were added to the Chinese VC industry. The growth continued, and in 2002, over 160 domestic and 50 international venture capital firms were active in China (Bartzokas and Mani, 2004). VC investments in China have consistently grown. In 1997, only US$70 million of venture investment was recorded in the whole country; that figure increased to US$257 million in 2001 (Bartzokas and Mani, 2004), and by 2010 over US$35.1 billion of funds was invested in venture business. In the past year (2021), a total amount of US$195.1 billion was attracted by the Chinese VC industry. The success of the venture capital method in developing countries and their transition to the developed world lures policymakers in less developed regions, and policymakers have realized that while their countries host good opportunities for investment in infrastructure, the most important factor in achieving a higher level of wealth and sustainable economic growth remains creating an endogenous innovation ecosystem, of which financing is one of the most important pillars and the driving force behind the development of innovative activities. Therefore, many governmental programs are specially designed to address the financing problems of the innovation ecosystem.

The innovation financing market is facing structural market failure for various reasons, such as information asymmetry between actors and a high volume of uncertainty in this area, making optimal financial resource allocation difficult. Therefore, governments intervene in the innovation financing market and try to address some of its shortcomings. As they do so, however, they do not limit their initiatives to the basic reasons for intervening but tend to interfere in all of this market's areas and aspects. Concern over the effectiveness of government intervention in the development of the venture capital market has been expressed worldwide (Zhang and Mayes, 2018).

Crowding out the private sectors is another issue in government intervention in the VC market. Researchers have found mixed shreds of evidence as to whether government intervention in the VC market improves or crowds out private resources (Del-Palacio et al., 2012; Jeng and Wells, 2000; Leleux and Surlemont, 2003).

By reviewing countries' experiences in designing appropriate tools, determining the government's intervention limits, and with the method and scope of government initiatives, knowledge regarding the development of this ecosystem can be expanded. To the best of our knowledge, most scholars have studied the ex-post issues of governmental programs in VC markets; few have emphasized the ex-ante issues facing governments that implement a venture capital investment plan. Moreover, most authors have focused on developed countries, generally omitting developing countries that have a friendly environment for venture investments. In summary, the chapter seeks to answer the questions below:

1. What issues and lessons are involved in implementing an intervention plan in the VC market of Iran as a developing region?
2. What policies are recommended to address these issues and lessons?

The next section provides a theoretical background of the rationale behind government intervention into the VC market. The following two sections comprise the methodology and a case study. In section five, seven INIF investment programs are discussed in depth. Finally, conclusions and recommendations are drawn.

2 Theoretical background

2.1 The rationale behind government intervention

Governments often justify their intervention in the innovation market by failures in the venture capital market and positive externalities to the public, such as job creation and boosting the economy of certain regions and sectors (Lerner, 2009; Murray et al., 2012). This study discusses the latter in a more general context of policy diffusion. In the next section, some theories of corporate finance are reviewed, and the main causes of failure are discussed. Then, regarding the framework introduced by Dobbin et al. (2007), four mechanisms of policy diffusion and their role in government intervention in innovation markets are reviewed.

2.1.1 Failure in the VC market

The classical theories of corporate finance, such as Modigliani and Miller's (1958, 1963) theory of "capital structure irrelevance," the theory of financial distress (Gordon, 1971), Jensen and Meckling's (1976) free cash flow hypothesis about "agency costs," and Myers and Majluf's "pecking order" theory (Myers and Majluf, 1984) address the issues of optimal capital structure, financing strategies for traditional firms, and analysis of their actors' motivation to achieve the optimal solution. However, these theories do not apply to businesses in the venture capital market. In other words, the behavior of VC and private investment players cannot be explained by standard corporate finance or structure theories. The pecking order theory, for example, emphasizes that companies consider sales of shares and divestiture methods as a last priority in prioritizing financing methods (Myers and Majluf, 1984); whereas for an innovative startup, linkage to a professional and smart venture capital fund is the preferred option and a priority. Generally, transaction costs associated with VC deals (Martin et al., 2005) and information asymmetries between investors and entrepreneurs (Colombo et al., 2016) are two common causes underlying the failure of VC markets (Stiglitz and Stiglitz, 2000).

2.1.1.1 INFORMATION-ASYMMETRY

The first cause of market failure that is often discussed concerns information failures and asymmetries, and the problems of moral hazard and adverse selection to which these give rise (Harding, 1999). Investing in innovative startups and innovative projects is inherently risky, and investors (both debt holders and shareholders) must consider many uncertainties in the decision process, the first of which is associated with the nature of the venturing concept that an innovative idea might never convert to a profitable business model. The second aspect is that the investors might not be able to evaluate the business properly, because the technology or idea is too sophisticated to comprehend or because the investee intentionally hides some critical information from the investors.

The former aspect would create a market where the risk-return preferences of the investors do not match the risk-return characteristics of the venture investments. These concerns about risks, uncertainties, and costs create a persistent gap in the VC market, where there are plenty of investment opportunities with attractive risk-return characteristics but few investors. If the majority of investors do not accept the risk-return tradeoff, the market will not shift toward equilibrium, and the gap will be sustained. Therefore, the government may decide to intervene in the market by manipulating the risk-return characteristics of investment opportunities or channeling its resources to the unattractive venture market.

2.1.1.2 TRANSACTION COSTS

The previous section discussed the gap between the VC market and the traditional stock market, and transaction cost is considered as a minor driver of the intermarket gap. This section takes the issue within the VC market and explains how transaction costs imply an even greater funding gap within VC market sectors. Transaction costs related to VC investment, costs of due diligence, in particular, are not proportional to the investment size (Martin et al., 2005). To put it another way, the costs of due diligence for a $250k or $5m business are not so different. Thus, the investment yield of a portfolio of early and seed-stage startups may not compensate for the accrued costs of their deals. As a result, a gap will emerge, with the cost/deal size ratio being the main culprit in the within-market gap scenario.

2.1.2 Policy diffusion or social and national strategical interests

The second justification holds that government intervention in the venture capital market is based on considerations that are far away from economic rationales; in particular, it is based on externalities such as job creation and regional economic boost (Lerner, 2009; Murray et al., 2012). Although the public benefits and externalities of a successful VC market are the claimed reasons for intervention, governmental interventions targeting these goals could be explained by another phenomenon, one that can provide insight into rationales underlying government actions, i.e., policy diffusion (Dobbin et al., 2007; Gilardi, 2016; Graham et al., 2013). Policy diffusion takes place when government policy decisions (in this case, market intervention in a given sector, region, or judication) are systematically conditioned by previous policy implementation in another sector, region, or judication (Maggetti and Gilardi, 2016; Schmitt, 2014). In the context of the VC market, it implies that government intervention is the result of interdependency between decisions made by political authorities rather than an independent decision-making process. Generally, four mechanisms are mentioned in academic literature for policy diffusion as follows.

1. **Economic competition**: In a market where competition for resources is constrained, the government should intervene to prevent suboptimal resource

allocation and welfare. In the case of the venture market, the government has to implement friendly policies in response to policies in a competing jurisdiction, because the funds, expertise, and human capital available for venturing is limited (Dobbin et al., 2007).

2. **Coercion**: Coercion is described as a mechanism in which an inferior or state authority is obliged to follow a superior or federal policymaker (Vogelaar and Stam, 2021). In the case of a unitary government, like Iran, a superior authority imposes its policy on many sectoral and geographical governmental bodies. With coercion, the policy is implemented involuntarily, in contrast to other diffusion mechanisms.
3. **Imitation**: The imitation mechanism, also referred to as emulation or constructivism, happens when a jurisdiction without genuine interest in the policy ratiocination structure imitates another leader jurisdiction policy (Dobbin et al., 2007; Shipan and Volden, 2008; Wavre, 2016). The imitation mechanism is usually observed when a socially accepted policy is benchmarked and implemented in a jurisdiction, notwithstanding its effectiveness in the adopting environment.

> (...) the 'burden of proof' changes over time as a function of social acceptance. When considering a radical policy innovation, the burden of proof rests on its advocates, but when it becomes widely accepted, it is the opponents of the policy who have to make their case compellingly to prevent its adoption.
>
> (Gilardi, 2016)

4. **Learning**: Although the implementation of a policy regardless of its diffusion mechanism might be successful, planning and imposing one through learning is preferable and superior. The learning mechanism leads to an adopted model, often originating from multiple jurisdictions, which is exclusively adjusted for the target business environment (Dobbin et al., 2007; Gilardi, 2016; Graham et al., 2013). Learning occurs neither when a policy is socially accepted nor because it is dictated by superior authority or regulatory competition. It happens when the policymaker believes that a policy has been successful in another jurisdiction and has potential for domestic success.

2.2 Intervention strategies

Although governmental participation in the VC market could not be precisely defined (Karsai, 2015) without regard to particulars or exceptions, the government takes two simultaneous roles in the VC market: the main regulator and the main public investor. As the main regulator, the government legally recognizes the venture capital players and prepares the legal framework for their operation. Moreover, it sets some purposeful boundaries and restrictions on VC investments to protect the inexperienced public and private investors. However, as an investor (debt, equity, or other means of financing), the government attempts to channel available financial resources to the venture capital business to cover market gaps and fulfill its strategic interest.

2.2.1 Government as an investor

As an investor, governments often create a central national or regional fund with the dedicated resources to invest or support investments in the VC market. The record of national venture capital investment programs in developed countries is extensive. The best well-known examples of government venture capital initiatives are the Small Business Investment Companies (SBICs) in the United States; the European Investment Fund (EIF); in 1997, the Innovation Investment Fund (IIF) in Australia; MTSs (Participation Companies for New Technology-based Firms) in the Netherlands; Belgium's Investment Company for Flanders (GIMV); and in Germany, the Beteiligungskapital fur Junge Technologieunternehmen (BJTU) (OECD, 1997).

Because of the extent of intervention, there is a range of models and approaches with different levels of governmental participation in the investment process. At the top of the range are programs in which absolute state-controlled funds and investments are executed, and on the bottom of the range are programs designed to minimize government involvement in the investment decision-making process (Karsai, 2015). With the former approach, known as the direct method, the government takes the position of general partner, while with the latter, known as the indirect method, its position is downgraded to a limited partner or a non-equity investor. Few programs could be assigned to one end of the range. Different covenants in investment contracts shift the approach toward the middle of the range. According to Murray (2007), some of these covenants are "capped returns to the state," "first in and last out," "guaranteed underwriting of investment losses incurred by the limited partners," and "buy-back options."

1. **Direct approach:** Fully state-owned venture capital funds are the most prominent example of a direct investment scheme, where the government often sets up a fund management company exclusively mandated to directing state-owned funds. With direct investment schemes, the government implements a hands-on approach. Not only does the government own the fund, but it is also directly involved in the process of selecting investee companies. Fund managers are selected by the government and are entrusted with the general party tasks (Karsai, 2015). The Biotech Fonds Vlaanderen in Belgium, the SITRA in Finland, DC Innovation in France, TBG in Germany, Piemontech in Italy, Axis Participaciones Empresariales in Spain, and the Scottish Enterprise in the United Kingdom are owned and directly managed by the relevant governments (Karsai, 2015).
2. **Indirect approach**: The Innovation Investment Fund in Austria, the Yozma program in Israel, the SBIC construction in the United States, the High-Tech Fund of Funds in the United Kingdom, the Vaekstfonde in Denmark, the Fund for the Promotion of Venture Capital in France, and the ERP-EIF

Dachfonds in Germany are instances of governmental efforts to indirectly invest in the VC market (Karsai, 2015). With the indirect approach, the government delegates the responsibility of managing funds and taking investment decisions to a second party which is mostly private. It takes a limited position in investment organization, and the private party acts as the general partner. The private party might manage the investment organization by itself or assign a professional managing team to it. With the indirect approach, the government strives to bundle the private party interests into the financial outcome of partnership as much as possible to control agency problems (Murray, 2007). Both pure direct and pure indirect programs are rare.

3. **Hybrid approach:** At the beginning of the intervention, the government generally prefers a more direct approach. Often in early government-backed VC funds, the government is the general partner. However, as time passes, due to the risk of market distortion and private investor exclusion, the government shifts to more indirect programs, and its position in the fund changes toward the limited partner (Karsai, 2015). As a result, the indirect approach is currently more prevalent among developed countries; according to a survey conducted by OECD (Wilson and Silva, 2013), 14 out of 32 OECD member countries are implementing direct venture capital programs, while 21 out of 32 members conduct indirect investment approaches such as co-investment.

2.2.2 The effectiveness of governmental venture capital programs

There are serious doubts about the ability of governments to address venture capital market failures (Lerner, 2002, 2009). In many developed countries, there is no shortage of funding for early-stage startups (Library House, 2006); therefore, it is hard to differentiate between startups which cannot raise money because of market gaps and ones that are not financially viable and thus unable to attract investors (Pierrakis and Mason, 2008). The government intervention in the second scenario not only is financially flawed but also results in the market in which the crowding-out effect drives down or, in the worth scenario, eliminates the private sector. Among other things, the knowledge and skill required for the complexity of the VC market and political interests are two important factors that may lead the government to biased investment decisions. In other words, the more involved the government is, the more biased are the decisions that are made. Although it seems reasonable for the policymakers to shift investment schemes to more indirect approaches, the government would not be able to reach its strategic targets if it is not sufficiently involved. Therefore, a trade-off between the level of involvement and the ability to follow strategic missions emerges.

It should be noted that as well as the governmental capabilities, the failure or success of governmental VC programs depends on the operational environment of the VC markets. For example, the current state of the economy, the development level of financial institutions, the condition of the job market, the amount spent on research and development, and the regulatory framework for the co-operation of venture capital investors and management companies are factors that affect the success of VC investments (Karsai, 2015). Therefore, it is difficult to detect the exact causes of failure or success of governmental VC programs. Figure 4.1 summarizes the rationales and mechanisms affecting market intervention programs.

On a final note,

> In many cases, there is likely to be a role for the government in stimulating a vibrant entrepreneurial sector, given the early stage of maturity of these activities in most nations. But at the same time, it is easy for the government to overstep its bounds and squander its investments in this arena. Only by designing a program that reflects an understanding of and a willingness to listen to the entrepreneurial process can government efforts be effective,
>
> (Lerner, 2009)

3 Methodology

This study has adopted the case study methodology as the main research method, because it is useful when the boundaries between the subject and the context are not recognizable (Yin, 2009). Indeed, the method studies the subject within its real-life context. The case description is presented to review the evidence. The analysis model is mainly exploratory. The paper uses explanation-building and pattern-matching techniques to conclude the recommendations. Interviews,

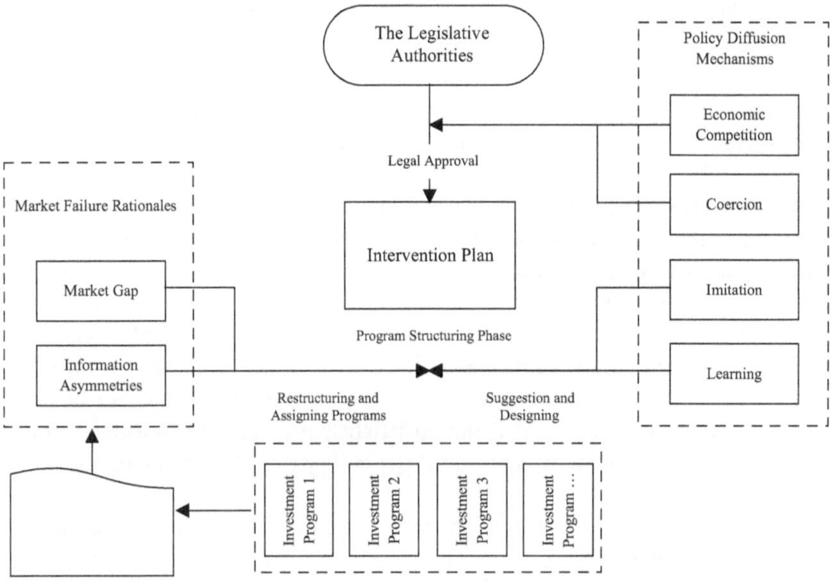

Figure 4.1 The Venture Capital Intervention Model.

internal and published documents, legal agreements, and direct observation are employed to collect case data.

The surveyed case consists of different programs. Therefore, multiple steps are needed to reach a holistic view of the case. The holistic view is essential, because no logical conclusion is reachable in a solitary analysis of the programs.

As mentioned, the data gathering method most widely used in this study is the interview, which is particularly useful in answering the study questions. Unstructured interviews were conducted with middle and top managers of the INIF, entrepreneurs, and legal authorities in 2021. Twenty-six interviews with fourteen candidates were conducted; some interviewees participated in up to three interview sessions. Among the interviewees are ten managers and legal authorities and four entrepreneurs. Interviews with managers of the INIF are of great interest for many reasons. First, the INIF is important in terms of its mission in creating the venture capital market in Iran. It is the largest governmental body dedicated to supporting venture activities in Iran. Second, although the institution was founded almost a decade ago, it just recently began supporting VC activities with equity-based programs. Therefore, we have the opportunity to follow the design, development, and execution of the INIF's investment program within the context of the organization. Interviews took 15–60 minutes. The interviewer used the case study protocols and took notes. The unstructured method helped the interviewer explain the questions of the study to the interviewee and discuss the issues within the context of the interviewee. Moreover, this method helped the interviewer easily revise and evolve the study questions.

Seven investment programs currently offered by INIF have been analyzed in this study. The programs are briefly described below and explained in detail in the case description section.

1. Private capital fund (PCF) and venture capital fund (VCF) program in which the INIF become the limited partner of public funds.
2. Co-investment with the Research and Technology Funds (RTFs) program in which the INIF co-invested as a limited partner with RTFs.
3. Co-investment with the accelerators program in which the INIF co-invested as a limited partner with accelerators.
4. Crowdfunding program in which the INIF guarantees the capital raised by crowdfunding campaigns.
5. Public offering program in which the INIF buys shares of a publicly offered tech-based project.
6. Project finance program in which the INIF finances innovative projects with specific contracts.
7. "Noavar" Islamic bonds program in which the INIF facilitates the issuance of "Noavar" bonds.

Venture capital investments in developed countries are made primarily in high-tech industries that contribute to innovation; however, the picture in Iran is different. Iranian venture capitalists invest primarily in ordinary production and service enterprises, which are not very risky, innovative, or young. Within the INIF investment programs, however, high-tech and high-risk investments are detectable.

With the results and conclusions extracted from the case description, the author(s) designed a series of policies to recommend to authorities in similar countries. The results are first suggested by the authors and have been revised and validated through post-interview discussions.

4 Case description: Iran National Innovation Fund

The Iran National Innovation Fund (INIF) is the most prominent public investor in the innovation ecosystem of Iran. This organization is one of the main Iranian governmental instruments for intervention in the venture market. INIF offers attractive interest-rate loans, grants, guarantees, investment programs, and many minor services to innovative startups. Here, a short background of the institution and its offered investment programs are described.

The Law on the Protection of Enterprises and Knowledge-Based Organizations and the Commercialization of Innovations and Inventions (PEKBOCI) (2010), approved by the parliament on October 28, 2010, is the legislative foundation of INIF. Article 5 of this law calls for the Fund for Innovation and Prosperity (later known as Iran National Innovation Fund-INIF) to be established with 30,000 billion Rials of committed capital.

The PEKBOCI act (2010), PEKBOCI act's codes of action (2015), and INIF's mandate (2011) effectively determined the structure of INIF's programs. Some determinative articles and their reflection on INIF's programs are presented below.

1. According to article 3 of the PEKBOCI act, only New Technology-Based Firms (NTBFs) are eligible to receive INIF's services with some exemptions in investment programs. Therefore, the operational domain of most of INIF's programs is restricted to slightly over 6,000 NTBFs. The INIF, however, is permitted to invest in innovative firms and VC funds whether or not they are mandated to invest in NTBFs.
2. The NTBF is an official title granted to knowledge-intensive and innovative businesses by another governmental body known as the Vice-Presidency for Science and Technology.
3. According to Article 1 of the PEKBOCI Act, all public firms, organizations, and legal entities (with state ownership of more than 50%) are ineligible for INIF programs.
4. According to Article 18 of the PEKBOCI Act's codes of action, INIF ownership in VC funds and firms shall not exceed 49%. In addition, another tighter restriction of 40% is imposed on INIF ownership in any legal entity by the National Competition Council of Iran, resulting in minority share and control in funds and other investments.

In summary, INIF investment programs must be dedicated to NTBFs or VC funds and firms, and there is a statutory prohibition against majority ownership in any investment.

The rationale behind the initiation of the INIF can be described in two parts. First, the coercion and imitation mechanism is apparent in the laws that permitted the establishment of the INIF. The second rationale is subtle in the statutes of the INIF and has shown itself after some time in the structure of the programs offered by the INIF. The venture capital ecosystem of Iran started with the private sector and a series of successful startups known as platformers. Because of the first-mover effect, the existence of few competitors, and the presence of experienced foreign investors, the first wave of Iranian startups easily grew and consolidated their market position. Therefore, there was no need for the government to invest or channel private sector investments into the VC market. As time passed, however, the ecosystem grew, and new demands emerged within the market. The situation became worse when the foreign investors decided to leave the market because of the imposed sanctions on the economy of Iran. Therefore, the second rationale behind the INIF programs was the growing financing gap that emerged because of increasing investment demands and the absence of private investors. These actions aim to motivate private investors and channel resources to innovative small and medium businesses (Carvalho, 2015).

4.1 Plans and programs

According to the INIF investment policy statement, which is demonstrated in Table 4.1, seven investment programs are currently being offered to innovative firms and startups. The programs can be categorized into two groups: First, programs in which the INIF acts as an investor or financer, including the PCF and VCF program, co-investment with RTFs program, co-investment with accelerators program, project finance program, and strategic investment programs;

Table 4.1 Target Portfolio for Two-Year Horizon

Program	*Commitment Size (Billion Rials)*	*Minimum Required Yield*	*Risk Level (Probability of Default)*	*Expected Return Adjusted by Risk*
PCF and VCF program	6,000	25%	Low (5%)	23.8%
Co-investment with RTFs program	3,500	20%	High (40%)	12%
Co-investment with accelerators program	450	21%	Very High (60%)	8.4%
Project finance program	500	21%	High (40%)	12.6%
Strategic investment programs including public offering	2,000	25%	High (40%)	23.8%
	Commitment size (billion Rials)	Risk level (probability of default)		Loss given default (billion Rials)
Crowdfunding program	900	High (50%)		450
"Noavar" Islamic bond program	8,600	Moderate (10%)		860

Source: INIF investment plan.

and second, programs in which the INIF is a facilitator and helps businesses raise money from different resources. In the next sections, the seven investment programs are explained, and Table 4.2 summarizes their characteristics.

4.1.1 Private capital fund and venture capital fund program

The first investment scheme implemented widely by INIF is the Private Fund and Venture Capital Fund program, which is claimed to address the gap between the VC market and the traditional stock market. To participate in a VCF or PCF, the INIF adopts one of these two approaches:

1. Less than 20% of controlling units, same amount of ordinary units, and one (out of five) representative on the investment committee.
2. 20%–40% of controlling ownership, same amount of ordinary units, right to veto, and two (out of five) representatives on the investment committee.

With the former, because the INIF takes one seat on the investment committee, it cannot have an overwhelming influence on investment decisions. However, with the latter, INIF is legally authorized to reject any decisions made in the investment committee and shareholder meetings. In a fund with both approaches, the INIF is neither a purely limited partner, nor a purely general partner; however, both incline to a limited position, and in the latter INIF has more influence.

It is worth noting that the INIF does not offer any incentive options to other limited partners in VCF and PCF programs. Therefore, all shareholders are equally compensated and take the same amount of risk. Incentives for the fund manager, however, follow the rule of thumb, and he/she charges unitholders a 2% annual fee and 20% carrying fee with a hard indexed hurdle rate.

4.1.2 Co-investment with the research and technology funds program

Research and Technology Funds (RTFs) are private special funds. They are independent of the government and the INIF. As with the INIF, RTFs invest in VC businesses, finance NTBFs, and offer guarantees; however, the size and extent of their operations are limited compared to INIF.

The program intends to cover the VC market gap by financing businesses and projects which are less appealing to private investors. Generally, accepted business plans have a lower investment yield or a high risk of failure compared to other programs due to leading-edge technology implementation. Co-investment with RTFs is one of INIF's direct investment programs. Indeed, the investment committee of the INIF directly selects the investment cases; however, some important eligibility criteria for investment must be met:

1. The business must qualify as an NTBF or, in the case of an initiative, meet the eligibility requirements of NTBFs.

2. The investee's business plan should be commercializing a strategic innovation, resolving a national issue, or make major contributions and externalities for the public.
3. An RTF must finance at least 25% of the required resources.

Policy diffusion is easily recognizable in the investment criteria, and the investment committee is particularly interested in business plans which would result in extensive externalities, for example, Covid-19 vaccines. Although the committee was aware of the poor odds of success, the committee agreed to invest in the program so that the capability and knowledge for developing similar products would be available domestically.

Although INIF's investment committee makes investment decisions, the co-investor is responsible for the management of the dedicated resources. Moreover, the co-investor should coach and consult the investee, represent the INIF in shareholder and board meetings, and eventually liquidate the investment and distribute the contributions.

The INIF is also responsible for the due diligence process which is often outsourced to licensed consultant firms. Moreover, it offers on a ratio of up to 4:1 of the out-of-pocket commitment (i.e., the INIF invests 40b Rials, and the RTF and other third parties put in another 10b Rials). It seems that this generous offered ratio enables RTFs to invest more so that the investment is spread more evenly across the cases. Furthermore, the program enables RTFs to finance projects which are far beyond their investment check size. The incentive options of the co-investment contract have been written so that risk-return characteristics of the investments are altered in favor of the co-investors. For example, the co-investor is not charged for due diligence, and the co-investor is awarded up to 4% management fee and 20% carrying fee with a hard indexed hurdle rate. Furthermore, the INIF delegates its voting right in shareholder meetings and board to the co-investor; thus, the co-investor can impose controlling measures to eliminate information asymmetries by electing board members or the CEO.

4.1.3 Co-investment with accelerators program

There are more than 120 accelerators in Iran's VC market (Echomotive, 2021). According to the official database, 83 of them are NTBF (Vice-Presidency for Science and Technology, 2021). The program claims to address the market gap within the VC market by boosting accelerators' investment in seed-stage startups. Co-investment with accelerators is the most indirectly executed program offered by the INIF. Although the investment committee selects the co-investor partners, they do not intervene in the combination of the accelerator's invested portfolio.

The investment ratio of the program is locked at 1:2, so that the INIF contributes two parts and the accelerator contributes one part of the committed capital. The accelerator may fulfill up to 30% of its committed capital by different services delivered to startups. For example, the INIF co-invests 10b Rials on a startup, and the accelerator invests another 3.5b Rials and delivers 1.5b Rials of services such as workplace and facilities to the startup. The non-cash settlement keeps the accelerator in line with its usual operations. Furthermore, the INIF grants up to 5% of the management fee to the accelerators. In addition, the accelerator will receive a 20–30% carrying fee with a hard indexed hurdle rate, if it successfully liquidates the invested portfolio before the maturity of the co-investment contract. The most important incentive of the program is the buy-back option granted to the accelerator on each investment case. The accelerator is offered an extra discount of up to 30% to buy INIF's share in startups. The INIF limits its committed capital in each co-investment contract to 40b Rials.

4.1.4 Crowdfunding program

Over recent years, crowdfunding has evolved from a limited over-the-counter funding source to a major financing method for entrepreneurs and small- and medium-sized businesses, and it is now legally registered and supervised by governments. In 2020, the global crowdfunding market value reached $12.27b USD and is predicted to double by 2027, growing at a compound annual growth rate (CAGR) of 11% (Statista, 2021b). The first Iranian crowdfunding platform was launched in the late 2020s. Within a few years, "Iran Fara Bourse" had developed and introduced the legal process for registration and entitlement of crowdfunding platforms. The first platform was officially registered on June 10, 2020 (Iran Fara Bourse, 2021).

The program serves early-stage startups by supporting their online campaign on crowdfunding platforms. Crowdfunding partners propose early-stage startups to INIF, and currently, only profit-sharing plans are accepted in the program. Except for the crowdfunding model, no conditions are placed on the proposed business plans; however, the investment committee of the INIF may decide to support businesses that are more aligned with its strategic interests. However, there is an important restriction on crowdfunding partners: the crowdfunding platform must be an NTBF. Although business plans are shortlisted by the INIF, the INIF claims that the final decision is made by a large group of investors who invest small amounts of money on the project. To put it another way, the program holds that promising projects are separated from non-performing ones by the wisdom of the crowd.

With the crowdfunding program, INIF does not invest in any project. To change the risk-return characteristic of the project, INIF offers a guarantee to investors in return for a tiny fraction of their profit. The guarantee covers losses of the plans of up to 100% of the invested capital. The profit-sharing agreement becomes effective when the return of the project meets a defined indexed threshold and increases incrementally as the return grows. The profit-sharing agreement is similar to the carrying fee with a soft indexed hurdle rate.

4.1.5 Public offering program

The initial public offering is the pinnacle of a successful startup. Few startups may survive the challenges of growth and go public. Entrepreneurs wish to list their investment in the capital market. Moreover, the capital market is not only an exit point for many investors but also the primary source of financing for massive funding rounds.

Businesses are frequently listed on Iran's capital market; however, the offered shares are almost always directly listed, and the company does not issue new shares. Therefore, the listing is just a liquidation mechanism. Contrary to usual direct listing practice, the Security and Exchange Organization of Tehran (SEO) recently devised a unique method for offering shares of newly established firms to the public (Codes of Action of Public Offering of Project Firms, 2021). The committed capital of the shareholders must exceed 500b Rials. The founders may satisfy their capital commitments by contributing operational assets to the project (Codes of Action of Public Offering of Project Firms, 2021).

As mentioned, one important rationale behind INIF intervention in the VC market is the failure of the market to provide the capital required for venture activities. Similar to early-stage businesses struggling to attract seed money, innovative projects with enormous minimum required investments are also unable to mobilize minimum initiation resources. With the public offering program, the INIF tries to cover the minimum requirements needed to start capital-intensive venture investments. The program could be considered a co-investment scheme with two parties: first, the trusted intuitional investors and second, the public. It is important to note that the risk of the corresponding projects is insignificant compared to other innovative startups in the ecosystem. Although innovation dramatically improves the yield of the projects, because of high investment in physical assets, the risk of failure is slight, and losses are recoverable.

4.1.6 Project finance (revenue sharing schemes) program

Project finance is a long-term financing method for major projects through financial engineering (Yescombe, 2013). This method is generally considered a debt instrument; however, compared to full debt or full equity financing, it stands as a hybrid approach.

The program requires that the project has a sale or service contract with a governmental or public organization, so that the risk to future revenues is avoided. Furthermore, a revenue-sharing agreement is settled, in which the INIF receives a fraction of the proceedings of the project. The agreement is valid until the internal rate of the INIF crosses a specified threshold. It is important to note that the terms of the agreement are quoted from the only project financed by the program, so it is reasonable to assume that the terms would be revised for every financing request.

'The devil is in details' is a favorite saying among projects financers and is used to show the efforts and difficulties inherent in determining the details of each project financing agreement. The same issue is expected with the program, and the program has to be specified for each financing request.

4.1.7 "Noavar" Islamic bonds program

Governments often support private and municipal bond issuances to support investing in infrastructure or humanitarian projects. One of the most famous subsidized bond plans is the American Recovery and Reinvestment Act (2009), in which the US Congress authorized or expanded several tax-advantaged alternatives for financing governmental infrastructure and public projects. The plan includes different bond programs.

Some subsidized bond programs which are specifically earmarked to raise money for climate and environmental projects are sometimes referred to as green bonds or climate bonds. According to the Green Bond Database (2020), since the inception of the climate bond programs in 2007, over US$1.3 trillion in bonds have been issued in the market. According to the same database (Climate Bonds Initiative, 2020), in just five years from 2015 to 2020, the annual issuance of green bonds increased sixfold from US$44.7 to US$290.1 billion. The green market is expected to continue to grow, and environmentalists hope the annual issuance of green bonds will reach US$1 trillion by 2030 (Jones, 2020).

Some scholars believe that the concept of the green bonds applies to the innovation ecosystem to "spur innovation, build knowledge, and increase the number of truly effective programs" (Butler et al., 2013). They discuss two reasons supporting the idea of the innovation bonds. First, the bonds can secure new resources for the ecosystem, and second, they ensure that only successful programs are financed (Butler et al., 2013). The INIF also maintains that innovation bonds may cover the financial gap of the high-end VC market. Therefore, similar to the Public Offering Program, the Noavar Islamic bonds program has been introduced to finance low-risk capital-intensive innovative projects and NTBFs.

Noavar bonds are the same as other Islamic bonds issued in Iran's security market. The terms and covenants of the bonds are similar to their corporate counterparts, except that the bonds are issued with the title of "Noavar" which is translated to "innovative." The INIF first designed subsidies for the program to reduce the effective interest rate of the bonds and claimed that the high cost of issuing bonds impedes NTBFs ability to raise money for their innovative projects; by lowering the cost of issuing bonds, it claimed, many NTBFs will be able to acquire the capital needed for their expansion. However, the initiation phase of the program revealed other issues preventing NTBFs from raising capital in the debt market. Generally, the yield of innovative projects is high enough to cover the cost of bonds; yet, NTBFs are unable to provide suitable collateral or a credible guarantor to pass the requirements imposed by SEO. In addition, the heavy formal procedures of issuance dissuade NTBFs in the middle of the process. Addressing these issues, INIF has revised the program. In addition to previous incentives, now the program offers NTBFs to guarantee their bonds based on their credit ratings.

4.2 Discussion and recommendations

In this section, the lessons extracted from the INIF investment programs are presented. Some notable issues which are useful for planning other intervention plans are discussed, and some recommendations for policymakers are concluded.

Recommendation 1: It is possible and recommended to consider the indirect approach as a triggering strategy in the intervention plan.

Contrary to the general trend from direct to indirect intervention (Pierrakis and Mason, 2008), the INIF's first investment programs are fully indirect or hybrid. With the PCF and VCF program, the INIF fully entrusts investment decisions to the investment committee of the funds, where the independent partners have taken the majority. With the RTFs co-investment program, investment is conditional on the participation of the RTFs. It seems that the private sector has already developed and acquired the capabilities and knowledge required for venturing, and it is possible to delegate the investment process to them. Similarly, the same knowledge and capabilities may be available in other less developed innovation markets; therefore it is recommended that the authorities consider the indirect approach as the primary method in their intervention programs in innovation markets from the beginning of the plan to avoid the consequences of direct investment approaches. It is important to mention that the indirect approach reduces the risk of agency costs and biased decisions, and it improves the financial performance of the portfolio; however, the indirect approach limits the ability of the government organization to fulfill its strategic interests. Table 4.3 summarizes the pros and cons of an indirect triggering strategy.

Conclusion and recommendation 2: With the fully indirect approach, the government may not carry out its mission or fulfill its strategic interests. A range of programs with different investment approaches is required.

As mentioned in the previous lesson, because of agency problems, the cost of biased investment decisions, and crowding out the private sector, direct investment approaches are inferior to indirect approaches. Considering the consequences of government intervention in the market, it would appear reasonable to promote indirect investment programs and shift the current direct approaches to indirect methods; however, with the fully indirect approach, the government may not carry out its mission or fulfill its strategic interests. The financial gap of the high-end VC market with capital-intensive projects, for example, is not coverable by any indirect schemes. Because of the high costs of failure, all participating parties prefer to keep their influence and supervision on the project by establishing fair corporate governance or a joint venture structure rather than delegating decision-making to the partner through the LP-GP structure. Moreover, in publicly offered projects, the supervising authority compels the non-public investors to adopt a standard corporate structure with a diversified independent board of directors to protect the interests of minor investors. The innovative projects with high externalities and long-term investment horizon are another example. The outputs of these projects are mostly non-financial, or the financial benefits of the project will not be accessible in the foreseeable future.

Table 4.2 INIF Investment Programs

Program	*Approach*	*Progressa*	*Description*	*Exit Incentive*
Co-investment with Accelerators program	Indirect	71%	The investment decision fully and the supervising tasks mainly are delegated to an accelerator who represents the INIF in the investee's board of directors. INIF does not interfere in investee operations.	20% carrying fee upon each successful exit. 30% to 5% discount on the fair price if the accelerator buys INIF shares. Early offers receive higher discounts; a 3-year settlement with attractive terms is available.
PCF and VCF program	Indirect	48%	The general partner of the fund is responsible for investment decisions and supervision. The general partner represents the INIF on the investee's board of directors, and the INIF has a representative(s) on the investment committee of the fund.	20% carrying fee after full portfolio exit.
Crowdfunding program	Indirect – Hybrid	50%	Decisions are made by a hybrid approach. Investment cases are proposed by the platform, shortlisted by the INIF, and selected by crowd wisdom. Supervision tasks are carried out by the platforms and legal authorities. No one interferes with the operations of the investee.	Exit risk is avoided; the agreement is revenue sharing and is terminated in less than 1 year.
Co-investment with RTFs program	Indirect – Hybrid	53%	Although, RTFs are the general partners of the investments, both general and limited parties must agree with the investment decision; the INIF carries out supervision procedures independently, and the RTF represents the INIF on the investee's board of directors.	20% carrying fee upon full exit. Moreover, a 3-year exit settlement with attractive terms is available.
Public offering program	Direct – Hybrid	50%	All partners should agree on the investment; the governance and the supervision are carried out through standard public corporate procedures; the legal authorities supervise and audit the corporation, and financial statements are available to the public.	Shares of the firm are publicly tradable after official registration.
"Noavar" Islamic bond program	Direct	0	Cases are selected by the INIF, and the legal authorities permit the issuance of the bonds. Supervision is carried out through standard public corporate procedures and the legal authorities.	Exit risk is avoided.
Project Finance program	Direct	18%	The INIF makes the investment decisions; supervision is carried out by the INIF and in the case of an emergency; INIF does not interfere with the operations of the project.	The partner may compensate the INIF so that the internal rate of cash flows to INIF exceeds 21%, thereby terminating the revenue sharing agreement.

The Gen-Therapy project, for instance, is at least ten years behind the commercialization stage, and the risk of failure is high. Therefore, almost no general partners are willing to invest in the project, and a more direct investment must be devised. Therefore, as summarized in Table 4.3, it is recommended that the authorities consider a range of programs with different investment approaches, even though the cost of directing such programs is considerably more than programs with a single approach and the portfolio of the institution would be unevenly distributed between programs.

Conclusion and Recommendations 3 and 4: The successful exit on a venture investment is strictly limited by outside barriers. The exit strategy should be carefully considered in the investment schemes, and cooperation with authorities to remove the exit barriers is essential.

Limited party investors, similar to the INIF, do not expect to end up with a portfolio of minor investments in different illiquid businesses after a long period of investment. The sustainability of the investment cycle requires that the limited investor be compensated in cash or other liquid assets; then the proceedings are reinvested in a new venture program. Exit incentives and covenants are essential in the investment agreement which aligns the general partner with the exit preference of limited partners; however, successful exit from a venture investment is strictly limited by the macro-business environment, structural barriers, and financial market development. An initial public offering, for instance, is considered the prime exit strategy of VC investments; yet, the Securities and Exchange Organization (SEO) of Tehran has declined all IPO requests from successful VC businesses. Moreover, the market of private equity in Iran is primitive and lacks experienced players. Exit strategies are carefully considered in INIF investment schemes, so that some of the programs are specially designed to avoid the risk of exit, for example, the crowdfunding and public offering programs; however, the INIF should utilize its special consultative status to remove the exit barriers in the market. The same is recommended to similar organizations.

Conclusion and recommendation 5: A comprehensive credit report and investment policy statement are essential and recommended.

The IPS provides a solid framework for designing investment program terms. It helps an organization optimize its influence on the market regarding resource and risk restrictions. By adding some key performances, the IPS may be able to evaluate the strategic targets of the programs. It is recommended that the IPS be created and periodically updated. Table 4.1 demonstrates the target portfolio of INIF's investment programs. The IPS is an essential part of the investment strategy, but another procedure is required for evaluating the performance of the investment program in terms of the strategic targets and externalities of the programs. A comprehensive credit report is also essential and recommended for risk appraisal of the portfolio. The INIF lacks both reports.

Conclusion and recommendation 6: The policy diffusion mechanism should be the key instrument justifying, presenting, and promoting venture capital programs.

Table 4.3 Lessons and Recommendations

Lesson	*Recommendation (s)*	*Pros and Cons*
Triggering strategy	Consider indirect approach as the primary method in intervention programs in innovation markets from the beginning of the intervention plan.	Pros: Transparency, lower agency costs, higher performance, unbiased investment decisions, reduced crowding-out effect. Cons: Inability to follow strategic interests.
Program spectrum	Implement a range of programs alongside the indirect-direct spectrum.	Pros: Ability to follow strategic interests, covering all emerged gaps in the market. Cons: High cost of managing and implementing a diverse portfolio of programs; the weight of investment in programs is highly uneven.
Exit as a success factor	1. Utilize the special consultative status and cooperate with policymakers to remove the exit barriers in the market. 2. Follow investment programs in which barriers to exiting are avoided.	- -
Investment Policy Statement and Risk Appraisal Report	1. Define a process for preparing and reviewing the IPS and risk report. 2. Add specific performance measures to IPS and risk reports to evaluate the strategic targets of the intervention plan.	Pros: Provide a structure for program design and specification, control the performance of the programs within the strategic targets of the institution. Cons: Implementing a process for risk evaluation is costly and difficult.
Policy diffusion strategies	Utilize the policy diffusion mechanism in promoting intervention programs instead of emphasizing market failure rationales.	Pros: Easy to understand, acceptable by both private and governmental sectors, easy to implement. Cons: The final executed program may diverge from its original intent.

Although market failure is mentioned as the primary reason for government intervention in the VC market, in reality, it appears to be difficult to persuade the government or the private sector to invest in the VC market for the market gaps, because measuring the gap, finding the referable examples, and justifying the investment opportunities aroused are practically impossible tasks. Therefore, market failure is the key principle in designing VC programs; it is recommended that the policy diffusion mechanism be the key instrument justifying, presenting, and promoting VC programs for authorities and the private sector.

5 Conclusion

The present study first introduced a framework for the introduction and evaluation of intervention plans. Then it discussed the rationales behind government intervention in the VC market; market gap and policy diffusion are mentioned as two important rationales. Next, different types of intervention strategies are introduced. After that, INIF investment schemes, as a case study, are described and discussed. The case study method is utilized to describe barriers and issues concerning the implementation of an intervention strategy in developing ecosystems and to find the challenges and impediments in developing a sustainable VC market. At last, some conclusions and corresponding recommended policies are explained and presented. The study suggests that policymakers consider the indirect approach as the initiation strategy; implement a range of programs alongside the indirect-direct spectrum; utilize their special consultative status to remove exit barriers; follow programs in which the barriers to exiting are avoided; prepare IPS and risk reports; add specific performance measures to IPS and risk reports; utilize the policy diffusion mechanism in promoting intervention programs.

aPerformance of each program is measured by comparing the amount of realized guarantees or investments with the two-year targets which were set by the INIF investment plan. It is important to note that the progress measured is achieved within the first year of the plan.

References

Act R (2009) The American recovery and reinvestment act of 2009. *Public Law* 111(5):5–30

Asian Venture Capital Journal (AVCJ) (2001) The 2001 guide to venture capital in Asia

Bartzokas A, Mani S (2004) *Financial systems, corporate investment in innovation, and venture capital.* Edward Elgar Publishing

Buchanan WT (1989) Venture funds: A special survey. *Singapore Business*, 14–15

Butler D, Bloom D, Rudd T (2013) Using social impact bonds to spur innovation, knowledge building, and accountability. *Commun Develop Invest Rev* 9(1):53–58

Carvalho L (2015) *Handbook of research on entrepreneurial success and its impact on regional development.* IGI Global

Climate Bonds Initiative (2020) Climate bonds green bond database. https://www.climatebonds.net/market/data/

Codes of Action of Public Offering of Project Firms (2021) (testimony of Security and Exchange Organization)

Colombo MG, Cumming DJ, Vismara S (2016) Governmental venture capital for innovative young firms. *J Technol Transf* 41(1):10–24

Cumming DJ, Grilli L, Murtinu S (2017) Governmental and independent venture capital investments in Europe: A firm-level performance analysis. *J Corp Financ* 42. doi:10.1016/j.jcorpfin.2014.10.016

Del-Palacio I, Zhang XT, Sole F (2012) The capital gap for small technology companies: public venture capital to the rescue? *Small Bus Econ* 38(3):283–301

Denis DJ (2004) Entrepreneurial finance: an overview of the issues and evidence. *J Corp Financ* 10(2). doi:10.1016/S0929–1199(03)00059-2

Dobbin F, Simmons B, Garrett G (2007) The global diffusion of public policies: Social construction, coercion, competition, or learning? *Annu Rev Sociol* 33:449–472

Echomotive (2021) NTBF Accelerators. https://ecomotive.ir/accelerators-list/

Gilardi F (2016) Four ways we can improve policy diffusion research. *State Polit Policy Q* 16(1):8–21

Gompers P, Lerner J (2001) The venture capital revolution. *J Econ Perspect* 15(2). doi:10.1257/jep.15.2.145

Gordon MJ (1971) Towards a theory of financial distress. *J Financ* 26(2):347–356

Graham ER, Shipan CR, Volden C (2013) The diffusion of policy diffusion research in political science. *Br J Political Sci* 43(3):673–701

Harding R (1999) *Venture capital and regional development.* Institute for Public Policy Research London WC2E 7RA

INIF's mandate (2011) (testimony of Research and Technology (SCSRT) The Supreme Council for Science)

Iran Fara Bourse (2021) List of Iranian cowdfunding platforms. https://www.ifb.ir/Finstars/AllCrowdFundingAgents.aspx

Jeng LA, Wells PC (2000) The determinants of venture capital funding: Evidence across countries. *J Corp Financ* 6(3). doi:10.1016/S0929–1199(00)00003-1

Jensen MC, Meckling WH (1976) Theory of the firm: Managerial behavior, agency costs and ownership structure. *J Financ Econ* 3(4):305–360

Jones L (2020) $1Trillion Mark Reached in Global Cumulative Green Issuance: Climate Bonds Data Intelligence Reports: Latest Figures. https://www.climatebonds.net/2020/12/1trillion-mark-reached-global-cumulative-green-issuance-climate-bonds-data-intelligence

Karsai J (2015) Squaring the circle? KÜLGAZDASÁG 1(Kln):62–93

Klingler-Vidra R, Kenney M, Breznitz D (2016) Policies for financing entrepreneurship through venture capital: Learning from the successes of Israel and Taiwan. *Int J Innov Manag* 7(3):203–221

Leleux B, Surlemont B (2003) Public versus private venture capital: Seeding or crowding out? A pan-European analysis. *J Bus Ventur* 18(1). doi:10.1016/S0883–9026(01)00078-7

Lerner J (2002) When bureaucrats meet entrepreneurs: The design of effective 'public venture capital' programmes. *The Econ J* 112(477). doi:10.1111/1468-0297.00684

Lerner J (2009) *Boulevard of broken dreams.* Princeton University Press

Library House (2006) Beyond the Chasm: The Venture-Backed Report 2006

Maggetti M, Gilardi F (2016) Problems (and solutions) in the measurement of policy diffusion mechanisms. *J Public Policy* 36(1):87–107

Martin R, Berndt C, Klagge B, Sunley P (2005) Spatial proximity effects and regional equity gaps in the venture capital market: Evidence from Germany and the United Kingdom. *Environ Plann A* 37(7):1207–1231

Modigliani F, Miller, MH (1958) The cost of capital, corporation finance and the theory of investment. *Am Econ Rev* 48(3):261–297

Modigliani F, Miller MH (1963) Corporate income taxes and the cost of capital: A correction. *Am Econ Rev* 53(3):433–443

Murray GC (2007) *Venture capital and government policy. In handbook of research on venture capital.* Edward Elgar Publishing. doi:10.4337/9781847208781.00011

Murray G, Cowling M, Liu W, Kalinowska-Beszczynska O (2012) Government co-financed'Hybrid'Venture Capital programmes: Generalizing developed economy experience and its relevance to emerging nations. *Kauffman international research and policy roundtable*, Liverpool, 1–29

Myers SC, Majluf NS (1984) Corporate financing and investment decisions when firms have information that investors do not have. *J Financ Econ* 13(2):187–221

OECD (1997) *Government venture capital for technology-based firms.* OECD Paris

PEKBOCI act's codes of action third edition (2015) (testimony of The Cabinet of Iran): Tehran

PEKBOCI: Protection of Enterprises and Knowledge Based Organizations and the Commercialization of Innovations and Inventions act (2010) (testimony of The Parliament of Iran): Tehran

Pierrakis Y, Mason C (2008) Shifting sands: The changing nature of the early stage venture capital market in the UK. National Endowment for Science, Technology and the Arts London. http://www.nesta.org.uk/publications/shifting-sands-changing-nature-early-stage-venture-capital-market (Accessed on Aug 24, 2022)

Schmitt C (2014) The diffusion of privatization in Europe: Political affinity or economic competition? *Public Adm* 92(3):615–635

SGX (2021) Catalist. SGX websit. https://www.sgx.com/securities/catalist

Shipan CR, Volden C (2008) The mechanisms of policy diffusion. *Am J Pol Sci* 52(4). doi:10.1111/j.1540-5907.2008.00346.x

Statista (2021b) Crowdfunding market size globally 2020. https://www.statista.com/statistics/1078273/global-crowdfunding-market-size/

Stiglitz JE, Stiglitz JE (2000) Economics of the public sector. Third Edition. New York: Norton & Company

Statista (2021a) Value of Private Equity (PE) and Venture Capital (VC) deals in Singapore. https://www.statista.com/statistics/1023247/singapore-pe-vc-deal-value/ (Accessed on Aug 24, 2022)

Vice-Presidency for Science and Technology (2021, September 21) NTBFs database. https://pub.daneshbonyan.ir/ (Accessed on Aug 24, 2022)

Vogelaar JJ, Stam E (2021) Beyond market failure: Rationales for regional governmental venture capital. *Ventur Cap* 23(3). doi:10.1080/13691066.2021.1927341

Wavre VL (2016) Mechanisms of policy diffusion in the telecommunications sector; Universal Service Obligation and Spectrum Management in Morocco, Egypt and Jordan

Wilson KE, Silva F (2013) *Policies for seed and early stage finance. OECD Science, Technology and Industry Policy Papers No. 9.* Paris: Organisation for Economic Co-operation and Development

Yescombe ER (2013) *Principles of project finance.* Academic Press

Yin RK (2009) *Case study research: Design and methods* (Vol. 5). Sage

Zhang Y, Mayes DG (2018) The performance of governmental venture capital firms: A life cycle perspective and evidence from China. *Pacific-Basin Finance J* 48:162–185

Section 2

Regulatory and policy framework

5 Regulatory frameworks of crowdfunding for startups in Singapore, Thailand, and Vietnam

Pornchai Wisuttisak, Nguyen Ba Binh, and Andrew Terry

1 Introduction

Through the innovative information and communication technologies, lending or sharing platforms have contributed to the new financial medium model, linking lenders and lendees directly through a virtual financial platform known as crowdfunding. The platform enables mass lenders to connect and provide financial support to those who need their business development. Under the peer-to-peer (P2P) consumer (or business) lending platform, crowdfunding is utilized as the new structure of banking and stock market, where people can readily be involved in the exchange of financial availability and support to businesses. In some cases, the platforms are recognized as lending-based crowdfunding platforms. The new crowdfunding structure allows small startups in households or micro-businesses to receive financing directly from many investors rather than begging for financial support from banks or financial institutions. The platforms are a part of the broader fintech reforms, which are often considered an opportunity to make financial intermediation more transparent, equitable, and efficient.

In some countries, crowdfunding platforms are becoming viable financial choices competing with bank credit and stock markets. Crowdfunding has become a pioneer financial provider which involves massive transactions between lenders and lendees. With the significant increase in crowdfunding, the financial market has faced both benefits and the side effects of potential financial fraudulence, where mass consumers can become targets of dishonest businesses. Governments aim to protect both lenders and lendees through issue-specific regulations governing crowdfunding. Government regulations also include the governance of the secondary financial market, coordination effects of the platform, market barriers, and institutional lenders. This chapter aims to focus on how Singapore, Thailand, and Vietnam respond to establishing regulatory frameworks of crowdfunding and will provide regulatory frameworks to display the similarities and differences in startup crowdfunding in Singapore, Thailand, and Vietnam. There is still a gap in research on the regulatory frameworks for crowdfunding in countries with ASEAN perspectives. With this comparative study, the current chapter can provide possible recommendations for the development of policy and a regulatory framework for crowdfunding. The chapter looks at

DOI: 10.4324/9781003220220-8

the empirical and case studies on regulation of crowdfunding for supporting startups' access to finance and investment. It also intends to add to the literature on how developing countries can shape their regulatory framework for crowdfunding to keep up with fast-changing finance innovation and technologies. The research aims to answer the question of what regulatory and legal requirements and solutions are there for developing crowdfunding. This chapter fits well with the scheme of the book, which seeks to study intuitional and regulatory innovation for supporting innovative financial technologies.

The chapter focuses on Singapore, Thailand, and Vietnam, because first, those three countries can broadly provide regulatory frameworks on crowdfunding in ASEAN countries, and second, they are on different levels of development based on world bank economic indicators. The chapter employs comparative study methodology to evaluate regulatory frameworks for crowdfunding for startups. The chapter is divided into five parts. The first part introduces the overview of the chapter. The second part gives an overview of crowdfunding and discusses regulatory frameworks on it. The third part explores regulatory frameworks of crowdfunding in Singapore, Thailand, and Vietnam. The fourth presents comparative views on regulatory frameworks of crowdfunding in those three countries. The fifth provides conclusions with regulatory implications.

2 Overview of crowdfunding and the regulatory framework on it

2.1 Concept of crowdfunding

During 1950–2000, financing fell predominantly into the domain banks and financial institutions, which tended to fully cover all financial services. With the invention of "financial technology" (fintech), however, the secure and profitable position of banking and financial institutions became shaky. Banks and financial institutions are set to be superseded by the increasing use of fintech. Fintech, especially crowdfunding through Internet platforms, enables lenders to provide financial support to lendees' businesses. Individuals or businesses can obtain financial help or investments by seeking loans from banks or issuing stock in stock markets. Thus, crowdfunding is increasingly changing and replacing the traditional financial frameworks of initialized banks and causing them to lean toward de-initialized financial services that enable participatory modes of financing (Fenwick et al., 2018). Crowdfunding is especially beneficial to SMEs or startups, as it presents them with opportunities to receive financial support directly from wide investors rather than relying on loans from banks (Ryu and Kim, 2016; Yang and Lee, 2019). Crowdfunding establishes a method for startups to acquire funding from various new venture capital by assisting business creators in attracting funding from many people or businesses (Mollick, 2014). In the case of newly established SMEs or startups, banks will not easily lend financing. However, if an SME or startup has business potential, it can resort to crowdfunding platforms to attract financing (Nisar et al., 2020). Over the last two decades, the Internet and social media platforms have transformed crowdfunding into the means by which SMEs and startups can propose business ideas to large numbers of people who may have some money they are prepared to donate or invest. As expressed in the Australia CAMAC Report, crowdfunding is an innovative financial service for persons seeking funds from the crowd through Internet platforms in ways previously unforeseen (CAMAC, 2014). The most common types of crowdfunding are presented below (Shneor et al., 2020).

- The Donation-based model – the provision of funding based on philanthropic or civic motivation without expectation of material reward.
- The Rewards-based model – the provision of funding in exchange for non-monetary rewards, most frequently in the form of pre-purchased products or services.
- The Debt-based model – the provision of funding through loans by individual or institutional lenders with the expectation of repayment of the principal and a set interest within a predefined timeframe.
- The Equity-based model – the provision of funding in return for an equity interest in the business.

While donation- and reward-based models are essential, they are non-investment models which are unlikely to raise sufficient funds to meet the financial needs of SMEs and startups and are, therefore, of limited use as sources of financing in this context. The investment models of debt crowdfunding (also known as lending crowdfunding, marketplace or crowd lending, or peer-to-peer (P2P) lending) and equity crowdfunding are the most viable. The latter model (also referred to as crowd-sourced equity funding (CSEF), investment-based crowdfunding, or simply, and increasingly, simply crowd-sourced funding (CSF)) is the focus of this chapter.

CSEF is a new and growing method of capital raising which refers to the arrangement through which a business can raise early-stage funding (CAMAC, 2013). It differs from other forms of crowdfunding through the provision of an equity interest in return for the investment.

The US adoption of the Jumpstart Our Business Startups (JOBS) Act provided the catalyst for the development of equity crowdfunding in the US. The Act provided a dedicated legal basis for equity-based crowdfunding and, in combination with increasing access to the Internet by the crowd, the foundation for modern crowdfunding. Online fundraising by way of crowdfunding is now an established, successful, viable, and increasingly influential strategy. It is emerging in those jurisdictions that have implemented the legal framework to support startups and SMEs as a means of drawing capital by issuing securities. The terms of the equity offer attract funding from hundreds of investors, who invest very small amounts in return for equity (Figure 5.1).

For SMEs and startups, the benefits of a successful crowdfunding campaign are likely to be even greater than those of raising funds that may not otherwise have been possible (Singh, 2021). Crowdfunding provides publicity for SMEs and startup concepts (which are unlikely to be widely known), validation of the

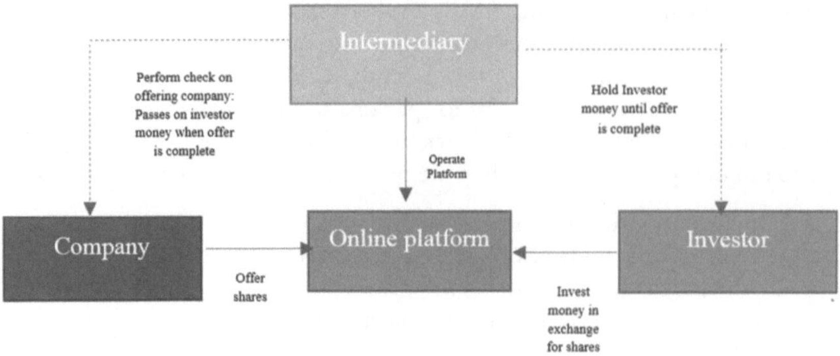

Figure 5.1 Equity-Based Crowdfunding.
Source: ASIC (2018).

company's credentials, and a body of investors who are not simply investors but brand ambassadors. Through crowdfunding, startups can bypass conventional institutional angel investors who have the resources to dictate rather than negotiate the terms of the offering. And, of course, CSEF is not an all-or-nothing strategy: traditional fundraising techniques remain open to the company. Nevertheless, there are downsides to crowdfunding for both the investor and the startup. Companies seeking crowd-sourced funding are usually at an early stage with no proof of profits. Investments through crowdfunding offers can become highly speculative, with a potential risk of failure and loss to equity investors (ASIC, 2020). Ironically, the crowdfunding initiative's success may result in the administrative challenge of a very large number of very small investors.

2.2 Regulation on crowdfunding from international perspectives

The increasing use of crowdfunding for SMEs and startups poses challenges to traditional banks or financial institutions and the government in having to govern crowdfunding to ensure that the public interest of funders is protected from fraudulent crowdfunding. Havrylchyk (2018) proposes that governments in 17 OECD countries have to reform their financial regulations that facilitate and govern crowdfunding. The new regulatory regimes allow businesses to raise funds from digital crowdfunding platforms (Fenwick et al., 2018; Ferrarini, 2017). In the US, the regulation to govern crowdfunding was adopted to promote the crowdfunding platform and guarantee that the risks to wide investors are protected against. The US Securities and Exchange Commission (US SEC) issued the Part 227 regulation of crowdfunding with the following vital rules:

- require all transactions under Regulation Crowdfunding to take place online through an SEC-registered intermediary, either a broker-dealer or a funding portal;
- permit a company to raise a maximum aggregate amount of $5 million through crowdfunding offerings in a 12-month period;

- limit the amount individual non-accredited investors can invest across all crowdfunding offerings in a 12-month period; and
- require disclosure of information in filings with the Commission and to investors in the intermediary facilitating the offering (US SEC, 2021).

The EU commission passed Regulation 2017/1129 and Directive (EU) 2019/1937 on European crowdfunding service providers (ECSP) for businesses to stimulate crowdfunding and ensure the interests of crowdfunding investors. The regulation defines crowdfunding as the matching of investment interests with business creators through crowdfunding platforms to facilitate the granting of loans and be the platform for transferrable securities. The regulation also contains the following:

- Uniform rules across the EU for the provision of investment-based and lending-based crowdfunding services related to business financing.
- Increase the availability of this innovative form of finance, which supports startup companies to tap into investments from crowdfunding platforms.
- Provide clear regulation on information disclosures for a startup who is a business originator and crowdfunding platforms.
- Strong and harmonized supervisory powers for national agencies overseeing the standard of crowdfunding platforms.
- Regulations applying to crowdfunding offers with consideration of value at EUR 0-5,000,000 which are to be calculated over a period of 12 months.
- Crowdfunding company must maintain investor protection measures by making a credit risk assessment, due diligence, individual portfolio management of loans, key investment information sheet, pre-contractual reflection period, complaints handling, conflicts of interest, and prudential requirements.

In Australia, to provide a regulatory framework for crowdfunding, the Corporations Amendment (Crowd-sourced Funding) Act 2017 was adopted along with the amendment of the Australian Securities and Investments Commission Act 2001(ASIC, 2021). The amendments reduce regulatory burdens for crowdfunding while maintaining appropriate investor protection measures (ASIC, 2021). The regulatory framework requires all crowdfunding operators to obtain an Australian financial services (AFS) license before any crowdfunding operation in Australia. In addition, the ASIC issued the regulation of RG 261 Crowd-sourced funding, a guide for companies to govern the operation of crowdfunding in Australia. The regulation defines crowdfunding as "*a company raising funds—usually through an online intermediary—from a large number of individual investors who make relatively small financial contributions to the company*" (ASIC, 2020). In addition, the regulation set out the following requirements:

- The crowdfunding company must be a registered proprietary or public company with its principal business and directors residing in Australia.
- The consolidated gross assets and annual revenue of the crowdfunding company and all of its related parties must not exceed the assets and annual revenue caps of $25 million.

- The crowdfunding company and its related companies must not raise more than $5 million in any 12-month period through crowdfunding offers.
- Retail investors have an investment cap of $10,000 per crowdfunding company in any 12-month period (the 'investor cap') and a cooling-off period allowing them to withdraw from a CSF offer up to five days after making an application.
- The crowdfunding company in making offers must prepare an offer document that includes the prescribed minimum information for clear and transparent information disclosure (ASIC, 2020).

Countries and regions have passed specific regulations on crowdfunding, creating an increasing wave of regulatory reforms for crowdfunding governance. What can be implied from the adoption of specific rules on crowdfunding is that countries accept the benefits of crowdfunding but remain distrustful of it, which may affect wide investors. Thus, the regulation mainly deals with a threshold of investments and technical requirements for all crowdfunding companies. This chapter will explore the regulatory frameworks of crowdfunding that help support startups in the ASEAN countries of Singapore, Thailand, and Vietnam. The three selected countries reflect different stages of development among ASEAN countries. Singapore is at a high development level being 2nd in the World Bank's ease of doing business category (World Bank, 2020) and is classified as a high-income country (World Bank, 2020). Thailand is at the middle level, being 21st in the World Bank's ease of doing business category (World Bank, 2020) and is classified as an upper-middle-income country (World Bank, 2020). Vietnam is at the middle level, being 70th in the World Bank's ease of doing business category (World Bank, 2020) and is classified as a lower-middle-income country (World Bank, 2020). Thus, these three countries can represent all ASEAN countries, which have different levels of economic development. The later part of this chapter, therefore, focuses on the regulatory frameworks of these three countries.

3 Regulatory frameworks of crowdfunding in Singapore, Thailand, and Vietnam

As mentioned above, various countries respond to crowdfunding by reshaping their regulations to enable crowdfunding for financing startups and SMEs. This part provides regulatory frameworks of crowdfunding for startups in the three countries and later displays a comparative analysis of the three countries.

3.1 Regulatory framework for crowdfunding in Singapore

3.1.1 Development of regulation on crowdfunding

Singapore is a country open to change and transformation. Regulatory frameworks for all business sectors are issued and reformed according to changing technology and business circumstances. The digital economy and smart nation were established as vital policies to drive Singapore's development. The Singapore National Plan of Smart Nation sets a practical approach to build up connectivity between digital transformation and private sectors to ensure Singapore's international competitiveness (SNDGO, 2018). In addition, based on the Digital Economy Framework for Action plan, Singapore adopted modernization on policy, regulation, and standards to create a system and environment that enables businesses while maintaining trust (IMDA, 2018). The adoption of modernization on policy and law directly connects to building up Singapore as a global financial hub, strategically located in Asia, connecting the financial world between east and west (IMDA, 2018).

Singapore's government has also put policy in place for financial promotion of SMEs and startups, i.e., the *Startup SG Equity*. Under the Startup SG Equity, the government provides a financial scheme of (1) Co-investment with independents; and (2) Investment in selected venture capital firms that can invest in eligible startups through a cooperative fund approach (Startup SG, 2021). The government funding scheme is shown in Table 5.1.

Singapore's government also takes into consideration that institutional funds are the main source of support for SMEs and startups, but it also recognizes that the crowdfunding platform is an important element in digital financial methods for developing SMEs and startups. The government reshaped its policy to enable crowdfunding platforms for supporting SMEs and startups established in Singapore. Before 2015, the financial and money markets regulations, a main source of funds for SMEs and startups, were very rigid. These regulations created a high compliant cost, obstructing SMEs and startups from accessing funding through crowdfunding (Hu, 2015). Later, the government reformulated policy and regulations with the rationale of facilitating crowdfunding in Singapore. The Money Authority of Singapore (MAS) issued the 2015 consultation paper proposing measures to provide SMEs and startups with more access to funding sources (MAS, 2016). The consultation paper came back with the following results: (1) MAS will ease financial requirements for financial dealing licensees but maintain regulatory frameworks for investor protection; (2) MAS will set regulations for lowering the base capital requirement for financial dealing licensees to $50,000;

Table 5.1 Investment Parameters Scheme for the Co-investment of Startups

	General Tech	*Deep Tech*
Investment Cap for Each Startup	*$2M from SEEDS Capital*	*$8M from SEEDS Capital*
Co-investment ratio	7:3 up to the first $250K from SEEDS Capital; 1:1 thereafter, up to $2M	7:3 up to the first $500K from SEEDS Capital; 1:1 from $500K to $4M 3:7 thereafter, up to $8M

Source: Startup SG (2021).

(3) MAS will relax specific financial requirements for capital market intermediaries; and (4) MAS will create a new investor classification for securities-based crowdfunding (MAS, 2016). After consultation, the Singapore government adopted specific regulations which facilitate crowdfunding for SMEs and start-ups. The current regulatory scheme of crowdfunding in Singapore is discussed in the next part of the chapter.

3.1.2 Regulatory frameworks on crowdfunding in Singapore

After consultation and consideration of changing financial technology, Singapore adopted specific regulations to facilitate crowdfunding for SMEs and startups with four main schemes: (1) small offers exemption, (2) private placement, (3) institutional investors, and (4) accredited investors.

Small offer exemption is based on section 272A of the Securities and Futures Act (Cap. 289) (SFA). SMEs or startups, by crowdfunding platforms, can issue individual offers of securities investment not exceeding SGD 5 million within a 12-month period. The objective of adopting the regulation of small offer exemption is to reduce the regulatory burden for SMEs and startups in being compliant with the prospectus requirements (see prospectus requirements in the SAL, 2019) for a small money-raising scheme (MAS, 2018b). In a normal situation, any business involving securities investments must prepare and be approved with prospectus requirements that are burdens to SMEs and startups. In addition, the regulation was adopted with the recognition that SMEs may raise investments from venture capital firms, business angels, and friends and family, who already have access to information about crowdfunding (MAS, 2018b). The regulation on small offers exemption thus aims to make fundraising more accessible for SMEs and startups. Therefore, any offers in crowdfunding that do not exceed 5 million in 12 months are exempt from following the Securities and Futures Act (Cap. 289). However, there are other regulatory requirements within section 272A which protect investors in the small offer in crowdfunding. Examples of requirements are transparency of company information, business report, and general meeting report (MAS, 2018b).

A private placement is based on section 272B SFA and is crowdfunding with no more than 50 investors within any 12-month period. The regulation was adopted for crowdfunding that involves a small group of investors and does not pose any high risks to wide investors. Section 272B on private placement has set out that any offer for private investment must not be an advertisement offer or promotional expense by commission fee by the holder of a capital market services licence under securities or securities-based derivatives contracts. The regulation ensures that licensed brokers in the security market may not be involved with private placement of crowdfunding outside the traditional securities market. The regulation further intends to facilitate the crowdfunding of small groups of private financial cooperation.

The institutional investors scheme is based on section 274 of the SFA. SMEs and startups can connect with institutional investors and directly request financial lending by resorting to a crowdfunding system. The regulatory requirement of crowdfunding with institutional investors is similar to that of a private placement. SMEs and startups must not offer through advertisement and must not be involved with any promotional expenses by commission fee for securities market services.

The accredited investors scheme is based on section 275 of the SFA and enables SMEs and startups to use crowdfunding with knowledgeable investors who understand crowdfunding and investment in digital platforms. The regulatory requirement of crowdfunding with accredited investors is similar to that of a private placement. SMEs and startups must not offer through advertisement and must not involve any promotional expenses by way of commission fee for securities market services.

The four crowdfunding schemes for SMEs and startups are the regulatory schemes that reduce legal and licensing burdens from the prospectus requirements, requiring all securities corporates to submit and prepare all financial and technical documents for MAS approval. The exemption for the prospectus requirements reduces regulatory costs for the financially weak recipient of funding (Hofmann, 2018). While all four regulatory schemes exempt crowdfunding platforms from prospectus requirements, crowdfunding platforms must obtain a capital market services (CMS) license under the SFA (MAS, 2018a). Licensees ensure that the platform operators know all financial requirements and risks from crowdfunding in financial markets.

3.2 Regulatory framework for crowdfunding in Thailand

3.2.1 Regulatory framework for crowdfunding in Thailand

Thailand has set policy on SMEs and startups concerning policy from other countries (Wisuttisak, 2021). The frameworks ensure that support is available to SMEs and startups, which are the backbone of Thailand's industrial infrastructure and economy (Turner et al., 2016; Yoshino et al., 2016). The SMEs promotional plan was formally set by the enactment of the Small and Medium Enterprises Promotion Act B.E. 2543 (2000) (SMEs Act) with the establishment of the Office of Small and Medium Enterprises Promotion (OSMEP). The SMEs Act section 34 stipulates that SME funds are to support SMEs and startups and to improve efficiency and capabilities. The 4th (2017–2021) SME Promotion Master Plan was adopted by digital development policies on SMEs and startups relating to access to investment funds, entrepreneurship training, revision of regulations on SMEs, promotional schemes for SMEs clusters, and a value-added startup. Thai SMEs and startups seem to have available support in terms of policy and financial help through government grants and specific bank loans. However, SMEs and startups in Thailand still face challenges to acquiring financial support. Punyasavatsut (2011) points out that while there are various policies to extend financial support for SMEs and startups, only 40% of Thai SMEs could gain access to credit from banks, because SMEs and startups tend to have less information about their businesses and less certainty of business journeys. This is different from large corporates, which have a solid financial statement that they can use in bargaining with banks. Banks consider SMEs and startups to be riskier, as they do not have clear accounting information but do have a limited credit history (Yoshino and Taghizadeh-Hesary, 2019). Thus, banks and financial institutions are not in an easy position to lend financial support to SMEs and startups. Table 5.2 presents the challenges facing SMEs in achieving access to funding from financial institutions in Thailand.

Although SMEs and startups face difficulty accessing funding from financial institutions, they still rely heavily on financial institutions. Only 40% of Thai SMEs and startups can gain access to credit support from a financial institution (Punyasavatsut, 2011). With the technological change of digital transactions and crowdfunding schemes in international markets, Thailand has gradually accepted crowdfunding. The Thai government has initiated the Thailand 4.0 policy on a national innovation system (NIS) for creating an innovative economy (Harris and Wonglimpiyarat, 2020). The 4.0 policy closely links with a crowdfunding platform to promote SMEs and startups in Thailand (Wonglimpiyarat, 2018). The Thai government has also reformed laws and policies related to fintech to keep up with contemporary technological developments (Jenweeranon, 2020). As regards crowdfunding, the Thai government has authorized the Securities and Exchange Commission (SEC) to be a regulator and issue any regulation governing crowdfunding in Thailand.

3.2.2 Regulatory frameworks on crowdfunding in Thailand

The regulation of crowdfunding falls under the governance of the SEC. Most of the rules issued by the SEC are meant to balance objectives between facilitating crowdfunding for SMEs and startups and investment protection. Crowdfunding is considered the issuance of financial securities subjected to the Securities and Exchange Act B.E.2535 (SEC Act). The SEC Act sets out rules and procedures of securities exchanges in Thai stock markets and other related financial means.

Table 5.2 Challenges to SMEs Access to Funding from Financial Institutions in Thailand

SMEs Perspective	*Bank Perspective*
• Lack of Information and advice from FIs • Complexity and inconvenience related to loan Application process • Inadequate qualification of SMEs • Expenses/fees and interest rate charged • Lack of collateral • Lack of information infrastructure for SMEs	• Inadequate collateral • Lack of business experience • Unreliable accounting system of SMEs • Lack of business planning of SMEs • SMEs' NPL history • High transaction and operational costs per SMEs' loan application • Strict government rules and regulations • Unlevel playing field

Source: Punyasavatsut (2011); Yoshino and Taghizadeh-Hesary (2018).

Based on the Act, the Securities and Exchange Commission (SEC) has the authoritative power to issue regulations ensuring the sustainability and growth of the securities market in Thailand. Sections 32 and 34 prescribe that any issuance of securities and offers to public investment must obtain SEC approval. Any limited company must not issue any securities by public offering unless the SEC provides an exemption. Thus, the SEC issued regulations that permit SMEs and startups to conduct crowdfunding to attract investments. The SEC also issued various subordinate rules to govern crowdfunding platforms. The necessary subordinate regulations are (Thailand SEC, 2021):

- Notification of the Capital Market Supervisory Board No. KorJor. 5/2562 Exemption for a report of a public offering of crowdfunding
- Notification of the Capital Market Supervisory Board No. KorThor. 6/2562 Rules and Conditions in advising on crowdfunding to the public, which is not classified as financial advice under financial businesses
- Notification of the Capital Market Supervisory Board No. ThorJor 21/2562 Rules on public offerings of crowdfunding

Based on the notification, the SEC adopted a regulatory framework of approval based on a crowdfunding platform. Thus, crowdfunding platforms must obtain SEC approval before issuing or exchanging any crowdfunding securities. By SEC regulation, the approved crowdfunding platform must (Thailand SEC, 2021):

- Screen companies (SMEs and startups) that will be offered for sale in crowdfunding by reviewing the identity and qualifications of the offering as specified in the announcement to build confidence for investors to a certain extent
- Disclose information about the offering
- Educating investors about risks
- Assess credibility and risk level and creditworthiness of crowdfunding

The funding portal also has to classify crowdfunding business levels as retail investor, non-retail investor, venture capital, private equity trust, and qualified investor. In addition, the regulation requires crowdfunding platforms to prepare the proper process of selling and buying securities on the platform and all crucial details of the company offering shares or securities on crowdfunding. The platforms have to prepare all reports for investors and the SEC audit. In addition, the SEC regulations require crowdfunding platforms comply with the limitation level of crowdfunding for investor protection, as shown in Table 5.3.

In addition to limiting retail investments, SEC regulations also obligate crowdfunding companies to evaluate retail investors regarding financial knowledge. The crowdfunding investment is not under the all-or-none shares, like the issuance of stock exchanges (Thailand SEC, 2021). If the crowdfunding can attract 80% of crowdfunding issuance, the crowdfunding can start their operation. The SEC has set regulations and policies to ensure that the issuance

Table 5.3 Thailand SEC Regulation of Crowdfunding Investment

Investor in CFS	*Raise Fund*	*Limitation of Investment*
(1) Retail Investor	The company can raise funds from retail investors up to 20 million Baht in the first 12 months, and the total funding limit is not more than 40 million baht (including stocks and debentures).	Investment is not more than 100,000 baht per company, and the total investment value is not more than 1 million Baht per year (including stocks and debentures).
(2) Non-retail investor (Institution or corporate investors)	No limitation.	No limitation.

Source: Thailand SEC (2021).

Table 5.4 Thai SEC's Regulatory Requirements on IPO and Crowdfunding

	Stock market IPO	*Crowdfunding*
Issuers	Thai SEC	Funding portal with approval from SEC
Criteria	Regulation of good governance	General license
Information disclosure	According to the Securities and Exchange Act, the filing must be submitted with a financial advisor approved by the SEC.	According to general guidelines of SEC
• During a selling of shares		Company information and financial report
• After the selling of shares	Prospectus Documents Financial statement and formal forms of report (56/1)	Contact point of funding portals – web page or online connection
Selling channels	By underwriter with compliance to sales conducts	Funding portal
Liquidity	Supplement with secondary market	No secondary market

Source: Thailand SEC (2021).

of crowdfunding in the financial market is different from the issuance of IPOs in Thai stock markets. The details of the regulatory differences are listed in Table 5.4.

The SEC's regulatory difference between IPOs and crowdfunding is from the feedback from SMEs and startups, indicating that they cannot satisfy the rigid rules on IPOs. The SEC thus reformed its regulations for crowdfunding by making fewer requirements (Kongsakul, 2020). The SEC also set the rules of a private placement for creating a platform bridging SMEs and startups with venture capital (VC) or private equity (PE) (Kongsakul, 2020). The SEC's private investments program is also meant to enable SMEs and startups to connect with potential angel investors.

3.3 *Regulatory framework of crowdfunding in Vietnam*

3.3.1 *Development of regulation and policy on crowdfunding in Vietnam*

Vietnam is considered the leading startup hub of ASEAN (Kaur, 2021). Vietnam has fintech growth and crowdfunding, because the country has a young and tech-savvy population and a rapid increase in mobile and Internet usage (Thu, 2020). SMEs and startups make up around 90% of the number of active enterprises, and they are expected to grow because of the government policy to promote startups (Hai et al., 2020). However, obtaining capital through such traditional channels as banks or securities exchanges is not easy for startups in Vietnam. In accessing external sources of capital, especially credit capital, SMEs and startups find it difficult to secure funding from financial institutions (Loan, 2018). As in other countries, crowdfunding has become an effective way of gathering capital for startup enterprises in Vietnam. Crowdfunding first appeared in Vietnam in 2003, and now, about 100 P2P lending companies are operating there (Năm, 2021). With the increasing number of startup enterprises and the necessity of crowdfunding for these companies, the legal framework is essential to supporting the sustainable development of crowdfunding in Vietnam. However, Vietnam differs from Singapore and Thailand in that it has not adopted specific regulations for crowdfunding. The current regulatory frameworks involving crowdfunding are (1) *Commercial Law* 2005 and *Civil Code* 2015; (2) *Law on Electronic Transactions* 2005; and (3) *Directive 09/CT-TTg* of the Prime Minister issued on Feb 18, 2020, about creating favorable conditions for startup enterprises.

3.3.2 *Commercial Law 2005 and Civil Code 2015*

Vietnam is heavily influenced by the civil law system, so business activities are mainly regulated by legal documents rather than case law. Nevertheless, it has not yet introduced any specific regulations on crowdfunding. Therefore, crowdfunding has been implemented based on an underlying commercial legal framework. Although there is no specific legal article on it, crowdfunding can now be operated based on the principle of freedom of contract under Vietnam's *Commercial Law* (issued in 2005) and Vietnam's *Civil Code* (issued in 2015). These are the main legal documents that startup enterprises (lendees), lenders, and lending-based crowdfunding platforms (LCP), and providers must obey when conducting crowdfunding.

Based on sections 1 and 2 of *Commercial Law*, the contract between LCP providers and startup enterprises [lendees] shall be considered a service contract. This contract can be oral, in writing, or in any communication determined by specific conduct according to article 74 of the commercial law. In general, articles 78–81 of *Commercial Law* permits the LCP provider and the lender to freely agree on rights and obligations. Such commitments and agreements are not prohibited by law, nor are they contrary to public order. According to *Commercial Law*, the LCP provider shall have the following obligations, unless otherwise agreed:

- To supply services and carry out other related work fully, in accordance with the agreement [of the parties] and according to this Law.
- To preserve materials and facilities delivered to perform the services and to return same to the client after completion of the work.
- To immediately notify the client of any instance of insufficient information and materials or inadequate facilities that fail to ensure the completion of the services.
- To keep confidential any information made known to the LCP provider during the provision of the services if so agreed [by the parties] or if required by law.
- If the nature of the particular service being provided requires the LCP provider to produce a certain result, then when providing the service the LCP provider must obtain an appropriate result in accordance with the conditions and objectives set out in the contract. Where the contract does not contain specific clauses on the standard of the result to be obtained, then when providing the service, the LCP provider must obtain an appropriate result in compliance with the ordinary standards applicable to that type of service.
- Suppose the nature of the particular service being provided requires the LCP provider to use its best endeavors to produce the desired result. In that case, the LCP provider must discharge the obligation to provide such service using its best endeavors and capacity.

In addition, according to *Commercial Law*, the lendee shall have the following obligations unless otherwise agreed:

- To pay for the provision of the service as agreed in the contract.
- To provide all plans, instructions, and other details for the service in a timely manner without delay or interruption.
- To cooperate in all other necessary matters to enable the LCP provider to provide the service appropriately.
- Where a service is to be provided jointly by a number of service providers or by one service provider in cooperation with other service providers, then the client shall be obliged to coordinate the operations of all service providers so as not to impede the work of any one service provider.

The LCP provider and the lendee are also free to agree on time-limits for completion of services, service fees, and payments. According to the *Civil Code*, the contract between the lendee and the lender is determined as the contract for a property loan (Section 4 Chapter XVI Civil Code 2015), which is a legally binding agreement covering the rights and obligations of parties sufficient to the freedom of contract. Although both parties can freely agree on the contract, several obligations are imposed by the *Civil Code*. The lender has to:

- Provide the property to the lendee in full based on the set contract following the quality and quantity and at the time and place agreed.
- Provide compensation of damage to the lendee in the case the property is not of the agreed quality.
- Refrain from requesting the lendee to return the property prior to the due date.
- The *Civil Code* imposes only one obligation on the lendee to repay loans as follows:
- Where the property lent is a sum of money, the lendee must repay the lender the loan in full within the agreed period of time. If the property is a movable property, the lendee must provide a movable property of the same type, quantity, and quality to the lender, unless there is another arrangement between lender and lendee.
- Where a lendee cannot deliver a movable property, lendee may, with the consent of the lender, repay the value of the borrowed movable property.
- The place for repayment of a loan can be the residence or the lender's head office, unless there is another arrangement between lender and lendee.
- If the lendee fails to repay all or any installment of an interest-free loan, the lendee has to pay overdue interest until the date of payment completion.
- If the lendee fails to repay, in whole or in part, a loan with interest, the lendee must pay interest on the principal as agreed in proportion to the overdue loan term and interest.
- The lender and the lendee can agree on the interest rate, but it must not exceed 20% per annual.

For the performance of contracts, the Code divide the loan contract into two types: (1) contract for loan without fixed term, and (2) contract for loan with fixed term. With a contract for a loan without a fixed term with no interest, the lender may reclaim the property, and the lendee may repay the debt at any time. If the contract is for a loan with interest, the lender may reclaim the property and can receive interest until the completion of return on property. However, the lendee may return the property at any time by giving prior notice to lender. The lendee has to pay interest until the date of repayment completion. Furthermore, if the contract for loan with a fixed term is an interest-free loan, the lendee may return the property at any time by giving prior notice to the lender. The lender may reclaim the property before the due date, but the lender must obtain lendee's consent. If it is the contract of a loan with interest, the lendee may return the property before the contract period but must pay interest for the entire term.

Although the lender and the lendee can conduct crowdfunding based on the above-discussed commercial and civil regulations, many important issues related directly to crowdfunding have not been legally addressed. The legal issues include conditions for LCP providers, scope of lendees, capital limit of lendees, and duties of LCP providers to lendees, which may lead to difficulties and risks for the parties when implementing crowdfunding.

3.3.3 Law on electronic transactions

Because LCP is an online platform, it is important for LCP providers, lenders, and lendees to consider regulations on electronic transactions. In 2005, Vietnam passed the *Law on Electronic Transactions* to govern e-transactions in operations (Article 1). The law contains important rules regarding electronic contracts that would regularly be signed between the LCP providers and lendees and between the lendees and lenders. According to this law, data communication can be 'electronic information exchanges, electronic documents, e-mails, telegram, telegraphy, faxes, and other similar forms' (Article 10). Where the law requires information to be in writing, data communication can be classified as writing in the case of the referenceable e-document (Article 12). In addition, the court must not deny the validity of the electronic data for the sole reason that it is an electronic data communication (Article 11).

The electronic message shall have validity as an original copy if: (1) its content is ensured being unchanged since its first origination in the form of a complete data message; and (2) the contents of the data message are accessible and referenceable. Therefore, all data messages used in LCP among LCP providers, lenders, and lendees can be recognized by laws. The law also prescribes the validity of electronic contracts and electronic signature.

Where the law requires a written document, the e-signature would validate the document if: (1) it is checkable that the e-signature signor gives consent to the contents of the data message; and (2) such method is sufficiently reliable and appropriate for the purpose of electronic communication (Article 24). Although the Law on Electronic Transactions initially created a legal framework that makes online transactions related to LCP possible, there still exists a number of ambiguous issues in this law, such as electronic identification, electronic authentication, and security of electronic transactions (VGP, 2021), that may constrain the development of LCP. Vietnam's Ministry of Information and Communications is proposing to revise this law to resolve these problems, in particular, and to create a better legal framework for electronic transactions, in general.

3.3.4 Initial steps toward building a specific legal framework for crowdfunding

Although there are no specific regulations on crowdfunding, Vietnam's government has recently expressed its intent to issue a particular legal framework. The aim to issue the specific regulation is in response to startup enterprises that have been encouraged to develop and have received much support from the government. In 2016, Vietnam first introduced a draft law on small and medium-sized enterprises, including several crowdfunding regulations. However, these regulations had been removed before the *Law on Small and Medium Enterprises* was passed on June 12, 2017.

Last year, Vietnam's prime minister issued *Directive 09/CT-TTg 18 Feb 2020* to provide a favorable environment for startup enterprises. According to *Directive*

09, the *Law on Investment* shall soon be revised to favor foreign investors in establishing, contributing capital, buying shares or capital of the Innovative Startup Investment Fund in Vietnam. In particular, this *Directive* requested Vietnam's Ministry of Finance to build a project of establishing capital exchange for startup enterprises and report this project to the prime minister in 2020 or 2021. In November 2020, the Ministry of Finance also announced that it is actively building a project of crowdfunding (Vietnam Ministry of Finances, 2020). Although there is a significant need for specific regulations on crowdfunding, the content and outcome of this project are still unclear.

4 Comparative views on regulatory frameworks of crowdfunding

From the exploration of regulatory frameworks on crowdfunding in the three selected ASEAN countries, it can be seen that there are differences and similarities in the regulatory frameworks, such as (1) the objective to support SMEs and startups, (2) specific regulations enabling crowdfunding, (3) regulatory governance on investment thresholds, and (4) institutional regulators. The comparison of differences and similarities are displayed in Table 5.5.

The exploration of regulatory frameworks on crowdfunding for startups in the three studied countries indicate that they are similarly concerned about the difficulties startups face in obtaining financial support. Crowdfunding becomes a viable method for SMEs and startups, but governments have to maintain their regulatory roles to ensure secure crowdfunding for small-wide investors. However, it is noted that among the three selected countries, Vietnam is the only one that has not adopted specific regulations on crowdfunding. Although specific regulation is not the only answer for crowdfunding governance (Wasiuzzaman, 2021), regulation can at least assure the certainty of investor perception on crowdfunding for startups. Singapore and Thailand have amended their regulatory frameworks with the purpose of supporting the proliferation of startup crowdfunding. There is a difference in the regulations on investment thresholds linked with capital market development. With its mature financial markets, Singapore prefers relying on exemption schemes that relax the restricted prospectus requirements for crowdfunding. With developing financial markets, Thailand chooses licensing-based schemes and requires all crowdfunding to satisfy regulations of license approval. The difference in regulatory schemes can lead to different results of crowdfunding for startups.

5 Conclusion and policy recommendations

Crowdfunding is a vital platform for a startup in assessing investment funds for wide investors. It helps close the gap in financial availability which traditional banks have not provided to SMEs. The chapter explores the concepts of crowdfunding contributing to the new landscape of financial support of SMEs and startups. By relying on financial technology and Internet platforms,

Table 5.5 Comparison of Regulatory Frameworks on Crowdfunding in Singapore, Thailand, and Vietnam

Regulatory Framework	*Differences and Similarities*
1. Government objective to support startups crowdfunding	*Singapore and Thailand* set their policy and regulations. There is also a practical implementation of the policy to support startup crowdfunding *Vietnam* has pronounced its policy to support startup crowdfunding, but there is still no practical implementation.
2. Specific regulations enabling crowdfunding	*Singapore and Thailand* adopted specific regulations for crowdfunding. Singapore has amended the Securities and Futures Act (Cap. 289) (SFA) to provide exemptions for security crowdfunding. Thailand has issued subordinate regulations under the Securities and Exchange Act B.E.2535 (SEC Act) to enable crowdfunding for SMEs and startups. The amendment and issuance of the rules facilitate the creation of crowdfunding for SMEs and startups. *Vietnam* has not adopted specific laws on crowdfunding. The crowdfunding activities still rely on civil commercial codes and regulations on electronic transactions. Thus, the traditional rules of loans and investments are applied to crowdfunding. However, according to *Directive 09*, the *Law on Investment* is expected to be revised to support crowdfunding.
3. Regulatory governance on investment thresholds	*Singapore* sets a policy of exemption by permitting all crowdfunding by (1) small offer exemptions (up to SGD 5 million within a 12-month period); (2) private placement (no more than 50 investors); (3) institutional investors (fund support of startup through institutional consultation); and (4) accredited investors (fund support of startup by expert investors). *Thailand* relies on license-based regulations on crowdfunding. For retail crowdfunding, all crowdfunding must have licenses and can raise crowdfunding from retail investors up to 20 million Baht in the first 12 months with a limitation on total funding, not more than 40 million Baht (including stocks and debentures). There is no investment limitation for institutional investors in startups. *Vietnam*, by no specific law on crowdfunding, has a limitation of supporting crowdfunding for SMEs and startups.
4. Institutional regulator on crowdfunding	*Singapore* entrusts the Money Authority of Singapore with supervising and regulating crowdfunding. *Thailand* relies on the Securities and Exchange Commission (SEC) to regulate and supervise crowdfunding. *Vietnam*, with no specific regulation, has no specific regulator on crowdfunding.

Source: Authors' compilation and comparison.

crowdfunding permits direct investment in startups instead of requesting financial support from a financial institution. Crowdfunding also benefits startups and, in a broader view, increases productivity, economic growth, and employment. In the EU, the USA, and Australia, governments accept the benefits of crowdfunding and establish regulatory frameworks to facilitate crowdfunding while maintaining rules for investor protections (Goethner et al., 2021). The chapter later focuses on the regulatory frameworks of crowdfunding in Singapore, Thailand, and Vietnam, which differ in each jurisdiction. While Singapore and Thailand have adopted specific regulations on crowdfunding for the support of startups, Vietnam has not adopted specific regulations on crowdfunding. The regulations for investment thresholds on crowdfunding are also different according to the financial ambit of countries. Singapore focuses on exemptions-based crowdfunding rules, while Thailand concentrates their regulation under licensing-based crowdfunding. It seems that Singapore and Thailand recognize the benefits of crowdfunding and aim to create certainty in crowdfunding through rules and regulations. In Vietnam, crowdfunding activities open opportunities for startups, but the government is in the early stage of developing regulations for crowdfunding. From the comparative study of the regulatory frameworks, there is a conclusion with policy implications that:

- ***Specific Regulation*** – Regulation is vital to create certainty in crowdfunding and to protect investors. In traditional financial markets, investors are certain that they are protected from any fraudulent offers in financial markets by government regulations (Schwartz, 2013). For crowdfunding, it is also important that the government provides regulatory certainty and ensures wide investors that there is governance on any unfair or fraudulent conduct in crowdfunding. By specific regulations, investors are convinced to maintain their investment in crowdfunding, which later translates to crucial financial support for SMEs and startups. It is recommended that governments issue specific regulations to liberate crowdfunding from the costly regulations of traditional financial markets (Schwartz, 2013). The OECD has recently displayed that many ASEAN countries have improved their regulatory frameworks to encourage SMEs' wider take-up of crowdfunding (OECD, 2020). Vietnam may have to consider swiftly adopting regulations on crowdfunding to keep up with the technological changes of financial technology with crowdfunding platforms.
- ***Regulation with adaptation*** – Regulation is essential to build up investment confidence in crowdfunding, but the government has to bear in mind that regulation must easily evolve to harmonize with capital raising models in changing financial technology (Hopkins and Hopkins, 2013). Regulations have to be flexible rather than rigid and resistant to change. Regulatory frameworks have to achieve their purpose of facilitating easier access to capital through crowdfunding for small businesses. One example is special taskforce committees from both government and private sectors to keep regulatory checks with the advancement of financial technology. Crowdfunding may not involve conventional currency and investment but instead be linked by blockchain and new digital or cryptocurrency.
- ***ASEAN crowdfunding regulation*** – From the regulatory frameworks of crowdfunding in Singapore, Thailand, and Vietnam, there must be cooperation on regulatory frameworks on crowdfunding at the regional level. If possible, there should be regional regulatory frameworks on crowdfunding in ASEAN. The regional regulatory frameworks can contribute to investment facilitation in trans-ASEAN in line with the ASEAN Comprehensive

> Investment Agreement 2007 that aimed to create investment liberalization, protection, and investment promotion in ASEAN. Regional regulation can harmonize legal understanding and reduce potential conflict when facing cross-border crowdfunding (Lazzaro and Noonan, 2021). It can also help deal with borderless investments under crowdfunding with financial technology in ASEAN. However, if the ASEAN regional regulations on crowdfunding cannot easily be established, it is proposed that there must be harmonization in crowdfunding regulation. One example is from the *ASEAN Regional Guidelines on Competition Policy*, where all members can adapt their competition law and policy but only on the same page with the principle of the guidelines.

It is accepted that lending crowdfunding is not really a viable option for startup businesses, because there is less attraction for investors who would like to have a stake in the SMEs and startups. The specific regulation may create a relatively strong expansion of equity crowdfunding. Government in ASEAN and other developing countries should create regulations that can keep up with the changing pace of crowdfunding to ensure that SMEs and startups are able to tap into the financial benefits of crowdfunding. Beyond the specific focus on regulatory frameworks of crowdfunding, there should be policy cooperation between government and private sectors in encouraging advocacy of crowdfunding to SMEs and startups. The policy cooperation for supporting all types of crowdfunding will later contribute to the awareness and growth of crowdfunding markets that will replace the traditional financial markets in the long term (OECD, 2020).

References

ASIC (2018) RG 262 Crowd-sourced funding: Guide for intermediaries. Available via https://asic.gov.au/regulatory-resources/find-a-document/regulatory-guides/rg-262-crowd-sourced-funding-guide-for-intermediaries/

ASIC (2020) Crowd-sourced funding: Guide for companies. Available via https://asic.gov.au/media/5702668/rg261-published-19-june-2020-20200727.pdf

ASIC (2021) Crowd-sourced funding. Available via https://asic.gov.au/regulatory-resources/financial-services/crowd-sourced-funding/#csf-legislation

CAMAC (2013) Re: Corporations and Markets Advisory Committee, crowd sourced equity funding

CAMAC (2014) Corporations and Markets Advisory Committee, crowd sourced equity funding. Available via https://www.camac.gov.au/camac/camac.nsf/byheadline/reportsfinal+reports+home.html

Fenwick M, McCahery JA, Vermeulen EPM (2018) Fintech and the financing of SMEs and entrepreneurs: From crowdfunding to marketplace lending. In Cumming D, Hornuf L (Eds.), *The Economics of Crowdfunding: Startups, Portals and Investor Behavior* (pp. 103–129). Cham: Springer International Publishing

Ferrarini G (2017) Regulating fintech: Crowdfunding and beyond. *Eur Econ* 2:121–142

Goethner, M, Hornuf, L, Regner, T (2021) Protecting investors in equity crowdfunding: An empirical analysis of the small investor protection act. *Technol Forecast Soc Change* 162:e120352. doi:10.1016/j.techfore.2020.120352

Hai HV, Xuan ND, Thao TD, Hien PTT (2020) The effects of strategy and market orientation on the performance of Vietnamese startups. *Manag Sci Lett* 11(4):19. Available via http://growingscience.com/beta/msl/4454-the-effects-of-strategy-and-market-orientation-on-the-performance-of-vietnamese-startups.html

Harris WL, Wonglimpiyarat J (2020) Dynamics of crowdfunding and FinTech challenges. *Int J Bus Innov Res* 23(4):15. doi:10.1504/IJBIR.2020.111762

Havrylchyk O (2018) Regulatory framework for the loan-based crowdfunding platforms. Available via https://www.oecd.org/officialdocuments/publicdisplaydocumentpdf/?cote=ECO/WKP(2018)61&docLanguage=En

Hofmann C (2018) An easy start for start-ups: Crowdfunding regulation in Singapore. *Berkeley Bus. LJ* 15(1):48

Hopkins J, Hopkins K (2013) Not all that glitters is gold: Limitations on equity crowdfunding regulations. *Duq Bus Law J* 16(1):20

Hu Y (2015) Regulation of equity crowdfunding in Singapore: National University of Singapore

IMDA (2018) Digital economy framework for action, Singapore. Available via https://www.imda.gov.sg/-/media/imda/files/sg-digital/sgd-framework-for-action.pdf?la=en

Jenweeranon P (2020) Thai regulatory approaches to technology-driven innovation in financial services. In Fenwick M, Van Uytsel S, Ying B (Eds.), *Regulating FinTech in Asia: Global Context, Local Perspectives* (pp. 97–114). Singapore: Springer Singapore

Kaur D (2021) Why Vietnam is the leading startup hub of Southeast Asia. Available via https://techwireasia.com/2021/05/why-vietnam-is-the-leading-startup-hub-of-southeast-asia/

Kongsakul J (2020) Unlock SMEs/Startups by crowdfunding and private placement (translated from Thai Laguage). Available via https://www.sec.or.th/TH/Template3/Articles/2563/190363-SMEs-Startup.pdf

Loan PT (2018) Crowndfuding: A new form of capital mobilisation for Small and Medium Enterprises (SMEs) in Vietnam. Paper presented at the 5th IBSM International Conference on Business, Management and Accounting, Hanoi University of Industry, Vietnam. Available via http://www.caal-inteduorg.com/proceedings/ibsm5/SME1-31.pdf

Lazzaro E, Noonan D (2021) A comparative analysis of US and EU regulatory frameworks of crowdfunding for the cultural and creative industries. *International Journal of Cultural Policy* 27(5):590–606. doi:10.1080/10286632.2020.1776270

MAS (2016) Response to feedback received – Facilitating securities-based crowdfunding. Available via https://www.mas.gov.sg/-/media/MAS/News-and-Publications/Consultation-Papers/Crowdfunding/Response-to-Feedback-Received--Facilitating-Securitiesbased-Crowdfunding.pdf

MAS (2018a) Frequently Asked Questions (FAQs) on lending crowndfunding. Available via https://www.mas.gov.sg/-/media/MAS/Regulations-and-Financial-Stability/Regulations-Guidance-and-Licensing/Securities-Futures-and-Fund-Management/Regulations-Guidance-and-Licensing/FAQs/FAQs-on-LendingBased-Crowdfunding-8-Oct-18.pdf

MAS (2018b) Guidelines on personal offers made persuant to the excemption for small offfers. Available via https://www.mas.gov.sg/-/media/MAS/Regulations-and-Financial-Stability/Regulations-Guidance-and-Licensing/Securities-Futures-and-Fund-Management/Regulations-Guidance-and-Licensing/Guidelines-on-Personal-Offers-made-pursuant-to-the-Exemption-for-Small-Offers-SFA-13G19_8-Oct-2018.pdf

Mollick E (2014) The dynamics of crowdfunding: An exploratory study. *J Bus Ventur* 29(1):1–16. doi:10.1016/j.jbusvent.2013.06.005

NămT(2021)Gọivốncộngđồngcrowdfundingvànhữngcáibẫy[Crowdfundingandthetraps]. Available via https://hvnclc.vn/goi-von-cong-dong-crowdfunding-va-nhung-cai-bay/

Nisar TM, Prabhakar G, Torchia M (2020) Crowdfunding innovations in emerging economies: Risk and credit control in peer-to-peer lending network platforms. *Strateg Change* 29(3):355–361. doi:10.1002/jsc.2334

OECD (2020) Alternative financing instruments for ASEAN SMEs. Available via https://www.oecd.org/finance/Alternative-financing-instruments-for-ASEAN-SMEs.pdf

Punyasavatsut C (2011) SMEs access to finance in Thailand. In Harvie C, Oum S, Narjoko DN (Eds.), *Small and Medium Enterprises (SMEs) Access to Finance in Selected East Asian Economies* (pp. 193–230). Jakarta Indonesia: ERIA Research Project Report 2010–14

Ryu S, Kim K (2016) Crowdfunding success as a quality signal to venture capital. Paper presented at the 22nd Americas Conference on Information Systems: Surfing the IT Innovation Wave, AMCIS 2016

SAL (2019) Corporate Finance and securities regulation, Chapter 17. Available via https://www.singaporelawwatch.sg/About-Singapore-Law/Commercial-Law/ch-17-corporate-finance-and-securities-regulation#:~:text=4%20The%20prospectus%20must%20be, from%20its%20date%20of%20issue

Schwartz AA (2013) Crowdfunding securities. *Notre Dame Law Rev* 88(3):33

Shneor R, Zhao L, Flåten BT (2020) Introduction: From fundamentals to advances in crowdfunding research and practice. In Shneor R, Zhao L, Flåten BT (Eds.), *Advances in Crowdfunding: Research and Practice* (pp. 1–18). Cham: Springer International Publishing

Singh VK (2021) Policy and regulatory changes for a successful startup revolution: Experiences from the startup action plan in India. In Taghizadeh-Hesary F, Yoshino N, Kim CJ, Morgan P, Yoon D (Eds.), *Investment in Startups and Small Business Financing* (pp. 33–67). Singapore: World Scientific Publishing

SNDGO (2018) Smart nation: The way forward. Available via https://www.smartnation.gov.sg/docs/default-source/default-document-library/smart-nation-strategy_nov2018.pdf?sfvrsn=3f5c2af8_2

Startup SG (2021) Startup SG equity. Available via https://www.startupsg.gov.sg/programmes/4895/startup-sg-equity

Thailand SEC (2021) Fundraising through a crowdfunding service provider. Available via https://www.sec.or.th/TH/Pages/LAWANDREGULATIONS/CROWDFUNDINGREGULATORYSUMMARY.aspx#Screening

Thu, N (2020). Exploring Asia's youngest consumer market: Why Vietnam now? Available via https://wecreatecontent.asia/content-marketing-blog-asia/2020/3/2/exploring-asias-youngest-consumer-market-why-vietnam-now

Turner M, Sermcheep S, Anantasirijkiat S, Srisangnam P (2016) Small and medium-sized enterprises in Thailand: government policy and economic development. *Asia Pac J Public Adm* 38(4):251–269. doi:10.1080/23276665.2016.1256545

VGP (2021) Proposal to amend the Law on Electronic Transactions (Tranlated from Vietnamese laguage). Sociallist Repulic of Vietnam Online Newspaper of the Government. Available via http://baochinhphu.vn/Chinh-sach-moi/De-nghi-sua-doi-Luat-giao-dich-dien-tu/413021.vgp

Vietnam Ministry of Finances (2020) Continue to promote financial market restructuring (Translated from Vietnamese language). Available via https://www.mof.

gov.vn/webcenter/portal/tttc/r/m/ts/ts_chitiet?dID=198171&dDocName=-MOFUCM185343&_adf.ctrl-state=15qr5supqr_4&_afrLoop=5474471714218655

US SEC (2021) Regulation crowdfunding. Available via https://www.sec.gov/smallbusiness/exemptofferings/regcrowdfunding

Wasiuzzaman S (2021) Regulations, perceived information quality and perceived risk of equity crowdfunding: A study of Malaysian investors. *Strateg Change* 30(4):353–366. doi:10.1002/jsc.2429

Wisuttisak P (2021) Comparative study on regulatory frameworks for promotion of startup businesses and SMEs in Japan, Republic of Korea, Malaysia, and Thailand. In Taghizadeh-Hesary F, Yoshino N, Kim CJ, Morgan P, Yoon D (Eds.), *Investment in Startups and Small Business Financing* (pp. 33–67). Singapore: World Scientific Publishing

Wonglimpiyarat J (2018) Challenges and dynamics of FinTech crowd funding: An innovation system approach. *J High Technol Manag Res* 29(1):98–108. doi:10.1016/j.hitech.2018.04.009

World Bank (2020) The world by income and region. Available via https://datatopics.worldbank.org/world-development-indicators/the-world-by-income-and-region.html

Yang Q, Lee YC (2019) An investigation of enablers and inhibitors of crowdfunding adoption: Empirical evidence from startups in China. *Hum Factors Ergon Manuf* 29(1):5–21. doi:10.1002/hfm.20782

Yoshino N, Taghizadeh-Hesary F, Charoensivakorn P, Niraula B (2016) Small and Medium-Sized Enterprise (SME) credit risk analysis using bank lending data: An analysis of Thai SMEs. *J Comp Asian Dev* 15(3):383–406. doi:10.1080/15339114.2016.1233821

Yoshino N, Taghizadeh-Hesary F (2019) Role of SMEs in Asia and the financing challenges they face. In Yoshino N, Taghizadeh-Hesary F (Eds.), *Unlocking SME Finance in Asia Roles of Credit Rating and Credit Guarantee Scheme.* (pp. 2–22). Abingdon, Oxford: Routledge

6 Institutional and regulatory requirements for innovative Fintech market in Bangladesh

Why do they matter?

Sakib Bin Amin, Farhad Taghizadeh-Hesary, Juhi Jannat, Mahatab Kabir Khandaker, and Farhan Khan

1 Introduction

Characterized by artificial intelligence (AI), robotics, and the Internet of Things (IoT), the fourth industrial revolution is considered as a platform that can undoubtedly proliferate the competitiveness of all industries, leading to more diversity in goods and services and increased value-added. Financial technology (Fintech) is an example of a technological innovation that leads this revolution, which is changing the general nature of the financial market (Arner et al., 2015; Buckley et al., 2020). With the help of technology, fintech is enhancing financial activities by going beyond the capacity of the conventional banking system apart from promoting competent financial consulting. Fintech assists innovative businesses and start-ups in the present context to play an essential role in achieving sustainable economic growth, adequate job creation, poverty reduction, and technological progress in many countries around the world (Appiah-Otoo and Song, 2021; Chao et al., 2020; Pranata, 2019; Taghizadeh-Hesary and Yoshino, 2019; Wales, 2017; Yang et al., 2021). Lee and Shin (2018) argue that fintech is an enabler of sustainable innovation and a leader of the sharing economy. Shin and Choi (2021), Deng et al. (2019), Hinson et al. (2019), and Philippon (2016) further assert that fintech, through digitization, can lead to many different business revelations that can ultimately mitigate the existing distortions from traditional industries as well as help achieve the sustainable development goals (SDGs).

However, changes in the financial market caused by the augmentation of fintech have led to several challenges (Allen, 2020; Khalid and Kunhibava, 2020; Taylor et al., 2019). Among others, regulatory and institutional issues are at the top of the list and require rigorous attention both in developing and developed countries. The existing regulatory and institutional structures face challenges surrounding the dynamics of fintech innovations. Moreover, without proper regulatory frameworks and institutional aspects, the propensity of fintech activity development reduces significantly because of uncertainty regarding market stability (Alaassar et al., 2021; Buckley et al., 2020).

DOI: 10.4324/9781003220220-9

Bangladesh, located in the northeastern part of South Asia, earned its independence in 1971. The country inherited a deprived and undiversified economy with a predominantly agricultural economy with low productivity, a weak industrial sector, and poor infrastructure. Despite these adversities and resource constraints, however, Bangladesh's economy has experienced landmark success over the past five decades, as reflected in different socio-economic indicators (GED, 2020). On average, the GDP growth of Bangladesh has increased from about 3% in the 1970s to 7% in the 2010s and has surpassed 8% just before the Covid-19 pandemic disrupted the markets (Figure 6.1). Extreme poverty in Bangladesh was also reduced to 10.50% in 2019 from around 80% in the early 1970s (BBS, 2018).

One of the main reasons for this observed change in the growth trajectory is the remarkable structural transformation from an agrarian to an industry-based economy over the past three decades or so. From 2000 to 2019, the average joint contribution of the service and industry sectors in Bangladesh GDP was approximately 78% (Amin et al., 2020). Apparel, popularly known as readymade garments (RMG), being the flagship export product, is now considered the lifeblood for the Bangladesh economy. Bangladesh has exhibited dramatic shifts in its export composition in which the share of the so-called traditional exports (such as mainly raw jute and jute goods, tea, leather, and frozen fish) has fallen from more than three quarters to just about 10%.

In 2021, the United Nations Committee for Development Policy (CDP) approved the graduation of Bangladesh from the list of Least Developed Countries

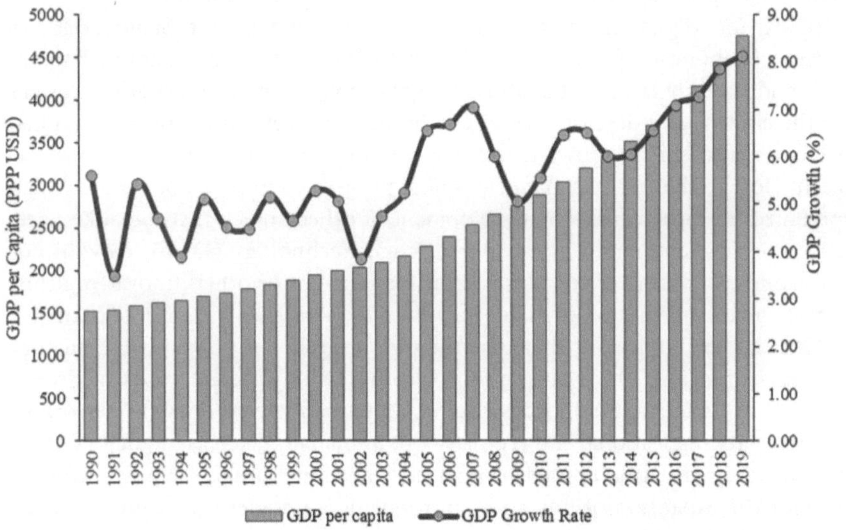

Figure 6.1 GDP Growth and Per Capita Income in Bangladesh.
Source: World Bank (2020).

(LDC), as it had satisfied the eligibility standards with regard to per capita income, human resources, and economic and environmental vulnerability for the second time in a row since 2018. With aspirations to become a high-income country by 2041 and reduce extreme poverty by 2030, Bangladesh currently focuses on achieving sustained economic growth by generating more employment opportunities; enhancing the standard of health and education, energy and transport infrastructure, and governance; and reinforcing anti-corruption procedures (GED, 2020). Accordingly, the energy industry is recognized and prioritized as part and parcel of this sustainable development for Bangladesh's future economy.

Though the Covid-19 pandemic unexpectedly left the country in a worse economic downfall, Amin et al. (2021a) simulated a dynamic model and revealed that the economic growth rate in Bangladesh would be around 4.5% in the long-run, greater than many other countries. This growth prediction is consistent with forecasts from the International Monetary Fund (IMF) and lies approximately between predictions of the Bangladesh government and the World Bank.

The development of fintech started in Bangladesh in the late 2000s because of increased internet penetration and a large unbanked population. According to the Global Findex Database published by the World Bank in 2017, financial inclusion in Bangladesh had increased from 3% to 21% in 2011. Mobile financial services (MFS) (such as bKash, M-cash, Sure-cash, Upay, Nagad, Rocket, etc.) have played a considerable role in this regard. Although financial inclusion has improved in Bangladesh, gender inequality still exists. Demirgüç-Kunt et al. (2017) showed that 36% of the female population in Bangladesh has access to mobile banking compared to 65% of their male counterparts. Two key reasons behind such skewness are a lack of digital literacy and cultural norms.

To expand digital financial services, the Central Bank of Bangladesh has started collaborating with the a2i (Access to Information) program in Bangladesh and recently launched a lab that works to create more innovative services for the citizens and develop a rural e-commerce market. Different conventional banks are also shifting toward user-friendly digitization to increase their outreach. Despite the fact that Bangladesh has progressed in terms of fintech which specializes in e-payments, the development of other fintech methods like peer-to-peer (P2P) lending, AI, distributed ledger technology (DLT), crowdfunding, cloud computing credit rating firms for start-ups or other innovative firms, partner financing, and blockchains still have not seen the light of development.

This chapter points out that that the prevailing institutional and regulatory drawbacks in Bangladesh cause the slow progress in different types of fintech utilization. Bangladesh still does not have any distinctive policy framework or the necessary institutional and regulatory requirements (such as regulatory sandbox, market regulation approach, institutional set-up and subsequent reforms, etc.) for the expansion of fintech by introducing a broader spectrum of fintech methods (such as MFS). Moreover, it has been found that certain existing policies hinder the entry of many fintech methods into the market. Based on recent literature, statistical evidence, government policy initiatives, and case studies, the chapter proposes an effective framework for fintech market development in Bangladesh given the sustainable development agendas for meeting the goals of Vision 2041 and beyond.

The rest of the chapter has the following parts. Section 2 presents some stylized facts on the fintech development in Bangladesh. Section 3 briefly covers some case studies of fintech development across Asia. Section 4 holistically scrutinizes the importance of institutional and regulatory aspects for fintech development, followed by a framework for Bangladesh. Finally, Section 5 concludes the chapter with some key policy suggestions.

2 Fintech scenario in Bangladesh: policies and some stylized facts

2.1 Existing policies

The development of the financial technologies started in the late 2009 for Bangladesh, primarily due to the large unbanked population and increased internet penetration. The implementation of the dream of a "Digital Bangladesh" and "Vision 2021" consolidated by the present Awami League government jumpstarted the path to digital and financial inclusion in Bangladesh. The Government of Bangladesh implemented the Information and Communication Technology (ICT) Act 2009, ICT Policy 2009, and Right to Information Act 2009 that served as the foundation of the immense growth of the Bangladesh fintech environment. In January 2011, the A2i (Access to Information) program released the Strategic Priorities of Digital Bangladesh 2011, which highlighted the strategic priorities required to bring about more digitized, mobile, and developed forms of initiatives in Bangladesh. The Perspective Plan of Bangladesh released in April 2012 and 2020 also prioritized the growth of the ICT sector in terms of framing a universal access policy, developing a legal and regulatory environment for ICT development, and expanding digital content in government websites (GED, 2020). Moreover, the 8th Five Year Plan released in December 2020 focused on expanding devices and network connectivity, supporting access and communication and financial technologies, and digitization like sensors, artificial intelligence, blockchain, 5G broadband, data analytics, and cloud computing (GED, 2021).

The dream of a more financially mobile and inclusive Bangladesh was further propelled toward reality by the regulations and guidelines issued by the government of Bangladesh. The need for a simpler and easily accessible method of financial services, especially for the poor who had less access to them, gave rise to MFS in Bangladesh. The MFS Guidelines were released on September 22, 2011, by the Central Bank of Bangladesh, revised shortly afterwards in December 2011, and then were applied as the basis for the entire MFS industry in Bangladesh (Islam, 2021). Later on in 2018, the Central Bank brought forward the Bangladesh Mobile Financial Services (MFS) Regulations of 2018 that aimed to provide a regulatory structure to enable a competitive environment and promote the accessibility of affordable banking for the poor. These guidelines also ensured compliance with AML/CFT requirements, regulations, and guidelines provided by the Bangladesh Financial Intelligence Unit (BFIU).

2.2 Existing situation: stylized facts

The formulation of the robust regulations and guidelines by the Bangladesh government has propelled the country's financial arena to a higher standard than previous decades. The number of mobile phone subscribers has increased from 93.788 million in June 2012 to 176.41 million in June 2021, an increase of almost 88%, as shown in Figure 6.2. The number of mobile phone users has been consistently increasing, as has the number of internet subscribers in Bangladesh. Internet subscriptions in Bangladesh can be acquired mainly through three channels, mobile internet, Internet Service Providers (ISPs), and Public Switched Telephone Networks (PSTNs). In June 2012, only 26.629 million people in Bangladesh subscribed to internet services; by June 2021, this number had jumped to 120.95 million subscribers, an increase of almost 354.2%. Most of these internet subscribers made use of mobile internet services, and a very small percentage of internet users subscribed through ISPs or PSTNs. Mobile internet subscriptions increased from 25.016 million in June 2012 to 110.9 million in June 2021. Even though this drastic increase of almost 343.3% occurred, the percentage of mobile phone users without a mobile internet connection is still large. In June 2012, only 26.67% of mobile phone subscribers had access to

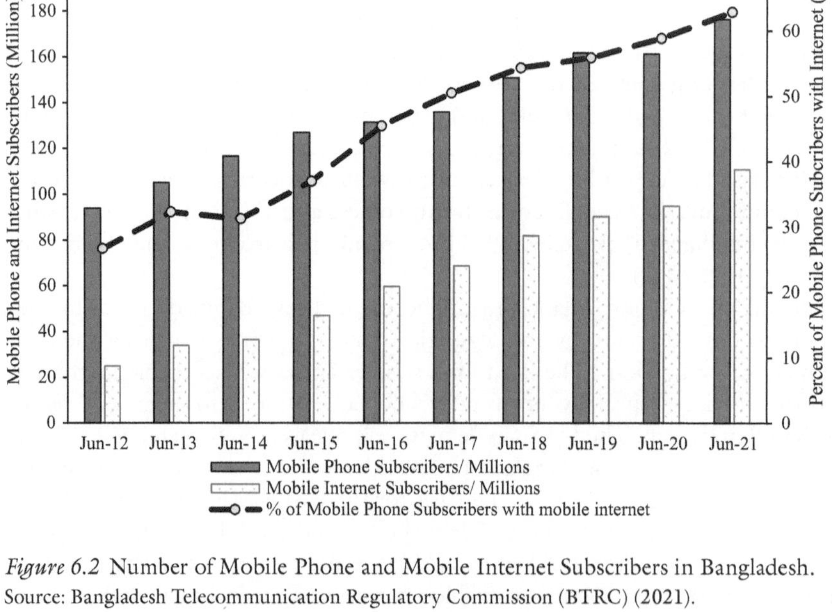

Figure 6.2 Number of Mobile Phone and Mobile Internet Subscribers in Bangladesh.
Source: Bangladesh Telecommunication Regulatory Commission (BTRC) (2021).

mobile internet. Nonetheless, the situation has improved significantly; as of June 2021, almost 62.86% of mobile phone subscribers had access to mobile internet.

Moreover, the 4G network coverage in Bangladesh has improved drastically over the last few years. In 2018, it reached 79%, as shown in Figure 6.3, and then it increased to 95% network coverage by 2020.

With the improved accessibility of mobile Internet in the form of 4G network coverage, there has also been a significant improvement in the mobility of financial services that are facilitated through mobile internet. As shown in Table 6.1, there has been a persistent increase in the number of MFS accounts and, consequently, the number of active accounts. MFS agents numbered 746,475 in May 2017 and 1,086,018 agents in May 2021, an increase in the number of MFS agents of almost 45.49%, according to the data provided by Bangladesh Bank (2021). The number of registered clients increased from 52,684,000 in May 2017 to 98,132,000 in May 2021, while the number of active accounts increased from 21,446,000 in May 2017 to 39,650,000 in May 2021, as shown in Table 6.1. However, there has also been an increase in the number of inactive accounts, which soared from 31,238,000 in May 2017 to 58,482,000 in May 2021. This has kept the percentage of registered clients with an active account increasing at an almost constant rate over the past few years as shown by the

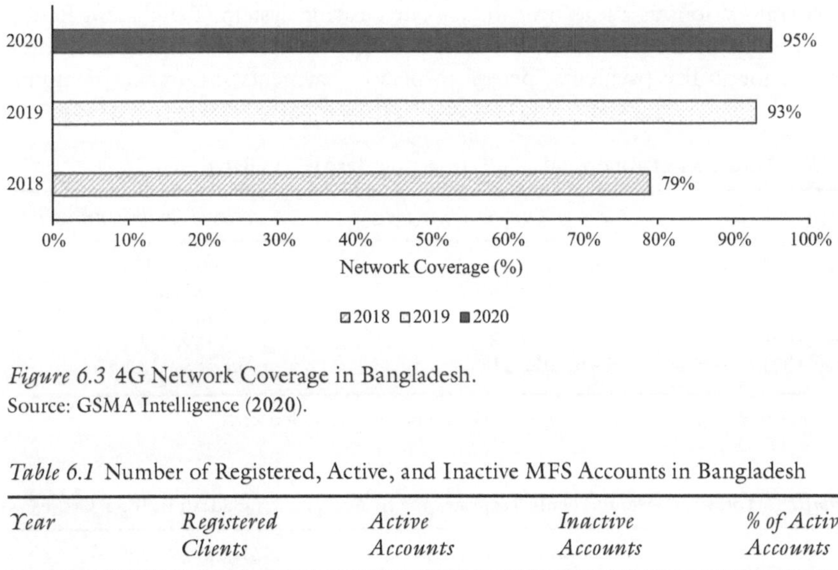

Figure 6.3 4G Network Coverage in Bangladesh.
Source: GSMA Intelligence (2020).

Table 6.1 Number of Registered, Active, and Inactive MFS Accounts in Bangladesh

Year	*Registered Clients*	*Active Accounts*	*Inactive Accounts*	*% of Active Accounts*
May 2017	52,684,000	21,446,000	31,238,000	40.71
May 2018	61,323,000	22,909,000	38,414,000	37.36
May 2019	70,456,000	32,129,000	38,327,000	45.60
May 2020	87,939,000	35,461,000	52,478,000	40.32
May 2021	98,132,000	39,650,000	58,482,000	40.40

Source: Bangladesh Bank (2021); Note: MFS = Mobile Financial Services.

last column in Table 6.1, with an average of around 40.88% of registered clients with an active account, and a maximum of 45.60% of registered clients with an active account in May 2019. Thus, there is still plenty of room for improvement in mobile financial services, and there is still immense potential to increase the mobility of financial technologies.

Furthermore, the number of total transactions by MFS has increased persistently, from 152,048,135 total transactions in May 2017 to 346,701,611 total transactions in May 2021, an increase of almost 128% (Table 6.2). Similarly, there has also been an increase in the number of daily transactions by MFS from 4,904,779 in May 2017 to 11,183,923 in May 2021, an increase of around 128%, identical to the percentage increase in the number of total transactions.

The monetary value of MFS transactions has also persistently increased in the past few years. The total MFS transaction amount equaled 26,171.28 BDT crores in May 2017 and increased to 71,246.88 BDT crores in May 2021, a drastic increase of approximately 172.23% (Table 6.3). Consequently, the average daily MFS transaction amount in May 2017 was 844.23 BDT crores; this figure soared to 2,298.29 BDT crores in May 2021, also a 172.23% increase.

With the robust development of mobile financial services, the Bangladesh Electronic Funds Transfer Network (BEFTN) has shown exemplary development. BEFTN was established in February 2011 and is Bangladesh's first paperless electronic inter-bank funds transfer system that deals with both credit and debit transactions as a lead over the cheque clearing system (Bangladesh Bank, 2021). It accommodates all types of electronic payments including online transactions for utility payments, person-to-person payments, insurance premium

Table 6.2 Number of Total and Daily Transactions by MFS in Bangladesh

Year	*No. of Total Transaction*	*No. of Daily Transactions*
May 2017	152,048,135	4,904,779
May 2018	185,478,845	5,983,189
May 2019	231,379,578	7,463,857
May 2020	281,780,662	9,089,699
May 2021	346,701,611	11,183,923

Source: Bangladesh Bank (2021); Note: MFS = Mobile Financial Services.

Table 6.3 Total and Average Daily Transactions by MFS in Bangladesh in BDT Crores

Year	*Total Transaction/ BDT Crores*	*Average Daily Transaction/ BDT Crores*
May 2017	26,171.28	844.23
May 2018	32,822.83	1,058.80
May 2019	42,236.23	1,362.46
May 2020	47,601.28	1,535.53
May 2021	71,246.88	2,298.29

Source: Bangladesh Bank (2021); Note: MFS = Mobile Financial Services.

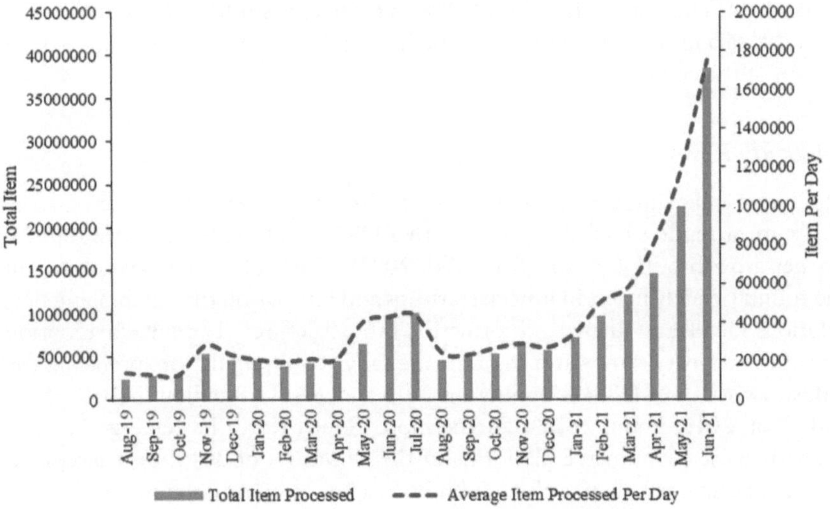

Figure 6.4 Total and Average Number of Items Processed by BEFTN.
Source: Bangladesh Bank (2021).

payments, etc. As shown in Figure 6.4, the total items processed monthly by BEFTN increased by almost 1519.2% from August 2019 to June 2021, with the most drastic increase occurring in the first six months of 2021. The number of monthly items processed increased from 2,380,575 in August 2019 to 38,546,894 in June 2021. Moreover, the total transaction amount increased from 14,211 thousand BDT crores to 54,490 thousand BDT crores in this period. The average number of items processed per day also increased drastically from 140,034 in August 2019 to 1,752,132 in June 2021.

This shows the immense progress made in the number of transactions occurring through electronic services, mobile financial systems, and financial technologies in Bangladesh.

3 Lessons in Fintech development from selected Asian countries

This section briefly discusses the progress of the fintech market development in selected countries, namely South Korea, Iran, Indonesia, Singapore, and China. The rationale behind choosing these countries is twofold. First, selected countries represent Asia with similar socio-cultural traits (such as faith, ethnicity, preferences, family traditions, etc.). Second, the countries capture the income differences within the region. For instance, Iran and Indonesia are lower-middle-income countries like Bangladesh, while South Korea, Singapore, and China are high-income and upper-middle-income countries, respectively. The aim is, therefore, to gather knowledge regarding the underlying changes, mainly institutional and regulatory, each country has gone through to reach the current status given the embedded regional common traits and economic differences (or similarities). The knowledge obtained from these case studies will be utilized in formulating a fintech market framework for Bangladesh, as discussed in the next section of the chapter.

3.1 South Korea

The burgeoning fintech industry of South Korea is chiefly prioritized, as the government renders its full support (with a US$16 million budget in 2020) for further growth of this sector (Slawinski, 2021). The leading financial players of the country widely invest in fintech start-ups and innovation labs, embracing new solutions for IT and financial information infrastructures. The fintech adoption rate of the country stands at 67% of the digitally active population, prefacing the industry growth of US$18.9 billion in 2013 to US%111.8 billion in 2018 (Shin and Choi, 2019; Yoon, 2021). Furthermore, South Korea has emerged as one of the biggest e-commerce platforms in the world. As of 2019, open access to payment networks in banks along with open application programming interface (API) initiatives and lower transaction fees had led to a significant (approximate) 14.6-times increase in digital transactions within two years. The Covid-19 pandemic escalated the trend in digital payments, reducing cash dependency in the ever-growing business-to-consumer (B2C) market (Global Data, 2020). Tech-savvy investors have also popularized alternative financing options such as crowdfunding and P2P lending.

South Korea has undertaken strategies involving thorough revision and refinement of current policies to ensure greater development opportunities for innovative fintech solutions. For instance, the South Korean Financial Services Commission (FSC) devised a virtual sandbox scheme to promote financial innovation and digital finance by nurturing fintech (England, 2021). This regulatory sandbox program is a collaborative measure, influencing local and overseas fintech firms to provide a rollout environment free from certain regulations.

3.2 Iran

Fintech is gaining momentum in Iran as the country's financial institutions, central bank, and other state-run bodies are constructing reforms to transform the capital, Tehran, into a digital hub. Iran Vision 2025, which aims to establish Iran as a developed nation by 2025, encompasses such measures of financial innovation. According to recent statistics, about 50 fintech start-ups are operating in Iran's financial markets, which is noteworthy considering that the country is still in its prime of innovative fintech (Moradi et al., 2020). The Central Bank of Iran (CBI) also announced plans in 2019 to tap blockchain technology to decentralize the banking system. Furthermore, an innovation center named "Polwinno" was launched in 2019 to guide the implementation of smart technologies including minor electronic transactions, mobile banking, e-wallets, financial services, e-commerce, and AI in the banking sector. In 2020, a new regulatory framework for the CBI was instituted to help fintech firms facilitate micropayments with electronic wallets.

On the flip side, the absence of a unique regulatory body and a proper legal framework are hindrances to growth in Iran's potential in innovative fintech. Additionally, transaction cost payments have been an unresolved issue in the case of e-payments; however, the CBI has proposed a resolution that encourages negotiation among market players instead of a fixed-fee regimen. The future plans of the CBI also hold the launch of a regulatory sandbox with an agenda to resolve the existing flaws in the fintech industry and facilitate licensing so as to spur innovation.

3.3 *Indonesia*

The flourishing economy and transition of people's interest toward ease and speed in accessibility have carved a clear path to promoting fintech start-ups in Indonesia. With rapid income growth and high Internet penetration of more than 50%, the country now engages in various fintech applications such as deposit devices, loan tools, and payment instruments (Batunanggar, 2019). The industry totaled 249 fintech firms in 2019 and recorded distribution of about US$1.62 million through eleven local P2P platforms in 2017 (ASEAN Fintech Census, 2018). Moreover, e-payments have also been one of the fastest-growing fintech areas, with a six-fold US$840 million rise in e-money transactions between 2012 and 2017, as highlighted in the Daily Social (2018).

Bank Indonesia and Financial Services Authority or Otoritas Jasa Keuangan (OJK), are the two main supervising bodies for the Indonesian fintech industry. According to the Indonesia Fintech Report (2021), all financial institutions have undergone risk monitoring, screening, and joint solutions to improve credibility standards amid the Covid-19 pandemic. With the fast-growing fintech businesses, OJK has issued a new regulatory framework for financial stability to assist financial institutions and micro-, small, and medium-sized enterprises (MSMEs) in response to Covid-19 and has further proposed the Digital Finance Innovation Road Map and Action Plan 2020–2024 to amplify the integration, development, and talent training of the fintech industry. However, Bank Indonesia has also contributed to develop the digitization of payment systems by facilitating cooperation between banks and fintech firms to widen the access of MSMEs and the public to financial services. A recent study in Indonesia showed that embracing ethical digital technologies can help enhance the Islamic finance markets, thus promoting financial inclusion across Muslim-majority countries (Fintechnews Indonesia, 2021).

3.4 *Singapore*

Singapore has evolved as a center for fintech innovation and remains among the world's most technologically advanced and digitally interlinked countries with an exponential increase in fintech firms and succeeding employment opportunities.

Within the span of merely five years, the government of Singapore established a comprehensive support system that encourages growth in the fintech and digital asset sectors. Singapore is also ranked highest among Asia's fintech cities, as stated by the Global FinTech Index (2020). Entrants into the industry prevail, rising from 100 to more than 1000 new entities from 2015 to 2020 (Wyman, 2020).

Singapore has acknowledged numerous initiatives that boost innovation by experimenting with updating financial services, comprising programs that provide financing from the public sector to early-stage start-ups, and establishing innovation labs for mentorship, support, and funding. Presently, the regulatory framework in Singapore recognizes fintech, which innovates and contributes to the existing industry. In 2019, the previous regulatory sandbox was augmented with sandbox express for better testing in the market for financial innovation. In November 2018, the Monetary Authority of Singapore (MAS) founded APIX, a collaborative platform that revolutionized the development of open banking. It is also renowned as the first cross-border regulatory sandbox in the world. Lastly, Singapore has pledged its services to provide solidarity grants for the recovery of start-ups, as Covid-19 affected several industries and posed fundraising challenges, sending a strong message that the government must prioritize innovation (Wyman, 2020).

3.5 China

China, deprived of appropriate financial services during the early 2000s, has created a promising opportunity to develop non-bank payments. The government tactfully delayed the entrance of foreign financial institutions to allow its domestic fintech industries to flourish, leading to its emergence as an indispensable segment of the global market as it continues to develop. Chinese fintech firms utilize highly innovative technological systems such as blockchain, big data, cloud computing, AI, and IoT (Zhu, 2021), and they have prospered because of the government's relentless push toward a more financially inclusive ecosystem by rapidly adapting innovative and digital finance (Hua and Huang, 2021). China's dynamic industry persists as the frontrunner of fintech facilities since 2018, when China's investment accounted for 46% of the total global fintech investments, with Ant Financial having a record US$14 billion funding and Du Xiaoman Financial raising US$4.3 billion (Accenture, 2019). China's P2P lending industry has also significantly expanded compared to other countries, from 214 P2P loan firms in 2011 to 1,544 P2P loan firms in 2014; however, it has remained unregulated for a long time (Appiah-Otoo and Song, 2021).

The Chinese government also adopted a general regulatory guideline for developing the fintech market in 2015. The regulatory guideline was prepared by the Central Bank of China in collaboration with nine other government agencies. It advocated two critical aspects for fintech market development: First, stimulating market validity by changing consumers' preferences with the help of innovation and internet platforms, and second, a proper monitoring mechanism for sustainable fintech market development (ADBI, 2019; Wildau 2016; Yiqing 2016; You, 2018). The regulatory structure of the Chinese fintech market is fragmented in nature. Mainly, four government agencies monitor and regulate different sectors; however, the fragmented nature led to numerous regulatory issues, especially in the case of P2P and other types of lending (You, 2018). As a result, by 2016, a separate regulatory regime was introduced for refining the nature of the lending market dynamics.

Moreover, there has been a gradual paradigm shift in financial services, as China started to advance toward consumption-driven rather than investment-driven growth models. The swift development of fintech in China has been closely connected to the growing needs of consumers and the implementation of digital technology (Chen, 2016). Bigtech firms such as Alibaba and Tencent in China have played a crucial role in improving traditional banking in China by disseminating banking services to underserved customers and customers in rural China (Huang et al., 2020). Given the regulatory efficacy, the giant Chinese fintech firms have concentrated their efforts on extending credit to the previously financially underserved countryside rather than just wealthier urban consumers. Focusing on rural people who now have access to the internet via mobile phones has created a range of potential new markets for a variety of goods and services (Kong and Loubere, 2021). Moreover, the growth and inclusion of financial technologies have further accelerated the efficiency in providing different financial services. For example, they are processing large numbers of loan applications, restructuring large loans, and restructuring risk assessment concisely. As a result, the degree of regulatory measures has also started to change quickly to ensure market stability.

In 2020, the fast-paced fintech industry witnessed heavy reforms within payment services, intelligent investment advisory services, online lending, cryptocurrency, and blockchain due to the controversy of Ant Financial and the suspension of its IPO (Lai, 2021). Reform of the fintech market began with the tightening of legislative measures. For example, the government has more access to data related to businesses, consumers, and financial information of fintech firms. Government has also banned big firms from sharing their data overseas. China has also tightened the market entry requirements for fintech firms. To avoid any uncertain issues, the Chinese government has made it mandatory for insurance-focused fintech firms planning to enter the market to have robust internet security systems. Moreover, the government has taken the initiative to restrict the flow of information between the fintech firms that focus on bank and non-bank services. Recently, the Chinese government passed a stricter consumer protection law. Furthermore, the Central Bank of China has already redesigned its regulatory guideline to restrict non-bank payment fintech firm activities to mitigate risks associated with the growing payment sector.

4 Institutional and regulatory requirements

This section will discuss two important aspects. The first sub-section discusses the importance and dynamics of institutional and regulatory requirements in the context of emerging fintech markets. The second sub-section elaborates on a novel framework for Bangladesh, an emerging country in the South Asian region (Ahmed et al., 2021).

4.1 Scrutinizing institutional and regulatory requirements: why do they matter?

Historical evidence suggests that the financial services industry is one of the most dynamic industries and one of the most regulated industries due to its association with high risk and volatility. The emergence of fintech after 2009 has led to massive structural changes and raised concern regarding the existing regulatory frameworks and conventional approaches of regulatory power practices (Stayton and Mangematin, 2019; Taylor et al., 2020). Regulators faced challenges from various aspects, such as the speed of adoption, higher disintermediation, convergence in industries, borderless platforms, and a high degree of heterogeneity in services (Allen, 2020; Knight, 2016), because the existing traditional institutional setup had failed to address these problems.

Brummer (2015) points out that the emergence of new players due to the speedy development of fintech is creating problems for regulators who are trying to keep the market within control; it had been easily controlled by relying on different intermediaries such as broker-dealers or financial analytics firms. Furthermore, it has been observed that the rules that increased consumer welfare are now behaving like obstacles for fintech firms, because they prevent the entry of fintech firms that lack resources for meeting conventional compliance standards. However, fintech could have served adequately and arguably could have changed the market behavior in a positive manner (Knight, 2016). Therefore, reform analysis of the assumptions regarding the institutional and regulatory processes and the validity of the financial decision loops within the administrations (both public and private) are getting immense momentum in the recent body of literature for creating a safe and better financial services environment for all the stakeholders (Alaassar et al., 2021; Allen, 2020; Taghizadeh-Hesary and Yoshino, 2019).

Another aspect of interest is the issue of regulators. A quintessential question of "who will regulate" is both important and challenging to answer, because different types of regulators have different levels of jurisdictions, procedures, and means of enforcement. Apart from the mentioned criteria, to further the discussion, it is necessary to define the characteristics of regulations as used in this chapter. Therefore, the chapter defines regulations as formalized rules (both from public and private perspectives) for monitoring all the activities under the scope of the market. Regulations ensure a level playing field for all stakeholders. These rules also allow regulatory entities to exercise legal power, if certain aspects of the regulations are broken or distorted by the market players.

Broadly speaking, there can be two types of regulators considering the above-mentioned criteria, namely government and private regulators. Compared to a private regulator, a government regulator is much more powerful in regulating the fintech market for various reasons, such as the power to impose monetary and other penalties if rules are broken or any fraud activities are perpetrated. Unlike a private regulator, a government regulator can govern the whole industry directly and proactively. Moreover, because of its acceptability and power exercising ability, a government regulator can connect with a relatively broader spectrum of stakeholders, who are attached to the fintech market directly and indirectly, leading to a stronger foundation of legitimacy (mostly cognitive and normative) (see Amin et al. (2021b) for more details on the legitimacy dynamics). As a result, it has been seen that countries that are now transitioning toward more innovative fintech and consist of highly fragmented services mostly rely on government-based regulators, such as Indonesia, China, Iran, Hong Kong, and South Korea. However, some problems exist that have led some countries to focus on not only government but also private regulators. According to the existing literature, one of the key issues with government-based regulators is the lack of institutional robustness, especially in the case of developing and emerging countries. Among others, Amin et al. (2021b), Imam et al. (2019), and Cai and Aoyama (2018) explicitly argue that because of the fragmented nature in the instructional set-up, the essence of regulatory legitimacy becomes somewhat sluggish, leading to distortions in the market as well as diminishing accountability among stakeholders. As a result, many of the European Union (EU) countries, the United Kingdom (UK), and the United States of America (USA) follow a mixture of government and private regulative arrangements to ensure maximum stability of the fintech market.

4.2 The proposed framework for Bangladesh

In this sub-section, the chapter introduces the proposed framework for the development of an innovative fintech market in Bangladesh for achieving future sustainability (Figure 6.5). The proposed framework has three distinct phases ordered chronologically: dynamic policy framework, regulatory sandbox, and market regulation.

The framework starts with a dynamic policy framework, because Bangladesh still does not have a dedicated policy framework for different types of advanced fintech (P2P lending, DLT, blockchain, AI, crowdfunding, etc.) other than MFS. In the first phase, the main aim is to properly formulate a dynamic policy framework and eradicate the existing barriers (policy and institutional), which will pave the way for local and international fintech firms to enter Bangladesh's fintech market. It should be noted that blockchain, bitcoin, outward crowdfunding, and cryptocurrency are restricted in Bangladesh by various policies such as the Foreign Exchange Regulation Act, 1947, the Finance Institution Act 1993, the Banking Companies Act, 1991, the Money Laundering Prevention Act 2012, and the ICT Act 2006. Insurtech is also restricted in Bangladesh under section 23 of the Bangladesh Insurance Act 2010.

Under the jurisdiction of the Ministry of Finance (MoF), a national committee will be formed. This national committee will consist of representatives from different stakeholders related directly or indirectly to the fintech market development. For example, the national committee will comprise representatives from the central bank, fintech community, regulatory body, and some auxiliary agencies (such as consumer welfare agency or other government agencies that can provide the necessary advice). The national committee will first review all relevant documents to understand the overall situation. It will also seek help from other countries that already have developed fintech markets to gather knowledge on policy formulation's market characteristics and dynamics. Next, a draft policy guideline will be formulated and sent to the MoF for clearance, after which, the national committee will finalize the policy framework, which will be used in the second phase.

The second phase is known as the regulatory sandbox. The creation of a regulatory sandbox for fintech market development is highly appreciated in recent theoretical and empirical literature (Alaassar et al., 2021, 2020; Allen, 2019; Arner et al., 2017, 2015; Batunanggar, 2019; Buckley et al., 2020; Khalid and Kunhibava, 2020). The Financial Conduct Authority (FCA) implemented one of the first regulatory sandboxes to ensure such practices of testing and simulating the effects of innovative fintech in the UK (Jenik and Lauer, 2017), and other countries soon followed. For example, the Monetary Authority of Singapore (MAS) implemented a regulatory sandbox in Singapore as an important tool to measure the consequences and cost of failure of fintech (Fan, 2018).

Among others, Alaassar et al. (2021) argue that regulatory sandbox is a dynamic fintech incubation model for fintech market development that is able to provide experimental and time-limited licenses to potential fintech firms for testing their products or services within a controlled environment and under proper regulatory jurisdictions. The regulatory body within the sandbox comes mainly from the public institution and has the power to impose any instrument listed in the regulative agenda. It also establishes a consultation process through which the relevant stakeholders shape the entire ecosystem. It is worth pointing out that a regulatory sandbox differs from conventional business incubators (BIs) or business accelerators (BAs), given the higher degree of flexibility. Unlike BIs and BAs, it assists fintech firms with the regulatory knowledge for better market performance. The regulatory sandbox also focuses on consumer exposure to risk side by side with market stability, on which BIs/BAs do not focus. These features make the regulatory sandbox a good component to be included in the framework.

Within the regulatory sandbox environment, the regulatory body along with other entities will start the induction process with the previously formulated policy. Fintech firms will be given membership after the eligibility of interested applicants is checked. This approach is similar to the one used by Hong Kong and Singapore. Membership eligibility will be checked against several criteria. Interested firms will first apply to enter the market. Then, the eligibility checking team will sort out potential firms by first confirming that the firm has a business license (i.e., trade license) provided by the government of Bangladesh. Such a license is mandatory for firms to do any business activities (approved by the government) in Bangladesh. If any applicant does not have a trade license or is still in the process of acquiring one, the eligibility checking team will defer the application for the next round. Once the licensing issue is investigated, the eligibility checking team will analyze the products or services the firm wants to provide to consumers with the main objective of confirming whether the proposed products or services coincide with Bangladesh's socio-economic perspective. Because the fintech market is just at its preliminary stage, activities not matching consumers' preferences may lead to a sluggish speed of transition to the next stage of market development. Once the market reaches a stable situation, more experiments could be done with non-conventional firms to increase the spectrum of products and services. However, if any international firm aims to join, the eligibility team will thoroughly the firm's business records after it is confirmed that the products or services match Bangladesh's perspective and the firm has a trade license. Moreover, an international firm that is successful and experienced in developing fintech businesses will be offered to join the fintech development program with some incentives.

The selected fintech firms will then be supervised by a team appointed by the regulatory body. Supervision will be divided among different teams. The first team will deal with products or services and will be formed by product and service experts and academic scholars. The second team will help with market structure. This team will be formed by appointing experts who have substantial knowledge of Bangladesh's existing financial market structure and fintech market transition process. Academic scholars who have shown research rigor in terms of market feasibility analyses, institutional aspects, and regulatory reforms will also be included on this team. The third and final team will aim to train the selected firms on different legal aspects and prevailing financial regulations. It will be formed by government officials (from the finance ministry, planning commission, economic division, etc.) and legal practitioners. This supervision team will aim to guide fintech firms through the overall process and assist them in understanding the market features, consumer preferences, regulatory measurements, testing features, collaboration techniques with the available BAs if needed to expand the products or services' horizon, enhanced communication with the regulatory body, and product and services refurbishment. After supervision is complete, the fintech firms will be examined with tests that are highly heterogeneous given the scope and objectives followed by countries around the world.

Given Vision 2041, for the case of Bangladesh, the chapter proposes four test criteria: usefulness of the products or services, acceptability among consumers, ability to face competition in the market, and market performance while the legitimacy and institutional aspects are accounted. For better results, a two-step testing procedure will be followed. The first step of the test will be conducted using an innovation lab, where the firms will be tested for their business strategies to promote the usefulness of the products or services in a hypothetical setup as well as on how quickly they can adapt to changes in market dynamics (i.e., both positive and negative externalities) caused by controlled changes in the exogenous and endogenous parameters. After successfully finishing the first stage, firms will move on to the second stage of the testing procedure, in which they will be introduced to the real financial market of Bangladesh. Different regulative features will control the market environment for completing the testing procedure effectively. The main objective in this stage is to analyze consumer acceptance and real consumer preferences, the firm's competitive nature in the market (i.e., degree of market competition), and institutional legitimacies. Special focus will be placed on competition dynamics when domestic and international firms both enter the market with similar types of products or services. This will provide meaningful insights into several aspects: First, whether there is a need for market protection for domestic firms; second, productivity differentials between international and domestic firms; third, potential loopholes in the regulative arrangements; and fourth, potential revisions for the fintech firm selection process.

If a fintech firm performs adequately in all criteria, then it will advance toward the exit procedure and obtain a license for real market activity and launch as soon as the permit is given by the regulatory sandbox authority. If any fintech firm fails to fulfill the selected criteria, it can go for another round of testing or it can exit the regulatory sandbox. It is worth mentioning that the parameters under each criterion that is used to test the fintech firms are not fixed but dynamic in nature, and the regulatory body has the authority to change or impose more parameters if needed for the test procedures. However, if changes are made to the test procedures, the regulatory body will notify the MoF so that it can notify the national committee regarding the changes to be incorporated as "alternative parameters" for future endeavors. For regulative measurements to be improved, the regulatory body can always collaborate with the BAs for consultations through the dedicated collaboration cell. The chapter also proposes the novel concept of a sandbox within a sandbox in the framework. The concept is defined as a monitoring and testing procedure of the main regulatory sandbox's ability to conduct all the listed activities. Upon analysis, the information will be provided to the stakeholders of the first phase to bring changes to the sandbox approach if necessary. The obtained information will also help identify institutional loopholes and lead the authority for targeted institutional reforms.

The final phase is the market regulation. All licensed fintech firms will start market activities obeying the general guideline. The central bank and the auxiliary agencies will provide the assistance necessary for maintaining market stability from both the demand and supply sides. In doing so, these entities will monitor the fintech firms. As the induction of fintech firms may create some degree of anomaly, all key financial indicators will be frequently checked by these entities, so that any indication of instability can be captured and addressed accordingly. However, the central bank and associated agencies will also form a framework (similar to the existing framework for conventional financial institutes) to regularly check the performance. Reports on performance indicators will then be sent to the regulatory body to undertake timely reform strategies for further assessments. Moreover, the regulatory body will monitor all activities of the fintech firms and can practice power if it necessitates under its jurisdictions

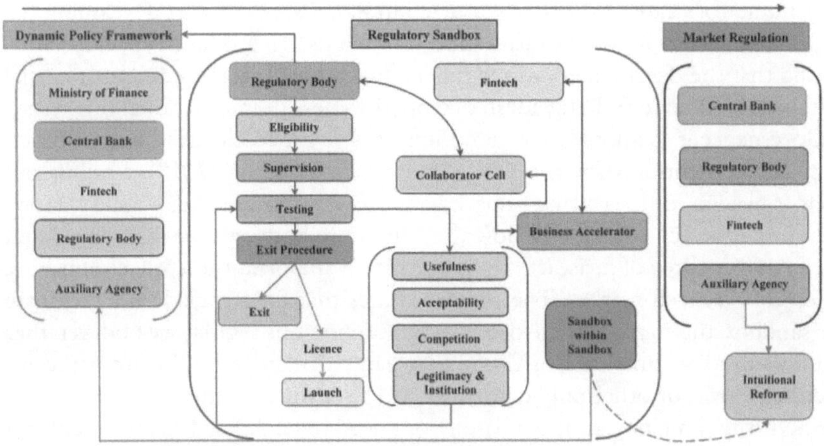

Figure 6.5 Proposed Framework for Fintech Development.
Source: Authors' Own Elaboration.

specified in the policy framework. A key point to be noted here is that the regulatory body responsible in the final phase is mutually exclusive from the regulatory body of the second phase (i.e., a different entity). Here, the regulatory body will be responsible for market-related reforms. If a single entity is used in both phases, then the outcome may not be optimal. One of the main reasons for this is that the type of regulation is not the same in both phases. Another reason is the loss of relative focus due to the workload division within the regulatory body. Also, given the discussion on the regulation techniques, it is proposed that this regulatory body will be purely government-based. However, a hybrid regulatory body (public and private) can be introduced in the framework as the market becomes more efficient in the long run. In this case, a proper feasibility study will be needed to determine the optimal approach of the regulative authority and institutional set-up. Finally, market activities will be used to apply any institutional reforms to boost market efficiency and expand market outreach.

5 Conclusion and policy recommendations

The main aim of this chapter has been to critically discuss the emergence of innovative fintech in Bangladesh and its institutional and regulatory requirements as well as fintech development's recent progress. The development of fintech in Bangladesh began in late 2009 due to the increase in internet penetration and the large unbanked population. Bangladesh's fintech has progressed and is specialized in e-payments because of well-crafted policies and regulatory frameworks. However, available statistics and information have revealed that the development of other fintech methods like P2P lending, crowdfunding, DLT, credit rating firms for start-ups or other innovative firms, partner financing, and blockchains have still not been developed. This chapter has proposed a fit-for-purpose framework by explaining the importance of institutional and regulatory aspects. This framework can be effectively utilized in Bangladesh to start developing the fintech market through innovative fintech methods other than MFS. It is worth noting that the development of the fintech market will promote future financial sustainability and level Bangladesh's competitiveness in international markets.

Governance is as important as adopting a policy for accelerating fintech development. As mentioned by the UN Environment Program (2018), a regulatory body is needed for measuring impact as well as ensuring market stability. However, important concerns as to how the regulatory body will be introduced and clarity in its degree of jurisdictions are extremely important to aptly establishing an efficient fintech market. The chapter argues that for Bangladesh to regulate the sandbox and market, there needs to be autonomous regulatory bodies rather than a subsidiary institute of the mainstream regulatory bodies from the related ministries or other public institutions. Also, the dynamics (i.e., short-run, medium-run, and long-run) of jurisdictions need to be defined clearly to enforce the regulatory rules efficiently and ensure market stability rather than linking with regulatory bodies from other ministries.

Cyber security is a major issue in the context of fintech market development in Bangladesh. To improve cyber security, it is essential to link the ICT division of Bangladesh with the digitization process. The central bank can collaborate with the ICT division for preparing a regulatory technology wing to monitor illegal activities that could be perpetrated with the digital platform. Moreover, institutional reforms to facilitate fintech market development should come from strengthening the regulatory legitimacy, which can be defined as the structure of standard rules, policies, and effectiveness in the bureaucratic process. It is worth recalling, too, that many institutional fragmentations within a centralized system is a general trait that can be observed in most South Asian countries (Amin et al., 2021b). Such characteristic spurs countless institutional loopholes in South Asian countries like Bangladesh that have resulted in the slow progress of many development agendas. Therefore, we advocate reforms for establishing regulative legitimacy that need to start from key public entities, and urgency should be given to reforming institutions affiliated with the financial system, technology and infrastructure development, planning and diffusion, and decision-making process. Furthermore, it is very important to ensure political stability for the intended green initiatives in Bangladesh.

Strategic collaborations between financial institutes (i.e., both conventional banks and non-bank financial institutes) and fintech firms may lead to some complications throughout the collaboration journey in Bangladesh, because the concept is totally new and comes with a high level of asymmetric information. Therefore, it would be wise to prepare action plans or a set of standards before confirming collaboration between financial institutes and fintech firms in Bangladesh. Here, collaboration among government entities, for example, planning commissions, the economic and finance divisions, and think tanks, could be initiated for preparing an effective action plan. Emulating the successful collaborative models used in other countries like Canada, China, Indonesia, Singapore, and

Spain would be very effective. In addition, identifying appropriate collaboration partners seems to be complicated for both parties, as to a certain extent, cultural reasons and consumer awareness hamper the process. To avoid such consequences, BIs and BAs could play an active role in connecting fintech firms and financial institutes, thus maximizing both parties' expected returns. Therefore, creating scopes for the development of BIs and BAs would be a practical policy option.

What's more, there is an immense need for interdisciplinary research from the Bangladeshi academia and think tanks. Without enough research and development (R&D) programs, there will be no next stage after the initial ones in developing the process of achieving a sustainable and efficient fintech market. Universities in Bangladesh can introduce innovation hubs, incubators, start-ups, competitions, offer scholarships for new innovations, and conduct interdisciplinary collaborations to form teaching curricula on the development of innovative fintech products and services. Private sectors also need to come forward in alliance with the government.

We further emphasize that the approach (in terms of the framework) used in this chapter could be adaptable for other developing and emerging countries that show development agendas and macroeconomic characteristics similar to Bangladesh to scrutinize the development of the fintech market. Additionally, policy implications elaborated for the case of Bangladesh could be specifically adjusted by developing and emerging countries to ensure sustainable and equitable financial market development.

An avenue for the possible extension of this chapter is to analyze and prepare regulatory frameworks for different categories of fintech in Bangladesh. Another interesting continuation of the chapter could be to conduct critical case studies on the regulatory and institutional set-ups in neighboring countries to propose a way forward in constructing an inter-country or inter-region collaboration. This will not only make the fintech market more competitive and robust but will also increase accessibility for consumers. Finally, an empirical exercise on the proposed framework is also appreciated as a new channel of contribution in the prevailing body of the literature.

References

Accenture (2019) Global FinTech investment surged in 2018 with investments in China taking the lead. Retrieved from: https://newsroom.accenture.com/news/global-fintech-investments-surged-in-2018-with-investments-in-china-taking-the-lead-accenture-analysis-finds-uk-gains-sharply-despite-brexit-doubts.htm (accessed 14 February 2022)

ADBI (2019) *Fintech for Asian SMEs*. Asian Development Bank Institute (ADBI), Tokyo

Ahmed ABA, Amin S, Harvie C, Nepal R (2021) The nexus between energy and trade in South Asia: A panel analysis. *J Appl Econ* 40(2):134–151

Alaassar A, Mention AL, Aas TH (2021) Exploring a new incubation model for FinTechs: Regulatory sandboxes. *Technovation* 103:102237

Alaassar A, Mention AL, Aas TH (2020) Exploring how social interactions influence regulators and innovators: The case of regulatory sandboxes. *Technol Forecast Soc Change* 160:120257

Allen HJ (2020) Experimental strategies for regulating FinTech. *JL & Innovation*, 3:1

Allen HJ (2019) Regulatory sandboxes. *Geo Wash L Rev* 87:579

Amin SB, Ahmed A, Khan AM, Khan F (2021a) Policy paper on the post Covid-19 sustainable energy options for power generation in Bangladesh. *Int Energy J* 21(1A):9–20

Amin S, Jamasb T, Nepal R (2021b) Regulatory reform and the relative efficacy of government versus private investment on energy consumption in South Asia. *Econ Anal Policy* 69:421–433

Amin SB, Al Kabir F, Khan F (2020) Energy-output nexus in Bangladesh: A two-sector model analysis. *Energy Strategy Rev* 32:100566

Appiah-Otoo I, Song N (2021) The impact of FinTech on poverty reduction: Evidence from China. *Sustain* 13(9):5225

Arner DW, Barberis J, Buckley RP (2017) *FinTech and RegTech in a Nutshell, and the Future in a Sandbox*. CFA Institute Research Foundation

Arner DW, Barberis J, Buckley RP (2015) The evolution of Fintech: A new post-crisis paradigm. *Geo J Int'l* L 47:1271

ASEAN Fintech Census (2018) Census report. Retrieved from: https://assets.ey.com/content/dam/ey-sites/ey-com/en_sg/topics/financial-services/ey-asean-fintech-census-2018.pdf?download

Bangladesh Bank (2021) Recent Statistics. Government of the People's Republic of Bangladesh

Bangladesh Telecommunication Regulatory Commission (BTRC) (2021) Recent Statistics. Government of the People's Republic of Bangladesh

Batunanggar S (2019) Fintech development and regulatory frameworks in Indonesia ADBI Working Paper Series No. 1014. Asian Development Bank Institute (ADBI), Tokyo

BBS (2018) Recent Statistics. Government of the People's Republic of Bangladesh

Brummer C (2015) Disruptive technology and securities regulation. *Fordham L Rev* 84:977

Buckley RP, Arner D, Veidt R, Zetzsche D (2020) Building FinTech ecosystems: Regulatory sandboxes, innovation hubs and beyond. Wash. *UJL & Poly*, 61, 55

Cai Y, Aoyama Y (2018) Fragmented authorities, institutional misalignments, and challenges to renewable energy transition: A case study of wind power curtailment in China. *Energy Res Soc Sci* 41:71–79

Chao EJ, Serwaah P, Baah-Peprah P, Shneor R (2020) Crowdfunding in Africa: Opportunities and challenges. In: Shneor R, Zhao L, Flåten BT (Eds) *Advances in Crowdfunding*, Palgrave Macmillan, Cham, pp. 319–339

Chen L (2016) From fintech to finlife: the case of fintech development in China. *China Econ J* 9(3):225–239

Daily Social (2018) Fintech Report. pp 16–35. Retrieved from: https://dailysocial.id/report/post/fintechreport-2018

Demirgüç-Kunt A, Klapper L, Singer D, Ansar S, Hess J (2017) *The Global Findex 2017: Measuring Financial Inclusion and Fintech Revolution*. The World Bank

Deng X, Huang Z, Cheng X (2019) FinTech and sustainable development: Evidence from China based on P2P data. *Sustainability* 11(22):6434

England J (2021) South Korea launches Virtual Sandbox for fintech development. *Fintech Magazine*. Retrieved from: https://fintechmagazine.com/financial-services-finserv/south-korea-launches-virtual-sandbox-fintech-development

Fan PS (2018) Singapore approach to develop and regulate FinTech. In: Chuen DLK, Deng R (Eds) *Handbook of Blockchain, Digital Finance, and Inclusion*, Elsevier, Volume 1, pp. 347–357

Fintechnews Indonesia (2021) Digital technologies to bolster Islamic finance market in Indonesia. Retrieved from: https://fintechnews.sg/54574/sponsoredpost/digital-technologies-to-bolster-islamic-finance-market-in-indonesia/

GED (2021) 8th Five Year Plan: July 2020–June 2025. Bangladesh Planning Commission. Government of the People's Republic of Bangladesh

GED (2020) Perspective plan of Bangladesh 2021–2041. Government of the People's Republic of Bangladesh

Global Data (2020) Data Bank. Retrieved from: https://www.globaldata.com/

Global Fintech Index 2020 (2020) The global fintech index city rankings report. *Findexable.* Retrieved from: https://findexable.com/wpcontent/uploads/2019/12/Findexable_Global-Fintech-Rankings-2020exSFA.pdf

GSMA Intelligence (2020) Annual Report. Retrieved from: https://www.gsma.com/mobileeconomy/wp-content/uploads/2020/03/GSMA_MobileEconomy2020_Global.pdf

Hinson R, Lensink R, Mueller A (2019) Transforming agribusiness in developing countries: SDGs and the role of FinTech. *Curr Opin Environ Sustain* 41:1–9

Hua X, Huang Y (2021) Understanding China's fintech sector: Development, impacts and risks. *Eur J Finance*, 27(4–5), 321–333

Huang Y, Zhang L, Li Z, Qiu H, Sun T, Wang X, Berger H (2020) Fintech credit risk assessment for SMEs: Evidence from China, IMF Working Papers, 2020(193): A001. Washington, DC: International Monetary Fund

Imam MI, Jamasb T, Llorca M (2019) Sector reforms and institutional corruption: Evidence from electricity industry in Sub-Saharan Africa. *Energy Policy* 129:532–545

Indonesia Fintech Report 2021 (2021) Advance AI. Retrieved from: https://f.hubspotusercontent10.net/hubfs/5877117/Marketing%20Content/Reports/Indo%20Fintech%20Rerpot%20(EN).pdf

Islam SMM (2021) Regulatory oversight in MFS industry. *Financial Express.* Retrieved from:https://thefinancialexpress.com.bd/views/regulatory-oversight-in-mfs-industry-1612534358

Jenik I, Lauer K (2017) Regulatory sandboxes and financial inclusion. Working Paper, Washington, DC: CGAP

Khalid M, Kunhibava S (2020) Fintech regulatory sandboxes in Australia and Malaysia: A legal analysis. *IIUM Law J* 28(1):1–35

Knight B (2016) *Fintech: Who Regulates It and Why It Matters.* Milken Institute

Kong ST, Loubere N (2021) Digitally down to the countryside: Fintech and rural development in China. *J Dev Stud* 57(10):1739–1754

Lai K (2021) Companies look for alternatives as China tightens IPO rules. *International Financial Law Review.* Retrieved from: https://www.iflr.com/article/b1rljg84bprsjg/companies-look-for-alternatives-as-china-tightens-ipo-rules

Lee I, Shin YJ (2018) Fintech: Ecosystem, business models, investment decisions, and challenges. *Bus Horiz* 61(1):35–46

Moradi S, Naderi N, Delangizan S (2020) Analyzing fintech startups development process in Iran. *J Entrep Develop* 13(1):121–140

Philippon T (2016) *The Fintech Opportunity.* Cambridge, MA: National Bureau of Economic Research

Pranata N (2019) The role of digital payments fintech in accelerating the development of MSMEs in Indonesia. In: Nemeto N, Yoshino, N (Eds) *Fintech for Asian SMEs*, Asian Development Bank Institute, Chiyoda-ku, pp. 145–166

Shin YJ, Choi Y (2019) Feasibility of the fintech industry as an innovation platform for sustainable economic growth in Korea. *Sustainability* 11(19):5351

Slawinski S (2021) Fintechs in South Korea see the launch of a new virtual sandbox. *Global Fintech News*. Retrieved from: https://globalfintechnews.com/fintechs-in-south-korea-see-the-launch-of-a-new-virtual-sandbox/

Stayton J, Mangematin V (2019) Seed accelerators and the speed of new venture creation. *J Technol Transf* 44(4):1163–1187

Taghizadeh-Hesary F, Yoshino N (2019) Application of distributed ledger technologies to improve funding in the startup ecosystem. In Nemeto N, Yoshino N (Eds) *Fintech for Asian SMEs*, Asian Development Bank Institute, Chiyoda-ku, pp. 30–50

Taylor MCR, Wilson C, Holttinen E, Morozova A (2020) *Institutional Arrangements for Fintech Regulation and Supervision*. International Monetary Fund

UN Environment Programme (2018) *Digital Finance and Citizen Action: In Financing the Future of Climate-Smart Infrastructure*. Geneva

Wales K (2017) *Peer-to-Peer Lending and Equity Crowdfunding: A Guide to the New Capital Markets for Job Creators, Investors, and Entrepreneurs*. Santa Barbara, CA: Praeger

Wildau G (2016) China P2P regulations target Hucksters and risktakers. *Financial Times*. 24 August

World Bank (2020) World Development Indicators (WDI)

Wyman O (2020) Singapore Fintech Landscape 2020 and Beyond, Singapore Fintech Association (SFA) Retrieved from: https://www.oliverwyman.com/content/dam/oliver wyman/v2/publications/2020/dec/singapore-fintech-landscape-2020-and-beyond.pdf

Yang Y, Su X, Yao S (2021) Nexus between green finance, fintech, and high-quality economic development: Empirical evidence from China. *Resources Policy*, 74: 102445

Yiqing W (2016) Surge in P2P scams leads to stronger supervision. *China Daily*. Retrieved from: http://europe.chinadaily.com.cn/business/2016-10/09/content_27000442.htm

Yoon L (2021) Fintech adoption rate South Korea 2017–2019. *Statista*. Retrieved from: https://www.statista.com/statistics/1125349/south-korea-fintech-adoption-rate/

You C (2018) Recent development of FinTech regulation in China: A focus on the new regulatory regime for the P2P lending (loan-based Crowdfunding) market, *Cap Mark Law J*, 13(1), 85–115

Zhu V (2021) China's FinTech: The End of the Wild West. Institut Montaigne. Policy Paper. Retrieved from: https://www.institutmontaigne.org/en/publications/chinas-fintech-end-wild-west

7 The role of government in digital innovations

Case of Turkish startup ecosystem

Yener Coskun and Esra Alp Coskun

1 Introduction

Today, technological innovations of startups and digital entrepreneurship play critical roles in the evolution of economic activities and contribute significantly to economic growth and employment. However, conditions in developing countries make it difficult for innovative startups to access stable and low-cost financing channels. In addition to financing, the economic and cultural ecosystems in the developing world may pose additional risks for technological improvements as well.

This chapter aims to discuss the role of government in innovations in startups and to analyze real-world examples to highlight the practical issues concerning the actual problems of the innovation process in the case of startup ecosystems, specifically in developing countries, by using the Turkish startup ecosystem as a case study. This paper contributes to the literature in two ways. First, this introductory essay represents the first comprehensive attempt to analyze the role of government in the startup ecosystem in Turkey in the light of Peak Games, Dream Games, Hepsiburada, Getir, and Trendyol as recent globally successful case studies. These case study analyses would specifically be found interesting, because they originated in the high-risk environment of the Turkish economy. Various international data such as credit rating notes or country CDS premium levels have long suggested that Turkey is a high-risk economy. The main limitation of our investigation is the lack of empirical literature and company-specific dynamic market information for the analyzed companies. Second, this chapter demonstrates that governments may contribute to digital entrepreneurship, however, the named success stories have not involved explicit government support. We argue that this picture implies emerging countries' digital startup and entrepreneurship ecosystems may have chances to create a global impact without or limited government support, thanks to globally highly active venture capital (VC) investments. Despite the country's high level of macroeconomic risks, Turkey's experience is an example of a market-based success story with a large international VC investment.

This chapter proceeds as follows. In the following sections, we discuss theoretical context from the perspective of both advanced and emerging countries,

DOI: 10.4324/9781003220220-10

followed by the decision-making process of governments in startup financing. In Section 3, the Turkish startup ecosystem and its financing strategies are analyzed by focusing on selected case studies. The chapter concludes with some policy implications for the role of the government in financing startups and financial innovations.

2 Literature review

2.1 The role of governments in technological progress and digital innovations

Despite some challenges, new firms are the engine of economic growth. Supported by different financing channels and entrepreneurship systems, specifically high tech, startup ecosystems make significant contributions to technological advancement. Gornall and Strebulaev (2015) suggest that VC-backed companies account for 41% of total US market capitalization and 62% of US public companies' research and development (R&D) spending. Among public companies founded within the last fifty years, VC-backed companies account for half in number, three quarters by value, and more than 92% of R&D spending and patent value.

The state complements the dynamism of entrepreneurship (Ebner, 2006). Policy interventions and state investments are also important in the digital age (Hanna, 2018). For example, Mazzucato (2013b) indicates that US startups (i.e., Google) have historically utilized various public VC funds. The World Economic Forum (2012) emphasized that the transition from an efficiency-driven to an innovation-driven economy also requires active government policies. In this perspective, the government should play an active role in the economy as an entrepreneur in the case of risky but promising investments. Risky projects usually involve infrastructure investments as currently/previously observed in all economic systems. In line with this idea, the Industry 4.0 ecosystems also imply the same "developer role" for governments, usually for high technology and R&D investments, innovations, and startups. It seems that these government incentives are of particular importance for startups that serve as driving forces behind innovation and technology-based economic growth in both advanced and emerging countries.

Mazzucato (2013b) asserted that in many technological revolutions, key early-stage funding has come from the state. For example, biotechnology, nanotechnology, and 3D printing are recent examples of how government investments may drive technological change and the landscape of industries (see, Dickinson, 2018; Mazzucato, 2016). Block and Keller (2011) also argue that this leading role of the state remain "hidden" for political reasons. This has made the US one of the most interventionist economies in the world (Mazzucato and Wray, 2015). Mazzucato and Wray (2015) also argue that space travel and fighting climate change are driven by creating new markets. State investment in space travel would be a good example of government-led technological improvements.

As a recent case for state investment in technology firms, Sheetz (2020) indicated that U.S. equity investment in space companies totaled $5.4 billion in 2020/Q1. As an example of PPP in space investing, NASA launched a manned flight to the International Space Station on a commercially developed U.S. rocket in May of 2020 (see Web Link 1).

Therefore, to increase long-term economic development, the literature reveals that governments may support mission-oriented investments and, more importantly, take an active role in supporting technological advancements through startup ecosystems in the digital age by being an interventionist. This proactive state intervention may represent a further step beyond the traditional market failure approach and imply that public money may be spent for Industry 4.0 companies that may provide long-term positive externalities for economic growth.

2.2 Startup ecosystem and the role of government

2.2.1 Startup ecosystem and financing problems

Innovation requires patient financing because of its uncertain nature and high operating costs. Finding the required funding from short-term profit-motivated private initiatives for innovative startups may prove difficult (Dorfleitner et al., 2017; Lazonick and Mazzucato 2013; Mazzucato 2013a). Traditional financing routes, such as credit or stock-market channels, may not suffice to fill the finance gap of startups because of various restrictions, as regulations may limit VC financing; for example, the Basel Capital Accord prevents financial institutions from lending to risky sectors. Securities regulations may also have some limitations for risky capital investments aimed at protecting small investors. The financing problem of startups seems obvious, especially in bank-based and volatile financial markets. Therefore, seeking innovative financing methods is essential to giving these enterprises easy access to stable and cheap financing, which may have a significant role in technological advancement, especially in developing countries. These innovative financing methods for startups, such as various forms of VC financing, are specifically important during the early idea and early stages of firm development (Table 7.1).

Among the problems, it seems that the lack of sufficient access to traditional and alternative finance channels is the biggest problem of technology and all startups. Considering a sample of 386 Italian tech startups, Colombo and Grilli (2007) found that only a limited number of firms may use external financing with small bank loans. Using 1,933 high-tech startups that received at least one financing round from a business angel (BA) as their sample, Croce et al. (2018) found that startups combining BA and VC financing find additional VC financing. Gornall and Strebulaev (2020) argue that most successful VC-backed companies went public within 3–8 years of their initial VC funding.

This brief review implies that despite some financing options, it is difficult to argue that startups may easily obtain a sufficient amount of financing through credit, stock market, or VC channels because of restrictions such as the lack of

Table 7.1 Startup Financing: Life Cycle Risks and Finance Channels

Stage	*Financial Needs*	*Barriers*	*Type of Capital*
Seed	Low	High risk Unfavorable risk-return relation The threat of mission drift Legal form Lack of managerial skills	Grants from charities Corporate grants Grants from government agencies HNWI Retail (crowdfunding; peer-to-peer lending), Business incubators
Start-up	High	Information asymmetry Performance measurement and monitoring Moral hazard Legal form	Equity (crowdfunding) Hybrid financing forms Patient capital Mezzanine financing Venture philanthropy
Early Growth	Very High	Information asymmetry Lack of collateral Lack of financial skills Fear of failure	Public procurement Social impact bonds Microfinance Term debt with flex features (social banks) Subordinate debt
Growth	Medium	Size Mission lock requirements	Commercial debt Equity (social impact fund)

Source: Arena et al. (2018).

business history, limited financial literacy, inflexible rules, etc. As extensively documented in the finance-growth nexus, declining access to finance is bad news for output growth; this problematic picture requires a sound solution. In response to this issue, the literature reveals that the public sector may play an important role in solving some of the financing problems facing startups. For example, to support a startup ecosystem, the state may establish technology centers, provide subsidies and/or tax advantages for R&D investments, create revenue through purchase programs, and become a strategic investor/partner for startups. Dees and Dolby (1996, cited in Arena et al., 2018) argue that agreements with the state signal an impact on other liquidity providers. However, the efficient use of public money requires an accountable distribution metric for financing startups. This important point is discussed in Section 2.2.3.

2.2.2 Other problems of startup ecosystems

Despite a positive outlook in terms of continuing to grow in number, market size, and revenue stream, startups may face several barriers to further development. Taking into account the significant role of the digital economy in global GDP growth, this may translate as slowing economic growth and declining employment for both advanced and emerging economies. Based on data from 35 countries over the period from 1996 to 2002, Anokhin and Wincent (2012) argue that the relationship between startup rates and innovation depends on the development level of a country.

Although Covid-19 resulted in increasing digitalization (Amankwah-Amoah et al., 2021), it is generally agreed that the level of development and readily available VC financing may further support formations of more fintech startups (Haddad and Hornuf, 2019). Government policies may improve the innovation and digitalization of startups if markets do not support them, as indicated by Bryan and Williams (2021). However, the success of governments is related to how the challenges surrounding startups are addressed. The most notable problems of further development other than financing in global fintech startups are broadly discussed in the literature and policy documents. For example, in their country-level analysis, Berg et al. (2020) classified the key challenges of fintech development in selected developing countries as a lack of financing/investments in R&D, lack of support system for innovation, poor information and communications technology (ICT) infrastructure, lack of a clear strategy by policymakers, lack of flexibility in the taxation, and scarcity of skilled talent. Therefore, we may argue that the role of governments in improving startup activities should focus on these challenges as well.

2.2.3 Decision-making of governments in emerging innovations and startups

2.2.3.1 US INNOVATION AND STARTUP POLICIES: IN BRIEF

Pickernell et al. (2013) emphasize that not all startups contribute equally to an economy. The question then arises: "Which startup companies should be financed by the government?" According to Acs (2008), the most significant contributions to the economy were achieved by fast-growing "gazelle" firms (Box 7.1), often referred to as high potential firms (Senyard et al., 2008). Shane (2009) also states that the use of public funding would more efficient if used by high-growth companies.

Box 7.1 Understanding Gazelle Firms

Lopez-Garcia and Puente (2012) state that Gazelle firms may be classified by size and growth rate. Ahmad (2006) defines "gazelles" as high growth firms less than five years old with rapid employment growth.

The U.S. government has had the most "visible hand" in innovation policy, investing actively in key areas, providing both research funding as well as early-stage capital financing (Block and Keller, 2011; cited in Mazzucato, 2013b). All the "radical" technologies, such as the Internet, GPS, touchscreen display, personal assistant 'SIRI', make Apple's iPhone a 'smartphone, were funded by the U.S. government's Small Business Investment Company program (Mazzucato, 2013b). Today, across the world, there is evidence that some of the most radical green investments are being made by public agencies/governments, from the Advanced Research Projects Agency-Energy (ARPA-E) in the US to the China Development Bank (CDB). Google's algorithm was also funded by the U.S. government's National Science Foundation (Mazzucato, 2013c).

On the other side of the coin, financing risky investments may have some consequences for governments. Inherently, innovation involves very high risk and uncertainty in the Knightian sense, and the majority of projects may fail. For voters, several failures may be acceptable for private investors/innovators, but it is hard to accept numerous failures of government-funded projects. Mazzucato (2013c) also argues that government should never have an exclusive license or hold a large portion of the value of an innovation that can result in a crowding-out effect.

Government investments in emerging technologies and startups may have various positive externalities. Mazzucato and Wray (2015) suggest that government does not need to get fast profit. Another incentive for governments investing in a company with high capital intensity and great technological risk is that they do not require tax reductions or low-interest rates, as the private sector does. The state has played a crucial "entrepreneurial" role in establishing completely new sectors, such as information technology, biotech, nanotech, and green tech, in some of the world's most well-known innovation hubs. The government, for example, has served as a strategic investor in Silicon Valley through a decentralized network of public organizations such as the Defense Advanced Research Projects Agency, NASA, the Small Business Innovation Research Program (SBIR), and the National Science Foundation (Web Link 2).

2.2.3.2 EMERGING MARKET PERSPECTIVE

As a cornerstone of technological advancement in the age of Industry 4.0, startups have their unique features. For example, startups are not the kind of firms that have strong balance sheets and income statements and can easily find financing. Moreover, they mostly need liquidity injection before it is too late, as they do not earn as much as they spend on innovation, prototypes, or new technologies. These two reasons make so vital the long-term and patient financing of startups. Mazzucato (2013c) suggests that VC investments would be highly possible once government funding is provided. The examples of government investments, particularly in the US, imply that strategic sectors should be supported by investing directly.

From the emerging market perspective, high-tech industries and startups may also play major roles in economic development through their innovation ecosystem. Booz and Hamilton (2014) argue that there are three reasons for the increase in startups in emerging markets: better ease of doing business scale, state support, and competition among emerging markets. Ernst (2014) indicate that starting in 2000 with the introduction in the Philippines of Smart Money (the world's first electronic cash card linked to a mobile phone), mobile payment services have gained traction in several emerging markets, such as in Kenya and Pakistan. All the above reasons suggest that as they increasingly become crucial for economic development, startups may be also financed by the governments. As alternative financing, government funds have several advantages vis-a-vis private investors or banks.

Interestingly, some countries are lucky to attract multinationals that may help develop entrepreneurship, innovation, and start-up ecosystems, such as India (Bhagavatula et al., 2019) and China. Some countries implement strict policies for technology and startup development. For example, Liu et al. (2012) discuss that government intervention may have a positive impact on high technology start-up innovation in China. Maune (2017) found that spending on R&D, cooperation between industry and university, policy targeting and government support, military research, and an efficient technology transfer system for commercialization have played critical roles for the development of innovation and high-tech startups in Israel.

Governments may use public funds to support technological advancements through startups; however, sound decision-making in the public sector is challenging. For example, the literature reveals that governments may fail to catch the latest technological improvements (Norris and Reddick 2013; Rocha et al., 2019); have a less efficient investment framework (Alperovych et al., 2015; Grilli and Murtinu, 2014); or lack sound analysis and selection criteria during investment decision-making (Bertoni et al., 2011), proper monitoring (Afful-Dadzie and Afful-Dadzie, 2016), well-educated officials, and sufficient funding channels. Moreover, a bigger risk may arise from politically connected public investments (Cumming, 2007; Lerner, 2002). Taking into account obvious problems in public decision-making, one may argue that developing sound and unbiased metrics for state-support in startup investments would be highly problematic, especially in developing countries. For example, Prashantham and Yip (2017) indicate that less reliable information, weak property rights, and unsound governance are the leading challenges for immature entrepreneurial ecosystems. Rocha et al. (2019) discuss that Brazil lacks digital industrial policy and financial incentives for digital entrepreneurship. More importantly, Industry 4.0 is also hindered by government-related obstacles. Ramesh (2020) argues that inept institutions characterized by bureaucracy and corruption are among the reasons for the instability of the business environment in India.

Overall, for developing countries, we may suggest at least some major rules for government intervention in an innovative startup ecosystem. First, as discussed in Arena et al. (2018), government investments or grant programs may specifically focus on the seed stage, which involves higher risks and financing needs for startups. Second, as indicated by Lerner (2002), government VC investments may work in selected sectors defined by the lack of private VC financing, and the invested startups may be selected by their potential positive externalities. As an interesting attempt, Afful-Dadzie and Afful-Dadzie (2016) suggest criteria set for selecting a startup business in a government-run VC. In this work, the authors suggest that the government investment may analyze the following items in her investment decision-making: entrepreneur (team personality and experience), product/service potential, financial characteristics, market characteristics, and societal impact/contribution.

3 Turkish startup ecosystems and the role of government

The recent global attention on Turkish gaming and technology startups brings the startup ecosystem in Turkey into consideration. In this section, we investigate it by reviewing selected stylized facts and case studies, such as Peak Games, Dream Games, Hepsiburada(.com), Getir(.com), and Trendyol(.com). In case study analyses, we specifically consider financing channels of firms and the role of government.

The Turkish experience is an interesting case study for two reasons. First, Turkish startups represent a success story despite their high economic risk environment. Second, the success stories represent globally successful market-based developments rather than a sample of policy-oriented or government-supported results.

3.1 Overview of the Turkish startup ecosystem

Classified as a permanent club member of Fragile Five economies along with Brazil, India, South Africa, and Indonesia, Turkey has some of the highest inflation rates, interest rates, and CDS premiums in the world. Selected statistics explicitly confirm that Turkey is a high-risk economy. Therefore, despite her demographic window of opportunity and economic growth potential, data suggests that the Turkish economy has a high level of uncertainties due to macroeconomic imbalances and explicit financial risks. This economic environment may imply that Turkey would be a difficult place for any entrepreneurship involving technology.

As an overview, the startup ecosystem in Turkey may be analyzed by using international statistics and rankings. In general, industry reports suggest that Istanbul has become one of the leading start-up centers in her region. For example, Startups Watch (2021c) suggests that Istanbul became the 11th city in Europe where the most startup investments were made. KPMG (2021) indicates that ranked 10th in Europe and 2nd in MENA in terms of deal size, Turkey's startup ecosystem successfully managed to attract foreign capital. According to the Global Fintech Index 2020 report (Findexable, 2020), Turkey ranked 44th and Istanbul ranked 21st in Europe and 56th in the world as the best fintech city. Startups Watch (2021a) also reports that in terms of total angel and VC funding, Turkey ranked immediately below Poland among European countries.

The total amount of new funds raised equaled 328 million USD in 2020, the largest total funding base to date.

FinTech Istanbul (2019) reported that as of 2018 (2019), the investment in fintechs in Turkey was US$12.2 (8.4) million. However, according to the latest report to date, Startups Watch (2021c) suggests that 63 startups raised a total of US$746 million from angels and VCs in Turkey as of 2021 Q2. This may translate as Turkey rose to 8th among countries receiving the most investment in Europe in the first quarter, while in the Middle East and North Africa it took 2nd place after Israel. In the Middle East region (excluding Northern Africa), Israel, the UAE, and Turkey stand tall as the top three countries with the most fintech. It is estimated that startups and fintech startups numbered around 1,000 and 200, respectively, in Turkey as of 2021 (Web Link 3). These statistics along with the recent successes of Turkish startups suggest that Turkish digital entrepreneurs have done a good job recently, despite various risks and macroeconomic imbalances.

3.2 Globalized Turkish startups-unicorns and financing strategies

3.2.1 SMEs in Turkey: financing channels, use of technology, and R&D investments

The Turkish economy is dominated by labor-intensive SMEs, and start-up ratios are particularly high in Turkey (Calvino et al., 2015). According to Turkish Statistical Institute (TurkStat) data as of 2019, SMEs comprised 99.8% of all firms and 72.4% of all employment in Turkey (Web Link 4). To finance their businesses, SMEs mostly use credit-financing and public debt; non-bank financing channels involving VC investment are limited. For example, according to OECD (see Web Link 5), as of 2018, the total outstanding business loans of SMEs was around 890.2 billion Turkish Lira (TL). In 2018, new investments in VC or private equity for SMEs was 0.9 billion TL, and its growth rates were 154%, 27%, and 108% as of 2016, 2017, and 2018, respectively. This picture suggests that despite the growing volume of VC investments, SME financing has fewer alternatives and depends heavily on the banking channel in Turkey. Moreover, TurkStat (Web Link 6) suggested that as of 2019, the use of high technology was only 0.5% (1.5%) in micro (small) SMEs. This is in line with the low level of R&D expenditures in Turkey. As of 2017, the R&D expenditures-to-GDP ratio was 2.145 in the world but 0.469 and 0.96 in Turkey in 2003 and 2017, respectively (Web Link 7).

Interestingly, despite problems of SMEs and specifically technology (tech) startups in Turkey (Tanrıkulu and Ermis, 2021), Turkish startups have recently attracted increased global attention. According to Startups Watch data, as of October 2019, over 250 fintech startups were operating in 13 different fields in Turkey, such as payments, banking, finance, crowdfunding, big data, and crypto coins (Yazici, 2019). In this section, we briefly analyze the stories of globalized leading tech and gaming startups in Turkey, namely Peak Games, Dream Games, Hepsiburada, Getir, and Trendyol.

3.2.2 Gaming startups in Turkey: the cases of peak games and dream games

KPMG (2021) indicated that based on deal sizes and transactions, the gaming industry continued to maintain its leading role in the Turkish startup ecosystem. In addition to its local impact, Turkish mobile games account for 20% of the most downloaded games in the US (Web Link 8), and overall 2% of all game publishers on Google Play are from Turkey (Web Link 9). The latest VC investments attracted by Turkish gaming startups may also imply that Turkey is becoming a hub for gaming startups. Therefore, we assess that the Turkish gaming startup industry would be a good starting point in an analysis of the tech startup ecosystem in Turkey.

According to the gaming snapshot of Turkey as of June 2021, there are still 426 "alive" gaming startups in Turkey, and the exit size of the industry during 2018, 2019, and 2020 was US$250 million, US$210 million, and US$1,986 million, respectively. However, interestingly, gaming startups obtained a very low number of angel and VC deals. The deal volume and the number of firms obtaining investment were as follows during 2018, 2019, and 2020, respectively: (US$0.6 million; five firms); (US$8.3 million; five firms); (US$8.3 million; 14 firms). As of June 22, 2021, however, 28 gaming startups in the industry had obtained US$68.2 million in angel and VC investments (Startups Watch, 2021b). In the gaming startup ecosystem of Turkey, two firms attracted global attention: Peak Games and Dream Games. From the financing perspective, the common point of both is their use of international VC investments.

Ersoy (2021) reports that game developers in Turkey have attracted more than US$2.5 billion in investments over the past six years. For example, as the first unicorn of Turkey and Istanbul-based game developer, Peak Games and Rollic Games were acquired by Zynga in 2020 with values of US$1.8 billion and US$168 million, respectively (Teknopark Istanbul IQ, 2021: p.65). Startups Watch (2021a) also suggests that Peak Games was the largest VC-backed exit in Europe in 2020. Another Turkish mobile gaming startup, Dream Games, obtained the largest Series B VC financing, with a valuation of $1 billion, after its game Royal Match reached the top-20 grossing games in the US, UK, and Germany in three months (Web Link 10). KPMG (2021) reported that the company previously attracted 50 million USD early VC stage funding from international investors with a 25.23% stake.

In addition to VC investment, acquisition is another financing strategy in the industry. In this respect, Gram Games, an Istanbul- and London-based mobile gaming startup, was acquired by Zynga for $250 million in cash. Founded in 2012 and launching its first game in 2013, Gram Games has been backed by Hummingbird Ventures since its founding (Web Link 11).

3.2.3 Global success of Turkish (.com) tech startups: Hepsiburada, Getir, and Trendyol

In line with the financing method of gaming startups, globally successful Turkish tech startups have also attracted large international VC investments recently. Below, we briefly overview Hepsiburada, Getir, and Trendyol as case studies.

Turkey has a highly competitive and internationalized e-commerce market (Box 7.2). As the second-largest e-commerce platform in Turkey (HSBC Global Research, 2021), Hepsiburada.com (meaning "you can find anything you want here"), founded in 2000 and launching its platform in 2015, raised US$680 million as the first Turkish IPO (through American Depositary Shares; or ADS) in Nasdaq with a US$4.4 billion market value (Bradshaw, 2021b; Web Link 12). According to Form F1 submitted to the U.S. Securities and Exchange Commission (SEC) on May 28, 2021, Hepsiburada is one of the few female-founded technology companies globally. In Form F-1, the company indicates that Hepsiburada is one of the early pioneers of the digitalization of commerce in Turkey. The company has integrated e-commerce solutions for logistics, delivery, online payments, and personalized ads. It is indicated on Form F1 that the company has not had material long-term financing needs because of the high level of cash generated by the business and currently a large number of credit limits with various Turkish banks (Web Link 13). Hepsiburada is an interesting tech startup case study, as it achieved global success in a short time. However, using traditional financing channels, mostly banking finance, is not usual for many tech startups, such as in the case of Getir and Trendyol.

Perhaps two of the most interesting Istanbul-based tech startup cases are Getir, a rapid grocery delivery app, and Trendyol, an online shopping platform. Founded in 2015, Getir provides delivery in ten minutes with many convenience-store items in Turkey, the UK, and the Netherlands. Startups Watch (2021c) suggests that Getir became the most invested Turkish startup and unicorn. From the financing perspective, Bradshaw (2021a) says that Getir tripled its valuation to $7.5 billion after a series of new capital injections from international VC investors. Getir raised nearly 1 bn USD from VC investors and reached its market value after the third round of investment in a Series D funding in 2021 (Web Link 14).

The biggest e-commerce startup in Turkey, Trendyol was founded in 2010 and is estimated to reach US$16.5 billion market value after a series of VC financing. This makes the company the largest startup, the first decacorn, and the highest valued company in Turkey (Web Link 15). Previously, the company raised US$2 million and US$10 million VC investment rounds. In 2011, the market value of the company was estimated as roughly US$150 million after an investment from Kleiner Perkins, a US-based VC firm (Web Link 16). In 2018, Alibaba Group Holding Ltd., the world's largest online and mobile commerce company, acquired 86.5% of the firm's shares by paying US$728 million (Web Link 17). In 2021, the company acquired US$1.5 billion in additional funding from several VC firms (Bradshaw, 2021b).

Box 7.2 E-commerce Market in Turkey

The E-commerce market in Turkey has had a growing international investment stream since the mid-2000s. Like the earlier case, Yemeksepeti, an online food delivery startup based in Istanbul, distributed her services to some other countries and was acquired in 2015 by Delivery Hero, a Berlin-based German firm, for $589 million in cash.* HSBC Global Research (2021) indicated that the e-commerce market in Turkey is highly competitive. After taking over Trendyol in 2018, Alibaba became the market leader, Amazon entered the market in 2018, and eBay market share is 4.4% through GittiGidiyor, another e-commerce platform in Turkey.**

* Available at: https://techcrunch.com/2015/05/04/delivery-hero-turkey/ (accessed on: July 18, 2021).

** Available at: https://www.bloomberg.com/nesws/articles/2021-07-29/trendyol-valuation-set-to-hit-16-5-billion-in-fundraising-round?s=03 (accessed on: July 18, 2021).

Comparing government-supported startup initiatives in emerging/advanced countries (Kim and Park, 2017 for Korea, Islam et al., 2018 for the US, Bertoni et al., 2019 for Spain), it seems that the Turkish case has an interesting place, specifically in the developing world, in the sense of her market-based tech startup financing structure. The above success stories imply that digital entrepreneurship in Turkey has a global impact. None of these cases involved organized government support, but they are full of bright ideas, entrepreneurial success, and international financing such as VC and IPO. It seems that the synergy of the startup ecosystem in Istanbul has a positive impact on tech startup growth in Turkey (Bradshaw, 2021b) as well as a positive outlook on entrepreneurship in Turkey (Box 7.3). For this network externality, Belli (2016) indicated that the key strengths of Istanbul are a young talent pool, cheaper labor costs, and increasing brand value. However, summarized as high tax burden, lack of tax incentives (Demirhan et al., 2019), low access to financial resources, lack of financial data, macroeconomic risks, lack of sufficient investors (OECD, 2018; Yazici, 2019), and poor relations with financial services firms (Sakarya and Aksu, 2021), the problems of (fin)tech startups in Turkey imply that government support might play a significant role in market development.

3.2.4 Startup ecosystem of Turkey and weak role of government

As the highest level government planning document, The Eleventh Development Plan (Plan) for the period 2019–2023 includes some principles to support fintech ecosystems. The Plan suggests that the fintech ecosystem will be supported through international good practices. Among others, it is suggested that

Box 7.3 Intellectual Property Rights, Entrepreneurship, and Doing Business in Turkey

According to the Global Entrepreneurship Index (GEI) rankings of Zoltan et al. (2016), Turkey is ranked 28th in Europe. In the entrepreneurial aspirations sub-index, Turkey is ranked as 18th in the world and shows a better ranking value than Korea and Japan, for example. Moreover, according to the World Bank Doing Business Report, out of 190 economies, Turkey ranked 33rd in the world, but her ranks for starting a business and resolving insolvency were, respectively, 77th and 120th as of 2020.* However, in the Intellectual Property Rights Index published by Property Rights Alliance, Turkey's global rank was 66th out of 126 countries in 2020. The above rankings suggest that although there is room for development specifically for intellectual property rights, entrepreneurship and doing business may have a relatively positive environment in Turkey.

*Available at: https://www.doingbusiness.org/content/dam/doingBusiness/country/t/turkey/TUR-LITE.pdf; https://www.doingbusiness.org/content/dam/doingBusiness/country/t/turkey/TUR.pdf (accessed on: August 13, 2021).

** Available at: https://www.internationalpropertyrightsindex.org/country/turkey (accessed on: August 13, 2021).

Regulatory and Industry Sand Boxes will launch, and the open banking legal infrastructure will strengthen (Presidency of Strategy and Budget, 2019). Moreover, based on the Plan, the Ministry of Development broadly discusses some plans for Turkish fintech ecosystems (Kalkınma Bakanligi, 2018). This study involves several aspects of fintech with a focus on "what the state should do in the future." As briefly discussed below, despite well-calibrated bureaucratic words, the records and market facts reveal that state support for the startup ecosystem in Turkey is limited.

First, as a startup financing channel, VC investment is a regulated and licensed financial activity in Turkey. The Capital Markets Board of Turkey (CMB) issued regulations for crowdfunding, VC investment funds (VCIF), and private equity/VC investment companies (VCIC) in Turkey (Web Link 18). However, to date, it is difficult to argue that there is a big market development based on these regulatory frameworks. For example, there are only two licensed crowdfunding firms, and these companies did not aid much in significant market development in startup financing (Web Link 19). However, according to the 2020 annual report of the CMB, the number of VCIC (VCIF) and their total assets are, respectively, US$10 firms (38 funds) and US$926 (435) million (Web Link 20).

The market figures suggest that in 2020, 165 startups raised a total of US$139 million from angels and VCs, setting a new record for the ecosystem (Figure 7.1).

Second, as a method of government intervention in the startup ecosystem, the Ministry of Treasury and Finance (MTF) has regulated and licensed angel investors and networks in Turkey since 2013 (Web Link 21). SWTIO (2020) indicated that as of March 2020, MTF had accredited 524 angel investors, of which 300 are active, while the number of active, accredited angel networks has reached 11. The volume of investment of angel investors was 11.7 million Turkish Lira (TL, or roughly US$1.4 million) as of June 18, 2021. The investment volume of the angel investment network without a tax incentive as of 2019 was 20.8 million TL (or roughly US$2.4 million) as of June 18, 2021 (Web Link 22). Therefore, despite tax incentives (SWTIO, 2020; Teker and Teker, 2016; Web Link 23), it seems that the existing official framework for business angels has resulted in a low volume of investment and, hence, has limited positive outcomes.

Third, SWTIO (2020) indicated that with contributions from the private and public sectors, the number of startup accelerator programs in Turkey reached 57 as of 2019. Banks, corporates, technoparks, and KOSGEB (SMEs Development Organization of Turkey) have accelerator programs for fintech and startups. From a private sector perspective, as of 2019, while the number of Corporate VC (CVC) entities was 26, 30 private companies also made a direct investment in startups without a separate CVC. As other state organizations, The Scientific and Technological Research Council of Turkey (TUBITAK) and Regional Development Agencies also support startups. As of 2019, TUBITAK and KOSGEB had provided US$32.5 million to startups in the early/idea stages. Startup Watch (2021a) underscored that "as it is quite difficult to raise funds from the angel (networks) at the idea stage, the largest 'angel' at this stage is the Turkish government." For example, in 2019, 568 idea-stage startups received a total of

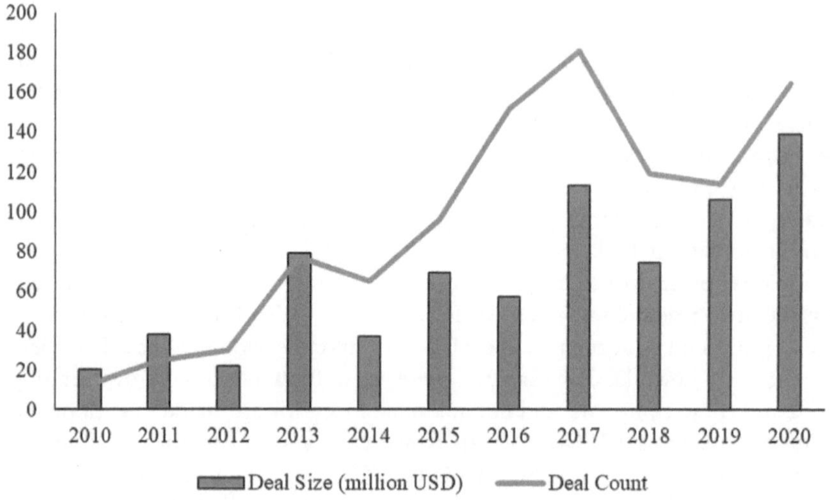

Figure 7.1 Annual Angel and VC Deal Activity (2010–2020) in Turkey.
Source: Startups Watch (2021a).

US$4 million in grants from TUBITAK TEYDEB; in 2020, 531 such startups received a total of US$7 million in grant funding. State support looks good during the idea stage, but obviously, the funding level is limited. As an explanation for this low-profile result, Dursun et al. (2017) assert that strict procedures and bureaucracy may discourage entrepreneurs, and hence, angel investors may represent a better, less complicated alternative for startups in Turkey.

Fourth, representing an alternative startup financing channel with various incentives, the recent developments in "technoparks" may suggest that startups may secure sizable tax benefits and develop commercialized technology through state-supported technology development zones (TDZs) in Turkey. According to data from the Ministry of Industry and Technology (2010: 27; 2020: 107), in 2010, the number of firms (persons) in these centers was 1,492 (12,735), and the volume of export was US$0.5 billion. As of 2020, the number of active TDZs in Turkey was 72. The number of firms (persons) in these centers reached 6,267 (64,866), and the volume of sales (export) was 106 billion TL (US$5.5 billion).

4 Conclusion and policy recommendations

Value discovery has always had its adventurous "free-spirit" entrepreneurs from pirate organizations (Durand and Vergne, 2012), maritime initiatives, to most major Arctic discoveries (Karpoff, 2001). For example, Dennis (1981) stated that the discovery of America was essentially "a VC project." The first and second industrial revolutions were mostly related to pure entrepreneurship, but the growing impact of competition among countries since World War 1 has also resulted in a more interventionist approach for technology development. The digital revolution of Industry 4.0 comes with its unique (digital) entrepreneurship. Not surprisingly, the financing structure of digital initiatives mainly utilizes private initiatives in many countries. However, redefining the concept of public benefit during the information age may bring new motivations for state interventions in technology development. The US and China may be leading examples of state intervention in terms of developing an active intervention framework for digital startups. Literature review and anecdotal evidence revealed that states may support digital entrepreneurship using various activities, such as providing grants, being a strategic investor, or issuing low-cost and long-term credit.

In this chapter, we examined the role of government in the development of innovation in a digital startup ecosystem using Turkey as the case study. Turkey's startup ecosystem represents a valuable case in the context of her cultural framework, which might shed some light on other emerging economies. We considered both the startup ecosystem and the recent global successes of Turkish gaming and tech startups, namely Peak Games, Dream Games, Hepsiburada, Getir, and Trendyol. Turkish economy is dominated mainly by low-labor-intensive SMEs. The existing SME structure involves a pattern of low equity, less diverse but costly financing options, a high level of macroeconomic uncertainties, low wage-low productivity, and mostly local-level goods and services supply. It is difficult to imagine that this chronicle will end with a technology startup boom despite the classical challenges of startups in a developing country (Berg et al., 2020; Prashantham and Yip 2017) and lack of effective digital policy for startups in Turkey. In the last couple of years, despite a high level of risks and weak internal VC investment framework (Haddad and Hornuf, 2019), many Turkish technology startups have attracted global VC investments and some of these firms even transformed into global startups.

Our tentative investigation suggests that government has some support for the startup ecosystem in Turkey; however, the above success stories have not involved explicit significant government input. It seems that this outcome is not in line with the arguments advocating the positive impacts of state intervention for the innovation ecosystem (Mazzucato, 2013c). As a similar result for some Korean digital start-ups, Yin et al. (2019) argue that their internationalization has not been directly accelerated by government support. The available, mostly anecdotal, evidence suggests that Turkish startups have relied extensively on international VC investments to finance their businesses or implement their exit strategies, and this seems to be mostly a market-based entrepreneurial success. However, we argue that the government may still play a more pivotal role in market development beyond bureaucratic rhetoric. Providing more research funding and early-stage capital financing (Block and Keller, 2011), establishing a government-run VC (Afful-Dadzie and Afful-Dadzie, 2016), and defining targeted sectors for purchase programs to create revenue streams for startups would be effective policy tools for further market development in digital startups.

The discussions presented in this research give some ground to improving the efficiency of startup ecosystems. In this respect, we conclude by drawing out the lessons from the Turkish experience to support the argument that public policies should adopt some specific (non-) financial targets to improve startup ecosystems and select high-growth potential startups. As a successful policy response in both developing/developed countries, the state may specifically prioritize its technical and financial support to some specific industries and their startup ecosystems. In light of the U.S. case among others, we argue that this may eventually result in commercial as well as public benefits.

As a future research direction, we should note that digital entrepreneurship in emerging markets is a largely unexplored topic in the literature. We expect that specifically empirical studies may significantly contribute to our knowledge in this area.

References

Acs ZJ (2008) Foundations of high impact entrepreneurship. Found. *Trends Entrep.* 4(6):535–620

Afful-Dadzie E, Afful-Dadzie A (2016) A decision-making model for selecting startup businesses in a government venture capital scheme. *Manag Decis* 54(3). https://doi.org/10.1108/MD-06-2015-0226

Ahmad N (2006) A proposed framework for business demographic statistics. OECD Statistics Working Paper Series, STD/DOC(2006)3. Paris: OECD

Alperovych Y, Hübner G, Lobet F (2015) How do governmental versus private venture capital backing affect a firm's efficiency? Evidence from Belgium. *J Bus Ventur* 30(4):508–525

Amankwah-Amoah J, Khan Z, Wood G, Knight G (2021) COVID-19 and digitalization: The great acceleration. *J Bus Res* 136:602–611

Anokhin S, Wincent J (2012) Startup rates and innovation: A cross-country examination. *J Int Bus Stud* 43(1):41–60

Arena M, Bengo I, Calderini M, Chiodo V (2018) Unlocking finance for social tech startups: Is there a new opportunity space? *Technol Forecast Soc Change* 127:154–165. https://doi.org/10.1016/j. techfore.2017.05.035

Belli M (2016) Banking and FinTech. Bankalar Arası Kart Merkezi. Available at: https://bkm.com.tr/wp-content/uploads/2016/02/Banking-and-FinTech.pdf (accessed on: July 21, 2021)

Berg G, Guadamillas M, Natarajan H, Sarkar A (2020) Fintech in Europe and Central Asia: Maximizing benefits and managing risks. February. The World Bank Group. Available at:https://openknowledge.worldbank.org/bitstream/handle/10986/33591/Fintech-in-Europe-and-Central-Asia-Maximizing-Benefits-and-Managing-Risks.pdf?sequence=1 (accessed on: July 24, 2021)

Bertoni F, Colombo MG, Grilli L (2011) Venture capital financing and the growth of high-tech startups: Disentangling treatment from selection effects. *Res Policy* 40(7):1028–1043

Bertoni F, Martí J, Reverte C (2019) The impact of government-supported participative loans on the growth of entrepreneurial ventures. *Res Policy* 48(1):371–384

Bhagavatula S, Mudambi R, Murmann JP (2019) Innovation and entrepreneurship in India: An overview. *Manag Organ Rev* 15(3):467–493

Block FL, Keller MR (2011) *State of Innovation: The U.S. Government's Role in Technology Development.* Boulder, CO: Paradigm Publishers

Booz RK, Hamilton BA (2014) The rise of emerging market startups. Available at: https://www.ge.com/news/reports/the-rise-of-emerging-market-startups (accessed on: 28 June, 2021)

Bradshaw T (2021a) Getir valuation triples to $7.5bn as investors chase grocery app craze. June 4. *The Financial Times.* Available at: *Financial Times* (ft.com) (accessed on: July 14, 2021)

Bradshaw T (2021b) How Turkey became a star of European tech. August 12. *The Financial Times.* Available at: *Financial Times* (ft.com) (accessed on: August 13, 2021)

Bryan KA, Williams HL (2021) Innovation: market failures and public policies. In *Handbook of Industrial Organization* (Vol. 5, No. 1, pp. 281–388). Elsevier

Calvino F, Criscuolo C, Menon C (2015) Cross-country evidence on start-up dynamics, OECD Science, Technology and Industry Working Papers, 2015/06, OECD Publishing, Paris. http://dx.doi.org/10.1787/5jrxtkb9mxtb-en

Colombo MG, Grilli L (2007) Funding gaps? Access to bank loans by high-tech startups. *Small Bus Econ* 29(1):25–46

Croce A, Guerini M, Ughetto E (2018) Angel financing and the performance of high-tech start-ups. *J Small Bus Manag* 56(2):208–228

Cumming D (2007) Government policy towards entrepreneurial finance: Innovation investment funds. *J Bus Ventur* 22(2):193–235

Dees JG, Dolby N (1996) Sources of financing for new nonprofit ventures. *Harv. Bus. Rev.* https://scholar.google.com/scholar?hl=tr&as_sdt=0%2C5&q=Dees+JG%2C+Dolby+N+%281996%29+Sources+of+financing+for+new+nonprofit+ventures&btnG=

Demirhan D, Temel S, Durst S (2019) The role of public entrepreneurship programs in fostering technology-based entrepreneurship: A Turkish case study. In: Dana LP and Ratten V (Eds.), *Societal Entrepreneurship and Competitiveness*, Emerald Publishing Limited, Bingley, pp 5–28. https://doi.org/10. 1108/978-1-83867-471-720191003

Dennis RW (1981) Venture capital, technology and taxes. *Technol Soc* 3(1-2):107–111

Dickinson H (2018) The next industrial revolution? The role of public administration in supporting government to oversee 3D printing technologies. *Public Adm Rev* 78(6):922–925

Dorfleitner G, Hornuf L, Schmitt M, Weber M (2017) The fintech market in Germany. In *FinTech in Germany*, Cham: Springer, pp 13–46

Durand R, Vergne JP (2012) *The Pirate Organization: Lessons from the Fringes of Capitalism.* Boston: Harvard Business Press

Dursun E, Tekin F, Karaosmanoglu A (2017) Functioning of angel investor ecosystem in Turkey: A study on Aegean region angel Investors. *J Multidiscip* 2(1):32–40

Ebner A (2006) Institutions, entrepreneurship, and the rationale of government: An outline of the Schumpeterian theory of the state. *J Econ Behav Organ* 59(4):497–515

Ernst Y (2014) Mobile money: The next wave of growth. Available at: http://www.ey.com/ (accessed on: 29 June, 2021)

Ersoy E (2021) 'Royal Match' Game Developer Soars Five-Fold in 4 Months to $1 Billion Value. 1 July. Bloomberg. Available at: 'Royal Match' Game Developer Dream Games Soars to $1 Billion Value. Bloomberg (accessed on: 14 July, 2021)

Findexable (2020) The Global Fintech Index 2020 Report. Available at: Findexable_Global-Fintech-Rankings-2020exSFA.pdf (accessed on: 14 July, 2021)

FinTech Istanbul (2019) Türkiye'de ve Dünyada FinTech 2019. Available at: https://bkm.com.tr/wp-content/uploads/2015/06/Turkiyede_ve_Dunyada_Fintech_2019-1.pdf (accessed on: July 21, 2021)

Gornall W, Strebulaev IA (2015) The economic impact of venture capital: Evidence from public companies, Working Paper, Stanford University

Gornall W, Strebulaev IA (2020) Squaring venture capital valuations with reality. *J Financ Econ* 135(1):120–143

Grilli L, Murtinu S (2014) Government, venture capital and the growth of European high-tech entrepreneurial firms. *Res Policy* 43(9):1523–1543

Hanna N (2018) A role for the state in the digital age. *J Innov Entrep* 7(1):1–16

Haddad C, Hornuf L (2019) The emergence of the global fintech market: Economic and technological determinants. *Small Bus Econ* 53(1):81–105

HSBC Global Research (2021) Hepsiburada (HEPS US). Available at: https://www.mediafire.com/file/jg018wc84f4a8nc/Hepsiburada_USA_IC_Internet_catalog_retail_4_aug_2021.pdf/file (accessed on: August 10, 2021)

Islam M, Fremeth A, Marcus A (2018) Signaling by early stage startups: US government research grants and venture capital funding. *J Bus Ventur* 33(1):35–51

Kalkınma Bakanligi (2018) On Birinci Kalkınma Planı (2019–2023) Finansal Hizmetlerin Geliştirilmesi Özel İhtisas Komisyonu Raporu. Available at: https://www.sbb.gov.tr/wp-content/uploads/2020/04/FinansalHizmetlerinGelistirilmesiOzelIhtisasKomisyonuRaporu.pdf (accessed on: July 15, 2021)

Karpoff JM (2001) Public versus private initiative in Arctic exploration: The effects of incentives and organizational structure. *J Polit Econ* 109(1):38–78

Kim S, Park KC (2021) Government funded R&D collaboration and it's [*sic*] impact on SME's [*sic*] business performance. *J Informetr* 15(3):101197. https://doi.org/10.1016/j.joi.2021.101197

KPMG (2021) Turkish startup investments review 2021 Q1. Available at: https://assets.kpmg/content/dam/kpmg/tr/pdf/2021/04/turkish-startup-investments-q1-2021.pdf (accessed on: 9 August, 2021)

Lazonick W, Mazzucato M (2013) The risk-reward nexus in the innovation-inequality relationship: Who takes the risks? Who gets the rewards? *Ind Corp Chang* 22(4): 1093–1128

Lerner J (2002) When bureaucrats meet entrepreneurs: The design of effective public venture capital programmes. *Econ J* 112(477): F73–F84

Liu Y, Woywode M, Xing Y (2012) High technology start-up innovation and the role of guanxi: An explorative study in China from an institutional perspective. *Prometheus* 30(2):211–229

Lopez-Garcia, P, Puente, S (2012) What makes a high-growth firm? A dynamic probit analysis using Spanish firm-level data. *Small Bus Econ* 39(4):1029–1041

Maune A (2017) Developing competitive advantage through startups and venture capital in emerging markets: A view from Israel. Risk Governance and Control. *Financial Mark Inst* 7(3):85–115

Mazzucato M (2013a) *The Entrepreneurial State: Debunking the Public Vs. Private Myth in Risk and Innovation*. London and New York: Anthem Press

Mazzucato M (2013b) Financing innovation: Creative destruction vs. destructive creation. *Ind Corp Chang* 22(4):851–867

Mazzucato M (2013c) Taxpayers helped apple, but apple won't help them. *Harvard Business Review*. https://hbr.org/2013/03/taxpayers-helped-apple-but-app (accessed on July 20, 2021)

Mazzucato M (2016) From market fixing to market-creating: A new framework for innovation policy. *Ind Innov* 23(2):140–156

Mazzucato M, Wray LR (2015) Financing the capital development of the economy: A Keynes-Schumpeter-Minsky synthesis (No. 2015/14). LEM Working Paper Series

Ministry of Industry and Technology (MIT) (2010; 2020) 2010 and 2020 Annual Reports. Available at: https://www.sanayi.gov.tr/plan-program-raporlar-ve-yayinlar/faaliyet-raporlari (accessed on: July 14, 2021)

Norris DF, Reddick CG (2013) Local e-government in the United States: Transformation or incremental change? *Public Adm Rev* 73(1):165–175

OECD (2018) OECD Economic Surveys Turkey. July. Available at: OECD Economic Surveys: Turkey 2018 (accessed on: July 14, 2021)

Pickernell D, Senyard J, Jones P, Packham G, Ramsey E (2013) New and young firms: Entrepreneurship policy and the role of government – evidence from the Federation of Small Businesses survey. *J Small Bus Entrepreneurship* 20(2):358–382. https://doi.org/10.1108/14626001311326770

Prashantham S, Yip GS (2017) Engaging with startups in emerging markets. *MIT Sloan Manag Rev* 58(2): 9

Presidency of Strategy and Budget (2019) The Eleventh Development Plan (2019–2023). Available at: https://www.sbb.gov.tr/ (accessed on: July 14, 2021)

Ramesh S (2020) Entrepreneurship in China and India. *J Knowl Econ* 11(1):321–355

Rocha CF, Mamédio DF, Quandt CO (2019) Startups and the innovation ecosystem in Industry 4.0. *Technol Anal Strateg Manag* 31(12):1474–1487. https://doi.org/10.1080/09537325.2019.1628938

Sakarya S, Aksu M (2021) Fintech ecosystem in Turkey: An evaluation in terms of financial markets and financial stability. In *The Impact of Artificial Intelligence on Governance, Economics and Finance*, Volume I, Singapore: Springer, pp 11–31

Senyard J, Davidsson P, Steffens P (2008) Improving Methodologies of High Potential Nascent Entrepreneurship Researchi 28th Babson Entrepreneur Conference, North Carolina, USA 5-8th June 2008

Shane S (2009) Why encouraging more people to become entrepreneurs is bad public policy. *Small Bus Policy* 33(2):141–149

Sheetz M (2020) The US government is helping get cash to private space companies, replacing frozen venture capital. April 24. Available at: https://www.cnbc.com/2020/04/24/us-government-getting-cash-to-private-space-companies-replacing-venture-capital.html (accessed on: 8 August, 2021)

Startups Watch (2021a) Turkish Startup Ecosystem 2020. February 23. v3.2. Available at: Reports / Startups.watch; (accessed on: 14 July, 2021)

Startups Watch (2021b) Gaming Snapshot for Turkey. V0.2, June 22. Game Snapshot v0.2 (startups-watch-production.s3-eu-central-1.amazonaws.com) (accessed on: 15 July, 2021)

Startups Watch (2021c) Turkish Startup Ecosystem in Q2 2021. July 13. V1.0. Available at: Reports/Startups.watch; (accessed on: 14 July, 2021)

Startups Watch and Presidency of the Republic of Turkey Investment Office (SWTIO) (2020) The state of Turkish startup ecosystem. Available at: https://www.invest.gov.tr/ (accessed on: 20 July, 2021)

Tanrıkulu F, Ermis M (2021) Technology entrepreneurship and access to financial resources in Turkey. In Dincer H, Yulsel S (Eds.), *Management Strategies to Survive in a Competitive Environment: How to Improve Company Performance*, Cham: Springer, pp 107–120. https://doi.org/10.1007/978-3-030-72288-3_8

Teker S, Teker D (2016) Venture capital and business angels: Turkish case. *Procedia Soc Behav Sci* 235:630–637

Teknopark Istanbul IQ (2021) Turkey's startup ecosystem is growing. Issue 1, pp 62–65. Available at: https://www.tgbd.org.tr/content/upload/bulletins/documents/iq240221-20210316145205.pdf (accessed on 15 July, 2021)

World Economic Forum (2012) The Global Competitiveness Report 2012–2013. Available at: https://www3.weforum.org/docs/WEF_GlobalCompetitivenessReport_2012-13.pdf (accessed on 2 Feb, 2022)

Yazici S (2019) The analysis of Fintech ecosystem in Turkey. *J Bus Econ Financ* 8(4):188–197

Yin W, Moon HC, Lee YW (2019) The success factors of Korean global start-ups in the digital sectors through internationalization. *Int J Glob Bus* 14(1):42–53

Zoltan A, Szerb L, Autio E (2016) *Global Entrepreneurship and Development Index 2016*. Verlag: Springer

Web links

1. https://www.morganstanley.com/ideas/investing-in-space (accessed on: August 8, 2021).
2. https://www.weforum.org/agenda/2015/04/what-is-governments-role-in-sparking-innovation/ (accessed on: June 28, 2021).
3. The-Fintech-Times_Fintech-Middle-East-Africa-2021-Report-2.pdf (fintr.org) (accessed on: July 16, 2021).
4. https://data.tuik.gov.tr/Bulten/Index?p=Kucuk-ve-Orta-Buyuklukteki-Girisim-Istatistikleri-2019-37548 (accessed on: July 16, 2021).
5. https://www.oecd-ilibrary.org/sites/8d33927c-en/index.html?itemId=/content/component/8d33927c-en (accessed on: July 20, 2021).

6. https://data.tuik.gov.tr/Bulten/Index?p=Kucuk-ve-Orta-Buyuklukteki-Girisim-Istatistikleri-2019-37548 (accessed on: July 20, 2021).
7. https://data.worldbank.org/indicator/GB.XPD.RSDV.GD.ZS?locations=TR (accessed on: July 20, 2021).
8. Report: 20% of most downloaded mobile games in US developed by Turkish studios | Game World Observer (accessed on: July 16, 2021).
9. Turkey Mobile Gaming Statistics in 2021 (42matters.com) (accessed on: July 14, 2021).
10. https://www.businesswire.com/news/home/20210630005241/en/Turkey%E2%80%99s-Dream-Games-Raises-155-Million-with-a-1-Billion-Valuation-in-a-Series-B-Round-Led-by-Index-Ventures-and-Makers-Fund. https://techcrunch.com/2021/02/28/istanbuls-dream-games-snaps-up-50m-and-launches-its-first-game-the-puzzle-based-royal-match/ (accessed on: July 18, 2021).
11. https://investor.zynga.com/news-releases/news-release-details/zynga-acquires-leading-global-mobile-game-developer-gram-games;https://www.gram.gs/our-story.html (accessed on: July 18, 2021).
12. Turkish online retailer Hepsiburada raises $680 mln in U.S. IPO | Nasdaq; https://www.nasdaq.com/articles/turkeys-hepsiburada-valued-at-%243.6-bln-in-strong-nasdaq-debut-2021-07-01 (accessed on: July 14, 2021).
13. https://www.sec.gov/Archives/edgar/data/1850235/000104746921001156/a2243271zf-1.htm (accessed on: July 18, 2021).
14. https://www.retail-insight-network.com/comment/getir-grocery-delivery-expansion/. https://wintercapital.com/tpost/xvenaxrop1-winter-capital-partners-invests-in-deliv (published in: 09 Jun 2021, accessed on: August 10, 2021).
15. Alibaba-Backed Trendyol Seeks Over $1 Billion to Fund Growth (bloombergquint.com). https://www.bloomberg.com/news/articles/2021-07-29/trendyol-valuation-set-to-hit-16-5-billion-in-fundraising-round?s=03 (accessed on: July 14, 2021).
16. https://techcrunch.com/2011/07/22/turkish-private-shopping-site-trendyol-scores-a-big-round-from-kpcb-tiger-global/; https://www.sec.gov/Archives/edgar/data/1577552/000104746918005257/R11.htm (accessed on: July 14, 2021).
17. https://www.trendyol.com/resources/documents/Press_280618.pdf; https://ecommercenews.eu/ alibaba-raises-stake-in-trendyol/ (accessed on: July 14, 2021).
18. https://www.cmb.gov.tr/Sayfa/AltSayfa/96; KFS_Is_ve_Islem_Kurallari_Yonergesi.pdf (mkk.com.tr); https://www.cmb.gov.tr/Sayfa/Index/4/5/3; https://www.cmb.gov.tr/Sayfa/Index/1/7; https://www.cmb.gov.tr/Sayfa/Dosya/133; https://www.cmb.gov.tr/Sayfa/Dosya/137; https://www.cmb.gov. tr/Sayfa/Dosya/146 (accessed on: July 14, 2021).
19. https://www.ikv.org.tr/images/files/emre_sakizli_kitlesel_fonlama.pdf (accessed on: July 20, 2021).
20. https://www.spk.gov.tr/Sayfa/Dosya/1342 (accessed on: July 14, 2021).
21. https://en.hmb.gov.tr/duyuru/launch-of-the-regulation-on-business-angel-scheme (accessed on: July 14, 2021).
22. https://ms.hmb.gov.tr/uploads/2019/05/BKS-%C4%B0LERLEME-RAPORU-1.%C3%87eyrek. pdf (accessed on: July 14, 2021).
23. https://www.oecd-ilibrary.org/sites/8d33927c-en/index.html?itemId=/ content/componen t/8d339 27c-en (accessed on: August 13, 2021).

Section 3

Innovations in institutions, products, and processes

Best practices and policies

8 Deploying machine learning and big data to promote MSMEs' access to finance in Japan and its application to other countries

Megumi Sagara and Lan H. Nguyen

1 Introduction

1.1 MSMEs' access to finance

Improving micro-, small, and medium-sized enterprises' (MSMEs') access to funding is a challenge for every economy. Since the loan principal for MSMEs is relatively small, it is difficult for financial institutions to raise the cost of credit checking and to examine the business operations of MSMEs. Lenders mainly choose to lend only to companies that hold collateral, which is only a small fraction of MSMEs, leaving other MSMEs to struggle to find access to financing. To improve this access issue, it is essential to identify how to reduce the cost of credit checking and how MSMEs' business information transparency can be improved.

Recently, MSMEs have begun enjoying several innovative fund-raising opportunities. Traditionally, they obtained funding from financial institutions through credit lines or term loans. More recently, with numerous innovations in fintech, MSMEs have started borrowing from alternative sources, such as online lending, crowdfunding, social lending, and online factoring. Amid significant differences in services, speed, and fees, one aspect that traditional banking and alternative banking have in common is the approach they take toward assessing borrowers' creditworthiness: the lenders always want to know if the borrowers are capable of repaying on time. Unfortunately, MSME borrowers' data is often insufficient for lenders to undertake a correct and timely assessment. If a database of MSMEs' information is available, it would become the essential financial infrastructure for the economy as well as the MSME sector.

Given the constraints inherent in MSMEs' data, this chapter attempts to summarize available financial information and credit assessment methods for MSMEs in Japan and present an on-going project that is introducing Japan's practice to other countries. We have found that not only is financial data useful in credit assessment for MSMEs, but alternative data such as cash transactions data could also be valuable in improving financial clarity for this sector. Financial and alternative data, if available, could work together to provide both short-term and long-term assessments of the MSME's repayment capability.

DOI: 10.4324/9781003220220-12

We have also found that in tackling high-frequency big-volume alternative data, machine learning performs better than traditional logistic regression.

1.2 Data available for MSMEs' credit assessment

The data available for MSMEs can be categorized into structured and unstructured data. Structured data refers to asset value information, financial ratios, cash-flows, and supply chain information that are conventionally relied on to generate a credit score. Such data is abundant for larger corporations but still missing for small businesses. In addition to structured data, banks and lenders are exploring unstructured data to seek an enhanced approach to assessing small businesses' creditworthiness. Unstructured data, such as insights collected from social media platforms, digital footprints, e-commerce payment history, and psychometric data that evaluate a person's willingness to pay are increasingly being applied and tested for their predictive power of default risk (HKMA, 2018).

Given the large pool of data needed when building a financial infrastructure for MSMEs, the data that is qualified must be valid, available, and reliable. Validity refers to the ability to evaluate the business prospects of MSMEs. Data uncorrelated with creditworthiness or unsupported by theoretical studies can distort predictions if included in the model. Availability refers to how long data can be continuously collected. Short-term data and interrupted data are not suitable for long-period and stable analyses. Reliability refers to the credibility of the data source. Banks consider credible sources of borrowers' data as they are validated and screened by the banks.

1.3 Financial methods and data

MSMEs have traditionally raised funds from financial institutions through bank loans and have only recently started using other funding sources. With the numerous innovations in fintech, MSMEs can now borrow online from alternative sources, such as crowdfunding, social lending, and online factoring.

(1) Online lending
Online lending is a funding method that allows MSMEs to access financing directly from individual investors without traditional financial intermediaries. For these methods to work, in addition to the existence of service providers and service users, the technological developments and legal frameworks of a country are essential in determining how popular such lending channels may become. There are also significant differences in government policies and legal requirements, financial institutions' attitudes, domestic fintech market development stages, and the reactions of MSMEs which seek loans.

Most online platforms process loan screening within a single day and undertake the whole process virtually, providing borrowers an entirely different experience from traditional loans. The regulations under which online lenders operate are less tight when compared to banks; as such, they can innovate new lending set-ups (Claessens et al., 2018). Borrowers' data is processed promptly, but much of it entails personal information of the business owners and not the potential growth of the business. The availability of data and the existence of a company that provides the data is a major factor in determining whether the business qualifies for the loan.

Online transaction lending for e-commerce stores is mainly conducted by e-commerce platforms, such as Rakuten, Amazon, and PayPal, whose database of e-commerce sellers has been accumulating. Rakuten began offering a wide range of financial products in 2013, while Amazon lends through its seller-lending program. Creditworthiness is judged based on the firm's characteristics (such as the age of the owners, money deposits, etc.), transactions volume (such as sales and cash flow), and at times, the evaluation score (from buyers).

Online lending based on big cloud accounting data is becoming popular for individual and business loans. In Japan, cloud accounting companies, such as Free and Money Forward, have partnered with financial institutions to provide loans to companies. In the US, JP Morgan has partnered with OnDeck to use this system for its own small business loans.

Online lending based on cash transaction data is also being explored by financial institutions. CRD and Resona Bank jointly developed a model using bank account transaction data, including deposit and withdrawal data, to determine creditworthiness. The bank requires applicants only to have a bank account with the bank for a certain period of time to be eligible to apply for a loan.

(2) Crowdfunding

Crowdfunding is a system in which a company that wants to receive investment pays a fee to a platform company, posts its project on the site operated by the company, and solicits funds. There are two types of crowdfunding: purchase-based, in which investors receive the results of the project (products and services), and equity-based, in which investors receive monetary returns. The latter is the riskier option between the two and is similar to the purchase of high-risk financial products. It also requires the creation of strict rules, including a system for risk disclosure. Many countries have issued regulatory frameworks for crowdfunding to protect investors (Ehrentraud et al., 2020).

(3) Social lending

Social lending is a system to connect investors and borrowers of funds on the Internet without going through financial institutions and the loan screening process. Platform companies rank borrowers and set interest rates according to the rank, and investors decide where to invest based on the combination of risk and return. As the platform is independent of financial institutions, it is possible to considerably reduce operating as well as other costs that are reflected in interest rates, but it is essential to create a mechanism for assessing creditworthiness. Moreover, in Japan, platform companies need to be registered as money lenders and follow the regulatory framework set forth by the regulator to protect investors. In Japan, services are provided by SBI Social Lending and other service providers.

(4) Online factoring

Factoring itself is a mechanism used to convert a company's accounts receivables into cash to support cash flow, and this form of finance has existed for a long time. Online factoring is a system that uses account receivables data to determine a company's creditworthiness based on its business partners and past orders, and the entire process is completed online. In Japan, companies affiliated with SBI Holdings, OLTA, and Money Forward Kessai have partnered with regional banks to provide this service.

As mentioned above, the variety of financing methods available to MSMEs is increasing, and these methods will contribute to their access to funding. It will be essential to consider how the data collected can be used to assess the creditworthiness of companies. Even if other financing methods are introduced with the development of fintech, the problem of evaluating will remain for lenders, and for these frameworks to function well, a financial infrastructure in the form of an information database must be created for assessing creditworthiness.

This chapter will introduce new approaches to financing MSMEs based on traditional banking and in line with the Japanese experience. While using big data to enhance lending methods and protect conventional banking methods and using alternative data and machine learning within the bank will reduce lending costs, monitor expenses, and expand the scope of lending. We believe that making the two frameworks work well to enable financing that is appropriate to the stage of development of the enterprise will create a valuable reference for improving access to funding for MSMEs in other countries.

2 Establishment of financial information infrastructure in Japan

2.1 What is the Credit Risk Database (CRD)?

The CRD Association was established in March 2001 as the initiative of the Small and Medium Enterprise Agency (SMEA) with the government's supplementary budget for the 1999 fiscal year to develop a system and conduct trial operations for the establishment of CRD to contribute to the facilitation of SME finance and the advancement of credit risk management (Kuwahara et al., 2019).

CRD is a member organization with a current membership of 169, including all 51 credit guarantee corporations in Japan, governmental and private financial institutions of various types, and other rating agencies. The Financial

Services Agency and other government agencies, such as the Bank of Japan and the SMEA, also use CRD services as members.

The database consists of the anonymized financial data of MSMEs collected from member financial institutions. As collecting information from a reliable source is an important factor in building a financial information infrastructure, CRD opts to collect data from megabanks, regional banks, and established credit guarantee corporations. CRD has been collecting the financial statement data of MSMEs since its establishment in 2001 and has now started collecting alternative data, such as deposit account data of MSMEs, in addition to the existing scope of data.

Financial statement and bank deposit data meets all of the requirements for validity, availability, and reliability. Financial statement data, which represents the financial health of a company itself, obviously meets the validity requirements for evaluating the future of the business. Considering availability, banks and credit guarantee corporations require MSMEs to submit financial statements when obtaining a loan or guarantee and thereafter for the duration of the loan or guarantee. The reliability of the data is guaranteed by the fact that the financial statements have been reviewed by banks and guarantee associations.

Deposit data also has validity in predicting the business prospects of MSMEs. Checking the changes in the balance of the deposit data provides an idea of the cash flow situation of the company. In addition to the cash balance, deposit data also shows the frequency of deposits and withdrawals along with transaction purposes. The data shows how the business is managing its cash flow, which is a vital management skill in risk management. Considering availability, the data on deposits are standardized, digitized, and already archived in the banks' account systems. As the data is archived automatically in the bank's accounting system, it should retain its reliability given the well-established internal systems of banks.

Default-related information is essential for constructing scoring models to evaluate the creditworthiness of SMEs. Statistical regression can predict which companies have a higher chance of continuing operations by using a combination of financial statement or deposit data and default data.

2.2 Credit risk scoring and other services

The scoring model, one of the main services that CRD provides to its members, analyzes the management of an MSME from the financial statements of the business and assesses its creditworthiness. The model, which is similar to standard financial analyses, analyzes the financial indices generated from the financial statements for stability, profitability, efficiency, and growth potential. Financial indices that are significant in determining default are picked up and combined into a well-balanced model that returns the highest accuracy. Generally, scoring models use approximately 20–30 financial indices. Similarly, the CRD corporate model uses a comprehensive list of approximately 30 financial indices to provide a highly accurate model.

As a borrower can borrow from different banks, there are instances where the same borrower's data is collected from different sources, but it is challenging to identify such instances when the borrower's name is anonymous. CRD has a methodology for identifying these borrowers by using a few key bits of information, such as foundation year, postal code, and key financial data. If two observations share the same key information, CRD considers these to be the same borrowers and make further efforts to select one.

In addition to scoring services, CRD develops a range of services based on the base credit-scoring model, such as internal rating construction and validation services or management consulting services. For internal rating services, CRD assists member banks to validate their internal system by mapping their internal ratings to the scores generated by the CRD model. It then investigates the reasons for and suggests adjustments to any discrepancies in the evaluation. For banks that do not have an internal rating system, CRD assists in the construction of such a system by adding qualitative criteria and overhead costs to the base CRD credit scores. The service is tailored for each bank's loan portfolio and risk profile. For management consulting services, CRD develops a benchmarking system from which each SME would be able to see their position in comparison to their peers in the same industry or segment. Benchmarking in terms of revenue and cost structure for SMEs is a unique feature that provides valuable information for both banks and their clients.

2.3 Alternative data and Machine Learning (ML) method

Since 2017, CRD has been developing scoring models for traditional credit risk assessment using financial statement data as well as for credit risk assessment using alternative data. Traditional models using financial statement data are sufficiently accurate for financial institutions and credit guarantee corporations to use in their operations; however, as most MSMEs prepare financial statements annually and some, including those in developing countries, prepare insufficient financial statements, it is necessary to determine how to increase the frequency of the data available as well as to compensate for the lack in financial statements. Utilizing transaction data, which has high frequency and is already available in the bank database, can effectively solve both problems.

Transaction information in lending has already been explored by financial institutions, as monitoring the movement of cash inflow and outflow from a client's deposit account can reveal the status of their business. While it is possible to study the cash flow of large corporate clients, this is not the case for smaller ones. Complex and voluminous transaction data makes it almost impossible to track individual clients with human eyes and without expertise. On the contrary, machine learning is efficient, as it recognizes patterns in a complex and large volume of data. Each deposit and withdrawal in the deposit data has categorical codes that indicate the purpose of cash inflow or outflow (Table 8.1). These categorical codes are sorted by their transaction purposes to create groups and based on the number of transactions, transaction size, deposit balance, and volatility cross time

Table 8.1 Summary of Cash Categories in AI Model

Cash Inflows	Sales/Revenue	Cash transfer received in payment for services or goods
	Investing Activities	Cash transfer for dividends, proceeds from trust funds
	Financing Activities	Cash receipts for loans, bank borrowings
	Others	Cash receipts for other activities
Cash Outflows	Cost of goods and services	Cash transfer to suppliers
	Variable costs	Tax payments
	Fixed Costs	Utilities payments
	Financing Activities	Cash lending, loan repayment
	Investing Activities	Cash investment in trust funds
	Others	Cash payments for other activities
Cash Balance	Average cash balance	

in each group, and we analyze the cashflow patterns. We also identify patterns of irregular and unstable cashflows that can lead to default. The greater the number of patterns recognized, the more accurate and stable the model will be. In a scoring model based on machine learning, the number of information features for finding default patterns can be a few thousand. For example, from the movement of deposits, we find that a declining number of cash inflows or volatile cash inflow and outflow patterns are often associated with defaults in loan payments.

Generally, machine-learning modeling faces the problem of over-learning which means a loss of generality due to overly fitting the dataset on which the model is built. Cross-validation is the process used during model building to mitigate this problem, which divides the data into multiple groups and shuffles the groups as training data and validation data to create a general-purpose model that is not affected by the characteristics of any specific datasets.

Although bank deposit data is highly effective in evaluating the creditworthiness of borrowers, a database for analysis must be constructed before we can take full advantage of it. As the data is very frequently accumulated in the core banking system as several complex transactions and the data was not prepared for analysis, we work on it to a great extent from the database construction stage. Nonetheless, the performance of the resulting model was extremely high. The accuracy of the scoring model is generally examined by several validation methods. One of them is the accuracy ratio, which is evaluated between 0 and 1, with 1 being the highest. The accuracy of the scoring model using transaction data is higher than 0.7, regardless of whether the random forest or XG boost is used (Nguyen and Sagara, 2020). This level of accuracy is as high as that of traditional models based on financial statement data.

Eleven financial institutions considering participation in AI model projects have implemented proof of concept (PoC) to confirm their data fit and obtained good results. Moreover, different financial institutions have other borrowers' portfolios depending on their size and type of business. Regardless of these differences, the AI scoring model's assessment of creditworthiness based on deposit data appears to be reliable. In addition to models for corporations, we are also developing models for sole proprietors, who have difficulty separating their personal lives from their businesses, and models for apartment loan management, which is often run as an additional business. It is possible to assess the creditworthiness of a small-business borrower based on the movement of deposit with the same level of accuracy as for a corporation.

We plan to build a joint database in the future to regularly validate and improve the scoring model and to improve it based on environmental changes.

2.4 Two scoring models

In this section, we compare the traditional model based on financial statement data and the AI model based on deposit data to clarify each model's characteristics.

First of all, the two models use different data. The financial statement data used in various traditional models is not completely the same, but the main explanatory variables are low-frequency financial indexes derived from data such as assets, liabilities, equity, and their breakdowns. However, the data handled by the AI model is complex data with a large amount of information and much higher frequency. Among data used in the AI model are transaction data and accounting data accumulated in Japan through accounting applications such as Money Forward and Free.

Second, the outcome of the two model types also differs. Generally, traditional models calculate the probability of default within one year, but they can predict up to one to three years ahead while maintaining a certain degree of accuracy. However, AI models are better at short-term predictions and can predict the probability of default up to three to six months in advance.

Traditional credit scoring models are mainly applied as financial evaluation models within the bank's internal rating system. They are also used at the time of loan screening for evaluation the credit risk of a client.

For banks that already have internal rating systems, the CRD scoring model can be used as an external validation tool. The AI model can be used as a simple rating and screening standard by evaluating companies with no or insufficient financial statements. In addition, owing to the high frequency of data, it is effective to use this system for mid-term management. While all financial institutions have a system in place to manage their business periodically, a large number of counterparties and a wide variety of financial institution businesses have shown in recent years that it is necessary to prioritize them effectively. Risk management would be more sophisticated if highly accurate models built from high-frequency data could select counterparties for enhanced monitoring and issue early warnings when the risk of default is detected.

Combining the two models is effective when used complementarily and credit risk management takes advantage of their respective characteristics. The traditional model with financial data can be used in loan screening, while AI model transactions can be used for short-term monitoring. In Figure 8.1, the lightly shaded area indicates borrowers with both high-risk profile measured by internal rating model and high short-term risk measured by the AI model. These are the accounts that need attention or immediate consultation from the bank.

2.5 *Analyzing COVID-19's impact using CRD*

The impact of the COVID-19 pandemic after 2020 is shifting the entire world to a situation that has never before existed. Generally, when the economy begins to worsen, a more significant impact is felt by small companies that have been poorly managed or have a weak financial base. However, COVID-19 has not affected everything in the economy. The manifestation of these changes differs depending on the business sectors and other factors. The CRD, a database of financial statements representing the business operations of SMEs, makes it possible to objectively identify which regions, industries, and sizes of enterprise are affected by the crisis and to what extent.

As CRD data is the microdata of individual companies, it can be used for a wide range of analyses. It can be used not only to aggregate data to observe overall or category-specific trends, but also for analysis using simulations to determine what types of change will occur in the future based on the current situation of individual companies.

BOJ (2021) uses CRD data to simulate the impact of infectious diseases on the default rate of SMEs for financial conditions up to FY2023. In Japan, large-scale corporate support measures, including a variety of benefits and virtually interest-free loans, have been taken to counter the effects of COVID-19, and this has resulted in companies having plenty of cash on hand, which has reduced the

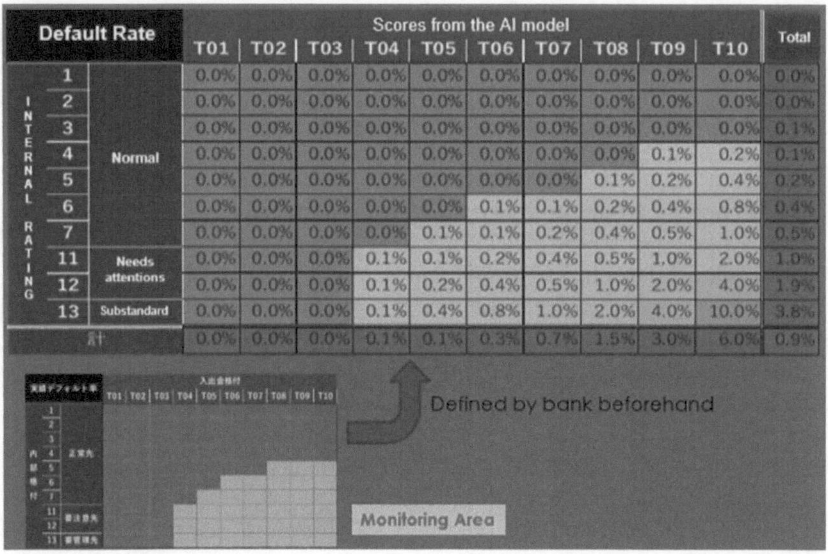

Default Rate			Scores from the AI model: T01	T02	T03	T04	T05	T06	T07	T08	T09	T10	Total
INTERNAL RATING	1	Normal	0.0%	0.0%	0.0%	0.0%	0.0%	0.0%	0.0%	0.0%	0.0%	0.0%	0.0%
	2		0.0%	0.0%	0.0%	0.0%	0.0%	0.0%	0.0%	0.0%	0.0%	0.0%	0.0%
	3		0.0%	0.0%	0.0%	0.0%	0.0%	0.0%	0.0%	0.0%	0.0%	0.0%	0.1%
	4		0.0%	0.0%	0.0%	0.0%	0.0%	0.0%	0.0%	0.0%	0.1%	0.2%	0.1%
	5		0.0%	0.0%	0.0%	0.0%	0.0%	0.0%	0.0%	0.1%	0.2%	0.4%	0.2%
	6		0.0%	0.0%	0.0%	0.0%	0.0%	0.1%	0.1%	0.2%	0.4%	0.8%	0.4%
	7		0.0%	0.0%	0.0%	0.0%	0.1%	0.1%	0.2%	0.4%	0.5%	1.0%	0.5%
	11	Needs attentions	0.0%	0.0%	0.0%	0.1%	0.1%	0.2%	0.4%	0.5%	1.0%	2.0%	1.0%
	12		0.0%	0.0%	0.0%	0.1%	0.2%	0.4%	0.5%	1.0%	2.0%	4.0%	1.9%
	13	Substandard	0.0%	0.0%	0.0%	0.1%	0.4%	0.8%	1.0%	2.0%	4.0%	10.0%	3.8%
計			0.0%	0.0%	0.0%	0.1%	0.1%	0.3%	0.7%	1.5%	3.0%	6.0%	0.9%

Figure 8.1 AI Model Used to Complement the Internal Rating Model (CRD Association).

default rate. This trend is true not only for borrowers with low credit risk, but also for those with high credit risk. The significant reduction in the shortage of cash reserves has resulted in a larger reduction in the default rate for borrowers with high credit risk. Simulations have also shown that the default rate will increase slightly in FY2023, when interest payments on the virtually interest-free loans begin, particularly in the face-to-face service sector, which was significantly affected by COVID-19. Similarly, CRD data can be used to confirm individual company trends in more detail, including companies that were more significantly affected by COVID-19, companies that benefited from government measures, and companies whose credit risks may worsen due to future economic trends.

The CRD data shows that the number of companies defaulting is low because of the various government measures taken against COVID-19. Some companies have seen a decrease in sales due to COVID-19. Conversely, they have simultaneously accumulated savings due to the subsidies. The government's measures will not last forever, and many companies will be forced to rebuild their business while this reprieve lasts. In terms of analysis, simulations are used to predict the future image of SMEs, but in the lending practices of financial institutions, it is desirable to use other data in addition to financial statement data to assess creditworthiness. While we believe that it is appropriate to base a company's basic baseline assessment on its financial statements, a 1-year update of information on the future outlook is only an inadequate forecast. We need data to be sensitive to changes and to sound the alarm about any growing uncertainty in the future. Previous analyses have shown the complementarity of the two models based on financial statements and deposit data, and the combination of reliably based assessments and more frequent monitoring not only work in normal times, but also under special circumstances, such as post-pandemic conditions.

3 JICA's technical cooperation project in the Philippines

3.1 Technical cooperation project's background

Efforts to build a database of SMEs, similar to Japan's CRD, and use it to assess their creditworthiness are underway in various countries.

In the Philippines, a project is currently in progress to establish CRD to improve access to financing for MSMEs; it is also an Official Development Assistance (ODA) project of Japan. Before this project, a feasibility study (FS) of CRD establishment was conducted by JICA with the cooperation of the three government-affiliated financial institutions in the Philippines, namely the Small Business Corporation, Development Bank of the Philippines, and Land Bank of the Philippines. Concerns about the challenging task of assessing the creditworthiness of MSMEs emerged in Japan before CRD and scoring models functioned as the financial infrastructure. Therefore, the feasibility of building up CRD in the Philippines was checked by CRD Business Support, a subsidiary of the CRD Association. This section summarizes the results of this feasibility study, while the detailed results are provided in JICA's final report (JICA, 2019).

To initiate this study, the terms of reference (TOR), which defines the purpose and content of the study, was approved in June 2016 by the Philippines Department of Finance (DOF), Bangko Sentral ng Pilipinas (BSP), Department of Trade and Industry (DTI), Securities and Exchange Commission (SEC), and the University of the Philippines (UPSS). Subsequently, "Minutes of Discussion on the Study for the Introduction of Credit Risk Database (CRD) in the Philippines" was signed by JICA and DOF, the Philippine counterpart of the study. DOF, BSP, DTI, SEC, and UPSS continued to work together as the working group members representing the Philippine side after the start of the study and providing comments and support for the study.

For the three government-affiliated banks to provide data for the survey, a request letter was issued by the DOF, the direct supervisory agency, to seek cooperation from each bank. Although the data was provided anonymously, a confidentiality agreement was signed with the cooperating banks before the actual collection of data.

- Feasibility study prior to technical cooperation
  For the study, a collection of a wide range of financial data is desirable, but most of the required data is not yet digitalized or ready to be shared. We asked the banks that have not digitized financial statements to centralize their paper-based financial statements at the headquarters, and we deployed encoding staff to input the data. For institutions that have partially digitalized their data, a dataset for analysis was created based on that data. For default data or loan performance data, we asked the bank to extract data from their system and arrange them into a pre-designed template.

- Dataset of the feasibility study
  The dataset in this study consisted of financial statement data (balance sheet, income statement), default-related data (monthly data corresponding to financial statement data), and non-financial data provided by the three Philippines' government-owned banks. The financial statements were dated from 2010 to 2016, and the associated default information was until 2017. The financial statement data was cleansed by checking for consistency and correcting the data, and ultimately, the data from 3,440 financial statements and 133 items of default data were used as the data set for analysis.

- Analytical method
  Following previous studies such as Yoshino and Taghizadeh-Hesary (2015), the financial indices representing the business's profitability, liquidity, efficiency, and business growth potential were created and tested for correlation with default.
  (i) Logit single regression
  A single logit regression analysis was used to identify financial indices that are significant for default discrimination. Continuous variables, categorical variables, and their transformations were used in the

regression. The transformed version of the data included logarithmization, neglog, and 3-, 5-, and 10-rank transformations.

(ii) Logit multiple regression

The significant variables in the single logit regression analysis were combined and modeled using multiple logit regression analysis.

(iii) Scoring trial

A scoring trial was conducted in which data from the Philippines was fed into a model built from data from Japan to check the accuracy of the model.

- Results of the feasibility study

As a result of logit single regression, 12 continuous variables and 35 discretized variables, all of which had a backing theory with reasonable signs, were identified as significant at the 5% significance level. The

As a relatively large number of variables were found to be significant in the logit single regression, several combinations of these variables are possible, and we selected a balanced combination of variables with high overall accuracy. The accuracy of the AR was 0.579 for the continuous variables and 0.612 for the discretized variables. Considering that most of the data in this dataset came from sole proprietors, this AR value is relatively high.

Japan's CRD model was used to conduct a scoring trial of the Philippines data set. The accuracy of the CRD model for this data set, in terms of AR, was 0.248, which is lower than the results of the model built from the data set for analysis. The lower results can be explained by the differences in variables that effectively identified defaults for the Philippines' and Japanese borrowers.

This study shows that it is necessary to build a scoring model specific for the Philippines and has led to the current technical cooperation project.

3.2 *Outline of the technical cooperation project*

- Background of the project

After the feasibility study confirmed the possibility of constructing a database of financial statements and developing a scoring model based on the database in the Philippines, the Philippines DOF and BSP requested the implementation of a technical cooperation project for the establishment and trial operation of the CRD so as to enable the future full-scale introduction of the CRD and establishment of an operational entity. As the implementing agency of ODA, JICA, together with the Ministry of Foreign Affairs of Japan and other relevant ministries, considered whether or not to adopt a project based on a request from the counterpart country. A comprehensive preliminary evaluation of the project was conducted based on the five evaluation items of "appropriateness, effectiveness, efficiency, impact, and sustainability."

According to the published preliminary assessment sheet (in Japanese only), JICA formed the following perceptions on the current status and challenges of the Philippines' financial sector development. The Philippines' government is supporting the development of small- and medium-sized enterprises (SMEs) as the engine of economic growth through "The Micro, Small, and Medium Enterprise Development Plan 2017–2022" (The Plan). However, due to various constraints and challenges, they have not yet been able to constitute the corporate layer that supports a multilayered industrial structure.

The vision of the Plan is "more globally competitive MSMEs that are regionally integrated, resilient, sustainable, and innovative, thereby performing as key drivers of inclusive Philippine economic growth." The Plan has three focus areas: business environment, business capacity, and business opportunities, and articulates improved access to financing for MSMEs with respect to the business environment in the focus areas (MSME Development Council, 2017). It further provides reasons why the target has not been met, although the law required financial institutions to lend 10% of their total lending to the MSME sector as of 2017. Financial institutions generally prioritize lending to larger firms with higher gain, lower credit risk, higher repayment rates, and perceived availability of collateral, while the traditional financial institutions' lending to MSMEs is limited by the lack of credit information.

JICA believes that introducing a CRD based on Japanese experience positions this project to contribute to strengthening credit risk management at financial institutions and solving the problems of SME financing.

The evaluation of JICA also found that JICA's contribution to the achievement of the Sustainable Development Goals (SDGs) is consistent with "Goal 8: Promote sustained, inclusive, and sustainable economic growth, full and productive employment, and decent work for all" and "Goal 9: Build resilient infrastructure, promote inclusive and sustainable industrialization, and foster innovation."

The project is also part of JICA's assistance to the Philippines' financial sector under its business strategy "Securing the Foundations and Drivers of Economic Growth," which aims to contribute to the establishment of financial institutions and systems that support economic activities in the Philippines. The following studies were undertaken prior to this project in the Philippines: "Information Collection and Verification Study on the Development of a Credit Risk Information Database," "Basic Information Collection and Verification Study on the Development of a Bond Market," and "Information Collection and Verification Study for Capacity Building on the Introduction of XBRL (Feasibility Study on Financial Information Systems)."

As a result of the evaluation, a strong need to support implementation of the project was identified, and the record of discussions (R/D) on the project activities and necessary measures was signed between JICA and Bangko Sentral ng Pilipinas (BSP) in February 2020. Furthermore, the "Project for Establishment of Credit Risk Database (CRD) in the Philippines" started as a technical cooperation (TC) project by the Japanese Official Development Assistance (ODA) in April 2020.

- Concept of the project

  The overall goal of this project is that a permanent CRD operation focused on promoting SMEs and business lending and strengthening the Philippines' financial sector will be established. The more specific project purpose is that a scoring model for SMEs' methodology for risk-based lending will be established with pilot operations and sustainable future planning, complementing the methodology currently used by the Philippines' financial institutions. There are four expected outputs from the project. The first is that a CRD system (both the database and statistical scoring model) with a sufficient accuracy ratio is built based on sufficient numbers and items of data from the Philippines' financial institutions. The second is that the CRD scoring service (objective and numerical risk evaluation information) is provided with a probability of default, and its preliminary service structure is created. The third is that the relevant staff acquires the necessary knowledge and technological skill on the operation/validation of the CRD system, including the scoring service. Finally, a concrete framework for a sustainable operation of CRD is prepared and discussed for its realization. It is expected that these outputs will be obtained during the three-year period of the project.

  A project implementation unit (PIU) has been established within the BSP, headed by a project director appointed from among the BSP staff, and consisting of a project manager, two data management specialists, and support staff. The CRD Business Support and the CRD Association are involved in this project as an expert team and are working with PIU staff to run the project. Considering Output 3 on technology transfer, the PIU staff is being prepared through an e-learning system, workshops, and on-the-job training through practical work. In addition, a joint coordinating committee has been established to coordinate among the organizations of the BSP, the Department of Finance, other relevant Philippines' ministries and agencies, and JICA and to approve, review, monitor, and evaluate the project. Various types of businesses, such as Thrift Bank, Universal and Commercial Bank, and Rural Bank, have been cooperating in providing data for this project.

- Challenges of the project

  Similar to the feasibility study, the study started with the establishment of a database for the analysis of financial statements, and as for this TC project, the SMEs' financial statements are not digitized in the system. Financial statements are either stored in paper-based folders at each branch office in the Philippines or are saved as spreadsheets with one sheet per borrower. To build a database for scoring model construction, we have asked the headquarters to centralize the PDF files of the financial statements and have arranged encoding staff in the Philippines to work on digitization in the bank or at the PIU office in BSP. Financial statements, which represent the financial position of a company are valuable, because they contain abundant information, and their value increases dramatically when they are digitized and made available for analysis. Paper-based or Excel sheet management is limited in its ability to identify trends, compare companies, or calculate the probability of a company's default. After the collection of encoded data, the project then proceeds to the model building and validation phase.

The technical corporation project started in a context where COVID-19 was globally widespread. In a standard technical cooperation project, Japanese experts go to the counterpart country and work there. In this project, Japan and the Philippines are physically separated by 3,000 kilometers. However, by improving the cloud and remote environments, we are implementing operations that are not blocked by distance. Data collected from financial institutions is stored in a database built on a cloud platform. Japanese experts and PIU staff can remotely share the PIU office set up in the BSP while maintaining, managing, and analyzing the data. These mechanisms can be carried out even in the environment of COVID-19 without the physical movement of people.

- Anticipations

  Dr. Benjamin E Diokno, Governor of Bangko Sentral ng Pilipinas (BSP, the central bank of the Philippines), expressed the expectations about establishing CRD at the virtual launch of the CRD project, December 9, 2020. He expressed that the project is a tangible step in building a sustainable financing ecosystem for SMEs.

  The first joint coordinating committee meeting of the TC project was held in March 2021 via web conference under the prevalence of COVID-19 and was attended by JCC members from BSP, JICA, DOF, SEC, as well as observers from Bankers Association, Chamber of Thrift banks, Rural Bankers Association, University of the Philippines, and Japanese Embassy. A lively exchange of opinions took place, indicating the high level of interest among the participants.

4 Conclusion and policy recommendations

In addition to traditional banking, we have introduced the use of big data and new methods, such as AI, used to improve the credit risk management framework.

In Japan, the traditional approach is to use balance sheet and income statement data to provide financial institutions with highly accurate scoring models. However, from the experience of building a Japanese scoring model, even if there is only income statement information, the model's accuracy can be significantly improved by incorporating alternative data such as transaction data. For countries in which MSMEs do not have a balance sheet, financial institutions can still use transaction data in their system to build a model with reasonably high accuracy to predict MSMEs' default using machine learning analysis. Model building using machine learning is described in more detail by Nguyen and Sagara (2020).

Countries may consider constructing a financial infrastructure of CRD and big data (financial statements data) to make traditional banking more robust. They can also apply machine learning and big data (alternative deposit data) to reduce lending and monitoring costs. Financial institutions can make the above two big data financial infrastructures work well together and establish a framework for assessment according to the development stage of the enterprise. When a company is small, healthy cash flow (working capital) is an important issue. Deposit data can represent well the movement of funds in the execution of a business, and machine learning is able to evaluate large and complex movements. As a company develops, larger loans for capital investment become necessary, and financial statements and traditional scoring models will be needed for a more comprehensive analysis of business stability, profitability, efficiency, and growth potential. We hope that the development of a database which satisfies validity, availability, and reliability and a scoring model based on such a database will be a solution for countries with high barriers for MSMEs to access funding, even though MSMEs are the backbone of the economy.

Our current experience in the Philippines shows that the understanding and involvement of the financial sector supervisory agency are critical in building a big database across banks. The BSP has been encouraging as well as reassuring participating banks of the necessity of the CRD and its services. It has also participated in streamlining the process of data collection and leading discussions on building a self-sustaining operating body that houses the CRD in the future. The permanent operating body is expected not only to maintain the voluminous database and its credit-scoring model but also to provide other necessary services for the financial sectors. The operation of CRD is considered a part of its national strategy for financial inclusion, and to date, the enthusiastic participation of BSP in the project has reflected its determination in working toward enhancing financial access for MSMEs.

References

Bank of Japan (BOJ) (2021) Kinyu System Report for October 2021

Claessens S, Frost J, Turner G, Zhu F (2018) Fintech credit markets around the world: Size, drivers and policy issues. *BIS Quarterly Review*, September

Ehrentraud J, Ocampo DG, Vega CQ (2020) Regulating fintech financing: Digital banks and fintech platform. FSI Insights No. 27. Bank for International Settlements

Hong Kong Monetary Authority (HKMA) (2018) Alternative credit scoring. White Paper. ASTRI

Japan International Cooperation Agency (JICA) (2019) The study for the introduction of credit risk database (CRD) in the Philippines: Final report. Japan Economic Research Institute Inc

Kuwahara S, Yoshino N, Sagara M, Taghizadeh-Hesary F (2019) Establishment of the credit risk database: Concrete use to evaluate the creditworthiness of SMEs. ADBI Working Paper 924

Micro, Small and Medium Enterprise Development Council (2017) Micro, Small and Medium Enterprise Development Plan 2017–2022

Nguyen LH, Sagara M (2020) Credit Risk Database (CRD) for SME financial inclusion. ADBI Working Paper Series

Yoshino N, Taghizadeh-Hesary F (2015) Analysis of credit ratings for small and medium-sized enterprises: Evidence from Asia. *Asian Development Review* 32(2):18–37

9 National Credit Bureau

An institutional financial innovation boosting SME financing in Thailand

Phadet Charoensivakorn

1 Introduction

Today, the importance of SMEs cannot be overlooked, because they make a significant contribution to GDP and will affect the economics of all countries, including Thailand. SMEs generate employment in countries, help investments grow, and stimulate the production of goods and services, which also supports spending in the economy and benefits all sectors in a country. Most of the SMEs in Thailand are not in the technology sector in the market. Many companies in Thailand are agricultural businesses where SMEs sell agricultural products, and it is very difficult for them to get loans from financial institutions. Another group of SMEs comprises the self-employed. This group is quite large, and they need funding to grow their businesses, but it is also very hard for them to obtain funding from financial institutions. Thai SMEs contributed 45% to national GDP in 2018. The new structure of SMEs is shown in Figure 9.1 (OSMEP, 2019), so we should support SMEs to help them grow each year. Unfortunately, SMEs cannot foreseeably grow in terms of systematic economic growth, because they face a serious pain point that stops these businesses from growing, and that is the difficulty they face in accessing financing. This pain point is happening not only in Thailand, but in other countries as well. Why can't SMEs access financing through financial institutions? If we look into the financing difficulties SMEs face, we will see that many issues are related to problems such as asymmetric information, the tools and technology used by lenders, collateral limitations, and the credit bureau law. Asymmetric information can happen when the credit information or some other sources of information are insufficient for lenders to make a credit decision. As regards lenders' tools and technology, we are now in the information age, and that data can be the new oil cannot be denied. Data can be made more powerful so as to be utilized very effectively. Similarly for financial institutions, information is powerful and can bring about a somewhat better understanding of the behavior of SMEs. Many financial institutions in other countries have long considered using this kind of information in their credit decision processes, but such utilization has only recently begun in Thailand. The last point related to the difficulties of SMEs to access finance is the law. Many laws address the use of information in the credit decision process, or tools such as the Credit

DOI: 10.4324/9781003220220-13

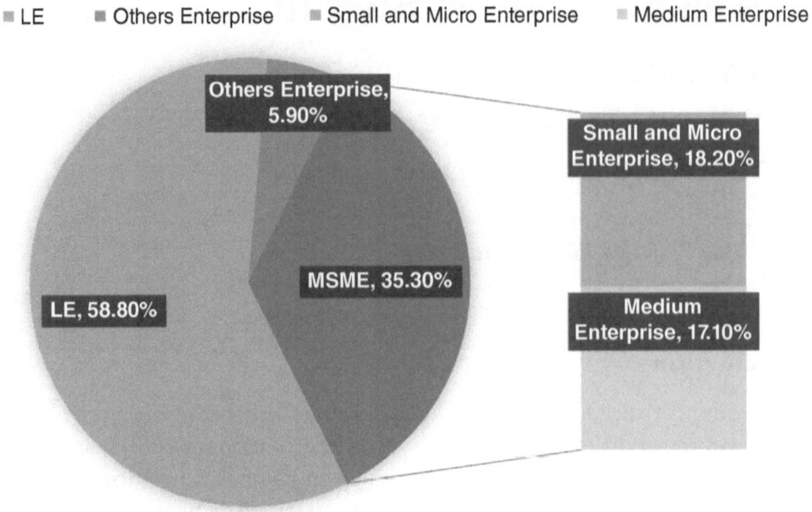

Figure 9.1 Structure of GDP in 2019 by Enterprise Size of SMEs.

Bureau Business Act, the Telco laws, the principal laws of sharing information, etc. Those laws need to be considered in order to make some resolutions to improve SMEs' access to financing. The credit bureau can help relieve the SME pain points in accessing funding by using credit information to enhance the credit underwriting process, but this in itself is not enough. At present, the credit bureau can only keep and provide credit information, which limits support for some SMEs that already have a financial history. Newcomer SMEs may also be limited or may never have had a credit history, a lack resulting in the absence of trust from financial institutions, and so they will face more difficulty in obtaining funding from them. Today, the credit bureau has changed the traditional trade process to an automated digital process, providing a tool to help SME finance approval and ultimately introduce alternative data to help lenders make credit decisions more efficiently but with the same limited data from the financial side. To change the SME pain points, it is necessary to change the law, which is the root cause of the pain points, especially the Credit Bureau Business Act. This act is very limited in many aspects, such as the financial institution type for credit bureau membership, the source of data for the credit bureau to process, and the tools and value added to products and services of the credit bureau. There are also other laws that need to be considered, such as data sharing and data utilization across the industry.

2 The background and history of credit bureaus in Thailand

The concept of establishing a credit data center was born in 1961, when the Thai Banker's Association discussed the idea with the Bank of Thailand, suggesting that there should be a center for the exchange of client data among commercial banks to reduce the risk of giving loans and to prevent the damages that may be incurred by commercial banks. The Bank of Thailand was asked to be the center to gather all the data, and it duly started the central credit registration in 1964, whereupon it was continuously developed until 1995, as the government through the Ministry of Finance, the Bank of Thailand, and the Securities and Exchange Commission, Thailand, collaborated to create a plan of financial system development. It was about establishing the credit data center on the proportion of financial organizations supporting development of the financial system. A committee was established in 1995 to study and seek a suitable approach to achieving the objective of establishing the credit data center. The committee acted until an agreement of joint venture with a company dealing with credit data in the United States was almost signed in 1996, when unfortunately an economic crisis gripped Thailand (the 1997 Asian Financial Crisis) (Wikipedia, August 2021), and many financial institutes were shut down. The resulting economic crisis became severe enough to obstruct the establishment of the credit data center (Figure 9.2). In 1998, the Minister of Finance supported the policy to establish the credit data center to be used to analyze loans and reduce the bad debt burden of financial institutions, which was a significant and urgent problem for financial institutions at the time. In July 1998, Dr. Pisit Lee-arthum, Deputy Minister of Finance, who controlled and monitored the Government Housing Bank (GHB), ordered the GHB to be the main office to establish the credit data center. Meanwhile, the Bank of Thailand proclaimed a policy for the Thai Banker's Association to quickly establish the credit data center. The Thai Banker's Association set up a team to complete the task afterwards. The establishment of the credit data center was divided into two sections, one set up by the GHB that established the Thai Credit Bureau Co., Ltd., and one being the Bank of Thailand together with the Thai Banker's Association that established Central Information Services Co., Ltd. Both companies were established with the same objective, i.e. being the center to gather clients' data to help reduce the risk and increase the efficiency of giving loans and preventing bad debt or non-performing loan problems in the economic system.

Central Information Services Co., Ltd., established by the Bank of Thailand and the Thai Banker's Association, was registered as a company on September 22, 1999, with the registered capital of 26 million baht, and whose shareholders were 13 Thai commercial banks, all members of the Thai Banker's Association. This company serves as a center for gathering loan data from financial institution members. It offers both consumer credit data and commercial credit data as a source of data for financial institutions to use when analyzing loans. Later in 2000, its two credit data reporting systems were developed: (1) Consumer Credit Reporting System developed by Trans Union International Co., Ltd., one of the world's leading credit data service companies, and (2) Commercial Credit Reporting System developed by Dun & Bradstreet Co., Ltd., one of the oldest and most famous commercial credit data service companies. Both system development companies are important allies in developing the system and augmenting the credit data service potential of Central Information Services Co., Ltd. Hence, to cooperate closely, continuously, and for a long time, in 2000 Central Information Services Co., Ltd. signed a joint venture contract with both Trans Union International Co., Ltd. and Dun & Bradstreet Co., Ltd. (through Business Online PCL, a joint venture company in Thailand). The capital was increased to 156 million baht, and the company name was changed to Central Credit Information Services Co., Ltd. on December 6, 2000. Nevertheless, the 13 commercial banks still hold equal shares totaling 50% of the whole, and TransUnion Inc. and Business Online PCL each hold 25% of the shares. The capital was again increased to 186 million baht with the same shareholding proportions.

In 2005, Central Credit Information Services Co., Ltd. merged with another credit data company, Thai Credit Bureau Co., Ltd. Central Credit Information Services Co., Ltd. had bought all the shares of Thai Credit Bureau Co., Ltd. and increased the capital to 250 million baht. The company name was changed to National Credit Bureau Co., Ltd. on May 19, 2005, and the shareholders included the original shareholders of Thai Credit Bureau Co., Ltd. and banks as well as government financial institutes. After the merger, shareholder portions consisted of Thai commercial banks holding the same portion of shares totaling 24.5%, while Business Online PCL and TransUnion Inc. held the same portions of 12.25% totaling 24.50%. The total proportion of shares held by shareholders of the former Central Credit Information Services Co., Ltd. amounted to 49%. The shareholders of Thailand Credit Data Co., Ltd. held 30%, i.e. GHB and PCC Capital Co., Ltd. holding 15% each. The remainder, amounting to 21%, were held by government financial institutes including Government Savings Bank, Dhipaya Insurance PCL, and the Small and Medium Enterprise Development Bank of Thailand with 9%, 6%, and 6%, respectively.

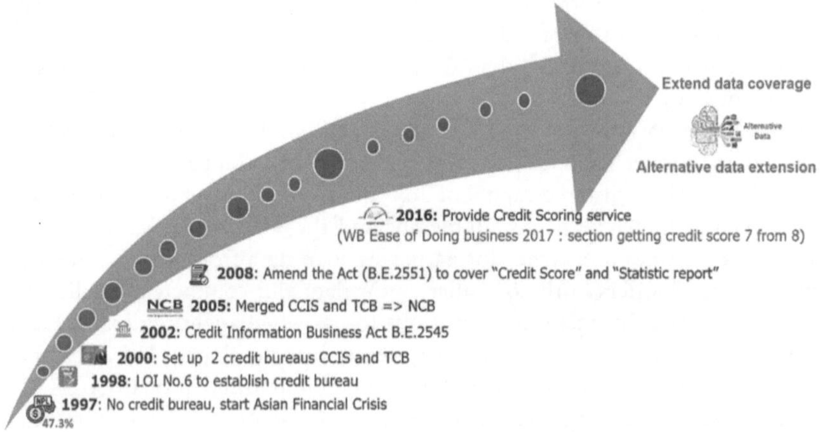

Figure 9.2 History of Credit Bureaus in Thailand.

3 The role of the National Credit Bureau (NCB) in the SMEs ecosystem

One of the main duties of the NCB is credit information processing as stated by the Credit Information Business Act B.E. 2545, which holds that "the Credit Information Company shall conduct information processing from information obtainable from the Member or from reliable Sources of Information, in accordance with the rules, procedures, and conditions as prescribed by the Committee" (Credit Information Business Act B.E. 2545). Therefore, the role of the NCB in the credit information process operation begins from collecting the credit data from members, processing the data to the credit information database, and disclosing credit information to members under the rules for disclosure consent. Credit data is submitted by members on a monthly basis, and the NCB processes the credit data into the credit information database on a daily basis. The law requires consent to access the credit information; only NCB members can gain access and only for loan request purposes.

In addition to credit information processing, the NCB also has other roles in financial literacy education for consumers. The NCB believes that financial literacy is fundamental for good credit for the consumer and, therefore, is working with the Bank of Thailand, the Thai Credit Guarantee Company, and other public education sector bodies to provide customers with knowledge of good credit behavior, how to create smart debt, and so forth. The following are the NCB's operations under the Credit Bureau Business Act.

3.1 Who can be a member of a credit bureau?

The law states that only those financial institutions described by the law can be members of the credit bureau; the financial institutions which are defined in the Act are

> commercial banks, finance companies, securities companies, credit financier companies, non-life insurance companies, life insurance companies, juristic persons who provide credit card services, juristic persons established under specific legislation to operate financial activities and services, and juristic persons who grant credit in the ordinary course of business described by the Committee
>
> (Credit Information Business Act B.E. 2545 Section #3)

The new businesses announced by the committee were hire purchase and leasing, the Saving Cooperative, Thai Credit Guarantee, and other financial institutions which can be announced in the future. This law, Section #3, hinders the Credit Bureau from accepting other types of members, for example, fintech companies or peer-to-peer lending firms. At present, the NCB has 110 members which are classified by industry such as commercial banks, special finance institutions (SFI), consumer finance, hire purchase, etc. (Figure 9.3).

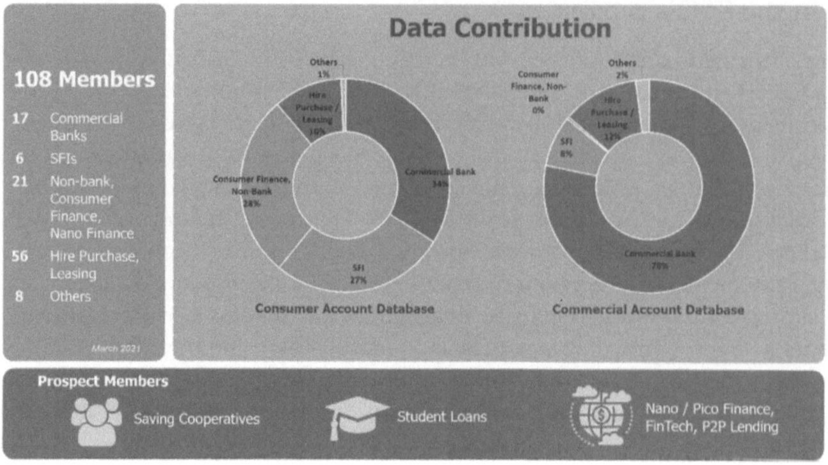

Figure 9.3 Member Type and Credit Data Contribution.

To become an NCB member is not mandatory but voluntary. Therefore, members can choose whether or not to become an NCB member. Members must pay a membership fee, which is the same for members of all sizes. There is no entrance fee for NCB membership.

3.2 How does the NCB collect the data?

The law only allows the NCB to collect two types of data, i.e., credit information (Credit Information Business Act, Section #3) and statistical data; in both cases, there are restrictions upon access and retention periods imposed by law. The credit information that the NCB collects is submitted by members and of two types: consumer credit information and commercial credit information. It is the duty of the members, by law (Credit Information Business Act B.E. 2545, Chapter III), to submit the credit information to the credit bureau (NCB) on a regular basis and provide updates when there are changes. The frequency of submission of data depends upon an agreement between the NCB and the member. At present, members submit credit information to the credit bureau on a monthly basis, so the credit bureau can update the information in the credit information database. The law allows the NCB to keep the credit information history for up to three years as the retention period. NCB members can access the credit information only with consumer consent. The NCB also collects another type of data which has no attached identity, known as statistical data according to the statistical data processing data law. The law allows the NCB to collect the statistical data (no identity) with no limit on the retention period, but there are limits to the entity and purposes when accessing the statistical data. The entities who can access the statistical data are the members of the NCB, government agencies or state enterprises, and research companies who access the data for the purpose of financial feasibility only and it is not possible to make a profit from the data.

The data to be collected by the NCB is limited to credit information only. This is a major pain point in this law, because there is other information that the NCB could collect to expand data coverage, and members could assess other aspects of borrowers' creditworthiness. Other types of data are alternative, such as telco and utilities data. Credit bureaus in other countries already collect such data, and Cambodian law was recently amended to allow them to collect alternative data (Cambodia Monthly Legal Update, July 2020), which will be beneficial for members, as it can help them understand consumer credit behavior better than in the past, allowing them to control a better NPL to their portfolio. A sample of the structure of the submission data of consumer and commercial credit data for the general credit bureau is shown in Appendix 1–2 (World Bank, 2019).

3.3 How the NCB analyzes the data

As the Credit Information Business Act allows the NCB to collect only two types of data as mentioned in the previous section, the NCB cannot analyze the credit information. It can, however, analyze the data through a statistical approach, because access to the credit information requires consent along with an objective from the loan request from the consumer and a credit review from the lender only. The statistical data law allows the NCB to make statistical reports, and therefore we utilize the statistical data for the crisis study and tracking the historical record of the financial industry with a crisis involved. At present, the NCB is tracking an issue related to the trend of household debt crisis in Thailand, and it provides early warning signs of debt status to the public and its members through MIS statistical reports. Some other entities from government agencies or state enterprises see the benefit of NCB statistical data, and they want to use it to study the effects and impact of the financial situation in Thailand. The problem of household debt in relation to GDP started in 2013 and continues to the present, with the percentage of household debt in terms of GDP increasing to 90%. Therefore, the Bank of Thailand studies the issue of household debt using the NCB statistical data. In 2018, the Bank of Thailand wanted to control the issue on the basis of a study of consumer behavior. It issued a policy to control the increase in household debt using measures such as a credit card control policy and LTV policy for home mortgages. The latest study was from a research company wanting to use NCB data to conduct a feasibility study concerning the impact of crisis or the policy issued to address the crisis, such as the debt moratorium relief program for the COVID-19 pandemic outbreak impact. A sample of the statistical report analyzed by the NCB shows the sample data analyzed by the NCB whereby the NCB brought the statistical information from new open accounts, 90 day+ delinquency accounts, new loan enquiries, and credit review enquiries to find a relationship between the percentage increase in household debt and the GDP on a quarterly basis. The results showed that during the increasing household debt crisis, financial institutions made more credit review inquiries instead of new loan inquiries, which reflected a smaller number of new accounts opening during the crisis.

The statistical data of the NCB is robust and not only allows the NCB to understand the micro-statistical data view, but also helps the NCB analyze the effects and implications of the micro-statistical data in terms of the macroeconomic situation, especially during the crisis of household debt. Imagine if the NCB statistical data could be used along with another source of data to provide more valuable analysis. For example, it might be possible to study the relationship between consumer debt behavior and their day-to-day behavior data. The sample of data connected to utilities can describe the utilization of water and electricity of SMEs in a particular area from which a loan is requested. The implications here suggest this information can be used to prevent fraud by the SMEs. Another source is trade finance, which can benefit SME supply chain funding through obtaining financing for their working capital to keep the company running.

One critical consideration when data is used for analysis is the privacy of that data. It is necessary to ensure there is a proper methodology to prevent the release of the identity of individuals whose data is accessed. The most common methodology in use is encryption to depersonalize the data, whereby the encryption key can be employed to link the data sources together with the NCB statistical data. This can support data portability while maintaining the data privacy standard.

3.4 Finance projection of the credit bureau in revenue and cost

Forecasting the credit bureau's revenue and costs is a critical task for the credit bureau. There are many factors involved in this forecasting, such as market status, data contributors, technology and security investment, etc. Similar to other credit bureaus, the NCB also projects the financing from revenue and costs as follows.

3.4.1 Revenue projection

The main revenue of the credit bureau comes from the number of credit reports and other value added services sold to members and consumers. Members request credit reports for lending and risk management purposes by law, and consumers request credit reports for their rights also defined by the law. Therefore, the pricing of credit reporting is very sensitive to the demand, and it affects the lender's operational costs. Therefore, the NCB needs to be careful with this sensitive pricing for products and services for members for whom pricing normally depends on the purposes of lending, volume commitment, and frequency of use. However, for credit report requests from consumers, the law sets a ceiling price for the consumer credit report, and the NCB cannot sell reports for higher than the ceiling price. These are the two main revenue factors for the NCB, and the other factors are membership fees and value-added products and services.

The NCB can do little about the products and services, because the law is very restrictive, and all products and services need approval from the regulator.

3.4.2 Cost projection

Cost projection factors also depend on the operational, technology, and security infrastructure investment along with the legal and compliance implications, audit services, and the products and services of the credit bureau. Those factors are correlated with each other. For example, if we want fancy and sophisticated products and services, the costs of other products and services will rise and, through loyalty fee sharing, will affect the owner of the product as well. NCB costs, for example, are credit operation set-up which needs to comply with the law, technology, and security infrastructure investment costs to ensure trust and address threats to protect stakeholders, and audit costs which are associated with those factor costs. Table 9.1 illustrates the hypothetical protection of a profit and loss statement (World Bank, 2019) for any credit bureau in the world.

Table 9.1 The Hypothetical Protection of Revenue and Cost

	Year 1	*Year 2*	*Year 3*	*Year 4*	*Year 5*
Total revenue (in USD)	0	500,000	1,000,000	1,750,000	2,625,000
% change in revenue	0		100	75	50
Cost					
Operating cost					
Labor	315,000	346,500	450,450	585,585	761,261
Rent	50,000	52,500	55,125	57,881	60,755
Utilities	1,500	1,800	2,160	2,592	3,110
Office equipment, supplies	7,000	8,000	8,000	8,000	8,000
Telecommunications	14,400	17,280	20,736	24,883	29,860
Audit, legal and other fees	12,000	12,000	12,000	12,000	12,000
Insurance	13,000	13,000	13,000	13,000	13,000
External data, marketing	20,000	25,000	30,000	37,500	46,250
Total operating costs	4,329,000	476,080	591,471	741,441	934,256
% of total cost	52	55	54	53	53
Fixed costs					
Rent, furniture, other fixed costs	20,000	20,000	20,000	20,000	20,000
System hardware and software	75,000	75,000	75,000	75,000	75,000
Technology platform	300,000	300,000	400,000	550,000	725,000
% of total cost	36	34	37	40	41
total fixed cost	395,000	395,000	495,000	645,000	820,000
Total cost ($)	827,900	871,080	1,086,471	1,386,441	1,754,256
% change in cost		5	25	28	27
Net income before interest & taxes ($)	(827,900)	(371,080)	(86,471)	363,559	870,744
Tax	0	0	0	109,068	261,223
Net income after taxes ($)	(827,900)	(371,080)	(86,471)	254,491	609,521

Source: FC.

4 How does the NCB maintain secrecy and protection?

The most important issue for all credit bureaus globally is data protection, and the NCB is no exception. The NCB collects credit information which belongs to the consumer, so the NCB needs to ensure the data is kept properly with confidentiality and proper access by authorized persons within the purpose of the law. Therefore, the NCB seeks the best security standards in the world to protect the critical credit information and ensure the data is accessed properly. The best security standard that most credit bureaus choose to implement to protect the security of data is the ISO27001 standard (ISO/IEC 27001). This is the international information security standard which helps the NCB prove that there is a proper system in place to manage the security of the credit information of members and stakeholders and, moreover, to generate trust in the security and data protection for their benefit. In the NCB, the credit information is classified as highly confidential information, according to the information security management policy, and its implementation is applicable in all NCB operations. The NCB does not leave any gap for any unauthorized employees or unpermitted persons to access the credit information database without permission under the law and the NCB information security policy. It has certified the standard ISO27001: 2013 Information Security Management System since 2008 and has maintained certification every three years continuously as the standard requires. The NCB thinks that if any credit bureau wants to create secrecy and confidentiality for the credit information, they should ensure that all security standards and procedures are checked and certified, such as the information security management certification, performing audit checks from internal and external perspectives, and preventing and protecting against cyber security threats through penetration testing and cyber drill practice. The credit bureau will not stop at only data security certification, but will also need to find other certifications to ensure trust and protection for their stakeholders. The new certifications that the credit bureau shall consider are those such as data governance and data privacy, because those are the new trends of data protection.

The NCB ensures that for credit information data processing, every transaction accessed is recorded properly so it can be traced back later as per request by the regulator. The NCB does not stop at the implementation and certification of information security standards, because the risk and threats to the credit information itself keep changing and become more advanced every day. Many data breach incidents happen regularly and often seriously, with the most recent examples being data ransom attacks from the cyber or digital world. Therefore, the NCB has to enhance and extend the existing security by adding more security strategies on both cyber resilience and cyber drills to increase trust in members while they are using credit information from the NCB. Another concern for many people is data privacy, because they do not want only their data, but also their privacy to be protected. The idea originated from the GDPR in Europe and PDPA in Asian countries, including Thailand. The Personal Data Protection Act (PDPA) (Personal Data Protection Act B.E. 2562) was announced in 2019 and purposes to protect the privacy of personal data. The Act does not affect the credit information for the NCB, because credit information is already protected by the Credit Information Business Act. However, the NCB has implemented the PDPA to ensure all data collected from the consumer is kept securely according to the Data Privacy Act.

5 How would credit information be used by financial institutions?

In 1997, when Thailand was facing the Asian financial crisis, there was a major collapse in the financial industry. Studies of the outcomes of the collapse found many reasons, but the main explanation concerned asymmetric information in the credit risk assessment process. Each financial institution was lending on their own information, because there was no credit bureau providing centralized information. After the credit bureau was established in 1998, the asymmetric information problem was resolved, as the financial institutions had centralized information to use in the credit risk assessment process. Now, financial institutions who were acting as lender could use the credit information to reduce their own risk and reduce the number of non-performing loans within the Thai economy.

Because credit information is considered highly confidential data which is protected by the Credit Information Business Act and also protected as security data by ISO 27001 which the NCB has certified as the data security protection standard, accordingly, it can only be accessed by financial institutions that are members of the NCB. Moreover, the Credit Information Business Act is clear that the purpose of accessing credit information is that the credit information company shall disclose or provide credit information to the member or the recipient of service who wishes to use such information for the purpose of analyzing credit or the granting of credit cards. Every time the aforementioned information is disclosed or provided, consent must be obtained in advance from the owner of the information, except when the owner of the information has otherwise given prior consent (Credit Information Business Act B.E. 2545). A member may use information from a credit information company according to Section 20, but only unidentified facts of the credit information owner can be used as factors to build a credit model with the consent of the owner of that credit information. A member can use the credit model according to the first paragraph only for the purposes of credit analysis, credit card issuing, and the member's internal risk management (Credit Information Business Act B.E. 2545).

Financial institutions that are NCB members must use the credit information from the NCB according to the objectives in Section 20 and 20/1 described in the Credit Information Business Act B.E. 2545. They use the credit information as supporting information in their credit underwriting process, which is required by the Bank of Thailand. The credit information is necessary data for the financial institution to estimate the creditworthiness from the borrower's payment history in the credit information report, as seen in Figure 9.4. Moreover, some

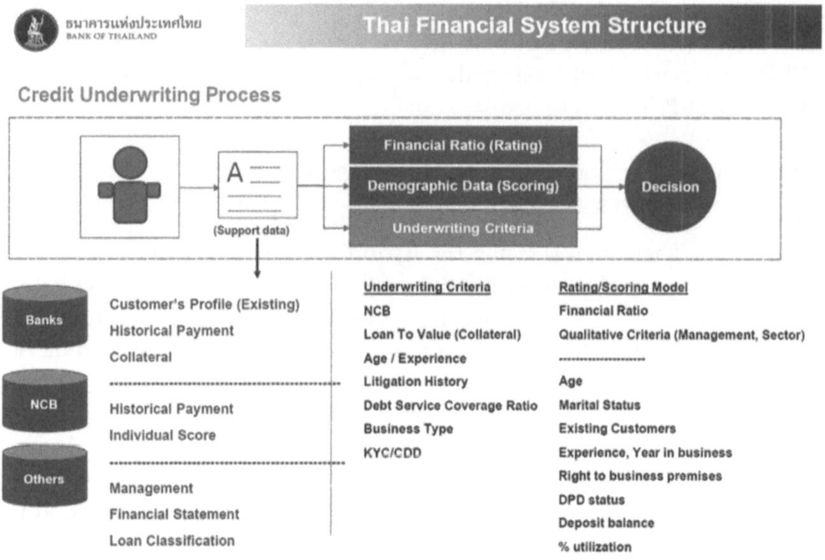

Figure 9.4 Thai Financial System Structure.
Source: Bank of Thailand.

NCB members also use the credit information (after removing identity information from it) that is received from the NCB as a factor to build the internal credit model as a tool to use in the credit underwriting process.

6 How the NCB uses the collected data

The concept behind "data is the new oil" is that just like oil, raw data is not valuable in and of itself, but rather value is created when it is gathered completely and accurately, connected to other relevant data, and done so in a timely manner. When properly refined, usable data quickly becomes a decision-making tool – information – allowing companies to react to market forces and be proactive and intentional in their decision-making (Rosebrough, 2020).

The NCB uses the collected credit data according to the World Bank framework as shown in Figure 9.4. It uses the credit information collected from members to produce products and services with limitations by law to support NCB members, such as credit reports and credit scoring. The NCB also uses statistical data, also limited by law, to produce statistical reports to support government agencies such as the Bank of Thailand, Ministry of Finance, and so forth, for use in feasibility studies in the finance industry and to issue a monetary policy to control the market. The NCB also uses the statistical data internally to track the household debt situation and provide early warnings, such as the NPL trend, to the public.

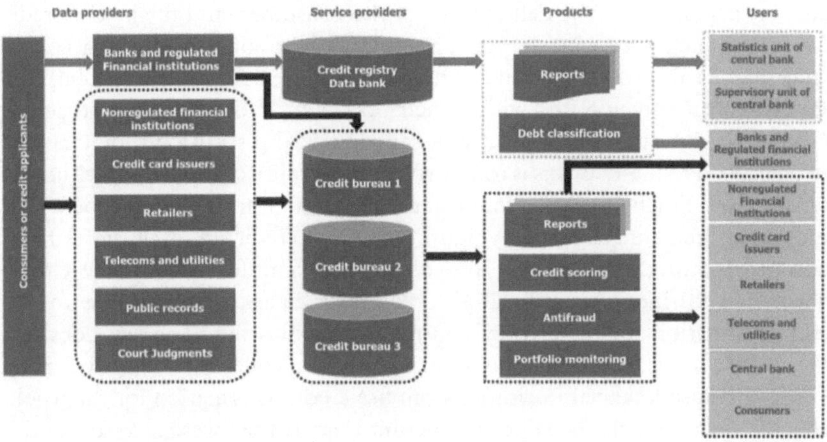

Figure 9.5 How the Credit Information Flows in a System with Both a Credit Registry and a Credit Bureau.

7 How would NCB data improve the performance of banks and fintech companies in Thailand?

Most financial institutions such as banks and fin-tech companies can use credit information from the NCB to improve their performance both directly and indirectly. Financial institutions measure their performance from revenue and their portfolio quality or asset quality. The consequences of quality portfolio or asset management will ultimately be reflected in the revenue. If the financial institution has good asset quality, they can control the expected NPL and therefore ensure some reserves in capital provisioning requirements as the regulator requires. In the Asian financial crisis of 1997, with the currency floating and the NPL rising, the banks did not have sufficient capital provisioning reserved, and they eventually collapsed. That was one example where banks should have achieved better performance, but they could not, because there was no information for them to use to prevent the loss (Japan Research Institute, Jun 1999, No. 44).

After that unpleasant experience for all financial institutions during that period, they are now more careful about their performance. A new regulation was introduced requiring more care in making capital provisioning reserves for the NPL by using the Basel III standard. Today, with centralized credit information from the credit bureau, financial institutions can use the credit information together with risk tools or services from the NCB to improve their performance, which can be measured from the quality of NPL. Financial institutions regulated by the Bank of Thailand are obliged to check the credit information every time they perform credit underwriting with regard to a customer. To do the credit information check from the NCB, they can perform an evaluation of the creditworthiness from the repayment behavior reflected by the credit report of the consumer. The credit report describes the payment behavior, outstanding debts, or in some cases the delinquency of the consumer, and finally the credit utilization which they can also calculate from the credit report. As a consequence, financial institutions can select good customers for their portfolio, and they can control their NPLs within their portfolio. It is noteworthy that the NCB has no right to determine whether the financial institution should accept or reject a loan request, as this is totally the responsibility of financial institutions by themselves. Financial institutions can use the credit information for the whole life cycle of credit management (Figure 9.5). The credit life cycle starts from credit provisioning, monitoring, and collection, but unfortunately, the Credit Information Business Act B.E. 2545 only allows financial institutions to use credit information for credit provisioning and monitoring. The law does not allow the use of credit information for marketing and collection. This would not be right, because financial institutions can use credit information for the whole credit life cycle, but the law does not permit that. If they were able to use the credit information for collection and some marketing, better credit performance in asset quality of the financial institutions could probably be expected in the future, in the view of the author.

That is how the financial institutions who are NCB members by law use credit information to improve their performance. However, those financial institutions who are not yet NCB members by law, such as fintech companies or peer-to-peer lending companies, can use the credit information from the consumer channel, which lets the consumer check their own credit and pass the credit report to the fintech company to do the credit underwriting. Today, fintech companies must send their customers to check their self-credit report. Then they use that information in the credit underwriting process together with an alternative score that most fintech companies use internally. As a result, fintech companies can lend small amounts of money through social media enterprise platforms with better creditworthiness of their customer. We have not yet seen their performance, but we can predict that the new lending platform can use the credit information from the NCB for their credit underwriting or credit decisions within a short period of time, and they can achieve both good revenue and good credit control of their portfolio with a controllable NPL target.

8 What would make a credit bureau better to boost SME finance?

8.1 New services and products to support financial institutions

In addition to the information security developed by the NCB to meet the international standard of security, the NCB has implemented systems for better choices for members, especially in credit risk management tools such as credit scoring.

> Credit scoring is a statistical analysis performed by lenders and financial institutions to determine the creditworthiness of a person or a small,

> owner-operated business. Credit scoring is used by lenders to help decide whether to extend or deny credit. A credit score can impact many financial transactions, including mortgages, auto loans, credit cards, and private loans (The Investopedia team, April 8, 2021)

Credit scoring will be one of the risk tools using statistical methods in evaluating the possibility of delinquency on the part of the borrower in the future.

NCB has developed two credit-scoring models, i.e., the Consumer Credit Scoring model and the Commercial Credit Scoring model for small- and medium-sized companies. The consumer model was developed by TransUnion, one of the top three credit bureaus in the US, while the commercial credit scoring was developed by Fair Isaac Company (FICO) in the UK. The NCB credit scoring ranges from 300 to 900, or is graded as AA-HH. This is a risk assessment tool which will be used to assess the borrowers' possibility of delinquency. The score will present the possibility of delinquency in the next 12 months for 10,000 people who have scores in the same range. For people who have a score in this range, there will be the possibility of on-schedule debt settlement from xxx people and the possibility of delinquency from yyy people. The financial institutions, hence, will consider this score with their credit policy and other factors to decide whether they will approve the granting of credit or to determine which interest rate should be given to the borrowers. This risk management tool was previously launched in 2016, and members have to subscribe to this service which helps them increase their efficiency in credit evaluation without any bias.

Moreover, the NCB has provided the early warning sign developed from the existing statistical database. This warning sign will provide an early warning in the statistical report which members can use to better understand the status of market conditions in order to reduce risk and increase the level of care in their credit analysis process. The notification of total accounts which have been in default for more than 90 days is one example of the early warning signs in the statistical report.

Even though there is only one credit bureau in Thailand for now, the NCB is always developing and improving its services and systems to operate regularly at a high standard. For example, the NCB can now reduce the time to access credit reports, whereby financial institutions can make credit information inquiries online within three to five minutes per transaction, depending upon the inquiry channel and connectivity type.

8.2 How does the NCB support members in the digital lending era?

Today, digital lending is a key to success for a new credit provider, as credit providers with new technology can serve their customers faster, better, and more securely than their competitors. Borrower behavior has changed the way they live and the way they access information from the Internet, and those changes have resulted in a customer-centric strategy that financial institutions are strongly considering at present. One strategy which is customer-centric is the notion of anytime, anywhere, and easy to access, which explains the increasing focus on mobile technology as a selling tool to the market. The NCB has foreseen the changes in the strategies that financial institutions are using, and the objective is to change from traditional lending to digital lending. The NCB has developed new services for credit information requests for members and consumers, and, of course, it must also comply with the laws. The NCB is now extending its credit information reports from being paper-based to electronic-based in PDF format through mobile requests. This allows both members and non-members, especially those who are limited by the law such as fintech companies, to utilize that data to speed up their creditworthiness evaluation. The consumer can apply for a loan from the lender and know the result within 15 minutes just using their fingertips through the mobile lending application. Also in the near future, the NCB will develop its own mobile application to allow self-credit report requests and receiving the report in electronic form in PDF format. In addition to the self-credit report request, the mobile application will also provide education in financial literacy and how to manage a credit history. There is also a simulation of the score calculation. This is one of the NCB objectives, to help customers learn how to make better use of credit for better consumer living.

8.3 How does the NCB foresee technology innovation supporting financial institutions?

Let us first consider what technology innovation is:

> Technology innovation is a new or improved product or process whose technological characteristics are significantly different from before. Implemented technological product innovations are new products (product innovations) or processes in application (process innovations) that have been brought to market. The product or process is considered to be an innovation if it achieves specified advantages for the enterprise concerned; these need not be new from the point of view of other companies or the market.
>
> (Thilastokeskus, 1995)

When the NCB develops technology innovation in its products, services, or processes, the Credit Information Business Act and the Bank of Thailand Financial Master Plan can be considered as factors to support current services along with the framework from the Bank of Thailand and the needs of the members, which will be used in developing new products and services or enhancing existing ones. The big shift in innovation is the use of blockchain technology to transform traditional consent to electronic consent through the Digital ID platform. The Digital ID platform provides identity and verification services which is the significant key to accessing credit information from the NCB. Financial institutions can enhance their KYC process by using this platform, as it will check and verify the borrower's identity from the service provider before gaining access to the data sources available in the ecosystem, such as the NCB data. The NCB is a data provider in the platform which requires consent before releasing the data; therefore, it is the NCB's duty to verify the consent before the credit information is disclosed to the financial institutions. At present, those consent verification processes are carried out manually, and the financial institutions are trusted to perform this duty at their premises with the borrower on behalf of the NCB and to send the consent paper to the NCB later. This process is costly to both the financial institutions and the NCB, because the NCB needs to keep the consent as log evidence of enquiry, and the bank also needs to keep the consent for the NCB for the audit process per request. After the NCB implemented this e-consent process through the Digital ID platform, the operating cost could be reduced for members deciding to change to e-consent. However, this is in the process of gradual change, because not all members are ready for this, as it needs a technology adjustment to enable this process.

Members who decide to use this e-consent process can enjoy the benefits and convenience of their digital lending process, which can improve efficiency in their credit decision-making process and result in more approved customers in the future, and it will ultimately boost SME funding. We foresee that this will be one of the major access channels for digital lending in the near future.

8.4 Limitations or pain points of the Credit Information Business Act

As the Credit Information Business Act B.E. 2545 was enacted in 2002, it has now been in use for more than two decades and there have been few amendments. The first amendment was in 2006 and changed the definition of credit. The second amendment was in 2008 and canceled the definition of credit information and made changes to the information concerning credit information and credit scoring. This change was to enable the credit bureau to process the statistical information. The third amendment was in 2016 and adjusted the duty of the committee of the Act. The fourth amendment was also in 2016 and adjusted the usage of the credit information received from the credit bureau by ensuring that the identity of the subject must be removed before use as a factor of a credit model.

Those changes show how slowly the Credit Information Business Act was amended within the period of almost 20 years, how the changes did not significantly improve the Act, and how they did not benefit the NCB and its members at all. One amendment in 2008, however, did benefit the NCB in providing the credit scoring service for members. Under the current Credit Information Business Act B.E. 2545, there are many limitations which prevent the credit bureau from competing with credit bureaus in other countries. The law tightly limits the definition of financial institutions that are allowed to be members of the credit bureau. From the World Bank survey of doing business in the credit bureau section, other financial institutions already exist in other parts of the world that can enhance or extend the data coverage of the credit bureau, for example, fintech companies, crowd funding, trade credits, telecoms, and utilities. Another significant pain point is data collection, which is related to the point of the limitation of the definition of financial institutions who can be members of the credit bureau. The law today allows the credit bureau to collect only credit data, known as traditional data, although the collection of other alternative data would also be beneficial for financial institutions to use in their credit decision-making process for a better understanding of the creditworthiness of the consumers. This can also improve the situation of SME access to financing.

Today, the Bank of Thailand, which acts as the secretary of the Credit Information Protection Committee, is considering amending the law again. In the next section, the author will describe the amendment to explain what the changes are and when they will become effective.

8.5 *New hope for the Credit Information Business Act, from pain points to policy implications*

As mentioned in the previous section, the Credit Information Business Act is changing slowly, and most of the changes are not beneficial to the credit bureau except for one change in 2008 which allowed the credit bureau to process credit scoring. In 2019, despite the misfortune of the Covid-19 outbreak that affected the whole world, one good thing happened, which was a new law amendment proposed by the Bank of Thailand.

The law amendment was initiated by the Bank of Thailand, and the idea was to resolve the pain points in the current Credit Information Business Act. The BOT has reviewed the Act and interviewed related people, including NCB members, focus groups, potential members, specialists in consumer protection, data owners, and related enterprises. The Bank of Thailand reviewed and concluded the outcome from those related groups and summarized the responses to make changes to the policy stance. There are six pain points to the current Credit Information Business Act B.E. 2545: 1. Type of information and scope of data collection; 2. Credit information system and members of credit bureau; 3. Data disclosure and utilization; 4. Data retention period; 5. Governance and compliance, and 6. Penalties. In this chapter, the author will discuss only two pain points that are related to the topic, and those are type of information and scope of data collection, and credit information and members of the credit bureau.

As we already know, the current Credit Information Business Act limits the scope of data for the credit bureau to collect, which is the traditional credit data from the loans side only. If we refer to the Memorandum on Economic Policies of the Royal Thai Government December 1, 1998, it states a Credit Bureau Bill was to be introduced allowing the establishment of credit bureaus to facilitate the exchange of information among creditors (Economy News, Tuesday, December 8, 1998, 18:17 – Ministry of Finance). The creditors would not only be financial institutions, but could also be trade creditors, utilities, etc. The information will let financial institutions try to better understand their customers' behavior on the basis of the data available from the credit bureau. Most credit bureaus in other countries collect alternative data, which allows companies to predict their clients' behavior, and in this way growth projections become more effective, optimizing decision-making and reducing the probability of risk. However, alternative data has to be used in the proper way, because it is relatively new and, at first glance, can raise several questions. There is a lack of historical records, plus not all alternative data is publicly accessible. Therefore, it is profoundly important to have an accurate understanding of from where information is coming and how its usage is limited (Credo Lab, May 14, 2021). There is a proven record in some countries such as the US and China that suggests alternative data will increase the predictive power of credit scoring and will be of benefit to financial institutions.

The second pain point is credit information and membership of the credit bureau, because at present, the Credit Information Business Act limits the type of member in the credit bureau and has done so since the law was enacted. To date, no amendments have been made in this area. Today, there are other finance institutions such as fintech companies, peer-to-peer lending, trade creditors, and telecoms who show the intention to become NCB members, but they cannot become members because of the legal limitations. The Bank of Thailand proposed to change this definition, but we do not know what the final definition will be. The new definition to be used should consider the new digital world, give more flexibility to the business model and should not add only the new list of types of financial institution. As change does not happen very often, this change should be considered beneficial to both the credit bureau and the financial institutions. The other part of this pain point is the credit information business which the current Act limits to the credit bureau business only. However, there is other business related to the credit bureau that should be open to it, so the credit bureau can bring the benefits in terms of credit information, such as becoming part of the new ecosystem in the digital lending world.

At the present, those six pain points have resulted in the proposal of six policy stances, but these changes cannot be accomplished instantly; as the idiom suggests, Rome was not built in a day (Wikipedia, June 2021). The next step is to rewrite the six parts to meet the objective, and it will take at least a few years to go through the legal process. The author does not know how this would go on to help other financial institutions become NCB members and enjoy the benefits of credit information together with other alternative data. Therefore, the credit bureau and other financial institutions in Thailand will have to wait until the time comes.

One additional pain point was left out of the current law amendment proposal. The author wants to persuade the reader to think along with the author beyond the legal implications on the credit bureau law within the country, because we need to support local consumers when they are doing business outside the country, especially SMEs who need access to funding to run their businesses effectively outside the country. Imagine if the reader were an SME in Thailand who wanted to expand their business to Japan and needed funding to finance the SME. This presents a difficulty for both the foreign SME borrower and the lender in Japan who must approve (or reject) the loan request without a credit history. The credit bureau faces a big issue in considering how to help Thai SMEs in foreign countries. Therefore, the idea of the cross-border credit data exchange which began a few years ago in various European credit bureau served as a pilot study for other countries. To start a cross-border credit data exchange is not easy, because there are many factors involved in the operation, i.e., technology, operations, security, and the most critical and difficult factor of all, which is the law. The author hopes the cross-border credit data exchange will succeed and that will bring the credit bureau beyond the confines of being simply a local credit bureau in the future.

9 Conclusions and policy recommendations

The primary purpose of the NCB is to keep credit information records from its members and to process and disclose them with the proper consent. The NCB collects information on consumers who use credit through the member data submission, and consumers can make self-credit report checks under the law. The financial institutions that are NCB members use these records when making decisions for the credit underwriting process about extending credit and the terms of credit offered. Credit reports may provide an understanding of future behavior and reflect the creditworthiness in that a person's ability to repay a debt is directly related to how they have handled debt in the past. Reviewing a consumer's credit portfolio can reduce the risk of lending and prevent NPL.

NCB products and services can benefit financial institutions and prevent them from experiencing crises similar to the Asian financial crisis of 1997. Moreover, they also benefit consumers and let them know that the right information is sent to the NCB, as this right is covered by the law. NCB products and services reflect the financial behavior of individuals from basic credit reports and risk tools with the technological innovation that the NCB tries to provide in support of the members to bring about the greatest benefits in the credit life cycle. Moreover, the NCB also provides statistical data for members to manage their credit risk and control the NPLs in their portfolio, while in the meantime, the NCB provides the public with an early warning from time to time. Today, NCB members can utilize the credit information to prevent NPL and achieve increased approval volume with confidence by using credit information. However, under the current law there are many pain points for both members and the credit bureau. Thus, there is more opportunity in the new normal or even in the new digital lending world, if the law amendment can proceed in line with the stated aims. Amending the law in the next few years will not be easy, because the process takes time and must pass many steps to complete the changes. If we take a look at the neighborhood in the credit bureau industry, we can see more opportunities in both data and other businesses that credit bureaus in other countries conduct. The NCB is still moving on and trying to do its best to support financial institutions by bringing new technology, new business models, and new opportunities to the credit bureau business in Thailand. The NCB is a data processor that can work together with other new eco-entities to help SMEs gain access to financing with good information and good technology in the future. Of course, the NCB cannot do this alone, as it also requires support from the law, which is the most significant challenge not only for the credit bureau in Thailand, but also for the other bureaus.

The keys to success for the Credit Bureau Eco-system, which will boost SME financing in Thailand, are law and policy changes. The changes in the current Credit Bureau Business Act, i.e. the six policy stances proposed by the Bank of Thailand, need to be expedited as soon as possible. Those six policy stances are the key pain points for both the credit bureau and the financial institutions, including not only the existing members of the credit bureau, but also the potential members. Other non-credit bureau policies also need to be considered, such as sharing information from other data sources and the credit decision process for SMEs, especially those who cannot access financing within the current policy. It is also necessary to consider SME collateral, because collateral is a significant factor to ensuring security for the financial institutions before they grant a loan to the SMEs. SME supply chain funding and modern trade policy data should be considered if we want to boost SME financing in Thailand as well as other countries.

Finally, the author hopes this information will be of benefit to the reader and hopes they will better understand the role and duties of the credit bureau and the benefits of the credit bureau to the financial industry and to the country of Thailand.

References

Cambodia Monthly Legal Update, July 2020, Available via https://www.dfdl.com/resources/legal-and-tax-updates/cambodia-monthly-legal-update-july-2020/ PRAKAS NO. B7–020–352 BR.K ON CREDIT REPORTING, DATED ON 26 JUNE 2020. (Accessed on May 24, 2022)

Credit Information Business Act B.E. 2545, Available via https://www.ncb.co.th/wp-content/uploads/2017/06/Creditinfo_acteng_5combined.pdf, Credit Information Business Act B.E. 2545 Section#3 (Accessed on May 24, 2022)

Credit Information Business Act BE2545, Available via https://www.ncb.co.th/wp-content/uploads/2017/06/Creditinfo_acteng_5combined.pdf, Chapter III Rights and Obligation of Credit Information Company, Member and Recipient of the Services

Credit Information Business Act B.E. 2545, Available via https://www.ncb.co.th/wp-content/uploads/2017/06/Creditinfo_acteng_5combined.pdf, section 20. (Accessed on May 24, 2022)

Credit Information Business Act B.E. 2545, Available via https://www.ncb.co.th/wp-content/uploads/2017/06/Creditinfo_acteng_5combined.pdf, section 20/1 (Accessed on May 24, 2022)

Credo Lab (2021) Available via: https://www.credolab.com/blog/benefits-and-challenges-of-using-alternative-data

Economy News Tuesday December 8, 1998 18:17—Ministry of Finance, Available via: https://www.ryt9.com/en/ryt9/14073 (Accessed on May 24, 2022)

ISO 27001, ISO.org/standard/54534.html, the ISO/IEC 27001:2013

Japan Research Institute (1999) Available via: https://www.jri.co.jp/english/periodical/rim/1999/RIMe199903npl/ (Accessed on May 24, 2022)

OSMEP. Available via: https://www.sme.go.th/en/page.php?modulekey=365Credit Information Business Act B.E. 2545, Available via: https://www.ncb.co.th/wp-content/uploads/2017/06/Creditinfo_acteng_5combined.pdf, (Accessed on May 24, 2022) Credit Information Business Act B.E. 2545, section 16, 17

PDPA, Personnel Data Protection Act B.E. 2562, section 4

Rosebrough M (2020) Available via: https://www.kenwayconsulting.com/blog/data-is-the-new-oil. (Accessed on May 24, 2022)

The Investopedia Team (2021) Available via: https://www.investopedia.com/terms/c/credit_scoring.asp, what is the credit scoring?

Thilastokeskus J (1995) Available via https://www.stat.fi/meta/kas/tekn_innovaatio_en.html (Accessed on May 24, 2022)

Wikipedia (2021a) 1997 Asian Financial Crisis, Available via https://en.wikipedia.org/wiki/1997_Asian_financial_crisis (Accessed on May 24, 2022)

Wikipedia (2021b) Available via: https://en.wikipedia.org/wiki/Rome_wasn%27t_built_in_a_day (Accessed on May 24, 2022)

World Bank Group (2019) Credit Reporting Knowledge Guide 2019, Chapter 5 Developing Credit Reporting Systems in Emerging Market, p 78

10 Role of credit guarantee schemes in funding technology-based firms in Iran

Seyed Ali Fatemi Khorasgani, Seyed Habibollah Tabatabaeian, Farhad Taghizadeh-Hesary and Vajhollah Ghorbanizadeh

1 Introduction

The weakness of major financial institutions in financing small- and medium-sized enterprises (SMEs) is a major challenge in economic development (Garcia, 2006). Accordingly, in the second half of the 1990s, credit guarantee schemes were designed as an institutional innovation to support SMEs in credit markets (Arping et al., 2009). The characteristics of these schemes were particularly appealing to policymakers, as they can leverage available financial resources to direct other resources, especially bank loans, toward SMEs and resolve the problem of information asymmetry (Green, 2003). Credit guarantee institutions also facilitate the lending process by obtaining and securing collaterals with higher agility and less cost (Cowling and Mitchell, 2003).

Although different countries use credit guarantee schemes to support SMEs, few have applied these schemes to technology-based firms to further innovation in the application context. In this regard, credit guarantee institutions can issue guarantees to new technology-based firms (NTBFs) by valuing and pledging intangible assets or taking other types of liabilities instead of collateral (Mullins and Toro, 2017). Moreover, credit guarantee programs eliminate the adverse effects of the information asymmetry and heterogeneity of NTBFs by relying on relationship banking (Liu et al., 2016).

In Iran, policymakers are attracted to credit guarantee schemes for financing NTBFs, and this orientation is reflected in various laws and regulations (Knowledge-based Institutions and Companies Center, 2020). Accordingly, research and technology funds are currently the only private institutions in this field that present various guarantees (loan and contract-based guarantees) under the supervision of the Research and Technology Funds Workgroup. In addition to private funds, four public guarantee funds (Small Industries Fund (SIF), Export Guarantee Fund (EGF), Advanced Industry Research and Development Fund (AIRDF), and Cooperative Investment Guarantee Fund (CIGF)) also provide guarantee services to NTBFs. The Iran National Innovation Fund (INIF) also facilitates access to bank guarantees for NTBFs and supports the loans of research and technology funds.

DOI: 10.4324/9781003220220-14

Nonetheless, the Iranian credit guarantee system has not yet played the expected role in financing NTBFs. The share of NTBFs from bank loans has been between 0.6% and 1.6% in the last four years, of which 8%–10% was based on guarantees (Authors' calculations based on data from the Iranian Central Bank). Thus, various scholars have identified the reluctance of banks to evaluate NTBF requests because of their small volumes (Banitaba Koupai, 2011), the weakness of financial institutions in evaluating the intellectual property of NTBFs (Banitaba Koupai, 2011) (Banitaba, 2016), failure in the formulation of laws required for the operation, governance, and supervision of guarantee funds (Banitaba, 2016), and weaknesses in the comprehensive validation of NTBFs (especially the lack of the required database) (Aboojafari et al., 2019) as the challenges of the credit guarantee system of NTBFs in Iran.

Full exploitation of the credit guarantee system requires continuous monitoring and improvement according to the context. Various researchers have analyzed the credit guarantee systems in different countries and regions and presented policy implications to improve this system (Agnese et al., 2018; Calice, 2016; Li and Lin, 2017; Ma et al., 2019). Thus, the present chapter aims to identify the patterns in credit guarantee schemes designed for Iranian NTBFs according to (1) ownership structure, (2) execution framework (provided services, liability distinction pattern, guarantee provision, and inclusion scope), and (3) legislative framework (governing institution, macro law, and public support models). Based on the findings, the development of the counter guarantee system, the directing of RTFs toward specialized services in the guarantee field, the development of loan guarantee service in INIF, the design of a plan for directing public funds toward financial sustainability, and the development of simplified tax regime are proposed as the first steps toward the development of credit guarantee schemes for Iranian NTBFs.

2 Credit guarantee schemes

One institution that should be given special attention in the development of technological activities is the financing institution (Fombang and Adjasi, 2018). This necessity arises from the gap in the financing of technological activities by conventional financial institutions, which has caused access to financial resources to be identified as the most significant obstacle to the growth of NTBFs (Garcia, 2006), firms that face challenges in obtaining financing from conventional financial institutions for the following reasons (Panetta, 2012):

1. Risk and uncertainty of technological activities: Technological activities have two characteristics: they are inseparable and non-competitive. In other words, the expected return on investment is lower with these activities than with conventional investments. Therefore, when an NTBF seeks to finance technological activities from its internal resources, the characteristics of these activities as a public good reduce the incentive to invest.

2. Information asymmetry: Conventional financial institutions cannot fully understand technological activities and their risks. As a result, they have difficulty distinguishing good and bad technological activities for further investment.
3. High operating costs: Conventional financial institutions have to spend vast amounts to address the issue of information asymmetry and identify the risk and credit of technological activities with a complex accreditation system; however, these high operating costs are not commensurate with the amount of funding requested by NTBFs, nor is it cost-effective for conventional financial institutions.
4. Lack of collateral: Conventional financial institutions demand public and easy-to-obtain collateral from their clients to understand their credit as well as their risk coverage. NTBFs, however, cannot provide the required documents, given their financial and asset structure.

In addition to these four considerations in the financing of these companies, other sub-factors have been identified as well (Cowling et al., 2018):

- Uncertainty about the future income from investing in technological activities
- The difficulty and high cost of the valuation of the intangible assets of NTBFs
- Reluctance of NTBFs to provide information for evaluation and assessment

These considerations lead to a different financing hierarchy for NTBFs compared with other firms. This hierarchy, called the "financial growth cycle," considers the level of a firm's growth and presents different financial resources accordingly (Berger and Udell, 1998). According to this model, governments have utilized two main instruments to facilitate the financing of technological activities: direct use of government resources and venture capital (Kersten et al., 2017).

Although these practices have been able to solve part of the problem of financing technological activities, empirical studies on the effects of these measures have also clarified aspects of their limited effectiveness. In other words, these countermeasures have not been successful in allocating the vast resources of the economy (including banking resources) to technological activities. In response to these challenges, in the second half of the 1990s, governments moved toward credit guarantee schemes as an effective tool to support small and medium-sized enterprises (SMEs) in credit markets (Arping et al., 2009). These programs were attractive to policymakers, as they provided the capacity to leverage available financial resources and thus direct more resources to technological activities by attracting huge bank loans (Green, 2003).

The success of a credit guarantee system is highly dependent on its design dimensions, which should be tailored to the context to provide the best performance for credit guarantee schemes. Although it is not possible to introduce a single framework for the development of the system, various scholars have proposed different dimensions for this framework. As the proposed frameworks offer various dimensions at different levels, a comprehensive framework is developed at the system level (Table 10.1). Accordingly, the ownership structure of credit guarantee institutions can be divided into the following four categories (Beck et al., 2010):

1. Public guarantee funds: Funds owned by the government mostly target specific stakeholders or sectors.
2. Public–private guarantee funds: The ownership and management of public–private funds are usually done in a hybrid way by the government and the private sector. In the most popular structure, ownership is assigned to the government and management to the private sector.
3. Private guarantee funds: These are funds that are privately established and managed.
4. Mutual guarantee institutions: In such institutions, a group of credit guarantee stakeholders (financing institutions or NTBFs in a field) establishes a fund as a cooperative.

The execution framework determines how the schemes are implemented according to the following criteria:

1. Provided services: The two main types of credit guarantees are loan guarantees and equity guarantees. In addition to these two main types, contract-based guarantees are also provided (European Commission, 2003).
2. Liability distinction pattern: In direct guarantee schemes, the provider of the credit guarantee service is the main guarantor, while the third party is ultimately responsible for guaranteeing the entire (or part of the) repayment in the counter-guarantee model (Navajas, 2001).
3. Guarantee provision strategy: In individual guarantee schemes, all customers of guarantee funds are covered separately by the guarantor. Thus, each entrepreneur requests a credit guarantee, and after evaluation, a guarantee is granted. In the guarantee portfolio model, the guarantee institution does not process the individual applications; instead, the bank is allowed to attach the credit of each customer. The bank then simply notifies the guarantee fund of the newly approved facility (for example, monthly) (Levitsky, 1997).
4. Inclusion scope: The credit guarantee scheme is open if there are no specific requirements for firms. However, if restrictive conditions such as specific industrial sectors determine the target firms, the scheme is targeted (Navajas, 2001).

Credit guarantee schemes must be integrated with the macroeconomic system to adapt to different economic circumstances and not undermine its stability with their risky behaviors (Daskalakis et al., 2017; Yamori, 2015). In the legislative and monitoring framework, the type of interaction between government institutions with credit guarantee funds and other stakeholders is determined in terms of law, protection, and supervision. This framework consists of the following elements:

1. Governing institution: The governing is either designated to an institution (with all the governing capacity) or assigned to a network of multiple institutions. Moreover, the relationship of the governing institution with the governing body of the macro-financial system must be specified. For example, the same institutions may be in charge of both the macro-financial system and the credit guarantee system (Gracey, 2001).
2. Macro law: The general law regarding the credit guarantee system shall specify the rules that credit guarantee institutions must follow during their establishment and operation. These rules include determining the capital requirements for the establishment of the institutions, determining the maximum responsibility of the institutions, applying/not applying restrictions in the areas of activity of the institutions, and rules of prudential supervision in the financial activities of the institutions. Depending on the status, scope, and role of the credit guarantee system, different countries either formulate these rules under monetary, financial, and public banking laws or establish a specific law (Vento and Porretta, 2012).

Table 10.1 Framework for the Analysis of Credit Guarantee Systems

Dimensions	*Sub-dimensions*	*Alternatives*
Ownership structure (Beck et al., 2010)		Public institutions Public–private institutions Private institutions Mutual institutions
Execution framework	Provided services (European Commission, 2003)	Loan guarantee Equity guarantee Contract-based guarantee
	Liability distinction pattern (Navajas, 2001)	Direct guarantee Counter-guarantee
	Guarantee provision strategy (Levitsky, 1997)	Individual guarantee Portfolio guarantee
	Inclusion scope (Navajas, 2001)	Open schemes Targeted schemes
Legislative and monitoring framework	Governing institution (Gracey, 2001)	Single institutions Multiple institutions
	Macro law (Vento and Porretta, 2012)	Under the laws of monetary, financial, and public banking Special rule
	Government support models (Vento and Porretta, 2012)	Participation in the initial capital provision Participation in risk coverage Evaluation infrastructure Facilitated tax regime

Source: Authors' compilation.

3) Government support models: In some circumstances, governments take specific measures to support credit guarantee schemes. These measures, which enhance the business environment or improve the economic conditions of the activities of credit guarantee institutions, include participation in the initial capital provision, participation in risk coverage, development of the evaluation infrastructure, and development of a facilitated tax regime (Vento and Porretta, 2012).

Various developed and developing countries with different financial systems have already developed successful credit guarantee systems. The comparative study of such experiences can provide useful insight for the analysis and further development of Iranian credit guarantee schemes.

3 Comparative studies of credit guarantee schemes

Various patterns in the implementation of credit guarantee schemes were identified by studying countries with different development levels (developed and developing) and various financial systems (bank-based and market-based). Considering the Human Development Index (HDI) (HDRO, 2018), International Monetary Fund (IMF) classification (IMF, 2019a), World Bank classification (World Bank, 2018), and income per capita (IMF, 2019b), Japan, Germany, the UK, and Chile are developed countries, while China, Argentina, Brazil, and South Africa are developing countries. Also considering the financial system index (Demirgüç-Kunt et al., 1999) and further calculations according to the ratio of bank capital to stock market investment (Demirgüç-Kunt et al., 2013), Japan, Germany, China, and Argentina have a bank-based financial system, but the UK, Chile, Brazil, and South Africa have a market-based one. For a comparative study of selected countries, their credit guarantee systems are briefly introduced, and then the frameworks of their credit guarantee systems are compared (Table 10.2).

1) Japan: The history of the Japanese credit guarantee system goes back to the establishment of the Tokyo Credit Guarantee institution in 1937, but World War II can be considered a turning point in the development of the Japanese credit guarantee system, as there were only three credit guarantee institutions in Japan before the war. Accordingly, several credit guarantee institutions began to operate after the war to help rebuild the Japanese economy with the support of local governments. Today, guarantee institutions operating under the Credit Guarantee Institution Act in Japan play an important role in accessing financial resources for SMEs. In Japan, credit guarantee companies are registered as associations (unions) and foundations and supervised according to the law of credit guarantee institutions. Currently, the Japan Credit Guarantee Corporations (Union of 51 Guarantee firms) and the Japan Financial Corporation are recognized as the complementing pillars of the Japanese credit guarantee system (JFC, 2014; Uesugi et al., 2010; Yoshino and Taghizadeh-Hesary, 2019).

2) Germany: The credit guarantee system in Germany has a decentralized framework that reflects the federal political structure and key sectors of the economy. In this framework, the performance of the credit guarantee system varies in different regions, but basic principles are upheld throughout Germany. Guarantee banks and credit guarantee associations now form the German credit guarantee network. German guarantee banks are a network of 17 non-profit guarantee banks that operate under German banking law (Hall, 2016; OECD, 2013). The German Association of Guarantee Banks represents 17 guarantee banks and 15 SME-oriented investment firms that are members of the European Association of Guarantee Institutions (AECM). Other actors in the German credit guarantee system are credit guarantee associations established by the business community, chambers of commerce, trade unions, banks, insurance companies, and other private sector organizations as mutual guarantee organizations that provide medium- and long-term credit guarantees (Mosburger and Benedicter, 2004).
3) The UK: The UK has long used government-sponsored loan guarantees. The Business Sharing Services Organization (under the Ministry of Trade and Industry) launched the Small Firms Loan Guarantee (SFLG) in 1981 to provide guarantees to small firms (Cowling et al., 2018; Ughetto et al., 2017). SFLG was then replaced by the Enterprise Finance Guarantee (EFG) in January 2009. The new scheme is managed by the British Business Financial Services Unit (a subsidiary of the Commercial Bank of England) but is still structurally subordinate to the Business, Energy, and Industrial Strategy (Agnese et al., 2018). Another CGS operating in the post-crisis years is the National Loan Guarantee Scheme (NLGS). Introduced in March 2012, NLGS aims to increase opportunities and reduce costs for SME lending from banks (Hall, 2016).
4) Chile: The first legislative framework for the Chilean credit guarantee system dates back to the early 1980s when FOGAPE as a public fund was established under the supervision of the Superintendency of Banks and Financial Institutions of Chile (SBIF). Then in 2007, the credit guarantee system was designed according to the experiences of Argentina and Spain. Accordingly, mutual guarantee corporations (SAGR) and mutual guarantee cooperatives (CGR) are identified as two types of credit guarantee institutions. Cooperatives are non-profit and only guarantee credit to their beneficiary firms, while corporations have a more general framework. In this institutional environment, FOGAPE is obliged to provide loans to SMEs guaranteed by these institutions and further guarantee them. Another critical institution is the Chilean Economic Development Agency (CORFO), which is responsible for implementing Chilean government policies to increase the competitiveness and development of SMEs and support the lending and guarantee schemes in partnership with the private sector (Cowan et al., 2015; Vento and La Colla, 2012).
5) China: The establishment of credit guarantee funds in China dates back to the late 1990s when the government guided the design of a credit guarantee system due to the severity of problems for SMEs in accessing financial resources with the collaboration of umbrella associations (Li and Lin, 2017).

China has benchmarked the experiences of foreign countries (particularly Japan) and designed a specific model for guaranteeing credibility with domestic indicators, which consists of a body, two wings, and three levels. In this context, the body expresses the need to exploit diverse financial resources, market mechanisms, corporate governance policies, and support mechanisms. The two wings emphasize the use of credit guarantee (public and private) and mutual guarantee simultaneously, and the three levels refer to the governance structure at the national, provincial, and urban levels (Yang, 2009). In particular, public guarantee institutions with local departments and agencies under the Ministry of Commerce, the Ministry of Finance, and public banks are vital elements of the Chinese credit guarantee system (Situ, 2011).

6) Argentina: The credit guarantee system in Argentina has special key features that have enjoyed considerable success and effectiveness in recent years. Argentina's credit guarantee framework is inspired by the Spanish model and emphasizes mutual guarantee institutions that offer a range of services to their stakeholders. An advantage of the Argentinian credit guarantee framework is the financial incentives offered to firms that invest as sponsors or contributors in mutual guarantee institutions. Mutual credit institutions are recognized under SME development policies and are legislated and supervised by the Deputy Minister of Small and Medium Enterprises and Regional Development of the Ministry of Industry and the Central Bank (Kramer, 2013; Vento and Agnese, 2012).
7) Brazil: The Brazilian SME law was adopted in 2006 as a framework for changing the relationship between government and small businesses. Subsequently, in 2007, a supplementary law encouraged the Brazilian government to establish a national credit guarantee system to facilitate the access of SMEs to financial services. Before that, the first generation of state-owned guarantee institutions (including Endorsement Fund for Micro and Small Enterprises (FAMPE), Guarantee Fund for the Promotion of Competitiveness (FGPC), and Guarantee Fund for Employment and Income Generation (FUNPROGER)) were established in the 1990s. Despite their relatively high initial financial outreach, these institutions lost their financial stability over the long term. Inspired by the models of Argentina, Italy, and Spain, the second generation of Brazilian credit guarantee models used the concept of credit guarantee societies where loan applicants are the direct or indirect beneficiaries of public–private funds (Kramer, 2013; Lanz, 2017).
8) South Africa: Khula was established by the Department of Commerce and Industry following the passage of the National Business Decree (Decree 102) in 1996 as a facilitator of access to finance for the creation and development of SMEs, specifically for previously disadvantaged individuals (PDIs). Khula's services include providing loans, stocks, credit guarantees, agricultural land empowerment facilities, and mentoring. Khula used to work with a wide range of banks; however, this process faced problems because of the banks' lack of attention to identifying potential businesses to guarantee

Table 10.2 Comparative Study Results

	Ownership Structure	*Provided Services*	*Liability Distinction Pattern*	*Guarantee Provision Strategy*	*Inclusion Scope*	*Governing Institution*	*Macro Law*	*Public Support Models*
Japan	3 public	Loan	direct guarantee and counter-guarantee	individual and portfolio guarantee	Open (excluded a few fields)	Credit Guarantee Association, Financial Services Agency, and Ministry of Economy, Trade, and Industry	Specific Law (Credit Guarantee Law and Credit Insurance Law for Small and Medium Enterprises)	Participate in risk coverage and development of evaluation infrastructure
Germany	4 public, 2 public–private, 3 private, 1 mutual	Loan	direct guarantee and counter-guarantee	individual and portfolio guarantee	Both targeted (specialized) and open	Credit Guarantee Associations, Lenders 'and Borrowers' Associations, Venture Capital Banks, and the German Financial Supervision Unit	Under the Banking Act, the German Credit Institutions Act, and the Citizenship Act	Participate in risk coverage and development of evaluation infrastructure
The U.K.	3 public, 1 mutual	Loan	direct guarantee	individual and portfolio guarantee	Open (excluded a few fields)	Small Business Support Organization (Department of Commerce and Industry), Department of Business, Innovation and Skills, International Settlement Bank, and Treasury	Under the macro law of the financial system	Participate in risk coverage and initial capital provision
Chile	4 public, 1 public–private, 1 mutual	Loan	direct guarantee	individual and portfolio guarantee	Open (only with a sale limit)	Cooperative Department of the Ministry of Economy and the Chilean Supervisory Bank	Specific Law	–

	Ownership Structure	*Provided Services*	*Liability Distinction Pattern*	*Guarantee Provision Strategy*	*Inclusion Scope*	*Governing Institution*	*Macro Law*	*Public Support Models*
China	4 public, 1 private	Loan	direct guarantee and counter-guarantee	individual and portfolio guarantee	Targeting specific groups (vulnerable/ deprived)	Organizations under the Ministry of Commerce, the Ministry of Finance and State Banks, the National Reform and Development Commission, and the Ministry of Economic Affairs	Mostly specific Law	Participation in initial capital provision
Argentina	2 public, 1 public–private, 1 mutual	Loan	direct guarantee and counter-guarantee	individual guarantee	Open (one with geographical limit)	Deputy Minister of Small and Medium Enterprises and Regional Development under the Ministry of Industry, Central Bank, Ministry of Production, Department of Local Development and SMEs, and Central Bank	Specific Law	Initial capital provision and facilitated tax regime
Brazil	4 public, 2 public–private, 1 mutual	Loan	Direct guarantee	individual guarantee	Open	State Bank of Brazil, Labor Support Fund, Brazilian SME Support Services, SME Forum under the Ministry of Development, Industry and Foreign Relations, the National Economic and Social Development Bank, the Sao Paulo SME Association, and the Ministry of National Integration	Under the SME Act	Participation in initial capital provision
South Africa	1 public	Loan	Direct guarantee	individual guarantee	Targeting specific groups	Department of Industry and Commerce	Under the Small Business Act	Participation in initial capital provision

Source: Authors' compilation based on JFC (2014); OECD (2006, 2013); Vento and Agnese (2012); Vento and La Colla (2012); Cowling et al. (2018); Li and Lin (2017); Kramer (2013). Accordingly, the following results can be extracted.

credit. Accordingly, in its new strategy, Khula cooperates with only one or two large banks and a maximum of four small banks (as niches; OECD, 2006; Sefa, 2019).

I. Ownership structure: In all countries except Germany, credit guarantee institutions are often state-owned. In other words, given the complexity and difficulty of establishing these institutions, the initial implementation of the credit guarantee model in all countries requires government intervention.
II. Provided services: Because of the difficulty of equity guarantee, all the countries, even those with a market-based system, have used the loan guarantee model.
III. Liability distinction pattern: The structure of the financial system of countries plays a key role in the liability distinction pattern. The ease of stock trade and the possibility of value decline and bankruptcy in the short term leads to a risk-averse approach in the market-based financial system. Thus, there is less possibility of developing counter-guarantee models in these systems.
IV. Guarantee provision strategy: The position of different countries in the path of institutional development affects the way they provide guarantees. Countries initially start with a single guarantee model, as it is easier and more reliable. Then, with the maturity and development of banks' capabilities, the portfolio guarantee model gradually acquires its place alongside the previous model.
V. Inclusion scope: In all countries, open schemes are used more to pay attention to development capacities in different sectors. However, in developing countries, supporting certain groups is considered the main goal of targeted schemes, while in developed countries, some traditional sectors are usually deprived of support, or pioneering sectors are highlighted.
VI. Governing institution: Numerous institutions such as the Ministry of Industry and Trade, the Ministry of Economy, banks, and associations are involved in the credit guarantee process in most countries (except South Africa), which is a somewhat inevitable situation due to the interdisciplinary nature of this financing model. As a result, concentrating on the design of a transparent governance model is the key to success for the credit guarantee framework.
VII. Macro-law: In most countries (except Germany and the United Kingdom), the general law is drafted under the SME Protection Act or in the form of a special law. As a result, it does not seem that this framework can be easily defined under monetary, financial, and banking laws.
VIII. Government support models: Different countries offer a variety of services to develop the credit guarantee model. Accordingly, while providing initial capital is more needed in developing countries, risk coverage is more needed in developed countries.

4 Iranian credit guarantee funds

Since 1996, several public funds have been established to support SMEs in various fields, with credit guarantees as a service in Iran. Accordingly, Small Industries Fund, Export Guarantee Fund, Advanced Industry Research and Development Fund, and Cooperative Investment Guarantee Fund also provide guarantee services to NTBFs. According to the authors' calculations, these institutions guaranteed $40 million in 2018 for NTBFs, which is less compared to 2012. The Iran National Innovation Fund also facilitates access to bank guarantees for NTBFs and supports the loans of private institutions. Accordingly, this institution has grown its services exponentially and facilitated access to $100 million in bank guarantees in 2020 (Iran National Innovation Fund, 2021. Table 10.3 summarizes the status-quo of the Iranian public funds.

In addition to public institutions, research and technology funds (RTFs) are developed according to Article 100 of the Third Development Plan to create opportunities for the private sector to participate and invest in technological activities. These funds were further emphasized in Article 45 of the Fourth Development Plan, the NTBF Supporting Law, and the Executive Regulations of Article 44 of the Law on Removing the Barriers to Competitive Production and Improving the Country's Financial System.

A review of the statutes of research and technology funds suggested that these funds can provide a variety of guarantees with a 2% annual fee and a 10%–15% deposit of total loan in the form of various forms of collateral. In 2019, 37 research and technology funds were established with a total guarantee amount of $31.6 million (tripled compared to 2013) (Employers' Association of Venture Capital Funds and Institutions of Iran, 2019).

5 Patterns of Iranian credit guarantee schemes for NTBFs

For the identification of patterns in Iranian credit guarantee schemes for NTBFs, first, the funds' guarantee services are briefly introduced:

1. Export Guarantee Fund: As the largest and oldest guarantee fund, EGF provides financial services to export activities. Most of the fund's services are allocated to large firms that have entered the export market. Of course, some NTBFs have also gained export potential in recent years and can use the services of this fund.
2. Cooperative Investment Guarantee Fund: CIGF has focused deeply on guarantee funds, and thus has devoted a small fraction of its financial resources to contract-based guarantees. The main services of this fund are dedicated to cooperatives, as this fund can only dedicate 30% of its resources to other organization types (including NTBFs). However, CIGF has agreed with the Vice Presidency for Science and Technology to further develop its services to NTBFs.

Table 10.3 Iranian Credit Guarantee Institutions

Credit Guarantee Institutions	*Type of Insurance/Guarantee*	*Total Received Commission (Premium)*	*Required Collateral*	*Government Participation in Risk Coverage*
Small Industries Fund	Loan guarantee and various types of contract-based guarantees ($12,000)	1.5% of the guarantee amount	Applicant's check worth 1.5 times the amount of the guarantee, with real estate collateral or promissory note worth 1.5 times the amount of the guarantee	The government provided its initial capital ($2 million) and public grants. The fund is supported by its backup fund, the applicant's collateral, and public resources
Export Guarantee Fund	Different types of export credit insurance policies, investment insurance policies, loan guarantees, coverage of bank guarantees (based on contract)	Insurance premiums for export goods: 0.5%–5% of the sum insured Guarantee fee: 2%–3% of the guarantee amount	Promissory notes and real estate securities worth a total of 1.2 times the amount of the guarantee	The fund is 100% state-owned and in some years the capital has been increased using the state budget. Guarantee support includes received premiums and public resources
Advanced Industries Research and Development Support Fund	Auction/tender, performance, and advance payment guarantees	Up to 1.5% depending on the type of collateral and the amount; up to 2.3% in the absence of insurance coverage	Combination of cash, promissory note, financial assets, property (at least 130% of the guarantee amount)	The fund is fully state-owned, and its loss is covered by the government
Cooperative Investment Guarantee Fund	Loan repayment guarantees, other types of contract-based guarantees	1%–2% for loan guarantee, 50% banking system fee for other guarantees	Real estate collateral, commercial documents of participation bonds and stock exchanges depending on the project, a deposit of at least 10% of the guarantee amount	The fund is 100% state-owned, and its loss is covered by the government
Agricultural Insurance Fund	Natural hazard insurance for agricultural and livestock activities	5%–50% of the insurance amount	Not necessary	10%–90% of the received premium is borne by the government. Also, Government grants are expected in the annual budget
Mining Investment Insurance Corporation	Investment insurance in the field of mining activities, credit insurance for loan repayment	–	Mining license, mine exploration license	The fund is fully state-owned, and its loss is covered by the government
Iran National Innovation Fund	Provide 50% cash deposit required for bank guarantee, a 30% discount on the bank guarantee fee	–	–	Total funding by the government

Source: Authors' compilation based on http://www.sif.ir, https://egfi.ir/, http://www.airdfh.ir/, http://cigf.ir/, http://www.sbkiran.ir/, http://www.iranmico.com/, https://www.inif.ir/ (accessed on February 23, 2021).

3. Small Industries Fund: SIF guarantees a maximum of 70% of the loan (85% in disadvantaged areas). The guarantee services of SIF had a good upward trend until 2017, but then they collapsed. The failure rate of SIF guarantees is 30%, a rate that indicates its risky and unsustainable approach.
4. Advanced Industry Research and Development Fund: AIRDF, which operated as the Electronic Industry Research and Development Fund until 2018, focused on providing financial funds and guarantee services in the field of electronics industries before changing its title. With the title change, its scope of services expanded to various industrial areas. Until 2014, AIRDF did not give much attention to guarantee services but has since added them to its portfolio.
5. Iran National Innovation Fund: Among the specialized public funds introduced in this section, INIF is the most important one focused on NTBFs. Although INIF can provide credit guarantee services according to its association statute, it has practically removed this service from its service portfolio. The only guarantee-related service of INIF is the facilitation of three types of contract-based guarantees (participation in tenders, prepayments, and good performance) by the banking network through its deposits in several banks.
6. Research and Technology Funds: Most RTFs do not consider guarantee services but focus on other services such as loans and leasing. RTFs have also neglected loan guarantees as one of the main types of credit guarantees. However, RTF guarantees have low failure rates which further enhances its sustainability.

Based on the dimensions of the selected framework, Table 10.4 identifies the patterns identified in the existing credit guarantee institutions.

Accordingly, the following patterns have been identified regarding credit guarantee schemes:

I. Non-use of various capacities of the executive framework in the credit guarantee system (especially reliance guarantee and guarantee basket): In terms of the two dimensions of liability distinction pattern and guarantee provision strategy, all credit guarantee schemes focus on providing direct and individual guarantees. In other words, there is no institutional capacity to provide a portfolio guarantee or counter-guarantee.
II. Non-use of various models of the ownership structure in credit guarantee institutions: Only public and private ownership structures were implemented, while alternative models (public–private and mutual institutions) were neglected.
III. Focus of existing institutions on contract-based guarantees: Credit guarantee institutions in Iran, especially public ones, have focused more on contract-based guarantees in their service portfolio. All five public institutions provide contract-based guarantee services, but only three nonpublic institutions provide loan guarantee services. Although research and

Table 10.4 Patterns of Iranian Credit Guarantee Institutions

Guarantee Institution	*Ownership Structure*	*Provided Services*		*Liability Distinction Pattern*	*Guarantee Provision Strategy*	*Inclusion Scope*	*Governing Institution*	*Macro Law*	*Public Support Models*
		Guarantee Services	*Other Financial Services?*						
Small Industries Fund	Public	Loan guarantees, other contract-based guarantees	No	Direct guarantee	Individual guarantee	Open schemes	Ministry of Industry, Mine, and Trade	Law on Establishment of the Small Industries Fund	Initial capital provision and participation in risk coverage
Export Guarantee Fund	Public	Loan guarantees, coverage of bank guarantees (contract-based)	No	Direct guarantee	Individual guarantee	Targeted schemes (exporting firms)	Ministry of Industry, Mine, and Trade	Law on Establishment of the Export Guarantee Fund, Law on How to Manage the Export Guarantee Fund	Initial capital provision, participation in risk coverage, and reduction of the interest rate of the loan
Advanced Industry Research and Development Fund	Public	Different types of contract-based guarantees	Yes	Direct guarantee	Individual guarantee	Open schemes	Ministry of Industry, Mine, and Trade	Law on the Establishment of the Electronic Industry R&D Support Fund	Initial capital provision and participation in risk coverage

(*Continued*)

Guarantee Institution	*Ownership Structure*	*Provided Services*		*Liability Distinction Pattern*	*Guarantee Provision Strategy*	*Inclusion Scope*	*Governing Institution*	*Macro Law*	*Public Support Models*
		Guarantee Services	*Other Financial Services?*						
Cooperative Investment Guarantee Fund	Public	Loan guarantees, other types of contract-based guarantees	No	Direct guarantee	Individual guarantee	Targeted schemes (cooperatives)	Ministry of Labor, Cooperation, and Social Welfare	Article 9 of the Law on the Amendment of Articles of the Fourth Development Plan	Initial capital provision and participation in risk coverage
Iran National Innovation Fund	Public	Facilitate the acquisition of bank guarantees (contract-based)	Yes	Direct guarantee	Individual guarantee	Open schemes	–	Law on the Protection of Knowledge-Based Companies and Institutions	Initial capital provision
Research and Technology Funds	Private	Loan guarantees, other types of contract-based guarantees	Yes	Direct guarantee	Individual guarantee	Open schemes	Working Group on Public Research and Technology Funds	Article 44 of the Law on the Elimination of Barriers to Production and its bylaws, Instructions for Granting and Revoking Licenses, Directing and Supervising the Activities of Research and Technology Funds	Initial capital provision and loan provision by Iran National Innovation Fund

Source: Authors' findings.

technology funds can offer both models, however, they also focus on contract-based guarantee services. Thus, loan guarantees only make up 23% of total guarantees (8%, 8%, 6%, and 1% by SIF, EGF, CIGF, and RTFs, respectively).

IV. Lack of specialized financial institutions providing guarantee services in the private sector: Although the development of specialized private institutions is allowed in the relevant laws, all research and technology funds generically provide guarantee services along with other financial services.

V. Limited selection of NTBFs for loan guarantee services: From the four institutions that provide loan guarantee services, two have a targeted scope and provide their services only to exporting firms and cooperatives. According to the list of NTBFs (published by the Vice-Presidency for Science and Technology), less than 3% of these firms are cooperatives. Moreover, according to statistics available at the Center for International Scientific Interactions of the Vice-Presidency, less than 7% of NTBFs have been exported in the last two years. Therefore, a significant share of NTBFs cannot use the services of the Export Guarantee Fund and the Cooperative Investment Guarantee Fund, and are thus left with two options for receiving loan guarantees. Of these two options, research and technology funds offer limited loan guarantees. This issue again narrows the choices of knowledge-based companies in this field. Thus, most NTBFs can only refer to one public guarantee fund to receive loan guarantee services. In terms of the volume of services, NTBFs have had a limited choice in receiving loan guarantee services, and in practice, a small volume of loan guarantee services have an open scope and are available to the general public (8% and 1% of total guarantees by SIF and RTFs, respectively).

VI. Simultaneous use of two instruments in most public funds (provision of initial capital and participation in risk coverage): Out of five public funds whose initial capital is completely funded by the government, four of them also benefit from government participation in risk coverage, and in the event of a claim on guarantees, they can count on government support to compensate for the damage.

VII. Non-use of risk-sharing instruments for private funds: Unlike public funds, private ones do not use risk-sharing tools; research and technology funds, however, can refer to the Iran National Innovation Fund to acquire loans.

VIII. Non-use of complex instruments by the government: Government funds do not use the "facilitated tax regime" and "participation in the development of evaluation infrastructure" as the more sophisticated instruments of government participation in the development of the credit guarantee system. Granting or reducing the interest rate of the loans is also implemented in a few funds.

IX. Lack of macro law for the financial supervision of the activities of institutions: There is no unique law for the establishment and supervision of the activities of these credit guarantee institutions; instead, each fund has its establishment law. These laws only deal with the establishment and governance of the funds and neglect financial regulation and supervision as the main pillars of fund regulation.

X. Existence of several accountable institutions for credit guarantee institutions: The Ministry of Industry, Mines, and Trade, the Ministry of Labor, Cooperation, and Social Welfare, and the Working Group of Research and Technology Funds are the three accountable institutions, as they supervise one or more credit guarantee institutions. This institutional multiplicity has taken place, while the relationship between these institutions and the institutions in charge of the entire financial system has not been determined.

6 Conclusion and policy implications

This chapter has evaluated credit guarantee schemes in different countries with different financial market structures. In developed countries, the credit guarantee system has evolved in the policy and operational environment following a long history and has reached a point of stability. Therefore, most studies on the credit guarantees schemes in these countries focus on the system components and not the whole system. In developing countries, however, the systemic approach to credit guarantee is inevitable given the short history of implementing the financial tool. In other words, most of these countries have not been able to achieve the policy ecosystem needed to develop the desired system. Therefore, the use of this instrument has remained at the level of schemes. Accordingly, the systematic and comprehensive approach paves the way for compensating for the limitations of some credit guarantee instruments with complementary tools and provides an integrated overview of the development and implementation of credit guarantee schemes. Therefore, various scholars have studied the credit guarantee systems of developing countries with a systemic approach (Singh and Wasdani [2016] in India, Maningo [2016] in the Philippines, Amornkitvikai and Harvie [2016] in Thailand, Li and Lin [2017], Ma et al. [2019] in China, Dang and Chuc [2019] in Vietnam, Nadeem and Rasool [2019] in Pakistan, and Yağcı, [2019] in Turkey). Of course, this approach is complementary (rather than alternative) to the study of system components and can even lead to the analysis of internal component mechanisms. In the present chapter, the Iranian credit guarantee schemes of NTBFs have been studied with a systemic approach. Therefore, while identifying the macro patterns of the schemes, the main reasons for the prevalence of the mentioned patterns among different schemes have been extracted:

1. Counter-guarantee is one of the executive frameworks used in guarantee schemes that enable risk-sharing among actors, increase guarantee institutions' ability to participate in higher-value projects, and allow governments to participate in risk coverage (Deelen and Molenaar, 2004; Kramer, 2013). However, the capacity of this instrument is still not sufficiently exploited in Iran (as in other low-income countries [Beck et al., 2010]). Private research

and technology funds cannot develop this model because of the lack of access to appropriate capital support. Furthermore, most public funds do not have the necessary confidence to issue counter-guarantees for non-government funds. Finally, the Iran National Innovation Fund does not have enough experience in issuing direct guarantees and has made little use of the possibility of cooperating with research and technology funds in recent years to issue a counter-guarantee. Given the increasing role of the Iran National Innovation Fund as an accountable institution, however, this capacity will soon be exploited.

2. Portfolio guarantees have numerous benefits, including lower operating costs for banks and especially for credit guarantee institutions, a reduced number of valuations for firms, less executive tightness, faster operation, and an increased possibility of risk-taking and providing loans to more risky customers in the loan portfolio (Beck et al., 2010; Deelen and Molenaar, 2004; Levitsky, 1997). Nonetheless, the use of this instrument is not common in Iran (as in other less developed countries [O'Bryan, 2010]). Accordingly, the lack of proper knowledge of banks about NTBFs, the lack of institutional relationship between banks and guarantee funds, and the reluctance of research and technology funds to use the guarantee portfolio model because of increasing pressure on service delivery processes to these funds are the most important challenges. Previous experiences regarding the reluctance of banks to evaluate NTBFs and refer them to the Iran National Innovation Fund also confirm this finding.
3. Although the public–private ownership structure (and, in particular, public ownership and private management) can reduce the involvement and interference of the government in the executive activities of funds, on the one hand, and increase the management of the credit institution, on the other (Beck et al., 2010), this pattern is not welcomed in Iranian credit guarantee institutions. There have been no similar experiences in other areas either, as ownership has often been transferred in the form of privatization, and management has been maintained under public authority. Also, the move toward public–private ownership for the current public funds has heavy political economy dimensions and at the same time faces many legal challenges that lead to lower transparency in practice.
4. The mutual guarantee model has various advantages, including the creation of a stable market for banks as a result of longer-term transactions, the reduction of the interest rates on loans provided to firms, the development of assessment capabilities of the credit guarantee system (Columba et al., 2010; Gai et al., 2016), the possibility of leveraging unconventional properties of NTBFs, and ultimately the increase in access of these firms to high-volume financial resources (Beltrame et al., 2019). This model, however, is not applied in Iranian credit guarantee institutions (as in other middle and low-income countries [Beck et al., 2010]), partly because of the possible conflict of interest between large and small firms as well as funding and new institutions. A lack of powerful guilds to support mutual guarantee services,

the high risk of financial crisis due to various economic fluctuations and challenges, and the lack of successful experience in starting and organizing cooperative models are the main barriers to the development of mutual guarantee associations.

5. In contract-based guarantees, the third party (recipient of the guarantee) is also a party to the contract and is more inclined to terminate the contractual obligations rather than to receive damages and request a guarantee. Accordingly, in many cases, the credit guarantee institution can negotiate to resolve the dispute and prevent the termination of the cooperation. In a loan guarantee, however, the third party can easily put financial pressure on the credit guarantee institution by terminating the cooperation and excluding the possibility of negotiation. Therefore, the higher risk of loan guarantees in the absence of a policy to support this type of guarantee leads to more funding for contract-based guarantees.
6. The general rules and statutes of research and technology funds issue licenses for the full range of financial services. Thus, institutions do not limit the range of their activities but provide all eligible services. However, specialized licensing focused on different types of guarantees leads to the formation of specialized institutions. Therefore, following the desire of research and technology funds to provide loans instead of issuing guarantees, the policymakers should provide targeted support and facilities to these institutions to direct them toward specialized guarantee services.
7. Most NTBFs (except export-oriented and cooperative ones) can only refer to the Small Industry Guarantee Fund for loan guarantees. However, the long queue of applying SMEs and the weakness of NTBFs in providing documents (compared to other SMEs) lead to a small share of these institutions from the total provided guarantees. Therefore, the Iran National Innovation Fund, as the financial institution accountable for NTBFs, should provide loan guarantees.
8. The lack of obligation of most government funds to maintain the initial capital of the fund, on the one hand, and their approach to development and promotion of NTBFs in the early years, on the other, have led to relatively high failure rates for guarantees provided. For these institutions to continue to provide services, accountable public agencies have been forced to cover the risk by compensating the loss. Thus, the provision of initial capital and risk coverage reduces the productivity of these funds, as the institutions are not accountable for their financial performance. Moreover, as public resources ultimately cover potential claims on these funds, firms' perceptions of these institutions change from financial service providers to rent distributors. As a result, firms that have not been able to obtain the services they need through conventional channels due to financial deficits may refer to these funds. However, among the five public institutions, the Iran National Innovation Fund is different in this respect, as it received its initial capital from the public budget only, and its possible risks are not compensated by

the government. These settings can increase the productivity of the Iran National Innovation Fund in the exploitation of public resources or lead to an excessive risk aversion approach.

9. Given the difficulty of profitability of the private guarantee funds, especially in the early years of development (Kramer, 2013), government participation in risk coverage helps private institutions be less financially disadvantaged and capable of continuing their activities (Beck et al., 2010; Leone and Porretta, 2012). However, for private funds, the accountable institution with the required financial characteristics has not been available. At first, the Commission of Article 100 (located in the Secretariat of the Ministry of Science, Research, and Technology) only granted licenses and had no financial interaction with the funds. The Working Group on Research and Technology Funds has behaved relatively similarly, but the improving role of the Iranian National Innovation Fund as the Secretariat of the Working Group can lead to increased interactions with research and technology funds and further risk coverage in the future.
10. In addition to providing loans, public funds in different countries use more sophisticated tools of government participation in the development of the credit guarantee system. Some countries design a facilitated tax regime for credit guarantee service providers, which creates more opportunities for the establishment of credit guarantee funds and guides institutions toward the provision of more credit guarantee services. These facilitated tax regimes can also reduce the cost of providing credit guarantee services (Panetta and Cascio, 2012). However, this instrument is not currently favored by the innovation ecosystem policymakers, as it lacks legal support.
11. Another instrument used by some countries, especially those with a bank-based financial system, to facilitate the credit guarantee system is participation in the development of data infrastructure and corporate evaluation. Accordingly, banks are usually more cautious in providing loans to SMEs because of the lack of development of capital markets and information asymmetry. Thus, the development of a rich database and comprehensive credit infrastructure can solve part of this challenge, as it would help the identification of healthy businesses by creating validation models (Kuwahara et al., 2016). However, the lack of an accountable institution to create the infrastructure for evaluation and the lack of proper institutional communication between the innovation finance institutions and the financial macro system has led to the absence of proper infrastructure development. Funding institutions, however, have not yet felt the need to move toward credit-based services, as their current services have been very well received by applicants. After the development of government transaction guarantee bylaws, however, the Sepas system, which guarantees NTBFs through research and technology funds for participation in government transactions, was launched to provide such a database.

12. There is no specific law in the system of financial supervision of guarantee funds for matters such as prudential supervision of financial activities, determination of financial limits of services, and financial responsibility. At the same time, all funds provide financial services to various firms, creating an accumulation of financial debts, the non-fulfillment of which affects the entire financial system. Therefore, the existence of financial supervisory laws to determine how these institutions are connected to the financial macrosystem is essential. Public institutions are structured with a board of trustees, where the law simply addresses the establishment of the institution, and its supervision has been left to the board without a clear macro-law. Research and technology funds also have a similar governance pattern, although their supervision is highlighted in lower-level policy guidelines. Of course, this challenge was recently addressed by the policymaker, where after the announcement of the duties of the Working Group on Research and Technology Funds (in the executive by-law of Article 44 of the Law on Removing Barriers to Competitive Production and Improving the Financial System of the Country), the instructions for granting/revoking licenses and the directing and supervising of the activities of research and technology funds were approved. Compared to other related laws, this directive has better insight into the financial supervision of funds and has established regulatory rules to guide and monitor the performance of funds; nonetheless, they are not comprehensive enough compared to similar laws in other countries. Moreover, the relationship between this instruction, the macro-rules of the financial system, and macro-supervisory institutions in this system is not clear, and the accountable institution for the obligations created by research and technology funds has not been determined. When liabilities have been regulated for various financial institutions, the lack of such regulation for credit guarantee institutions causes various stakeholders, especially larger ones such as banks and large corporations, to be more cautious in the approval of their guarantees.
13. Due to the gradual and evolutionary development of the credit guarantee system, the multiplicity of accountable institutions in this system is now inevitable. Various public agencies (such as the Ministries of Industry, Mines, and Trade, and the Ministry of Cooperation, Labor, and Social Welfare) first established government development funds according to their needs and acted as accountable institutions. Subsequently, with the development of research and technology funds, the relevant responsible institution has been developed in the structure of the government but outside the financial system. Thus, one main issue is the placement of the responsible institution outside the financial system, which is partly due to the Central Bank's limited experience in developing financial innovations and supporting the formation of new financial institutions. The role of the public institution (in each field) as the parent institution of the private institution can lead to the development of a hierarchy in the credit system.

References

Aboojafari R, Daliri A, Taghizadeh-Hesary, F, Mokhtari, M, Ekhtiari M (2019) The Role of Credit Guarantee Schemes in the Development of Small and Medium Sized Enterprises. In Yoshino N, Taghizadeh-Hesary F, *Unlocking SME Finance in Asia: Roles of Credit Rating and Credit Guarantee Schemes.* Routledge, Abingdon

Agnese P, Rizzo M, Vento GA (2018) SMEs finance and bankruptcies: The role of credit guarantee schemes in the UK. *J App Financ Bank* 8(3):1–16

Amornkitvikai Y, Harvie C (2016) The impact of finance on the performance of Thai manufacturing SMEs. In Vandenberg P, Chantapacdepong P, Yoshino N, *SMEs in Developing Asia: New Approaches to Overcoming Market Failure.* Asian Development Bank Institute, Tokyo, p 144–178. https://www.adb.org/sites/default/files/publication/214476/adbi-smes-developing-asia.pdf

Arping S, Loranth G, Morrison A (2009) Public initiatives to support entrepreneurs: Credit guarantees versus co-funding. *J Financial Stab* 6(1):26–35. https://www.sciencedirect.com/science/article/abs/pii/S1572308909000400

Banitaba Koupai SM (2011) *Criticism of the Methodologies of Equipping and Allocating Resources by the Banking System and Presenting Suggestion for Development* [In Persian]. Faculty of Economics, University of Tehran, Tehran

Banitaba SM. (2016) *SME Finance: Development of Credit Guarantee Institution* [In Persian]. Islamic Parliament Research Center of the Islamic Republic of Iran, Tehran

Beck T, Klapper LF, Mendoza JC (2010) The typology of partial credit guarantee funds around the world. *J Financial Stab* 6:10–25

Beltrame F, Floreani J, Grassetti L, Mason MC, Miani S (2019) Collateral, mutual guarantees and the entrepreneurial orientation of SMEs. *Management Decision* 57(1):168–192. https://www.emerald.com/insight/content/doi/10.1108/MD-11-2017-1077/full/html

Berger AN, Udell GF (1998) The economics of small business finance: The roles of private equity and debt markets in the financial growth cycle. *J Bank Finance* 22(6–8):613–673

Calice P (2016) Assessing Implementation of the Principles for Public Credit Guarantees for SMEs- A Global Survey. World Bank Group

Columba F, Gambacorta L, Mistrulli PE (2010) Mutual guarantee institutions and small business finance. *J Financial Stab* 6(1):45–54

Cowan K, Drexler A, Yañez Á (2015) The effect of credit guarantees on credit availability and delinquency rates. *J Bank Finance* 59:98–110

Cowling M, Mitchell P (2003) Is the small firms loan guarantee scheme hazardous for banks or helpful to small business?. *Small Bus Econ* 21(1):63–71. https://link.springer.com/article/10.1023/A:1024408932156

Cowling M, Ughetto E, Lee N (2018) The innovation debt penalty: Cost of debt, loan default, and the effects of a public loan guarantee on high-tech firms. *Technol Forecast Soc Change* 127:166–176

Dang LN, Chuc AT (2019) Nam, challenges in implementing the credit guarantee scheme for SMEs: The case of Vietnam. In Yoshino N, Taghizadeh-Hesary F, *Unlocking SME Finance in Asia: Roles of Credit Rating and Credit Guarantee Schemes.* Routledge, Abingdon, pp 364–393

Daskalakis N, Balios D, Dalla V (2017) The behaviour of SMEs' capital structure determinants in different macroeconomic states. *J Corp Finance* 46:248–260

Deelen L, Molenaar K (2004) *Guarantee Funds for Small Enterprises.* International Labour Organization

Demirgüç-Kunt A, Čihák M, Feyen E, Beck T, Levine R (2013) *Financial Development and Structure Dataset.* World Bank Dataset, Washington D.C.

Demirgüç-Kunt A, Levine R (1999) *Bank-Based and Market-Based Financial Systems: Cross-Country Comparisons.* The World Bank, Washington D.C.

Employers' Association of Venture Capital Funds and Institutions of Iran (2019) The Situation of Venture Capital in the World and the Performance Report of the Members of the Venture Capital Association in Iran [In Persian]

European Commission (2003) Raising EU R&D Intensity- Improving the Effectiveness of Public Support Mechanisms for Private Sector Research and Development: Guarantee Mechanism. European Commission

Fombang MS, Adjasi CK (2018) Access to finance and firm innovation. *J Financ Econ Policy* 10(1):73–94

Gai L, Ielasi F, Rossolini M (2016) SMEs, public credit guarantees and mutual guarantee institutions. *J Small Bus Enterp Dev* 23(4):1208–1228

Garcia E (2006) *The SME Financing Gap: Theory and Evidence.* Brasilia Conference. OECD

Gracey AD (2001) *Guarantee Mechanisms for Financing Innovative Technology- Survey and Analysis.* European Commission, Luxembourg

Green A (2003) *Credit Guarantee Schemes for Small Enterprises: An Effective Instrument to Promote Private Sector-led Growth?* UNIDO

Hall S (2016) Credit Guarantee Schemes in European Economies: The Potential Impact of Different Financial Systems. Master thesis at Lund University, School of Economics and Management. https://lup.lub.lu.se/luur/download?func=downloadFile&recordOId=8883112&fileOId=8883513

HDRO (2018) Human Development Indices and Indicators. pp 22–25. Retrieved 14 September 2018

Iran National Innovation Fund (2021) Iran National Innovation Fund performance (2021) [In Persian]. Iran National Innovation Fund

IMF (2019a) World Economic Outlook Database: Changes to the Database. www.imf.org. Retrieved 7 February 2019

IMF (2019b) World Economic Outlook Database. October 2019. www.imf.org. International Monetary Fund. Retrieved 16 March 2020

JFC (2014) Credit Guarantee System in Japan. Japan Federation of Credit Guarantee Corporations, Tokyo

Kersten R, Harms J, Liket K, Maas K (2017) Small firms, large impact? A systematic review of the SME finance literature. *World Dev* 97:330–348

Knowledge-based Institutions and Companies Center (2020) Legal documents and regulations for evaluation and recognition of qualifications and support of NTBFs. Knowledge-Based Institutions & Companies Center of the Vice Presidency for Science and Technology [in Persian]

Kramer D (2013) Credit Guarantee Schemes for Small Businesses: Between Euphoria and Scepticism. The University of Berlin

Kuwahara S, Yoshino N, Sagari M, Taghizadeh-Hesary F (2016) Role of the credit risk database in developing SMEs in Japan: Ideas for Asia. In Vandenberg P, Chantapacdepong P, Yoshino N, *SMEs in Developing Asia: New Approaches to Overcoming Market Failures.* Tokyo: Asian Development Bank Institute, pp 297–323

Lanz LQ (2017) The Potential Role of SME's Credit Guarantee Schemes to Promote Financial Inclusion in Brazil. Columbia University

Leone P, Porretta P (2012) A comparative analysis of credit guarantee systems. In Leone P, Vento G, *Credit Guarantee Institutions and SME Finance.* Palgrave Macmillan, pp 287–326

Levitsky J (1997) Credit guarantee schemes for SMEs – an international review. *Small Enterp Dev* 8(2):4–17. https://citeseerx.ist.psu.edu/viewdoc/download?doi=10.1.1.534.3309&rep=rep1&type=pdf

Li J, Lin X (2017) Assessing credit guarantee companies in China: Applying a new framework. *China Econ Rev* 44:98–111

Liu Y, Fujiwara K, Jinushi T, Yamori N (2016) How should banks support SMEs to manage funding risks in China? The role of relationship banking. In Boubaker S, Buchanan B Nguyen DK, *Risk Management in Emerging Markets*, Emerald Group Publishing Limited, Bingley, p 365–398. https://www.emerald.com/insight/content/doi/10.1108/978-1-78635-452-520161025/full/html

Ma Y, Jing X, Huang Z (2019) Research on the optimization path of China's SMEs credit guarantee ecological environment. *Ekoloji* 28(107):1761–1766

Maningo GV (2016) Credit surety fund: A credit innovation for MSMEs in the Philippines. In Vandenberg P, Chantapacdepong P, Yoshino N, *SMEs in Developing Asia: New Approaches to Overcoming Market Failure.* Asian Development Bank Institute, Tokyo, pp 324–350. https://www.adb.org/sites/default/files/publication/214476/adbi-smes-developing-asia.pdf

Mosburger R, Benedicter D (2004) Credit Guarantee Organisations; Country Survey Germany

Mullins W, Toro, P (2017). Credit guarantees and new bank relationships. Central Bank of Chile Working Paper, 820. http://gcfp.mit.edu/wp-content/uploads/2017/09/Mullins.pdf

Nadeem T, Rasool R (2019) Marketing: The crucial success factor for Pakistan's credit guarantee scheme. In Yoshino N, Taghizadeh-Hesary F, *Unlocking SME Finance in Asia- Roles of Credit Rating and Credit Guarantee Schemes.* Routledge, Abingdon, pp 291–315

Navajas AR (2001) Credit Guarantee Schemes: Conceptual Frame. Financial System Development Project

O'Bryan WE (2010) An Analysis of Small Business Loan Guarantee Funds. The University of Nebraska

OECD (2006) Finan, S. Entrepreneurship. *The SME Financing Gap*, 2006

OECD (2013) SME and Entrepreneurship Financing: The Role of Credit Guarantee Schemes and Mutual Guarantee Societies in supporting finance for small and medium-sized enterprises, Paris

Panetta I (2012) An analysis of credit guarantee schemes: Suggestions provided by literature. In Leone P, Vento GA, *Credit Guarantee Institutions and SME Finance.* Palgrave Macmillan, London, pp 11–37

Panetta IC, Cascio CL (2012) The guarantee system in Spain. In Leone P, Vento GA, *Credit Guarantee Institutions and SME Finance.* Palgrave Macmillan, London, pp 131–169

Sefa (2019) Annual Report: Presentation to Parliamentary Committee on Small Business Development. Khula

Singh C, Wasdani KP (2016) Finance for MSMEs in India: Sources and challenges. In Vandenberg P, Chantapacdepong P, Yoshino N, *SMEs in Developing Asia: New Approaches to Overcoming Market Failure.* Asian Development Bank Institute,

Tokyo, pp 270–296. https://www.adb.org/sites/default/files/publication/214476/adbi-smes-developing-asia.pdf

Situ P (2011) Working Group on Inclusive Finance in China Guarantee Funds for Inclusive Finance in China. China Papers on Inclusiveness No. 3, World Microfinance Forum Geneva. https://www.findevgateway.org/sites/default/files/publications/files/mfg-en-paper-guarantee-funds-for-inclusive-finance-in-china-english-version-apr-2011.pdf

Uesugi I, Sakai, K, Yamashiro GM (2010) The effectiveness of public credit guarantees in the Japanese loan market. *J Jpn Int Econ* 24(4):457–480

Ughetto E, Scellato G, Cowling M (2017) Cost of capital and public loan guarantees to small firms. *Small Bus Econ*, 49(2): 319–337. https://link.springer.com/article/10.1007/s11187-017-9845-y

Vento GA, Agnese P (2012) The guarantee system in Argentina. In Leone P, Vento GA, *Credit Guarantee Institutions and SME Finance.* Palgrave Macmillan, London, pp 211–243

Vento GA, La Colla A (2012) The guarantee system in Chile. In Leone P, Vento GA, *Credit Guarantee Institutions and SME Finance.* Palgrave Macmillan, London, pp 244–286

Vento GA, Porretta P (2012) Introduction. In Leone P, Vento GA, *Credit Guarantee Institutions and SME Finance.* Palgrave Macmillan, London, pp 1–10. https://link.springer.com/book/10.1057/9780230362321

World Bank (2018) World Bank Country and Lending Groups. https://datahelpdesk.worldbank.org/knowledgebase/articles/906519-world-bank-country-and-lending-groups

Yağcı M (2019) Credit guarantee scheme and small and medium-sized enterprise finance-The case of Turkey. In Yoshino N, Taghizadeh-Hesary F, *Unlocking SME Finance in Asia: Roles of Credit Rating and Credit Guarantee Schemes.* Routledge, Abingdon, pp 337–363

Yamori, N (2015). Japanese SMEs and the credit guarantee system after the global financial crisis. *Cogent Econ Financ* 3(1):1002600

Yang L (2009) An Analysis on Credit Guarantee System of Small and Medium-sized Enterprises in China. Enterprise Grows in Sustaining Efficiency and Effectiveness

Yoshino N, Taghizadeh-Hesary F (2019) Role of SMEs in Asia and the financing challenges they face. In Yoshino N, Taghizadeh-Hesary F, *Unlocking SME Finance in Asia: Roles of Credit Rating and Credit Guarantee Schemes.* Routledge, Abingdon, pp3–22.https://www.taylorfrancis.com/chapters/edit/10.4324/9780429401060-1/role-smes-asia-financing-challenges-face-naoyuki-yoshino-farhad-taghizadeh-hesary

11 The role of capital market in innovation finance

Parisa Alizadeh and Mohsen Rahmati

1 Introduction

Technology-based SMEs play an important role in creating jobs and growing the economy over the long term (Wellalage and Fernandez, 2019). Sufficient and suitable external financing is of great importance to these SMEs, especially startups, not only for national economic growth (Hall, 2010), but also for firm-level innovation (Wellalage and Fernandez, 2019). Although banks and similar deposit-taking institutions have traditionally provided external financing to SMEs, they prefer to deal with companies that have steady cash and collateral flows (Thompson et al., 2018). In past years, this tendency has been worsened because of substantial financial regulatory measures enacted as a result of the world economic downturn, which have decreased the issuance of bank loans, especially for SMEs (OECD, 2020; Shinozaki, 2014).

It should be considered that SMEs and startups, specifically, lack sufficient collateral, have restricted financial histories, and may not possess the ability to create detailed financial reports (OECD, 2018). Therefore, traditional bank financing presents problems to younger, creative, and fast-growing SMEs with greater risk-return profiles (OECD, 2015). The situation is more complicated for SMEs in developing countries, particularly micro and small enterprises, as they have more problems in obtaining financing to effectively scale up and expand their businesses (Zavatta, 2008).

From an investor's viewpoint, investing in innovation-driven firms is largely related to information asymmetries between the firms and the investors, which is a consequence of risky innovative activities (Hain and Christensen, 2020). This property makes investment in research and innovative activities different from routine ones (Brown and Lee, 2017). In fact, innovative activities have some characteristics that make financing them difficult. First, the result of RandD and innovative activities is known as public good, and its use cannot be entirely protected by a specific firm. Moreover, the risk of copying the result worsens the inherent uncertainty in RandD. In addition, RandD and innovation rely mainly on intangible assets (i.e., knowledge and expertise), which cannot be used as collateral for the bank's investment. RandD results are usually obtained over the long-term and thus, financiers are not able to evaluate the projects and invest in firms using debt, which is based on collateral and insurance of the definite result

DOI: 10.4324/9781003220220-15

(IOSCO, 2015). Table 11.1 compares the attributes affecting the access of SMEs and large firms to external financing.

Considering the above failures, different attempts could be made, such as formulating policy instruments and verifying financing mechanisms (e.g., crowdfunding or fintech endeavors addressed to some extent by the other chapters of this book) to strengthen the innovative finance system as a whole. However, new institutions constitute an undeniable component of the system, too. Among these institutions, capital markets are key players in bridging the financial gap by preparing alternative financing sources for SMEs, especially as their funding demands change during their life cycle (IOSCO, 2015). Therefore, the purpose of this chapter is to focus on some innovations in institutions and products, and explain the main financing options (private equity, debt instruments, and collective investment vehicles) available through stock markets for startups and SMEs. The venture capital (VC) mechanism as the most common instrument for private equity and Sukuk funds as a growing debt instrument are described in more detail under specific subsections. The comparative study section addresses the government's policies for strengthening SMEs capital markets, countries' experiences in expanding equity finance, venture capital, and establishing specific SMEs markets. Constraints of capital market financing for SMEs are also discussed under a separate section. The chapter ends with conclusion and policy recommendations for a widening and deepening capital market for SMEs in a new three-dimensional framework consisting of demand-side, supply-side, and infrastructure policies.

Table 11.1 Comparison of SMEs and Large Firms in Terms of Factors Influencing External Financing

Attributes	*SMEs*	*Large Companies*
External relationships	Lack of financial sources for exploiting scientific and technological opportunities	Financial ability for technology acquisition and better access to information
Risk and Liquidity	High risk and problem in fund raising through capital market, illiquidity	Ability of fundraising through financial markets and diversifying an investment portfolio
Economies of scale	Lack of financial and equipment's ability to set up production structure	Ability of benefiting from EOS via the appropriate investment on RandD, marketing, and production
Growth	Lack of access to external resources	Ability of production-based financial development
Knowledge and Skills	Lack of financial knowledge, bookkeeping, and accounting knowledge and lower level of marketing and sales skills	Good financial, bookkeeping, and accounting knowledge
RandD expenditures	Lower RandD expenditures	High investment in RandD and innovative activities

Source: Compiled by Authors from Yoshino and Taghizadeh-Hesary (2015, 2016); Gorelova et al. (2019).

2 Capital market capacity for innovation financing

Capital markets could act as intermediary entities in analyzing the potential of SMEs and startups, besides distributing the risk of RandD and innovative activities between the firm's owners and the external financers. Therefore, these markets are particularly well-suited for enterprises that are involved in riskier endeavors, especially, fast-growing startups, or settled enterprises that go through a hard transition, like a change in equities or rapid growth during their lifespan (Thompson et al., 2018). SME financing options rely on different aspects such as their phase of expansion, business plan, industry sector, managerial background, and marketing capabilities. Equity capital is a more time-consuming process than other financing options and may be less efficient as a result. In addition, the legislative requirements make it more costly at first and more difficult to comply with in the future (Sarkar, 2016).

In contrast to financing through the bank system, there are some important reasons why stock markets could be regarded as an important source of financing for technology-based SMEs (IOSCO, 2015; Sarkar, 2016):

- Capital markets give access to financing through a well-structured, transparent, consistent, and dependable market.
- Through capital markets, SMEs do not have an obligation to make principal or interest payments. As a result, their cash flows are not affected.
- Listed companies can benefit from market discipline's positive effects on the quality of management, even if they are not listed on the main or secondary stock exchanges, in addition to more transparency for potential investors, suppliers, customers, institutional funds, etc.
- Better access to financing will be available for expansion through the possibility of fundraising at listing or later in the process (e.g., by issuing new securities).
- Implementation of employees' motivation plans will be easier through stock option programs.

The overall capital market is segmented into two main subdivisions: public capital market and private capital market.

Most of the demand in the private capital market originates from non-listed private companies, such as startups and SMEs, which can raise financing through venture capital (VC) or private equity (Binh et al., 2020).

The public market is open to all financiers and is addressed by a full arrangement of regulations about investors' protection endorsed by the official supervisory authority for the capital market. The private market, however, is open only to a limited number of "qualified" investors that are partially excluded from those regulations. In general, it is not necessary for businesses in the private market to obey public disclosure regulations, as the information is only shared confidentially among insiders who are professional investors, managers, owners, and intermediary entities. As a result, the transparency and liquidity of the private market is less than that of the public market (Thompson et al., 2018).

Keeping in mind that the full classification of financial instruments has been provided by ISO 10,962 (This document specifies and describes the structure of codes for a valid international system of classifying financial instruments), the most important categories for financing innovative startups and technology-based SMEs through the capital market are (1) equities, (2) debt instruments, and (3) collective investment vehicles (CIVs).

2.1 Equities

Equity financing includes all financial resources provided to corporations in exchange for equity ownership. Because equity investors do not receive any security from the investee company, and investment returns are based completely on success, they take on entrepreneurial risk. Depending on whether a market exists, investors may be able to sell their shares or receive a share of the profits in case the firm is sold. To achieve long-term corporate investment, innovation, value creation, and company growth, equity financing is relevant and particularly essential for firms with a high risk-reward profile, such as new, innovative, and high growth ventures (OECD, 2015).

Equity finance has different forms. Informally, family and friends can provide equity financing. Equity seed investment and early-stage equity capital can promote firm formation and growth, whereas equity instruments such as special platforms for the public listing of SMEs can provide them with external public financial resources (Zavatta, 2008).

2.1.1 Public equity

Well-developed public equity markets play an important role in the entrepreneurial ecosystem, as they provide access to financing for flourishing technology-based firms. Through these markets, investors, such as venture capital firms (see Section 2.1.2.1), are able to exit their investments through an initial public offering (IPO) (and subsequently equity offering) (Bernstein, 2017). SMEs willing to raise funds through the public market must obey the regulations of disclosure and investor protection imposed by the official authority responsible for the market. These requirements can impose some burdens on SMEs, because their operations are not usually clear, and their information is not produced on the required scale. More exactly, SMEs face several important barriers as they attempt to enter the public markets: illiquidity, lack of transparency, concentration of ownership, and high costs of implementing and monitoring investor protection requirements (Thompson et al., 2018).

2.1.2 Private equity

Private equity allows investors to participate in a portfolio of firms that are through substantial changes such as expansion, recapitalization, ownership change, or mergers and acquisitions (MandA). The private equity investment manager tries to transform the company through active ownership over a period of three to eight years (five years on average) by incorporating outside capital and working closely with the company's management. At that point, the investors expect to exit by selling their shares in the business. Large businesses looking to make a strategic purchase as part of their corporate plan as well as bigger financial investors and stock market investors might be among the bidders (via IPO). A so-called "secondary" market occurs when a group of private equity investors buys a prior limited partner interest in a private equity fund. After a fund's lifecycle is complete (usually ten years), the aim is to liquidate its entire portfolio. While senior management is responsible for day-to-day operations, private equity investors who are represented on the board are involved in strategic initiatives, such as acquisitions, joint ventures, and reorganization, which can affect the capital structure and balance sheet of the company (Thompson et al., 2018). The most important investor categories in private capital markets are people, families, companies with high net worth, public entities, fund of funds, endowments or foundations (non-profit institutions such as hospital and universities), and typical institutional investors including pension funds, life insurers, and sovereign wealth funds (Çelik and Isaksson, 2013). Regarding the specification of the private capital market and the attributes of SMEs, this market is usually more suitable for financing those enterprises than the public capital market.

2.1.2.1 VENTURE CAPITAL

Increasingly, policy makers are looking to venture capital (VC), as innovation and entrepreneurship are crucial to achieving sustainable growth (OECD, 2015). VC financing is equity participation in funding high-risk businesses that is used to finance high-technology-based companies with considerable potential for growth. Megginson (2004) proposed a new venture capital concept and described it as a "professionally managed pool of money raised for the purpose of making equity investments in growing private companies with a well-defined exit strategy." VC influences the early stages of technology development and innovation, helping startups overcome the problem of obtaining financing. By cooperating with the management team of startups, VC also plays a great role in enhancing corporate value (Park et al., 2008). VCs seek dividends and growth in the price of company stocks. At the same time, they do not want to control a business's share eternally but within a defined time cycle, and they may exit their investments when the firm is listed on a stock exchange (often within a three–five-year period) (Metrick and Yasuda, 2011). Informal investors, such as family, friends, and business angels, fund the seed or early stages, and VC firms usually participate in the next phases of financing (OECD, 2015). Most VC firms which act as investment funds have the structure that is shown in Figure 11.1.

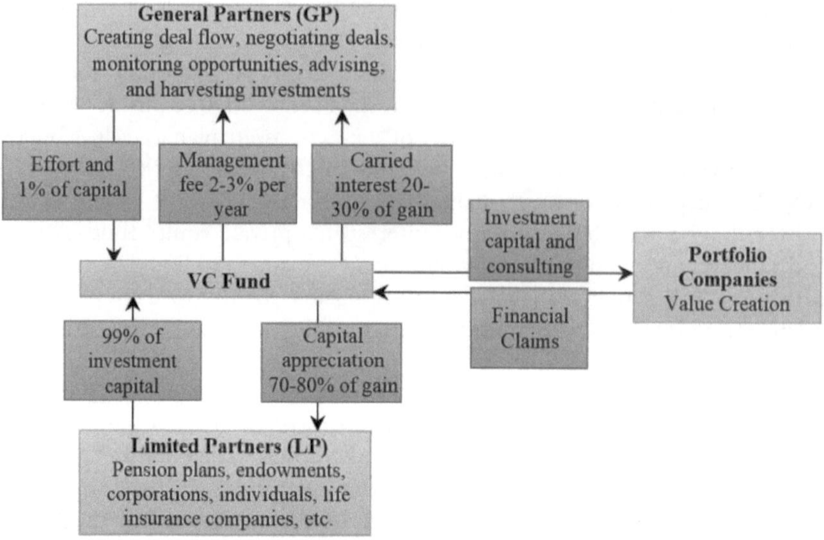

Figure 11.1 VC Fund Structure.
Source: Smith and Kiholm Smith (2004).

2.1.2.2 VC EXIT MECHANISMS

Fundraising, investing, and exiting are the stages of venture capital investments (Park et al., 2008). As a result, VC firms' returns are strongly influenced by the availability and liquidity of public equity markets, especially IPO markets, that allow them to sell their portfolios of investment through an IPO and exit (Bernstein, 2017; Wonglimpiyarat, 2013). This means that the IPO markets have an important role not only for publicly listed firms, but also for supplying capital for entrepreneurial activities and innovative startups (Bernstein, 2017).

Besides the IPO in the stock market, mergers and acquisitions (MandA) is another exit method for small firms (instead of VC firms). In an MandA process, private equity will be transferred through the joining of two similarly sized companies into a new single entity (a merger) or the acquisition of a smaller company by a larger company. The acquired company may continue to exist as a company with the same name but with new ownership, or it may be merged into the parent company and its business (Ren and Gao, 2011). Considering the advantages of MandA, some studies have shown that this exit method is becoming more attractive than IPO for VC firms to become involved in financing technology-based SMEs (Amor and Kooli, 2020). Table 11.2 compares the advantages and disadvantages of IPO and MandA in detail.

In general, the legal and institutional structure of a country as well as its stock market size are important factors that influence VC engagement in financing entrepreneurial SMEs (Wonglimpiyarat, 2013).

Table 11.2 Advantages and Disadvantages of VC Exit Methods

Initial Public Offering (IPO)	*Mergers and Acquisitions (MandA)*
Advantages: • results in higher profit than other exit manners preferred by investor companies • promote the reputation, credibility, and public profile of private equity • stocks produced can be used as rewards to stakeholders Disadvantages: • in general, higher time and costs are needed for private equity to complete exit only after the restricted stock trade period • much broader responsible investigation of the public market's authorities is needed • there is a risk of severe market fall and liquidity for private equity	Advantages: • quick and complete exit can be realized by private equity • execution process is much quicker and simple • the whole process is more flexible and controllable Disadvantages: • opposition of enterprise management may occur • the enterprise staff is unwilling to accept the method • potential buyers of the enterprise's stocks are limited

Source: Compiled from Ren and Gao (2011).

2.2 Debt instruments

Debt instruments in the form of corporate bonds could be private or public and are just as important as stocks when it comes to capital market products. Both bank loans and bonds allow money to be borrowed and lent. Issuing bonds allows a company to raise additional money from a variety of sources. In addition, bonds, unlike bank loans, can readily be exchanged between dealers on the secondary market (Binh et al., 2020).

2.2.1. Private debt

Through the private debt market (also called alternative lenders or professional loan funds), capital providers engage in debt financing rather than equity financing. Debt instruments have gained institutional and legal features and characteristics from the private equity market. Alternative lenders that have emerged as financial intermediaries in the private debt market are becoming more diverse as new types of institutions (e.g., large financial groups, banks, and even independent asset managers) enter the capital market. Recently, institutional investors are more willing to sponsor their own funds. Private debt markets have some important advantages, one of which is their superior capacity to accept liquidity and funding risks (in contrast to banks, which are faced more with withdrawals of deposits in severe market conditions). Although it seems that the private debt market is in competition with the traditional bank debt system, there are some complementary relations between these two systems of debt capital in a manner that SMEs with higher risk are more expected to be covered by the former (Thompson et al., 2018).

SMEs can issue debt securities to raise funds on a much more stable and long-term basis than they would have borrowing from the banks. Moreover, these securities are easily tradable, because first, their transparent prices talk about the performance and value of the issuer, and second, the ease of exit makes SMEs that issue debt securities attractive options for investment. Because of these features, SMEs enhance the governance of their internal operations as well as their communication with the outside world (IOSCO, 2015).

Liquidating bank loan assets in the debt capital market can be another indirect way to access financing through the debt capital market. The capital market securitization of banks' SME loans will offer a greater cushion for banks to raise loan amounts, thereby increasing the overall volume of cash given to SMEs. This asset-backed securitization, also known as a collateralized loan obligation (CLO), allows investors to split monitoring costs with banks. Likewise, banks can share exposure to credit risk with investors on the debt market, according to their perspective (Park et al., 2008).

2.2.2 Sukuk funds

Bonds are results of lending and borrowing, while Sukuks result from a contract between the issuers and the investors. Sukuk issuers securitize assets and issue them as bonds (Razak et al., 2018). There are two ways to classify Sukuks: by the type of structure, and depending on Shariah regulations (for instance, Murabahah or Ijarah). From the structural point of view, Sukuks can be divided into four types: asset-based, asset-backed, exchangeable, or hybrid. Sukuk issuance is largely asset-based (Lahsasna et al., 2018).

Sukuk subscribers or buyers will receive a certificate representing ownership of the asset, cash flows, and risk. The investors receive money equivalent to the value of the Sukuk upon maturity. This value depends on the value of the asset backing the Sukuk. In fact, Sukuks are distinguished from bonds by this feature (Razak et al., 2018).

Since the first Sukuk issuance in Malaysia in 1990, its performance has fluctuated significantly (Razak et al., 2018). Globally, the Sukuk industry has grown at the fastest pace in recent years. The majority of Sukuks are debt instruments that allow for risk-sharing; however, debt is often cheaper and more prevalent. SMEs can use risk-sharing Sukuk structures, as they are higher risk and attract a variety of investors such as private equity holders. The risk-sharing structure has been more successful in the past, especially where the banking system was less developed. Sukuks are mostly issued by government entities and corporations, but they can be issued by financial institutions. Although corporate Sukuk markets can complement the SMEs debt market, and the legal frameworks in some countries are in favor of them, they have not become very developed. In general, when a country lacks a strong banking system, Sukuks for SMEs tend to be more successful, and SMEs can be well positioned to raise capital through Sukuks in these circumstances (IOSCO, 2015).

2.3 Collective Investment Vehicles (CIVs)

There are several types of collective investment vehicles (CIVs), including investment companies, investment trusts, mutual funds, and unit trusts. CIVs in the form of funds help investors who may lack the required skills to invest profitably and appropriately in SMEs in diversified portfolios. The supervisory authority responsible for capital markets usually defines the legal structure and sets the regulations of the activities of CIVs to protect retail investors. The assets in the fund are valued at specified intervals under the formal regime set by the same authority. An investor purchasing a unit of the CIV acquires a proportional share of all the assets in the fund at net asset value (NAV) when purchasing and acquires the right to sell the share and have income generated by those assets in the form of interest, dividends, and capital gains (Thompson et al., 2018). Risk reduction through diversification, competent asset management, and possibly beneficial tax treatment are three key advantages of indirect investing in CIVs for regular investors (Fabozzi and Fabozzi, 2020).

CIVs in most countries are often open-ended funds; that is, no fixed number of investment units is issued. A certain number of open-ended CIVs that invest in the SMEs sector are found in OECD countries, but there are natural limits on the size of this market segment. The strongest factor limiting the development of open-ended CIVs investments in SMEs is that CIVs generally invest in publicly offered securities that are priced in a transparent manner and have liquid markets. Paradoxically, the securities which are issued by technology-based SMEs do not trade sufficiently and do not have a clear valuation or unlimited liquidity. Therefore, the better-suited CIVs for SMEs are closed-ended funds (CEF) which issue a fixed number of shares. These funds may invest in private or unlisted securities, i.e., those not issued on a public market and not subject to full official disclosure and investor protection regimes. Then, a CEF's net asset value (NAV) could be estimated using accepted accounting procedures and typically occurs quarterly or semi-annually.

Briefly, the common characteristics of CIVs for SMEs are (Thompson et al., 2018):

- CIVs usually take the form of closed-ended funds (CEF).
- CIVs mostly operate under special regulations enforced by the capital market responsible authority to protect retail investors.
- CIVs receive earnings in the form of interest and dividends from companies in its portfolio and distribute them through to final investors.
- CIVs may engage in direct managerial interactions with companies in their portfolios.

3 Countries' experiences

In this section, the experiences of different countries (both developed and developing) in deploying capital market potentials for financing technology-based SMEs and innovative startups are discussed. The focus will be on the initiatives and policy measures which are designed to exploit equity finance and VC, SMEs capital markets, and CIVs.

3.1 Equity finance and VC

A number of VC companies operate in the United States, Canada, Israel, and the United Kingdom (UNESCAP, 2017). There has also been an increasing wave of VC investments in East Asia in recent years (Bernstein, 2017). Among the Asian countries, Singapore, China, Korea, and India have built up a good VC industry. These countries' experiences show that economic growth and technological development are two main prerequisites for a growing VC industry (UNESCAP, 2017). The main share of overall investment in VC in Europe and the US is related to pension funds and institutional investors. In addition, in the US, MandA is more common than IPO as the main exit method for VC investors. In contrast, in most Asian countries, for example, Korea, the government is the main player in the VC market, and IPO is the main exit mechanism for VC companies (Park et al., 2008). It is also worth noting that VC funding is much rarer in some developed countries, like Japan, which is heavily dominated by banks. One of the most important reasons for this situation is the lack of a developed IPO market. Furthermore, some studies have indicated that IPOs are useful only for investing in existing companies but not in startups. Countries with a small internal market and low per capita income levels may have some difficulty in deepening their VC industry (UNESCAP, 2017).

Governments in different countries have introduced some initiatives to encourage access by SMEs to equity financing and VC. The experiences of five countries are reviewed below. Some countries were chosen from Asia (Taiwan, Korea, and China) which are expected to have more interventions from their governments in VC development process, especially in upcoming years. The cases of the UK and the US as countries which have longer experience in developing the VC industry are also presented. The case of Israel as the most successful case of integrating foreign investors with the domestic VC industry is also presented.

3.1.1 The government intervention for VC improvement: the case of Taiwan

Taiwan has recently achieved one of Asia's most remarkable rates of economic growth. Technology-based companies have been helped effectively by public funding, because innovation and technology development are a priority for the government (Wonglimpiyarat, 2013). "The Regulation Governing Venture Capital Business Management" was promulgated in 1983 to promote the growth of the VC sector in Taiwan. Since the late 1990s, Taiwan's venture capital industry has enjoyed high economic value due to its efficiency in enabling the creation of high-tech startups, particularly in the electronics sector. The "Taiwanese Private Equity and Venture Capital Association" (TVCA) was founded in 1999. Development funds and the SME development fund as well as venture capital firms play important roles in providing equity financing to promote industrial innovation. The Ministry of Economic Affairs now oversees the operation of VC funds. The government co-funds many VC funds that are run by public organizations or corporations with ties to the government (Wonglimpiyarat, 2012).

3.1.2 Support equity investors in SMEs: UK tax incentives

Three government programs are offered in the United Kingdom to provide tax incentive schemes to equity investors in order to encourage them to engage in smaller risky companies. Investments in these firms are tax-benefited under the Enterprise Investment Scheme (EIS) established in 1994. Investing in eligible shares can qualify the investor for tax breaks of up to 30% on investments up to one million GBP. Furthermore, in case of the sale of a current asset, the investors are able to defer capital gains tax by investing the proceeds in EIS shares during a specific time. Capital gains tax does not apply to profits generated by the sale of EIS shares. In some cases, a loss incurred by the investment may be deducted from income tax. A tax incentive program, called the "Seed Enterprise Investment Scheme" (SEIS), was created by the UK government in 2012 for investors in tiny, young businesses. In order to qualify for a 50% tax deduction on the cost of shares, up to GBP 100,000, a three-year holding period is required. Capital gains reinvested in SEIS are free from taxation by 50%. Capital gains on SEIS shares are not taxable if they are sold at a profit. In some cases, a loss incurred by the investment may be deducted from income tax. The third program, the "Venture Capital Trust Scheme" (VCT), was established in 1995 to encourage people to make indirect investments through intermediaries in higher-risk SMEs by providing tax relief of up to 30% of the investment cost, up to GBP 200,000. Among the requirements for VCT shares purchased by investors, they must be listed on a major stock exchange. Therefore, the VCT makes subsequent investments in eligible businesses, typically through stock or quasi-equity instruments. To qualify for the tax benefits, investors must retain their investment for a minimum of five years. Dividends and gains on capital on the VCT's shares are likewise tax-free (OECD, 2015).

3.1.3 Developing a domestic VC sector with foreign investors: Israeli Yozma initiative

The VC sector in Israel grew after government investment that was leveraged by overseas firms and organizations. The Israeli government invested USD 100 million in the Yozma group, a VC firm that invested in high-tech businesses (mostly biotech and information technology) in the early 1990s with the help of international investors from Germany and Japan, who were required to invest in Israeli startups. The group created ten hybrid public/private funds over three years, each with a capitalization of about US$20 million. Yozma began investing directly in startups around the same time. Private partners were granted a five-year option to buy out the government's stake of the company. In most cases, this option was used, which resulted in privatized VC money. Individual investments generally ranged from $1 to $6 million, with extra funds set aside for subsequent investments. The government provided equity guarantees to international funders as well as programs connecting Israeli businesses with global angel investors or Israeli venture firms exiting on international exchanges. In 1995, Yozma created its second fund relying on notable investors from North America, Europe, and Israel. The foreign partners made the majority of decisions about where and how to invest. Several of Israel's major academic institutions and technological incubators have also formed strong working connections with the Yozma Group. The Yozma III CEO Club was established as a part of the Group's attempts to integrate entrepreneurs and CEOs of successful businesses in Yozma's operations, and it has proven to be a key source of transaction flow. By the year 2000, the VC in Israel had progressed in a way that investments by non-public entities were outpacing the governmental sector (OECD, 2015).

3.1.4 Coordination between public and private sectors: the Korean experience

In Korea, public partnership in any kind of governmental borrowing or investment is a major resource used to invest in SMEs (Binh et al., 2020). However, the government is continuously trying to indirectly encourage (using deregulation) more private investors (e.g., financial institutions) to participate in the market. To do this, the government established "Korea Fund of Funds" (KFoF); in parallel, it removed the restrictions on investment placed by banks and insurers. Consequently, a market infrastructure suitable for investors that is coordinated with incentives has been formed. In addition, private fund managers are employed in the governance of KFoF and its subfunds to exploit their experience in improving fund performance and raising market standards (Park et al., 2008).

3.1.5 Diversifying VC exit mechanisms (US and China experiences)

Despite the benefits of IPO markets for innovative and entrepreneurial activities, there are also some possible disadvantages to making the switch to public stock exchanges. Experience indicates that the shift of China and US to public stock exchanges probably resulted in a decrease of technology development, in all likelihood as a result of immediate constraints and a rise in the management trend to concentrate on investments that fulfill short-term projects. Anti-takeover regulations, institutional investor holdings, and concentrated ownership can all help to protect a business from immediate limitations, let them consider further risks of long-term projects, and thus augment innovation and productivity within a company, even if it is a publicly listed one (Bernstein, 2017).

3.2 New markets for SMEs

Although the formal financial system for SMEs in most developing countries is based on banks (Wellalage and Fernandez, 2019), the capital market is still a critical component of the financial system that must be strengthened. Therefore, governments need to act as leaders in establishing secondary markets to assist SMEs, which are inherently risky. In other words, it is necessary for innovative SMEs to have a special stock market to assist entrepreneurs in obtaining the cash they need for operations. It is also one of the main channels for attracting VC funding, because an exchange prepares an exit path for investors through an IPO in the capital market. The SMEs capital market should have fewer listing guidelines and restrictions and should cover cheaper startup as well as ongoing expenses than a typical market (Wonglimpiyarat, 2015).

The secondary stock market in the US, known as NASDAQ (National Association of Securities Dealers Automatic Quotation System), offers entrepreneurs an essential exit path. The NASDAQ stock market's operations have aided the growth of the VC sector by providing a means for VC investors to achieve investment returns (Wonglimpiyarat, 2012).

Many nations have adopted the NASDAQ template in their efforts to develop a market for technology-based firms. For example, developed countries have had some successful exchanges, including the TSX Venture Exchange (TSXV) in Canada, the Australian Securities Exchange (ASX) in Australia, and the Alternative Investment Market (AIM) in the UK. Taiwan's GreTai Securities Market and Poland's Warsaw Stock Exchange (WSE) NewConnect are examples of market success in developing countries (Harwood and Konidaris, 2015). The Korea Exchange operates the KOSDAQ, which is the country's largest structured market for SMEs and VC firms. In July 2013, the Korea Exchange (KRX) created a special market for SMEs called KONEX, as KOSDAQ was becoming a fundraising venue for bigger businesses. Since June 1999, the Securities Exchange of Thailand (SET) has run an alternative investment (MAI) market, including SMEs as prospective issuers (IOSCO, 2015). Taiwan has two exchanges that deal with capital market financing: Taiwan's Stock Exchange (TWSE) and Gre Tai Securities Market, also known as Taiwan's over-the-counter (OTC) stock exchange. The TWSE market's listing standards are more stringent than those of the GTSM market. Both markets, however, provide technology-based sectors with adaptable regulatory requirements for market entrance (helping technology-based SMEs to access enough funds for growth). To be eligible for listing on the TWSE, a business must first get the results of an assessment by a central authority, namely the MOEA's Bureau for Industrial Development, to demonstrate its capacity to develop innovation. High-tech businesses can list on the OTC market, which offers a flexible listing process. Meanwhile, the OTC listing regulations also require MOEA to offer an expert judgment on the issuing firm's potential to innovate (Shinozaki, 2014). AltX, South Africa's Johannesburg Stock Exchange, was launched in 2003. From 2003 to 2008, market capitalization and the number of listings companies for AltX significantly increased. Since 2008, this has been heavily impacted by the financial crisis, and the number of listings has declined steadily (Harwood and Konidaris, 2015).

Hong Kong's GEM (Growth Enterprise Market), a secondary market for emerging companies, is operated by the Stock Exchange of Hong Kong Ltd. NEEQ, a successful Chinese equity market founded in 2013, was created to meet the demands of SMEs in any stage of growth. India National Stock Exchange (NSE) also started a specific platform for technology startups called Emerge (IOSCO, 2015).

In Iran, as another developing country, establishing SMEs capital markets is still in its infancy. Today, financing SMEs through the capital market is possible at the country's OTC market named Fara Bourse Securities Exchange (IFB) that is supervised by the Securities and Exchange Organization (SEO). The IFB was established on November 12, 2008, to help many businesses enter the capital market and enhance their business operations by simplifying the listing requirements. Financial instruments and institutions available at IFB, which are more specifically applicable for innovative SMEs, are Venture Capital Funds, Sukuk, and crowdfunding. In recent years, a growing number of VCFs have begun to participate in funding innovative startups and technology-based SMEs. Now, there are 16 active VCF at IFB, most of which are at the early stage of development (IFB, 2021). Figure 11.2 illustrates a brief structure of IFB supporting SMEs finance. In addition to primary and secondary markets of IFB equity market, recently established SMEs market helps SMEs activities with no volume limit or range of fluctuations in transactions.

Despite the fact that Asia's economic boom has created many SMEs in need of reliable financing, the capital markets for small- and medium-sized companies are already in their initial stage. This means that for many Asian equity markets to serve as funding platforms for SMEs, substantial government regulations and plans are necessary (UNESCAP, 2017). Table 11.3 summarizes some information on SMEs exchanges and listing requirements in some countries.

It is important to note that large corporations frequently issue corporate bonds, because obtaining credit ratings is easier for them, making them attractive to investors. However, bond financing is not often used by SMEs, because, for example, they do not have ratings. Because of this, they are less appealing to institutional investors; consequently, in terms of outstanding volume, the market

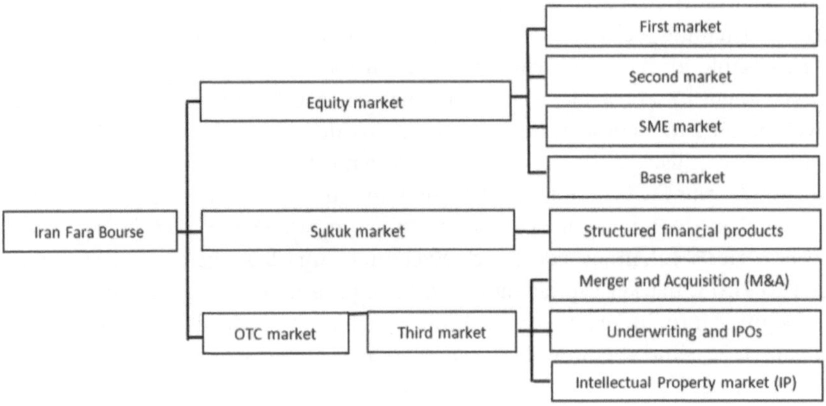

Figure 11.2 Brief Structure of IFB Supporting SMEs Finance (https://www.ifb.ir).

for SMEs bonds is very modest. The primary barriers to investing in these bonds include the lack of market liquidity, lack of transparency compared to bonds issued by large corporations, and insufficient coverage of ratings. To combat illiquidity in the market, issuers should list these bonds with less stringent listing criteria than large companies (UNESCAP, 2017).

In addition, government creates intermediate means in which bonds of small firms are pooled together to create funds, allowing investors to diversify their portfolios. Micado, a French micro-cap bond fund, is a case of this aggregation. Minibonds can be pooled in collective vehicles, and joint transactions between multiple originators in the form of partnerships will provide small- and medium-sized enterprises with the issuance volume needed to make it appealing to investors. Nevertheless, since many Asian nations' corporate bond markets (for large companies) are undeveloped in size, liquidity, and maturity, it may be more suitable for these governments to start with an SMEs bond market. Most SMEs may be able to grow into major companies as a result of this, boosting demand for corporate bond markets in these nations, particularly in low-income economies (UNESCAP, 2017).

China, on the other side, has created three different forms of SMEs bonds: (a) SMEs Collective Notes, (b) SMEs Joint Bonds, (c) SMEs Private Placement Bonds. Whereas SMEs Collective Notes, which are controlled by the People's Bank of China and the China Association of Financial Market Institutional Investors, are ramping up, SMEs Joint Bonds, which are exchanged on the interbank and exchanges and are controlled by the National Development and Reform Commission (NDRC), only offer a small number of bonds. The Securities Regulatory Commission (CSRC) supervises and regulates SMEs private placement bonds (IOSCO, 2015).

In the past decade, the issuance of bonds less than USD 15.6 million has increased in Europe. As a case in point, many exchanges in different regions of Germany have successfully developed platforms for SMEs debt. The exchanges of Düsseldorf, Frankfurt, Hamburg-Hannover, Munich, and Stuttgart have developed their own SME bond market platforms (UNESCAP, 2017).

3.3 CIVs

In many countries, public authorities implement equity finance support policies related to SMEs as part of their measures to encourage innovative startups and high-potential SMEs. In addition, many means of public investments and co-funding schemes were established. For example, a first call for proposals was launched by the Italian Fund for Sustainable Growth in 2009, with 60% of its total investment volume of €300 million (US$336 million) conducted toward SMEs. Chile has had the Early-Stage Fund (Fondo Etapas Temporanas) in place since 2013. In this fund-of-funds, equity financing is provided to high-growth SMEs by new investment funds. As part of its program to support SMEs equity financing, the Netherlands introduced in 2013 a fund of funds for later stage venture capital investments in cooperation with the European Investment Fund.

Table 11.3 Information on SMEs Exchanges and Listing Requirements

Country (Exchange)	*Launch Date*	*Target Companies and Startups*	*Minimum Operating Period*	*Minimum Capitalization*
Taiwan (GreTai)	1994	Does not target any particular industry, product, or size of company. Startups are not accepted.	Two years' experience required.	A minimum NT$50 million paid-in capital.
Hong Kong (GEM)	1999	Domestic and foreign small to mid-sized companies.	At least two years.	HK$200 million.
South Africa (JSE AltX)	2003	Company types or sectors not specified. Minimum share capital of $200,000. Not allowing startups.	Produce a profit forecast for the remaining financial year of listing and one full financial year thereafter.	SA Rand 2,000,000.
China (NEEQ)	2012	The nature of ownership of a shareholder is not restricted for companies applying for NEEQ listing. High-tech enterprise status is not mandatory for NEEQ listings.	At least two years.	Participation in the public equities exchange of listed companies is available to corporate bodies having registered capital equivalent to five million yuan or more; partnership enterprises with paid-in capitals of five million yuan or more, and qualified natural persons.
India (NSE India Emerge platform)	2012	Does not target a particular industry or kind of company. Capital raised after issuance > $4.16 million. Open to startups.	NSE – Minimum three years of experience, positive cash flow. Accruals for the past two financial years and net worth that is positive.	The paid-up capital is approximately $4,723,000.
Iran (IFB SMEs Market)	2018	No particular sector or industry is specified.	At least one year. It is also possible to accept the company at the beginning of its establishment.	Minimum equity of IRR 1 billion.

Source: Compiled from Harwood and Konidaris (2015), IOSCO (2015), Li et al. (2015), HKEX (2017), IFB (2021).

Requirements	*Public Shareholder When Listing*	*Sector Breakdown (2015)*
NT$4 million in pretax earnings must be achieved during the most recent fiscal year.	At least 50 shareholders are required	70% electronics, 14.5% biotechnology and health care, 8.4% traditional businesses, and 7.1% other
In the two financial years immediately preceding the issue of the listing documents, operating activities generated positive cash flow minimum of HK$20 million in aggregate.	100 holders	30% consumer goods and services industry, and 17% property and construction industry. The others were mainly in the information technology, industrials, materials and financial services sectors
The applicant must have control (at least 50% + 1 of the voting shares) over the majority of its assets.	Public holds a minimum of 10% of each class of equity securities	70% of the sectors are in financials, 15% in industries, 7% in technology, 5% in basic materials, 1% in consumer goods and the remaining 1% are in other sectors
An ongoing business with a well-defined business plan; good corporate governance; legally issued and transferred shares; recommended by a brokerage firm and subject to their ongoing monitoring.	10% for companies with a capital stock of over US$62 million	35% manufacturing, 27% computer and internet, 7% transportation and logistics, 6% energy, 6% service, 19% remaining sectors (2020)
Track record of at least three years of; The company should have annual revenue of not less than Rs. 10 crores and should have shown an annual growth of at least 20% in the past one year.	At least 50 shareholders are required.	80% manufacturing, 20% service industries
Good corporate governance; transparent financial and accounting background.	LLP companies.	40% food industries, 35% metals, 20% metal products, 5% others (2021)

In addition to encouraging the diffusion of information about this type of lending instrument, the government also promoted demand-side initiatives. The formation of a national SMEs development fund was announced in 2015 by China, supplemented by a 1.35 trillion yuan (US$6.35 billion) grant from the central government's budget and a 4.35 trillion yuan (US$6.35 billion) private investment. The fund concentrates on VC and private equity investments to foster startups in the seed and early-stage phases in key sectors and other promising, innovative sectors (OECD, 2020).

4 Constraints of financing SMEs through capital markets

Despite the opportunities that capital markets provide for financing SMEs, some impediments exist that prevent their complete use. SMEs cannot be listed on a stock market for two major observations: first, the substantial fixed expenses of an IPO (including the fees related to intermediaries, auditors, legal advisors, communication specialists, audit and accounting, and legal, underwriters, regulatory, listing, printing, public relations, investor relations, and communication services); second, the reporting obligations imposed on SMEs as a result of their high expenses. In certain situations, rigid limitations designed to protect investors' interests may prohibit SMEs from ever being listed on a major stock market (IOSCO, 2015).

There are also some failures regarding SMEs bonds: higher credit risk and higher transaction costs. A solution recommended for these imperfections is pooling SMEs together. If enough SMEs come together with different degrees of risk exposure to economic circumstances, then the portfolio may be less credit risky, and investors on the debt market may find it profitable. The high transaction costs of SMEs bonds could be handled with a sufficient deal size (Nassr and Wehinger, 2015).

The absence of institutional investor engagement is another issue that hampers the exchange's expansion in a country. The government imposes stringent criteria for investment assets, so these investors, including pension funds, mutual funds, and insurance companies, prefer to invest in larger businesses. SMEs stock markets, however, are more illiquid compared to stock exchanges where bigger listed companies trade and larger businesses are more likely than smaller organizations to issue additional stock (IOSCO, 2015).

Another major problem for the growth of capital markets for SMEs is the preference of investors to participate in SMEs that grow quickly, which makes capital markets unable to finance the seed and growth stages of a wide range of SMEs.

In brief, the most important impediments to SMEs being listed on an exchange market fall into four main categories (Wehinger et al., 2015):

a. Market infrastructure
   - Lack of timely and comparable information on the credit standing, financial position, and financial status of small- and medium-sized businesses

(SMEs) increases the asymmetries in information, which prevent the capital market financing of SMEs (particularly debt instruments) from expanding.
- Lack of a healthy ecosystem (including bank investors, SMEs-specific banks, brokers, market makers, and a range of independent consultants) serving the capital market must support SMEs in secondary markets.

b. Demand-side
  - Insufficient SMEs knowledge of financial instruments offered by the markets.
  - Insufficient skills needed for SMEs to handle issuance process.

c. **Supply-side**
  - Lack of liquidity in secondary markets makes investors unwilling to participate in SMEs capital markets and tend to move their capital away from SMEs into bigger capitalization markets.
  - Fewer regulations for small firms' issuances of equity with respect to financial disclosure, corporate management, or transparency that could negatively impact investors.

d. **Regulation**
  - Different equity and debt tax treatment in a way that debt is being favored over equity.

5 Conclusion and policy recommendations

Financial crises cause banks to become more risk-averse in a way that conventional bank-oriented mechanisms do not usually provide enough suitable access to financing for SMEs. As a result, financial policies for innovation are becoming more important for a country's entrepreneurial activities through SMEs and economic growth (Wonglimpiyarat, 2013). Recent studies found that capital market financing, which includes a wide range of stock and debt instruments as well as collective investment vehicles (CIVs), frequently supplements instead of substituting for bank funding (UNESCAP, 2017, Thompson et al., 2018).

In fact, a private capital market provides benefits to SMEs seeking financing, mostly through its more flexible terms and conditions, particularly for risky small businesses. As the operations of innovative startups and technology-based SMEs are usually unclear, they do not cover the requirements of disclosure and investor protection imposed by the official authority responsible for the public market; consequently, preferences lie with using private markets. Among the private equity financing instruments, VC firms or individual investors fund high-risk enterprises that are usually high-technology-based companies with considerable potential for growth. Once the companies are listed on a stock exchange, venture capitalists are required to exit the investments (often within a three–five-year period), thus the availability of liquid public equity markets, especially IPO markets, is an important factor for deepening the VC industry. The legal and institutional framework of the country and the size of the market also influence VC engagement in entrepreneurial firms SMEs finance. To deepen private equity financing in the form of VC firms, governments introduce some initiatives, such as the schemes that offer tax incentives to equity investors in SMEs (UK) and relying on the participation of foreign investors to develop a domestic VC industry (Israel's Yozma program).

Startups and SMEs could also be financed through CIVs in the form of closed-ended funds enveloping retail investors and operate under special regulations endorsed by the capital market responsible authority to protect the investors. Therefore, establishing a separate equity market with regulatory requirements tailored to SMEs (e.g., more flexible listing and disclosure requirements in comparison to the major markets) is necessary in every country.

In addition to the potentials of capital markets, there are also some constraints that should be alleviated by an appropriate and robust mix of policies by the governments in three dimensions to make a wider and deeper SMEs capital market (Abraham et al., 2019; IOSCO, 2015; Shinozaki, 2014; Wehinger et al., 2015).

Enhancement of the demand-side (SMEs)

- Improving SMEs' market literacy to increase awareness of financial instruments is offered by capital markets. To do this, government agencies should arrange educational programs, workshops, and seminars, for example, in collaboration with private partners from industry, banks, and capital markets. In addition, public or private entities could arrange some advisory centers, websites, or portals for providing a set of resources or information about the available financing mechanisms, investment opportunities and initiatives, or supportive programs provided by the government (Beyani, 2020).
- Building a set of skills (including strategic management, estimating, budgeting, accounting, planning for tax, financial report-writing, and relations with investors, etc.) for small- and medium-sized enterprises (SMEs) that will enable them to evaluate the suitability of debt vs. equity financing for their company, to assess their choices, and to meet market conditions.

Expansion of the supply-side (the investors' base)

- Allowing the entry of foreign investors or creating new types of investors, especially long-term institutional investors such as pension or mutual funds; for example, by designing tax incentive schemes for investors in innovative startups and technology-based SMEs.
- Individual investors can be encouraged to contribute to capital markets with the help of mutual funds, exchange-traded funds, and small public equity brokers who are specialized in SMEs financing.
- To broaden retail investor participation in the SMEs capital market, we must address the concerns about the riskiness of investing in the public equity of SMEs. This requires strong financial consumer protection and education, explaining the risks and benefits of diversifying savings portfolios.

Small issuers may be subject to different, even tighter, regulations and, in some cases, higher requirements than larger issuers in order to mitigate these risks.
- To create more market depth, stock exchanges can provide incentives for market participants, for example, a lower trading fee in exchange for lower trading requirements.

Improvement of market infrastructure

- Providing infrastructure and the databases maintaining expenses, in addition to the expenses of regular reporting by the issuers, should be addressed by central credit registers and data warehouses, which are held and operated by central banks and financial regulators. In Europe, such an initiative was launched by the ECB (European Central Bank) in 2013 through the European Datawarehouse. By mandating the gathering and sharing of credit data, governments could ensure that information on SMEs is complete and available. By gathering hundreds of financial reports and establishing a robust statistical model, the credit risk database (CRD) facilitates SMEs' access to financing by reducing the information gap between them and financial institutions (Kuwahara et al., 2019).
- It is also necessary to establish freely accessible data and information platforms on SMEs' creditworthiness, financial performance, and financing record to all qualified users such as institutional investors to have a more transparent SMEs market and better control over adverse selections and moral hazard risks.
- The regulation reforms have put a bit of strain on market-makers, who provide liquidity to secondary markets. For professional investors to participate in the SMEs equity markets, there must always be committed market-makers always providing information.

Financial market stability must not be compromised in the interest of promoting capital market instruments for small- and medium-sized companies. If it is used effectively, market financing for SMEs contributes greatly to economic recovery by freeing up resources and capacity to lend, enhancing investor diversification as well as helping to create a more stable financial system through improved risk-sharing in the economy.

Establishing SMEs exchanges in developing countries is harder, mainly because SMEs are estimated to have a relatively small size (Harwood and Konidaris, 2015), and several policymakers with little cooperation between them are responsible for the SMEs sector, in general (Kousari and Alizadeh, 2021), and financing, in particular (Sarkar, 2016). True integration between the demand-side (SMEs) and supply-side (government, regulators, market makers, securities companies, investors) is necessary for the development of the SMEs market. It is also a key requisite to increasing long-term financing opportunities for innovative startups and technology-based SMEs.

References

Abraham F, Cortina JJ, Schmukler SL (2019) The Rise of Domestic Capital Markets for Corporate Financing. International Bank for Reconstruction and Development / the World Bank. Available via DIALOG: https://documents1.worldbank.org/curated/en/312461569223225798/pdf/The-Rise-of-Domestic-Capital-Markets-for-Corporate-Financing.pdf Accessed 25 August 2021

Amor SB, Kooli M (2020) Do MandA Exits Have the Same Effect on VC Reputation than IPO Exits? *J Bank Financ* 111: 1–15. doi: 10.1016/j.jbankfin.2019.105704

Bernstein S (2017) Public Equity Markets and Innovation, ADBI Working Paper, No. 772, Asian Development Bank Institute (ADBI), Tokyo. Available via DIALOG: https://www.asean.org/wp-content/uploads/images/archive/22633-8.pdf. Accessed 17 August 2021

Beyani M (2020) Financial Education for the SMEs: Identifying SME Educational Needs, Alliance for Financial Inclusion. Available via DIALOG: afi-global.org/sites/default/files/publications/2020–09/AFI_SMEFWG_MSME_CS_AW_digital.pdf. Accessed 15 February 2022

Binh KB, Jhang H, Park D, Ryu D (2020) Capital Markets for Small- and Medium-sized Enterprises and Startups in Korea. *J Asian Finance Econ Bus* 7(12): 195–210. doi:10.13106/jafeb.2020.vol7.no12.195

Brown R, Lee N (2017) The Theory and Practice of Financial Instruments for Small and Medium-Sized Enterprises. EC-OECD Seminar Series on Designing better economic Development Policies for Regions and Cities. OECD Publishing. Paris. Available via DIALOG: https://www.oecd.org/cfe/regionaldevelopment/Brown_When-to-use-financial-instruments.pdf. Accessed 21 August 2021

Çelik S, Isaksson M (2013) Engagement Institutional Investors and Ownership. *J Financial Mark Trends* 2013(2): 93–114. doi: 10.1787/fmt-2013–5jz734pwtrkc

Fabozzi FJ, Fabozzi FA (2020) Chapter 5: Collective Investment Vehicles and Alternative Assets. In Fabozzi FJ, Fabozzi FA (eds) *Fundamentals of Institutional Asset Management*. World Scientific. doi: 10.1142/9789811221590_0005. pp 117–141

Gorelova I, Zemlyanskaya I, Surkova V, Chub M (2019) Assessing Small Businesses Tax Contributions to Redional Development. Assessing Small Businesses Tax Contribution to Regional Development. International Scientific Conference on Social and Cultural Transformations in the Context of Modern Globalism. doi: 10.15405/epsbs.2019.12.04.149

Hain DS, Christensen JL (2020) Capital Market Penalties to Radical and Incremental Innovation. *Eur J Innov Manag* 23(2): 291–313. doi: 10.1108/EJIM-07–2018–0144

Hall C (2010) The Decline of Bank Finance for SMEs in APEC. *Int J Entrep Small Bus* 11(1): 42–54. doi: 10.1504/IJESB.2010.034431

Harwood A, Konidaris T (2015) SME Exchanges in Emerging Market Economies a Stocktaking of Development Practices. World Bank Group. Policy Research Working Paper 7160. Available via DIALOG: https://documents1.worldbank.org/curated/en/102561468320934149/pdf/WPS7160.pdf Accessed 30 August 2021

HKEX (2017) Review of the Growth Enterprise Market (GEM) and Changes to the GEM and Main Board Listing Rules. Consultation Paper. Available via DIALOG https://www.hkex.com.hk/-/media/HKEX-Market/News/Market-Consultations/Consultation-Paper-on-Review-of-the-GEM-and-Changes-to-the-GEM-and-Main-Board-Listing-Rules/cp2017062.pdf. Accessed 16 February 2022

IFB (Iran Fara Bourse) (2021) About Us. Available via DIALOG: https://www.ifb.ir. Accessed 21 August 2021

IOSCO (2015) SME Financing Through Capital Markets (Final Report). The Growth and Emerging Markets Committee. Available via DIALOG: https://www.iosco.org/library/pubdocs/pdf/IOSCOPD493.pdf. Accessed 21 August 2021

Kousari S, Alizadeh P (2021) A Framework for Governing the STI System from the Perspective of Supply and Demand Policies; with the Aim of Legal and Functional Overlaps Elimination. *J Sci Technol Policy* 14(2): 81–98. [In Persian]. doi: 10.22034/jstp.2021.14.2.1334

Kuwahara S, Yoshino N, Sagara M, Taghizadeh-Hesary F (2019) Establishment of the Credit Risk Database: Concrete Use to Evaluate the Creditworthiness of SMEs. In Yoshino N, Taghizadeh-Hesary F (eds) *Unlocking SME Finance in Asia Roles of Credit Rating and Credit Guarantee Schemes.* OX: Routledge, Abingdon, pp 88–111

Lahsasna A, Hassan MK, Ahmad R (2018) Types of Sukuk, Their Classification and Structure in Islamic Capital Market. In *Forward Lease Sukuk in Islamic Capital Markets.* Palgrave Macmillan, Cham. doi: 10.1007/978-3-319-94262-9_4

Li Y, Meng X, Wei X. (2015) China's New Third Board Market: Opportunities and Challenges Procedia Computer Science 55: 1050–1059. doi: 10.1016/j.procs.2015.07.067

Megginson WL (2004) Towards a Global Model of Venture Capital? *J Appl Corp Finance* 16(1): 89–107. doi: 10.1111/j.1745-6622.2004.tb00599.x

Metrick A, Yasuda A (eds) (2011) *Venture Capital and The Finance of Innovation.* 2nd ed. John Wiley and Sons, United States of America

Nassr K, Wehinger G (2015) Unlocking SME Finance through Market-Based Debt: Securitisation, Private Placements, and Bonds. *Financ Mark Trends* 2015(2): 89–190. doi: 10.1787/fmt-2014–5js3bg1g53ln

OECD (2015) New Approaches to SME and Entrepreneurship Financing: Broadening the Range of Instruments. doi: 10.1787/9789264240957-en

OECD (2018) Enhancing SME Access to Diversified Financing Instruments. Discussion Paper. SME Ministerial Conference, 22–23 February 2018, Mexico City Available via DIALOG: https://www.oecd.org/cfe/smes/ministerial/documents/2018-SME-Ministerial-Conference-Plenary-Session-2.pdf. Accessed 21 August 2021

OECD (2020) Policy Developments in SME Finance a Decade after the Global Financial and Economic Crisis. OECD Publishing. Paris. doi: 10.1787/6bdd4eb7-en

Park JH, Lim BC, Koo JH (2008) Developing the Capital Market to Widen and Diversify SME Financing: The Korean Experience. Korea Institute of Finance. Report for Presentation at the Wrap-up Meeting of Consultants/Research Institutes of ASEAN+3 Research Group 2007/2008, 27 February 2008. Hanoi, Vietnam. Available via DIALOG: https://www.asean.org/wp-content/uploads/images/archive/22633-8.pdf. Accessed 21 August 2021

Razak SS, Saiti B, DİNÇ Y (2018) The Contracts, Structures and Pricing Mechanisms of Sukuk: A Critical Assessment. *Borsa Istanbul Rev* 19(1): 21–33. doi: 10.1016/j.bir.2018.10.001

Ren l, Gao Y (2011) Study on Exit Mechanism for Private Equity Investment in China. *Manag Engin* 05: 1838–5745. doi: 10.5503/J.ME.2011.05.010

Sarkar AN (2016) Financing Mechanisms to Support MSME and Startups: Role of the Capital Market. *Int J Adv Res Innov* 4(1): 244–255

Shinozaki S (2014) Capital Market Financing for SMEs: A Growing Need in Emerging Asia. Asian Development Bank Working Paper Series on Regional Economic

Integration. No 121. Available via DIALOG: http://hdl.handle.net/11540/1982. Accessed 21 August 2021

Smith RL, Kiholm Smith J (eds) (2004) *Entrepreneurial Finance.* 2nd edition. Wiley

Thompson J, Boschmans K, Pissareva L (2018) Alternative Financing Instruments for SMEs and Entrepreneurs: The Case of Capital Market Finance. OECD SME and Entrepreneurship Papers No 10. Available via DIALOG: https://www.oecd-ilibrary.org/economics/alternative-financing-instruments-for-smes-and-entrepreneurs_dbdda9b6-en10. doi: 10.1787/dbdda9b6-en. Accessed 21 August 2021

UNESCAP (2017) Small and Medium Enterprises Financing. Available via DIALOG: https://www.unescap.org/resources/small-and-medium-enterprises-financing. Accessed 15 August 2021

Wehinger G, Nassr K, Laboul A (2015) Opportunities and Constraints of Market-Based Financing for SMEs- OECD Report to G20 Finance Ministers and Central Bank Governors. Available via DIALOG: https://www.oecd.org/finance/financial-markets/Opportunities-and-Constraints-of-Market-based-Financing-for-SMEs.pdf. Accessed 27 August 2021

Wellalage NH, Fernandez V (2019) Innovation and SME Finance: Evidence from Developing Countries. *Int Rev Financ Anal* 66: 1–14. doi: 10.1016/j.irfa.2019.06.009

Wonglimpiyarat J (2012) Equity Financing and Capital Market Funding Policies to Support Entrepreneurial Development in Asia: Comparative Cases of Thailand, Malaysia, Singapore, and Taiwan. *J Priv Equity* 15(4): 10–24. doi: 10.3905/jpe.2012.15.4.010

Wonglimpiyarat J (2013) Innovation Financing Policies for Entrepreneurial Development: Cases of Singapore and Taiwan as Newly Industrializing Economies. *Asian J Manag Res* 24: 109–117. doi: 10.1016/j.hitech.2013.09.003

Wonglimpiyarat J (2015) *Technology Financing and Commercialization Exploring the Challenges and How Nations Can Build Innovative Capacity.* Palgrave Macmillan. doi: 10.1057/9781137

Yoshino N, Taghizadeh-Hesary F (2015) Analysis of Credit Risk for Small and Medium-Sized Enterprises: Evidence from Asia. *Asian Dev Rev* 32(2): 18–37. doi: 10.1162/ADEV_a_00050

Yoshino N, Taghizadeh-Hesary F (2016) Major Challenges Facing Small and Medium-Sized Enterprises in Asia and Solutions for Mitigating Them. ADBI Working Paper 564. Tokyo: Asian Development Bank Institute. Available via DIALOG: https://www.adb.org/sites/default/files/publication/182532/adbi-wp564.pdf. Accessed 17 February 2022

Zavatta R (2008) Financing Technology Entrepreneurs and SMEs in Developing Countries. Washington, DC: infoDev/World Bank. Available via DIALOG: http://www.infodev.org/publications. Accessed 28 August 2021

12 Financial innovations and Fintech solutions for migrant workers in the MENA region

Dharish David and Sanjana Bernadette Williams

1 Introduction

Financial inclusion allows both individuals and businesses not only to have access to, but also to use financial products and services to store and save money, send and receive payments. Furthermore, they may include access to credit and insurance (World Bank, 2018). Interestingly, as expected, financial inclusion has positive impacts on economic growth and poverty reduction, especially in low-income countries (Huang et al., 2021). Having access to formal financial services from a bank or financial organization at an affordable rate is crucial in helping those not in the formal economy to generate income (Le et al., 2019), escape poverty, improve the quality of life, invest in their future, safeguard against emergencies and losses in income through insurance, and avoid falling prey to predatory lending. Moreover, recent empirical studies have also shown that international remittances further enhance the effects of financial inclusion, strengthening economic growth in recipient countries (Chuc et al., 2022). As financial services are a highly regulated industry, new products and expansion beyond the home country has to be done in full compliance with the local laws, especially when it comes to migrant workers remitting their money from the host country to their country of origin.

Financial inclusion stands as a critical tool in assessing the competitiveness of the region with respect to raising incomes, creating employment opportunities, and eradicating poverty (Pearce, 2011). Over the past three decades, the Middle East and North Africa region has registered one of the highest rates of employment, in spite of its significant growth in efficiency and profitability. Despite the region's increased openness and liberalization, financial markets in the MENA region tend to remain underdeveloped and are potentially vulnerable to internal and external instabilities and shocks which are both financial and non-financial (Chancel, 2022). As one of the lowest levels of financial inclusions and highest in economic inequality in the world, the role of financial openness in the developing MENA region's financial sector and the interrelationships between financial integration and inclusion needs to be addressed.

At higher levels of policy governance, there is a clear relationship which shows that financial inclusion and stability go hand in hand. In some MENA countries,

DOI: 10.4324/9781003220220-16

microfinance and expansion of banks have not succeeded in reducing poverty levels, financial exclusion, and income inequality. It can be observed that the lack of financial access has a positive correlation with effect of economic growth (fall) and poverty alleviation. The pursuit of financial inclusion, which focused on drawing the "unbanked" population into a formal financial system, represents a great deal of pre-occupation for policy makers in the region (Pearce, 2011). However, globally, around 21%, or 1.6 billion people, are underbanked or unbanked, and the Middle East and North Africa region leads with 50% of their population being financially excluded (Ventura, 2021). Interestingly the MENA region has one of the fastest growing international migrant populations along with the most forcibly displaced in the world, doubling from 25 million to 54 million by 2015 according to Pew Research and the UN (PEW Research Center, 2016). Table 12.1 shows that many MENA countries also have the highest percentage of international migrant stock in the world. Therefore, improving financial inclusion in the MENA region is already a challenge, and so meeting the need for financial inclusion of those unbanked and underbanked, especially migrant workers and forcibly displaced populations, will be an even greater challenge.

In the past, having access to financial services was restricted by income levels but with the new normal, there is a great opportunity for fintechs to provide financial solutions through mobile phones and data-based economy where, with increasing mobile phone penetration and KYC regulations, there is a low entry barrier. Now, mobile money and blockchain technologies can be tapped by firms to provide solutions such as micro-credit, small loans, and remittances to those with almost no access to financing. Financial technology, or fintech, refers to the application of technology services and platforms revolutionizing finance and delivering financial services (Tajudin et al., 2020). Once underdeveloped, the banking sector in the MENA region has leapfrogged several stages, while fintech startups are tapping into the expanding digital economy and the rising penetration of mobile phones, access to the Internet, and digital payments ecosystem to provide more financial solutions.

Fintech-driven financial services are filling the gap left by traditional financial institutions (World Bank, 2021a). There is increasing anecdotal evidence that shows the support of financial inclusion through financial technology. Table 12.2 shows the key contribution of financial inclusion combining the traditional with fintech (digital) financial inclusion, ranging from access to payment services such as bank branches, ATMs, etc. The macro and micro implications have a positive impact on financial inclusion, which show that both financial access, lowering income inequalities, and promoting economic growth catch negative externalities on financial stability, provided it is based on a good regulatory ecosystem.

With the rapid growth in the number of migrant workers as a percentage of the labor force in many MENA countries in the past decades, this research will seek to understand the policy support and challenges for fintechs operating in the financial inclusion space especially to those out of the formal financial system. These solutions will tap into small value transactions and micro-credit

Table 12.1 International Migrant Stock as a Percentage of the Total Population (1990–2020)

Region, Development Grouping, Country	*1990*	*1995*	*2000*	*2005*	*2010*	*2015*	*2020*
WORLD	2.9	2.8	2.8	2.9	3.2	3.4	3.6
Northern Africa and Western Asia	6.1	5.9	5.7	5.9	7.5	8.7	9.5
Developed regions	7.2	7.9	8.7	9.6	10.6	11.2	12.4
Less developed regions	1.7	1.5	1.4	1.4	1.6	1.8	1.9
- Less developed regions, excluding least developed countries	1.6	1.4	1.4	1.4	1.6	1.8	2.0
- Less developed regions, excluding China	2.3	2.0	1.8	1.8	2.0	2.2	2.4
High-income countries	7.4	8.3	9.3	10.5	12.1	13.1	14.7
Middle-income countries	1.7	1.5	1.4	1.3	1.3	1.4	1.5
Upper-middle-income countries	1.6	1.5	1.4	1.5	1.6	1.8	2.0
Lower-middle-income countries	1.8	1.5	1.3	1.1	1.1	1.0	1.0
Low-income countries	3.0	2.6	1.8	1.6	1.7	1.7	1.8
Middle East	10.3	10.1	10.0	10.4	13.2	15.5	16.7
Bahrain	34.9	36.5	36.0	45.4	53.7	52.7	55.0
Iraq	0.5	1.0	0.9	0.5	0.4	1.0	0.9
Israel	36.7	34.0	31.1	28.9	26.6	25.2	22.6
Jordan	32.1	33.5	37.6	38.1	38.4	34.2	33.9
Kuwait	51.3	57.4	55.1	58.7	62.7	74.7	72.8
Lebanon	18.7	17.2	18.0	15.8	16.0	29.3	25.1
Oman	16.8	24.5	27.5	26.5	26.8	43.5	46.5
Qatar	65.0	70.4	60.7	74.6	78.5	65.8	77.3
Saudi Arabia	30.8	27.5	25.5	27.3	30.7	34.0	38.6
State of Palestine*	13.7	10.8	8.5	7.7	6.8	6.0	5.3
Syrian Arab Republic	5.7	5.8	5.1	4.8	8.3	4.6	5.0
United Arab Emirates	71.5	75.5	78.1	71.5	85.6	86.3	88.1
Yemen	1.0	0.9	0.8	0.9	1.2	1.4	1.3

Source: World Bank (2020).

Table 12.2 Relationship between Fintech and Financial Inclusion

Comprehensive Measure of Financial Inclusion (Financial Inclusion Index)	
Traditional (bank-based) Financial Inclusion	• Access to bank infrastructure • Macro and micro literature • Using financial inclusion through traditional means • Fintech services are not included in financial inclusion
Fintech-enabled Financial Inclusion	• Access to digital infrastructure • Micro and macro empirical studies • Descriptive stocktaking • Includes majority of the firm- (M-Pesa-micro-financing and ANT financial) and country-specific, which includes micro (example: North Africa). • Macro empirical studies seem to be non-existent and follow a piecemeal approach (focuses on one aspect).

Source: Authors.

for migrant workers and solve issues involving the lack of a credit history, collateral, identity proof, or a fixed resident address for such individuals. Many of these scalable solutions are still in their infancy, such as the use of blockchain and biometric identity, and providing peer-to-peer banking services, and they may need to be brought in from other countries and regions developing such solutions for the micro-economy. The needs of migrants and refugees will be a balance between micro-remittances, with minimal transaction charges, access to credit, and micro-savings and investments.

While the region is a complex web with many of the richest countries in the Gulf Cooperation Council (GCC) region such as Saudi Arabia, Bahrain, United Arab Emirates (UAE), Kuwait, Qatar, and Oman, it also attracts a large pool of poor migrant workers from South Asia, Southeast Asia, and Africa. With this situation, currently 85% of the fintech firms in the Middle East and North Africa (MENA) area operate in the payments and remittances space, as affordable money transfers have been such a challenge (Devanesan, 2021). Moreover, with its large refugee population, the region's fintech start-ups will also need to tap into financial inclusion through different fintech sectors such as peer-to-peer lending platforms, crowdfunding, e-payments, and other financing platforms (Zarrouk et al., 2021). For all this to flow seamlessly, support from government and regulators and support and financing from stakeholders will be crucial. Successful examples of support from fintech hubs and policy initiatives will be highlighted by looking into the policy measures and fintech case studies operating in this space.

This chapter will look at the latest developments in policy and regulatory support for fintechs in the MENA region, particularly for fintech solutions and innovations that provide access to credit, banking, and financial services to the underserved. This region is particularly interesting, as there is an exceptional demand for financial services, data, and technology innovations, and case studies of fintechs operating particularly in financial inclusion and overseas remittances deserve review. While having access to a bank account may seem to be a basic human right, for many migrant workers, refugees, or forcibly displaced people, financial inclusion is restricted by stringent banking rules and requirements. For financial inclusion, accessibility, availability, and affordability of financial products and services (which includes deposits, loans, insurance, credit guarantees, etc.) must be considered.

2 Systematic review of Fintech's impact on migrants and remittances

Improvement in financial inclusion among asylum seekers, migrants, and refugees has gained immense traction to access affordable but secure financial services, which has become a crucial aspect in promoting equitable economic growth, poverty reduction, and development. With the opportunity of open innovation among critical stakeholders in the emerging fintech industry, fintech brings about positive results to improve the response to the financing needs of the huge market segment that ranges from those underserved by banks due to credit risk to migrant workers (Serrao et al., 2013). Granting migrant workers access to basic financial services is at the core of financial inclusion in many of the more affluent countries in the Middle East and North Africa region (OECD, 2019). The main idea behind this is that financial services, such as providing a remittance platform, are a profitable business in host countries by enabling access to savings and investment opportunities while contributing to raising income and the GDP of recipient countries.

Despite the introduction of disruptive fintech services, the needs generated by unimproved conditions and protracted crises outstrip the resources available to meet them (Tajudin et al., 2020). Financial inclusion has recently become a crucial concern for policy makers worldwide. It is not new in the literature that financial development plays an important role in economic growth, and inclusive financial systems help reduce income inequality and smoothen consumption.

2.1 *Opportunities for Fintech technologies to provide financial inclusion for migrant workers in MENA*

This section fills the gap in the existing literature by bringing to the current knowledge of the fintech remittances infrastructure in the MENA countries, especially through fintech technologies, innovations, and solutions for the underbanked and unbanked on the margins. It employs a wide range of qualitative case study methodologies and conceptual analyses and provides an overview of how fintech start-ups facilitate cheaper and more efficient remittances and enhance financial inclusion in the MENA region by illustrating major fintech sectors such as online marketplace payments and peer-to-peer (P2P)/crowdfunding financing. The Middle East and North Africa region will be ideal for this study, as it hosts a large population of migrant workers, and in some cases, refugees will also be examined, provided case studies are available. Case study and qualitative approach will be used, as many of these fintechs use on-the-ground digital identification and authentication approaches such as through collateral, biometrics, credit worthiness, and developing credit score/rating.

The focus is first on the evolution of fintech in the MENA region and then narrows down to those that are working in financial inclusion and remittance services, which is critical for developing financial solutions to those in the margins, reducing poverty, creating jobs, raising incomes, and contributing to economic growth. It is important to review the systematic literature on how fintechs in the region and elsewhere positively impact migrant workers, refugees, and the marginalized by tapping into the most current technologies. There are still gaps in what kind of mechanisms they can access and how they use the financial footing as they integrate into the host economies (Velasco, 2021).

Through expanded alliances between traditional and fintech-enabled financial inclusion as well as migrant workers and refugees, fintech startups in the region will look into the solutions and innovations being tapped around user-friendly collaborative customer due diligence, data sharing, digital identity verification, payment schemes, AI, IoT, crowdfunding, and online peer-to-peer lending (P2P) platforms (Murthy et al., 2019). A new paradigm shift in financial and economic structure brought on by these technologies is required to respond to the challenges faced by the unbanked population. This chapter will also look into the financing and support of fintech hubs that are emerging in the region to solve the problems of financial inclusion within the population and for those who migrate into these countries.

3 Rise of FinTech in the MENA region

Fintechs will be enablers of the post-pandemic recovery in the MENA region with exciting long-term opportunities for the sector, says a white paper. Fintechs are currently in an exciting phase, with new entrants allowed to create compelling products for consumers, while challenging the status quo and influencing incumbent financial institutions. Within the fintech markets in the MENA region, the largest demand for services includes payments, transfer, and remittance solutions followed by crowdfunding, digital wealth management, and lending. The MENA region is one of the world's weakest regions in terms of financial inclusion (Demirgüç-Kunt et al., 2015) and has the highest gender gap in financial inclusion. In addition, the countries of the MENA are characterized by a large share of young people who are generally encountering major obstacles to accessing financial and banking services.

3.1 FinTech key sectors, ecosystem elements, and their development in the MENA region

In the MENA region, there are various opportunities that exist for investors to increase their exposure to the Fintech market with six main themes: emergence of super applications, fintech-enabled technologies, financial inclusion, digital currencies and banking, e-commerce and marketplaces, and the transition to a cashless society (Feyen et al., 2021).

The growth of Fintech as an industry in its own right is accelerating in the MENA region, and the reason is two-fold. First, the lack of legacy infrastructure gives emerging markets the agility to adapt to new and exciting technological advances, making them easier to integrate on a blanket basis. Second, major economies in the region, such as the UAE and Saudi Arabia, are currently mid-phase in their national transformation programs, which hold within them supportive regulatory plans and projects to support Fintech innovation.

Over the past decade, several mega-trends have emerged, such as greater connectivity, mobile penetration, and increasing customer demand, which forms the backdrop of an emerging financial ecosystem. Some of the mega-trends include increasing digitalization, change in the regulatory and competitor landscapes, and increases in customer demands and utilization of big data. As the Fintech arena grows, the demand for easier and faster financial technology solutions changes. Figure 12.1 gives us an overview of the main stakeholders which frame a financial ecosystem. Lee and Shin (2018) identified five elements of the ecosystem which differentiate from traditional financing in respect to its regulatory authorities, investments, infrastructure providers, and mainly, the technology which brings out the need for a cashless society.

A cashless society is no longer a far-off fantasy; rather, it is quickly becoming a reality through the increased adoption of cashless payments and supportive e-commerce market dynamics. Such dynamics have given non-bank lenders the impetus to emerge and incumbent governments to take digital and cryptocurrencies more seriously. Through the Dubai International Financial Centre (DIFC), Dubai is the home of building one of the region's most comprehensive cashless societies which brings in a diffusion of innovative digital technologies and venture capital environments, including cost efficient solutions, licensing and regulations, accelerated programs for early start-ups, and funding for growth-stage start-ups. Several countries have brought in different ambitions, like Saudi Arabia's Vision 2030, which has officially committed to achieving 70% cashless payments for all transactions upon completion of the program, a significant shift in consumer behavior that will likely continue to evolve further should the rate of financial technology innovation maintain its current trajectory (Minnock, 2020). Iran has launched the Iran Vision 2025, to make Iran the Mideast regional hub for financing and banking projected to reach US$128 billion by 2025 (Schroeder, 2017).

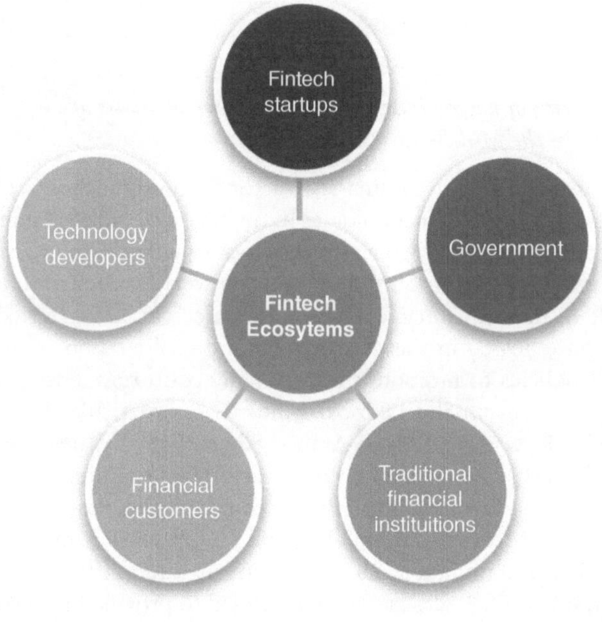

Figure 12.1 Fintech Ecosystem.
Source: Adapted from Lee and Shin (2018).

3.2 FinTech in the MENA region: overviewing and exploring FinTech solutions

The MENA region was an attraction for the low-skill workforce in the 1980s and 1990s. A clear upward social and economic mobility is evident among the foreign workers in the region. The Middle East and Africa lead with 50% of their population being financially excluded globally, comprising around 21%, or 1.6 billion people, who are underbanked or unbanked (ILO, 2020). West Asia and North Africa, especially the Arab States, are the main destinations globally for migrant workers comprised of migrants in the six Gulf Cooperation Countries (GCC) who account for over 10% of all migrants worldwide (Saudi Arabia is 3rd, and United Arab Emirates is 5th globally) (ILO, 2020). As of 2019, the total number of migrant workers in the GCC countries (including Jordan and Lebanon) was 35 million, with 31% of them being women. The global fintech market is worth at least $100 billion with an estimated 2,800 startups in the MENA region. Most regions in the Middle East and Africa are still unbanked and depend on traditional retail behavior despite the rapid rise of e-commerce as an online and mobile payment infrastructure (except for Israel and UAE).

Though financial inclusion through traditional banking services is on the decline, expanded access to digital solutions and services is on the increase. Fintechs can increase financial inclusion by providing customers with open application program interfaces, streamlining processes to reduce costs, and meet regulations. Trends abound in the Middle East and Africa include a large number of migrants, high unemployment, lack of financial literacy, building a credit score, and nascent financial systems.

3.2.1 Background of key regional trends and developments of FinTech in the Middle East region

The digital transformation in the financial sector has brought about a glaring consequence in the adoption of technologies in the financial industry and instigated the growth of the fintech (financial technology) market. Fintech startups are part of the emerging startup ecosystem in many wealthy countries, particularly in the Middle East. Regulatory regimes of the fintech industry started emerging in 2017 and have helped in the development and proliferation of Fintech hubs and a slew of policies to promote them in many countries. These policies and institutional support will also be looked into with a particular focus on UAE, Qatar, Bahrain, Kuwait, and Saudi Arabia. Since 2015, VC investments in the Middle East Fintechs have been doubling, reaching $78 million in 2017 (Figure 12.2). Estimates suggest that 465 Fintech companies in the Middle East will raise over $2 billion in venture capital funding by 2022 as compared to the 30 that raised nearly $80 million in 2017 (Milken Institute, 2019).

To understand how services are being extended to provide financial inclusion, the adoption of technology and how it will be accessed by the most marginalized, low paid migrants and forcefully migrated populations must be considered. Access to startup financing for fintechs includes early-stage ventures (seed

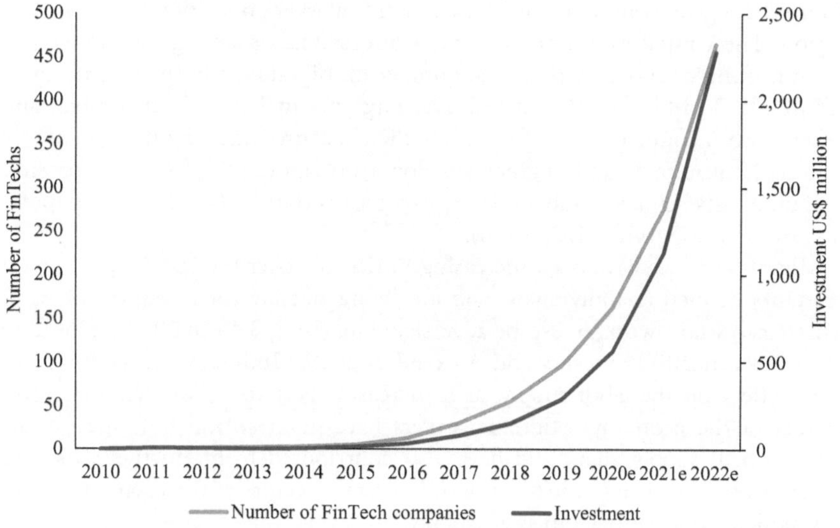

Figure 12.2 Venture Capital Investment into Middle East Fintech Companies (2010–2022e).

Source: Milken Institute (2019).

capital), as migrants and refugees do not fit into the impact investor investment hypothesis (Kluge and Mahoney, 2016), local talent with skills sets is lacking, and direct and indirect initiatives such as accelerator programs, venture capital, and angel investing are virtually unknown.

Another mega-trend to explore is the fintech ecosystem in the region. For example, Dubai has been recognized as one of the most successful emirates in the UAE which has transformed itself into a diversified economy (Schilirò, 2013). Fintech is experiencing tremendous growth in Dubai with a number of Fintech startups that commenced their journeys with crowdfunding sectors having now grown into SMEs across the region. The dynamic ecosystem plays an instrumental role in the growth of the fintech hive in Dubai. Many hubs, such as the Dubai International Financial Centre's Fintech Hive and the Qatar Fintech Hub, center their visions on keeping innovation as the main driver in growth followed by keeping the ecosystem conducive to new alternatives and continuously improving on their policies and initiatives to stimulate innovation through spill-over effects (Schilirò, 2021).

3.2.2 Rapid migration effect across countries in the MENA

The MENA region is home to some of the richest countries in the world as well as some of the poorest ones. The Middle East constitutes a remarkable geographical region in response to labor migration movements and has the world's largest percentage of expats and immigrant workers (Baldwin-Edwards, 2005). Figure 12.3 give us an overview of the migrant worker population in the MENA region. The United Arab Emirates and Saudi Arabia are among the top ten migrant hosting countries with a total number of migrants in both countries, i.e., around 18.3 million (IOM, 2018). The migrants in UAE, Saudi Arabia, and other MENA countries come from diversified backgrounds ranging from highly educated consultants and engineers to low-paid laborers. With a total of 8.84 million expats, United Arab Emirates expatriates outnumber the local population by a huge margin (ILO, 2020).

Migration levels have been increasing noticeably over the last 20 years, with migrants defined as individuals who are living outside their country of birth whether to study, work, or escape adversity comprising 3.4% in 2017, an increase from 2.8% in 2000 (Vickers and Alexander, 2019). Immigration has an enormous effect on the labor supply, as it increases the pool of workers in certain sectors of the economy. Migrant workers have filled critical shortages in the international supply chain and have also contributed to productivity and the GDP (gross domestic product) growth in certain sectors of the economy where low-skilled labor has been in short supply.

Many migrant workers who live and work in the Middle East come from developing nations in areas such as South Asia, southeast Asia, and Africa. Migrant workers have been the engine of the globalized economy, making the inability of labor move efficiently and have a high impact on remittances (Yaybokc, 2020). Migrant remittances are growing at an exceptional rate as an external source of capital in developing nations. Global foreign direct investments fell by having remittances as an important source for the countries that receive them, as they play a large part in the country's GDP. Within MENA, payments, transfers, and remittances make up around 85% of all fintech companies operating within that space.

3.2.3 Migrant workers on the Kafala system in GCC countries

Emerging in the 1950s, the Kafala system, also known as the sponsorship system, was formed to regulate the relationship between employers and migrant workers in the Gulf Cooperation Council (GCC) countries, which include Kuwait, Bahrain, United Arab Emirates, Saudi Arabia, and Oman along with other Arab states like Jordan and Egypt. In past years, the system often created irregular situations in both the employment and immigration status for migrant workers. Under the Kafala system, the migrant worker is legally bound to an individual employer or sponsor for their contract period. The migrant worker cannot enter the country for any reason without the permission of their sponsor (ILO, 2020). In 2021, Saudi Arabia ended the Kafala system for its foreign workers under its Labour Reform Initiative. Several GCC countries such as the United Arab Emirates are slowly moving away from the Kafala system for better conditions.

3.3 Remittance market in the Middle East and North Africa

Remittance flows to the MENA region rose by 2.3% to about $56 billion in 2020 following a rise of 3.4% in 2019 (World Bank, 2021b). The anticipated fall in the rate is attributable to the global slowdown caused by the pandemic as well as the impact of lower oil prices in Middle Eastern countries. This is due to the strong remittance flows from countries such as Egypt, site of the world's fifth largest remittance flow (Table 12.3), and Morocco. In parallel, as shown in Figure 12.4, the United Arab Emirates' outbound remittances fell by 3.9% to $43 million in 2020, while outflows from Saudi Arabia increased by 11% to $35

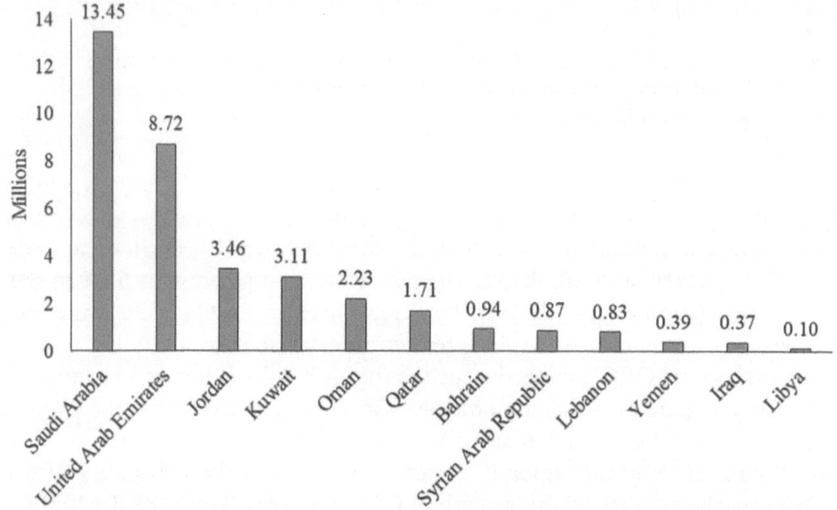

Figure 12.3 Migrant workers in the Arab States Region, 2020.
Source: IOM (2020).

Table 12.3 Top Remittance Recipients in the Middle East and North Africa (2020)

Region	*Remittance Flow ($ billion, 2020)*	*Remittances as a Share of GDP (%, 2020)*
Egypt, Arab Republic	29.6	32.2
Morocco	7.4	17.1
Lebanon	6.2	9.0
Jordan	3.9	8.2
West Bank and Gaza	2.7	6.5
Tunisia	2.1	5.3
Algeria	1.7	1.6
Iran, Islamic Rep.	1.3	1.2
Iraq	0.7	0.4
Djibouti	0.1	0.2

Source: World Bank (2021b).

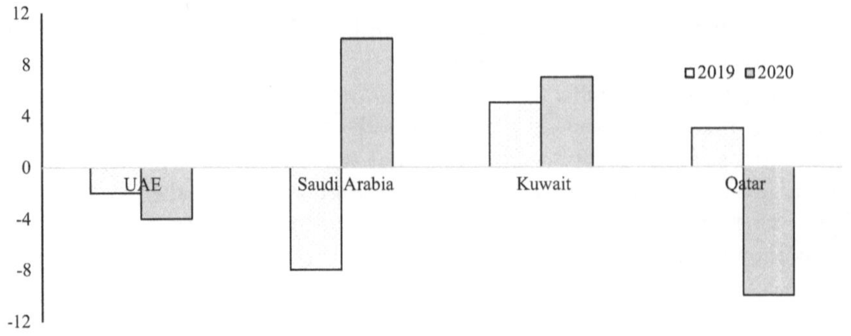

Figure 12.4 Outward Remittance Flows Varied Across Gulf Cooperation Council (GCC) Countries (% of Outbound Remittance Growth).

Source: Adapted from World Bank (2020).

million (World Bank, 2020b). This effect can also be shown in large recipient organizations such as Egypt, India, and Pakistan.

The average cost (sending) of $200 in the MENA region has declined to 6.6% in the first quarter of 2020, despite the pandemic, compared with 6.9% in the previous year (World Bank, 2021b). The global average for Q4 2020 was 6.5%. The average remittance cost varies across corridors; the cost of sending money from high-income OECD countries such as the United Kingdom to Lebanon remain high compared with sending money from GCC countries such the United Arab Emirates to Egypt or Jordan which remains at 3% in some corridors. The flow of remittances in the region is expected to recover at the slow pace of 1.6% considering the projected weak growth in GCC outflows (World Bank, 2021a).

4 Barriers to remittance services and the COVID-19 pandemic

Remittances generally consist of both transfer and income elements, defined by the IMF as personal transfers and compensation of employees (Reinke, 2007). The remittances industry seems to have been improving the lives of many families, particularly during the COVID-19 pandemic, increasing by 5.2% in 2020 in South Asia. Studies indicate that remittances tend to increase when the receiving households experience disasters or recessions (World Bank, 2021a).

While countries have already adopted several measures for facing the shock and fallout of the pandemic for migrant workers, more needs (in particular, to remittances) to be done, as both recipient (home) and sender (foreign) countries have been affected. Migrant workers employed in the Middle East, the European Union, and North Americas who were working mostly in contact-intensive services sectors have been particularly hard hit by COVID-19 (Bhattarai, 2021). The pandemic created another opportunity for firms to accelerate innovation and competition in digital platforms. Remittances play a decisive role when economies are hit, as migrant workers increase their volume of remittances to buffer the crisis. Despite the potential of remittances accelerating growth, the inefficiencies of the existing cross-border payments result in high costs, which minimizes the total benefits. The high remittance costs reduce the amount received by migrant families and might limit the use of a formal financial system for savings and investments. The factors that influence a high remittance/transaction cost include those discussed below:

I. **Transparency and Consumer Protection:** Consumers find it difficult to compare remittance prices, as there are several variables that make up the price. Remittance price is made up of the fee charged for sending a certain amount. A slight margin is taken from the exchange rate when the remittances are paid and received in different currencies. Sometimes, a fee is also charged on the recipient funds (World Bank, 2021b).
II. **Fees and Competition:** Remittance fees tend to be higher than the normal bar in corridors where the competition is low and the bank concentration is high.
III. **Legal and Regulatory Environment:** Regulatory and CDD (customer due diligence) policy decisions due to external shocks can cause the remittance cost to be high. Long-standing policies and regulatory issues must be addressed to improve resilience in the remittance market. Appropriate licensing and regulatory regimens based on each country's regulations must be undertaken with robust analysis of the risks due to new technology and players in the market.
IV. **Payment System Infrastructure:** In many countries, non-bank remittance service providers lack access to the national payment system infrastructure.

The financial technology industry has always been a game changer for migrant workers and has made international remittances cost-effective, secure, and swift. Among the factors driving the high-cost remittance cost in some corridors is the inconsistent data in cross-border payments. The vast majority of remittance service providers (RSP) have experienced an immediate reduction in the remittance volumes due the economic-induced crisis. This has opened the market for digitalization and financial technology. Digital-only remittance providers have brought a positive remittance growth and increase of volumes of remittance since the beginning of the pandemic. This is due to the temporary closure of many physical locations which consist of both sending and receiving and the risk of safety further encouraged the shift to digital channels.

5 FinTech remittance market and solutions for migrant workers

With remittances playing a crucial role as a source of income, it is appropriate to discuss the issues of costly remittance corridors, and a viable way proposed to overcome the challenges is through adopting Fintech services. To mitigate the socio-economic effects of various crises, including the COVID-19 pandemic, on migrants, it is necessary to evaluate the fintech startups operating in the MENA remittance corridors and develop a framework which assesses the supply and demand sides of the fintech services and new models for the latter for fintech-based remittance services. Despite the growth in the region, digital remittances still remain nascent which could reflect the behavioral inertia, the cost benefit analysis of digital over traditional services, and the impact of financial inclusion on financial stability, income inequality, and poverty. The main elements of the model must include a solution for migrant workers without traditional identity documents (expired refugee ids), high international transfer fees (transaction costs), the need to carry cash (savings) when forced to flee (dangerous and expensive to exchange), Internet access and access to smartphones, bad exchange rates, expensive P2P services, and financial risk (theft).

6 Scaling Fintech solutions and new models

Migrant workers face many challenges in sending money from abroad. Up to 77% of migrant workers have bank accounts but do not utilize them, citing a language barrier as the primary reason for this (Ponti, 2021). Moreover, many of these migrant workers do not have the know-how to use financial technology to manage their money. Two technologies that are acquiring more ground include blockchain and distributed ledger technology (DLT) and mobile money.

6.1 Blockchain and Distributed Ledger Technology (DLT)

Blockchain-based innovations have disrupted many traditional industries including the financial services industry (Soufaih, 2020). With migrant remittances representing the overall financial flow, particularly from the MENA region to other developing countries, blockchain has been seen as a promising technology which not only has served as an instrument for speculation, but now enables global remittances on the way we send and receive money. The terminology in this field is still evolving, the terms "distributed ledger," "blockchain," and "shared ledger" are used interchangeably. The fintech industry, which is currently going through a major transformation, has brought about several areas of rapid development, where blockchain can improve not just the formalization of remittances, but also financial inclusion. Blockchains are a type of distributed ledger technology that uses algorithmic and cryptographic models to validate and generate a continuously expanding data structure in the form of chains of blocks in a single depot on the distributed ledger (Papadaki and Karamitsos, 2021).

DLT is considered a possible solution to increasing costs in global remittances, particularly because of the difficulty in opening corresponding bank accounts. Cross-border payments are typically time-consuming and expensive. As shown in Figure 12.5, Ripple uses Integrated Ledger Protocol, an open-source distributed ledger that connects different banks' proprietary ledgers through

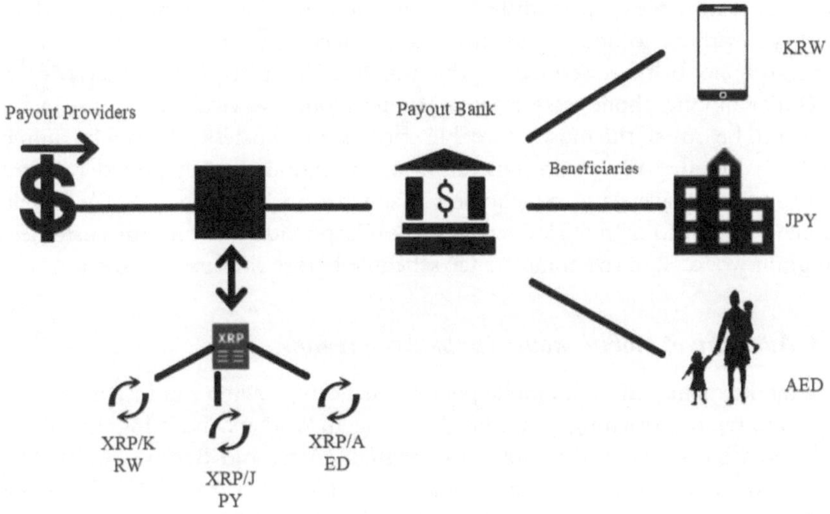

Figure 12.5 Distributed Ledger Process for Ripple (Notes: KRW: South Korean Won; JPY: Japanese Yen; AED: United Arab Emirates Dirham).
Source: Adapted from Ripple (2018).

connectors for the purpose of peer-to-peer transactions. Ripple has introduced its own product called the Xrapid that uses its own digital wallet called the XRP (Grayscale.co, 2019).

Blockchain technology is an innovative digital architecture that eliminates manual process requirements and provides any authentication through intermediaries. The United Arab Emirates, Dubai, in particular, is at the forefront of blockchain technology in the Middle East, while Bahrain and Saudi Arabia are in the initial steps toward adapting blockchain. Remittances are a key driver of blockchain in the Middle East due to its heavy expatriate population, and with blockchain, which is part of the distributed ledger technology solution, substantial cost savings and better customer service can be achieved. It allows storing data in the distributed ledger, allowing multiple stakeholders to share information confidently and securely (Accenture, 2020).

6.2 *Mobile money*

Mobile money has revolutionized the way financial services are provided across the globe. It is a good example of how technology can improve the efficiency of financial transactions. Provided by network operators and consisting of electronic wallets linked to the customer's phone number, these e-wallets allow individuals to use airtime as a form of currency, transfer funds, pay bills, and receive, withdraw, and deposit through their mobile phones. Other ways would be through the traditional person-to-person (P2P) transfers. New models include account-to-account (A2A) and government-to-person (G2P) transfers for international remittances, salary disbursements, and merchant payments (GSMA). Migrant workers do not require any internet access, nor do they need to own a smartphone for these services, as the mobile-cellular network connectivity in a regular mobile phone is sufficient. Mobile money services have consistently shown to be one of the most affordable options for transfers followed by online platforms. Figure 12.6 is an illustration of the mobile money provider model and the main players and stakeholders. Launched in 2018, the GSMA Mobile Money Certification requires certified mobile providers to inform customers (migrant workers) of the complete fee schedule before they use the service.

6.3 Adoption of mobile money in the Arab region

The market penetration of mobile phones has been growing significantly across the Arab region, reaching around 89% of foreign workers and bringing 59% of unbanked individuals to the formal ecosystem (Attia and Benson 2020). The promotion of mobile money has become a growing interest to the MENA policy makers, and this new trend prompts a great potential in the expansion of financial inclusion in the MENA region through adjustments in the regulatory framework and amplification of the technology reach. Although it has good reach, the impact of mobile money accounts is relatively low in the Arab countries in comparison with other corridors. Exploring new possibilities such as providing services without the need of an Internet connection can open the way to lowering the costs of financial services and increasing affordability.

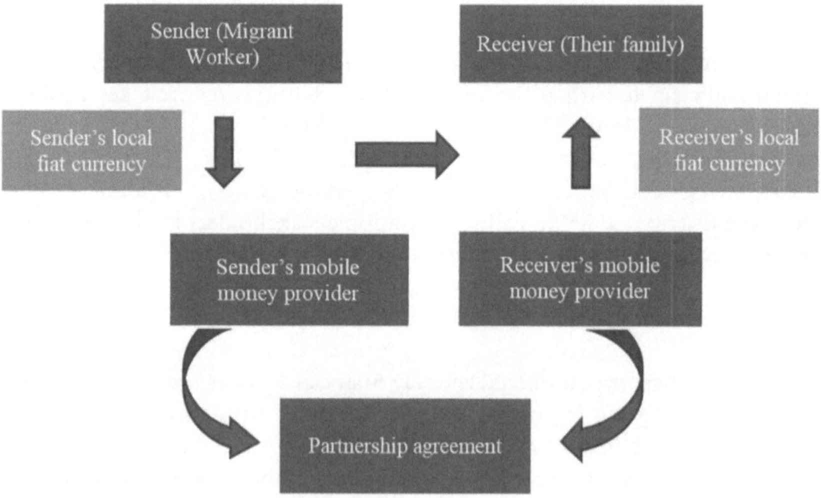

Figure 12.6 Mobile Money Provider Model.
Source: Adapted from Hahm et al. (2021).

7 Case studies of Fintechs

Case studies of fintechs operating in the MENA region provide solutions to the target population with the help of the trends in the technologies, innovations, and how solutions are being scaled up beyond the region too. Case studies of fintechs provide insights on their business models, the effectiveness of technology solutions, financial metrics that are more than just financial inclusion and reduce risks to economic empowerment. The shifting landscape of financial markets has challenged conventional thinking about relationships among technology, business models, and financial services (Gozman et al., 2018).

7.1 The Parlo Berhard's case and the potential of FinTech services for migrants

Parlo Berhad (Parlo), a Malaysia-based company trying to expand its reach to the MENA region, has been one of the most reliable and successful operators for leisure, corporate, and MICE (meetings, incentives, conferences, and exhibitions) travel, operating since 1996. The new normal has unfolded a huge disruption in the economy, demanding companies to redefine the "business-as-usual." The economic-induced crisis posed significant challenges to the tourism and travel industry, including Parlo Bhd, and had a substantially negative effect on the evolution of tourism demand (Varzaru et al., 2021).

With the growing pace in globalization, migrant workers have been hit hard by the pandemic, which has also impacted the downfall in remittances sent home by migrants. The supply of the foreign workforce in any region carries with it a complicated and multi-process step, and with the downturn in the pandemic, governments are in uncharted territory to carry additional requirements and contact traceability procedures. Parlo's example provides the dynamics and nature of the technological advancements in the fintech landscape for migrant workers and its usefulness in incorporating a similar business model for fintechs in the MENA region.

The pandemic offered the company an opportunity to generate a new revenue stream. The tourism company recorded the highest net loss of RM 3.68 million in 4Q2020 as compared to RM 61,000 a year before (NST Business, 2021). It was deeply affected by the COVID pandemic due to the travel bans which resulted in their recording higher losses or lower profits. With the uncertainties and to venture out and become a key player in financial digitalization, Parlo Bhd signed a definitive agreement with a Myanmar-based Diamond Palace for migrant workforce management services in Myanmar (Shanker, 2020). The travel management company ventured into travel and management arrangements for migrant workers to generate a new stream of revenue. The services entail travel, dormitory, and logistics arrangements, vocational training, medical examinations, and digital identity solutions (E-ID) for migrant workers (NST Business, 2021).

Figure 12.7 provides highlights the key technologies of Parlo Bhd's digital platform, which cover the main technologies that start-ups working in migrant

Technology	Description
E-wallet & Cashless	E-wallet for merchant payment and P2P payment
E-services	Merchant discovery, step-by-step health care, immigration, travel and arrangement
E-transfer	Money transfer to family
E-assistance	Assistance services on legal, medical, employment matters and notifications
E-financial mastery	Financial planner
Future expansion	Digitalisation services

Figure 12.7 Features of the Parlo Bhd Digital Platform.
Source: Adapted from the Edge Markets (2021).

related operations will need to incorporate. Parlo's platform ensures that all the information of foreign workers from Myanmar in countries such as Qatar, United Arab Emirates, Saudi Arabia, and Russia are digitized and presented in the form of digital identity documents, making it easier for KYC and verification.

Key technologies used by Parlo Bhd

1. **E-ID (Electronic Identification)**
   According to the latest International Labor Organization (ILO) estimates, migrant workers have increased to nearly 170 million worldwide, mostly concentrated in high-income countries which is nearly three times the number of foreign workers in 2020. The E-ID total solutions can serve and facilitate secure online transactions such as travel, insurance, banking, and other commercial services with authenticated and seamless processes at the migrant workers' convenience. Parlo has now secured around 160,000 workers in terms of logistics and travel services through its digital platform. This platform will allow migrants to register themselves, and registered users will be provided with a unique identification. MENA startups can

propose in offering both software and hardware solutions under the e-ID total solutions platforms in areas such as e-KYC (Electronic Know Your Client), key infrastructure, and identity management. The platform will make employment-related administration efficient and convenient through a mobile device.

2. **Biometric Digital ID Platform**

   Biometric technology has become a vital tool in the identification and migration movement process. The digital identity feature in this model, which will be embedded in model devices, are grouped based on enrollment and registration, encoding biometric and personal platform, and integration with mobile applications. A migrant worker's biometric and personal information will be collated to manage the registration and enrollment process, which includes money transfers to family, digital travel arrangements, and other assistance services in one place (Koslowski, 2019).

3. **Cloud Computing**

   Using artificial intelligence-driven property, Parlo Bhd uses multiple integrated elements to deliver and fulfill a seamless, controlled disbursement and speedy process. The platform uses cloud computing, which uses a network of remote servers on the Internet to accumulate, manage, and route the data. It uses the components of frontend and backend cloud computing architecture. Frontend or client side communicates with the backend through a network or the Internet and is visible to the end-user. The backend protects the data and responds to all queries raised by the frontend architecture (Borah, 2020). Figure 12.8 explains the backend platform model of Parlo Bhd, which is the biggest part of the cloud computing architecture. The whole cloud service is called the Backend-as-a service (BaaS).

   In the business setting, the backend architecture in the cloud empowers the frontend architecture. As Parlo Bhd offers both hardware and software, the architecture is located on the remote server. The components of the Parlo Bhd's backend architecture as explained in Figure 12.7 are:

   i. **User Application:** A substantial part of the backend architecture. It is the user interface that the backend platform offers to the end-user (migrant workers) to send queries and any requests or requirements (Borah, 2020).
   ii. **Service provider:** The service handles all the tasks that run in the cloud computing architecture. This layer of the backend executes a large array of tasks on the cloud runtime. In the Parlo Bhd model, the service providers include health care, immigration, and flights.
   iii. **Admin Portal:** The cloud admin portal is the administration console for managing various identification services. The current model for the admin portal includes user management (registration, termination, etc.), user journey management, and loan disbursements, among other services

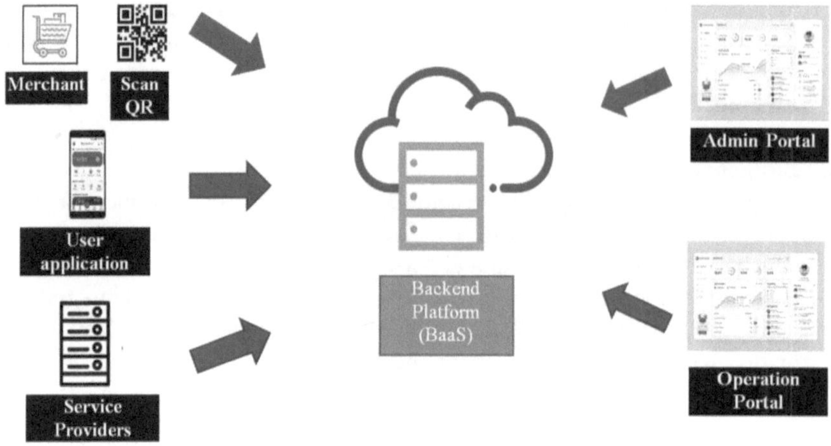

Figure 12.8 BaaS (Backend as a Service) Model of Parlo BhD.
Source: Adapted from the Edge Markets (2020).

iv. **Operation Portal:** A centralized access point where the company can manage deployments and instances. The Parlo Bhd model includes merchant management (registration, changes, terminations, etc.), merchant policy and provisioning, settlements, and transactions.

4. **Other Fintech Services Useful in the Future for the MENA Market**

Parlos share price rose 450% with the introduction of the digital platform and had an expected projection of RM 420 million (US$102 million) to close at 47 seen by the end of 2021 (The Edge Markets, 2021). Parlo plans to raise US$6.3 million through a private placement for a cashless e-wallet which will include future fintech solutions for financial management and a platform for e-services (reloads and bill payments) from both source and host countries, e-assistance (legal assistance, medical, employment and notification purposes), e-remittances, e-wages, and e-commerce. This new migrant workforce-related services business will help migrants repay bank borrowings. The new fintech platform will provide Parlo and its partnering firm, Diamond Palace, with a new revenue source, as they face a stalemate in the tourism industry due to the coronavirus crisis. The remittance alone from Myanmar overseas workers back to the country amounts to an estimated US$900 million a month (The Edge Markets, 2020).

Parlo's venture into foreign worker management covers Myanmar workers applying to work in or leaving countries in Singapore, Japan, South Korea, and the Middle East (only Gulf Cooperation Council countries) but will be extended to regions where the firm has forged strong relationships. The firm plans on integrating with mobile phones through optional embedded secure elements along with providing third-party logistics services for smartphones such as inventory planning and management, inbound and outbound services, logistics strategy, and reverse logistics management. The technology-enabled gadget will provide a base for migrant workers to replace physical identification documents through digitalization. For example, in today's world, debit and credit cards can now be easily accessed using mobile phone apps in smartphones and high-end secured hardware chips.

7.2 *Examples of MENA companies in FinTech operating in financial inclusion for migrants*

The changing paradigm of financial technology advances and digitalization in remittances are reshaping not just financial inclusion, but also financial literacy. Several factors have influenced the reshaping of fintech companies in the MENA region, including the proliferation of digital platforms and mobile devices, barriers to entry and greater competition, accelerating pace of change in the industry, and more supportive policy and regulatory responses for the fintech ecosystem.

In the last few years, a large number of fintech startups, particularly in the MENA region, have contributed to the significant growth of the remittance market and have had an impact on not only a more inclusive financial market, but also economic development. The remittance industry has seen a trajectory in financial inclusion due to the exceptional rise in the number of startups, particularly in our region of study. Table 12.4 gives an estimated number of fintech starts-ups in the Middle Eastern region. From blockchain technologies to mobile wallets, receiving digital licenses and launching their own debit and credit cards, fintech startups have created a revolution in future banking (Naderi, 2021). Interestingly there are a few examples operating in the MENA region and looking into their business models and focus services in the remittances market will be explained below.

7.3 *Case study of rise: a growth platform to eliminate remittance fees for expatriates (Country: United Arab Emirates; Key Technology: Online Platform/Mobile Application)*

One of the newest fintech startups in the MENA region is Rise that has a mandate to provide financial services to the underbanked population with the lowest

Table 12.4 Estimated Number of Fintechs and Startups in the Middle East Region

Country	*Estimated Fintech Startups*	*Estimated Startups*
Israel	750+	6000+
United Arab Emirates	400+	2300
Saudi Arabia	155	950+
Bahrain	100	200
Lebanon	40	100+
Kuwait	28	200
Jordan	28	500+
Oman	5	150
Qatar	5	250+

Source: Walker (2021).

costs and reducing entry barriers for its customers. Rise aims to democratize banking by building the world's first migrant financial service platform by helping 250 million migrants across international boundaries to seamlessly manage their finances between host and home countries (The Fintech Times, 2021). According to Rise, half of the world's population does not have access to bank credit and more than a billion people without access to a bank account, though there are 35,000 banks worldwide. Since its launch, the platform has grown over 50% month-on-month by value and brought over US$125 million of annualized income into financial services sector. In 2019, Rise also expanded its services by signing several partnership contracts with financial service providers, including insurance with AXA, cross-border unsecured loans in Philippines, the first 'pay-later' product in the GCC in partnership with Carrefour and a credit fund anchored by Astra Amco, (a large global hedge funds and an early-stage Rise investor) (MEVP, 2020). Interestingly, Rise has also moved into the financial literacy space by developing 50 e-learning courses and certification tools that cover topics such as financial literacy, health and safety, and regulations across the GCC.

For Rise challenges include three, control, credit history, and currency risk. With regards to control, the issues is that while migrant workers can send around 80% of their wages to their families in their home country, but once the money leaves the host country, there is no way to track how it is spent. Leading to what is known in the industry as the 'transparency trap'. According to Rise even with third party tracking, apparently 93% of senders also have no control on the spending, and many times it has caused tensions between senders and spenders (Ahmed, 2021). Moreover, there are hefty fees for this transaction due to the slow remittance process.

With the traditional financial service industry unable to serve underserved populations such as migrant workers as they require credit history, fintechs need to step in to create relevant products, which also extend into cross-border financial services. Due to the nature of these international transfers, currency risk is a big challenge especially as many of the developing countries may not have stable exchange rates.

Part of Rise's applications includes Xare, which is a mobile wallet application created especially with migrant workers in mind, where they need to financially support an extended family. To manage their finance smoothly Xare serves as a remittance substitute which allows family and friends anywhere to share access to their account or credit, eliminating the need to move money (The Fintech Times, 2021). UAE-based startup, Rise provides services to more than 300,000 customers in the Gulf region, and it is now actively expanding to markets in Asia, particularly to India and Southeast Asia. This mobile app allows users to divide the amount between several receivers instantly, safely, and securely, while they can also shut off access to the money when they choose. The mobile wallet application does not have grave FX risk as the conversion cost is only charged by the bank when the family spends in the home country (e.g., India), with a host country card (e.g., UAE). Of the cost of transferring money, forex spread charges are around 25% of the cost, while the transfer charges are the other 75%. Rise is currently negotiating with banks in getting preferred rates for its users.

Rise currently operating from the UAE, plans expand its services across the Gulf (starting with Saudi & Bahrain) to bring over 25 million migrant workers in this region under its financial services network. With the large demand, it aims to bring its services to over a million migrants in the next two years, mainly targeting the migrants from Indian, Philippines, Pakistan, and Bangladesh.

7.4 Key technologies being used by rise

7.4.1 Free-to-use mobile application

The new mobile application platform brings expatriate workers and families together to one platform and also eliminating remittance fees, whereby they can share real-time access to the their bank accounts with full transparency, security, and control to the worker. Users can instantly share access to their account and credit card with their families or friends setting daily/monthly monetary limits and expiry dates whilst without sharing any sensitive information and maintaining total control over how their earnings are spent. The main requirement for registration is a valid phone number reducing the whole process to just 30 seconds. A migrant flexibly changes their credit and spending patterns and adjust them based on their monthly budget, and generate micro-shares (Ahmed, 2021).

7.4.2 AI and cloud-based chatbot platform

Rise leverages a proprietary AI powered chatbot platform using the process of Natural Language processing, or NLP, AI technology and accessible interface to engage our customers in a conversational format across a range of financial knowledge, starting from financial literacy, financial planning, and health to opening bank accounts. Since its inception, Rise's chat bot has handled over 2.5 million messages and is currently serving over 20,000 unique users each week (ITP, 2019). The platform is accessible through a mobile application and offers a wide range of services such as providing a bank account with a fast and easy onboarding process, no minimum balance or salary, an accompanying debit card, remittance services, a pay-later product, insurance products, and a credit fund. Rise plans to give their customers a personalized customer service experience 24 × 7 with voice-powered AI.

Other uses of the application

- Rise offers customer loans to the migrant's home countries and the host country (UAE) along with a no minimum balance bank accounts in partnership with United Arab Bank, protecting these remittances with insurance solutions. The app can also set up expense accounts, send money to family members whose account details are hidden, and provide short-term loans through a credit card partnered with United Arab Bank. The program enables users to share credit, without the need for one party to get an expensive short-term loan. Even in many advanced economies, such as in the UK, short-term loans can cost up to 24% per month and are often predatory in nature for borrowers (Ahmed, 2021).

- Xare also provides a fair alternative, allowing individuals to help each other even if they do not have the cash to do so. Xare cards act as top-up cards where beneficiaries can use their card in thousands of stores to purchase products globally.

Xare's security system is highly innovative and secure making the card details always hidden from the beneficiary and not stored by Xare centrally, so that sensitive information cannot be hacked or compromised (Ahmed, 2021). The account holder topping up the card can turn on explicit authorization to make sure that no transactions occur without their approval on the Xare app.

7.5 *Case study of CWallet (Country: Qatar; Key Technology: Blockchain/E-wallet)*

CWallet is the first blockchain technology and multifunctional mobile wallet based in the State of Qatar. As the COVID-19 pandemic accelerated a shift toward a cashless society, CWallet used it as a rare opportunity to leverage their skills and assets, which was an innovation to recovery. The future of payment methods is to become digital and cashless, but the challenge lies in making the whole eco-system adopt the cashless society, which includes the unbanked workers around the world, millions of low-income communities, and expat-oriented regions. The mobile money wallet evolves in three main themes: payroll, payment, and remittance. The blockchain-powered wallet is designed and developed to be a one-step shop allowing users to receive their salaries on time, transfer and pay either online, on delivery, or onsite, allowing individuals to perform various financial transactions either locally or internationally (Agonia, 2021).

About one-fourth of the global population has no access to a bank or mobile money (World Bank, 2021c). CWallet's mission is to digitally empower individuals such as migrant workers, domestic helpers, and blue-collar workers in the region to access financial services that are currently unavailable to them by introducing the payroll and remittance system (The Fintech Times, 2021). Figure 12.9 shows an outline of the digital application for migrant workers. From the bank account, users can send money which will be converted to e-money. Users can pay bills using QR codes, transfer funds to their families using electronic money, and make cash withdrawals from the bank through e-money. The digital wallet application opens a platform for users to receive their payroll and send it directly to their families, enabling unbanked workers to buy scratch cards to put money in their digital wallet which can be later used for online payments.

Partnering with the Qatar Central Bank, the startup has obtained all the necessary licenses to launch its payroll and remittance feature. CWallet is not

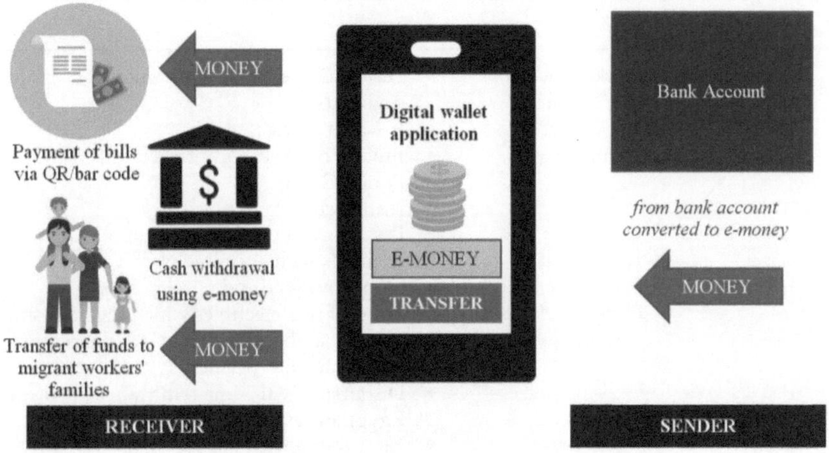

Figure 12.9 Outline of the Digital Wallet app for migrant workers.
Source: Adapted from CWallet (2021).

restricted to only e-wallet services, but also provides e-commerce platforms for merchants where they can use CWallet as a built-in wallet for the app through API (application programming interface) integration to exchange data sources.

7.6 Case study of NOW money (Country: United Arab Emirates; Key Technology: Mobile Banking)

Major remittances funds in the MENA region remain in the GCC countries, i.e., Kuwait, Qatar, UAE, Saudi Arabia, Bahrain, and Oman, which show the total remittance numbers to poor and middle-income would grow by 10% (World Bank, 2021b). With focus on migrant workers, NOW Money is a United Arab Emirates-based startup launched in 2015 to allow migrant workers to remit funds to their home countries. Individuals can also issue cards to use their money, receive their salaries through this account, and track their spending behavior.

NOW Money developed a digital client onboarding solution where they partner with employers of workers who are on a low-income level and provide them with smartphone-based accounts that will fully integrate in their mobile technology, and they can use mobile applications to buy mobile recharge cards, pay utility bills, use their money within the United Arab Emirates, or transfer the money to their home countries with an addition of a small transaction fee (Paracha, 2021). With $7 million in funds led by Anthemis Exponential Ventures raised by the firm in 2021, NOW Money will be further expanding its digital banking to the unbanked population across the MENA region. The digital accounts provided by the firm offers low-cost remittance and are provided with a VISA debit card and the NOW Money mobile application. The startup also plans to offer onboarding services and training sessions for blue collar workers. Bringing everything to the

Table 12.5 Summary Table of the other Startups in MENA Region

Company	*Country*	*Key Technologies*	*Features*
MyCash Online	Malaysia and Middle East	E-marketplace (Electronic marketplace technology)	• Performing express remittance or cross-border payments • E-wallet services • Buying bus and flight tickets • Phone Credit • Insurtech
Fawry	Egypt	E-commerce & E-payments platform created using blockchain technology	• Pay bills and other services in multiple channels such as online platforms, ATMs, mobile wallets, and retail points • Point of sale machines which includes small groceries, pharmacies and stationaries same like credit card payments • Disbursing real- time remittance payments for Egyptians via Fawry outlets
STC Pay	Saudi Arabia	Digital Financial Application with a help of Blockchain technology Mobile Wallet	• Partnership with Western Union which allows families of migrant workers to pick the transferred money from any Western Union location across the world. • First fintech unicorn Startup in Saudi Arabia to receive digital banking license • Evolved from a mobile app to a digital financial application which supports cross-boarder money transfers and other services
Rewire	Israel	Digital Banking App	• Operates on Electronic mOney Institution (EMI) and allows cross-border online banking services • Banking service free for migrants across Europe (monetises international services) • Pay social security insurance through the app.
Leaf Global Fintech	United States of America	Blockchain: Unstructured Supplementary Service Data (USSD) application	• Using blockchain to facilitate digital payments • avoid high transaction costs • risk of carrying physical cash • secure economic identity
Hawiyati	Amman, Jordan	Microfinance crowdfunding platform	• Open-source technology platform providing globally interoperable identify and verifiable credit history which enables financial institutions verify the identity and creditworthiness of clients
Ethis	Malaysia and Dubai	P2P Lending platform	• Islamic Crowdfunding platform; Shariah Compliant P2P lending licence, Developer of proprietary credit scoring system • Crowdfunding: Help low-income earners buy a house • Project financing

Source: Compiled and summarized by authors directly from company websites.

fingertips of the workers starting from no visits, no forms, no long queues to the money transfer center, an average user will be able to save about $1,800 in five years using NOW Money's remittance services (Dwyer, 2021). Table 12.5 shows the summary of other startups in MENA region.

8 Conclusions and policy recommendations

Fintechs provide a significant positive impact on the financial industry by providing opportunities for payment, crowdfunding, lending, capital market, wealth management, and insurance (Zarrouk et al., 2021). This growth has opened up a variety of opportunities for fintech startups that can disrupt the market and empower marginalized communities such as migrant workers, asylum seekers, and refugees by giving them access to basic financial services. Recognizing the disruptive effect of fintechs in the MENA region, there is a growing policy trend to steer the financial sector in the direction of a greater adoption of critically disruptive technologies for migrant workers. More coordination between the different stakeholders in the financial and economic landscapes of both sending and receiving countries would help reduce transaction costs and greatly improve the livelihoods of migrants and their families. These issues range from not just the business model but also access to talent and risk capital, partnerships for innovation, scaling up business activities, and improving the regulatory environment.

The potential for financial technologies in the remittance payment market is of great value, as there is a huge market opportunity; it also has socio-economic benefits for the marginalized and people with the least access to the financial system. Digital remittances have emerged as one of the crucial financial tools for migrant workers, especially amid the uncertainty of the COVID-19 crisis of 2020. Fintech case studies have provided the relevance and positive social impact to tap into remittances services that reduce the cost of transfers, which results in increased savings for migrants and their families. This work showcases the market opportunities available for fintechs to raise funds, while providing much needed solutions for migrant workers, capturing transaction data, and providing knowledge-based platforms for remittances.

Fintech startups have effectively leveraged financial technology and digital identification services such as eKYC and cloud and mobile payments. While transaction sizes are bound to be small and the absence of credit information makes migrants a high-risk category for traditional banking services, fintechs can provide them with banking and payment services to manage their money, make payments, and provide financial inclusion, social integration, and social security. Moreover, these populations also use their savings to make remittance transfers, not relying on credit which is riskier. While studies suggest that even with mobile transfers the average cost of remittances is quite high at around 7% of the transferred amount (World Bank, 2021c), e-remittances and digital identification solutions will also provide migrants with a digital trail, as accounts and transactions can be linked to proof of legal identity by supplemental documentation and also provide more credit information regarding migrant labor that regulators might find useful.

Mapping remittance, fintechs, and regulatory bodies in the MENA region using case studies adds to the literature on fintechs working on technology for good and social sustainability by empowering underserved populations such as migrant workers who are deprived of basic financial services. Financial technologies such as efficient and real-time payments systems, identity authentication (eKYC), blockchain, analytics, P2P, crowdfunding, and artificial intelligence allow startups and regulators to reimagine banking for communities at the bottom of the pyramid. There is huge scope of further work in this area, as fintechs are just starting to tap this market.

References

Accenture (2020) [online] Available at: https://www.accenture.com/_acnmedia/PDF-86/Acccenture-Unchained-Blockchain.pdf [Accessed 7 September 2021]

Agonia A (2021) *Qatar-based FinTech startup Cwallet secures $220,000 pre-seed funding, says founder.* [online] Qatar Tribune. Available at: https://www.qatar-tribune.com/news-details/id/205457/qatar-based-fintech-startup-cwallet-secures-220-000-pre-seed-funding-says-founder [Accessed 24 August 2021]

Ahmed A (2021) Rising to the Occasion: Dubai-Headquartered Startup Rise is Shaking up the Financial Services Sector. Available at: https://www.entrepreneur.com/article/365794 [Accessed 7 September 2021]

Attia H and Benson CC (2018) *Digital Financial Services: Payment Aspects for Financial Inclusion in the Arab Region.* Arab Monetary Fund

Baldwin-Edwards M (2005) Migration in the Middle East and Mediterranean: A Regional Study Prepared for the Global Commission on International Migration. Athens: Mediterranean Migration Observatory, Panteion University [Accessed 30 August 2021]

Bhattarai G, Subedi B (2021) Impact of COVID-19 on FDIs, Remittances and Foreign Aids: A Case Study of Nepal. *Millenn Asia* 12(2):145–161. doi:10.1177/0976399620974202

Borah R (2020) Cloud Computing Architecture: What Is Front End and Back End? [Online] *Clariontech.com.* Available at: https://www.clariontech.com/blog/cloud-computing-architecture-what-is-front-end-and-back-end [Accessed 12 August 2021]

Chancel E (2022) World Equality Report. Available at: https://wir2022.wid.world/www-site/uploads/2022/01/Summary_WorldInequalityReport2022_English.pdf [Accessed 12 February 2022]

Chuc AT, Li W, Phi NT, Le QT, Yoshino N (2022) The Necessity of Financial Inclusion for Enhancing of Economic Impacts of Remittances. *Borsa Istanbul Rev* 22(1):47–56

CWallet (2022) Available at: https://cwallet.qa/ [Accessed 12 February 2022]

Demirgüç-Kunt A, Singer D (2017) Financial Inclusion and Inclusive Growth: A Review of Recent Empirical Evidence. World Bank Policy Research Working Paper, (8040)

Devanesan J (2021) Fintech Helps Migrants in the Middle East and Africa Pay Their Dues. [Online] Tech Wire Asia. Available at: https://techwireasia.com/2021/02/fintech-helps-migrants-in-the-middle-east-and-africa-pay-their-dues/ [Accessed 8 August 2021]

Dwyer S (2021) Migrant Workers in the UAE get a Digital Banking Solution. Available at: https://www.accion.org/migrant-workers-in-the-uae-get-a-digital-banking-solution [Accessed June 6, 2021]

Feyen E, Frost J, Gambacorta L, Natarajan H, Saal M (2021) Fintech and the Digital Transformation of Financial Services: Implications for Market Structure and Public Policy. BIS Papers

Financial Inclusion in the Middle East and North Africa: Analysis and Roadmap Recommendations (English). Policy Research Working Paper; No. WPS 5610 Washington, D.C. World Bank Group

Gozman D, Liebenau J, Mangan J (2018) The Innovation Mechanisms of Fintech Start-Ups: Insights from SWIFT's Innotribe Competition. *J Manag Inf Syst* 35(1):145–179

Grayscale.co (2019) An introduction to XRP. *Grayscale Building Blocks* November 2019

Hahm H, Subhanij T, Almeida R (2021) Finteching Remittances in Paradise: A Path to Sustainable Development. *Asia & the Pacific Policy Studies* 8(3):435–453

Huang R, Kale S, Paramati SR, Taghizadeh-Hesary F (2021) The Nexus between Financial Inclusion and Economic Development: Comparison of Old and New EU Member Countries. *Econ Anal Policy* 69:1–15

ILO (2020) Labour Migration (Arab States) [online] Available at: https://www.ilo.org/beirut/areasofwork/labour-migration/lang--en/index.htm [Accessed 1 April 2022]

IOM (2018) IOM and Biometrics. Available at: https://cb4ibm.iom.int/ibm/pdf/14.pdf [Accessed August 6, 2021]

IOM (2020) Migration Data Portal. Total Number of International Migrants at Mid-Year 2020. Available at: https://www.migrationdataportal.org/international-data?i=stock_abs_&t=2020 [Accessed 17 August 2021]

ITP (2019) [online] Available at: https://www.itp.net/commsmea/18763-how-tech-and-ai-can-help-the-uaes-underbanked-according-to-rise-co-founder-padmini-gupta [Accessed 30 April 2022]

Kluge, J, Mahoney, C (2016) Building Successful Collective Impact Models. Presented at Ashoka-U Exchange, New Orleans, LA, February 24–25, 2016

Koslowski R (2019) International Travel Security and the Global Compacts on Refugees and Migration. *Int Migr* 57(6):158–172

Le TH, Chuc AT, Taghizadeh-Hesary F (2019) Financial Inclusion and Its Impact on Financial Efficiency and Sustainability: Empirical Evidence from Asia. *Borsa Istanbul Rev* 19(4):310–322

Lee I, Shin YJ (2018) Fintech: Ecosystem, Business Models, Investment Decisions, and Challenges. *Bus Horiz* 61(1):35–46. doi:10.1016/j.bushor.2017.09.003

MEVP (2020) Rise, GCC's Leading FinTech Platform for Modest-income Migrants Raises Seven-Figure Investment Led by MEVP, MAGNiTT. [online] Available at: https://magnitt.com/news/rise-gcc-s-leading-fintech-platform-for-modest-income-migrants-raises-seven-figure-investment-led-by-mevp-51662 [Accessed 1 April 2022]

Milken Institute (2019) The Rise of FinTech in the Middle East: An Analysis of the Emergence of Bahrain and the United Arab Emirates. Milken Institute. https://milkeninstitute.org/sites/default/files/reports-pdf/FinTech%20in%20the%20Middle%20East-FINAL-121119_0.pdf

Minnock O (2020) Saudi Arabia Aims for 70% Cashless Payments in Vision 2030 Following Introduction of Apple Pay. [online] *FinTech Magazine*. Available at: https://fintechmagazine.com/digital-payments/saudi-arabia-aims-70-cashless-payments-vision-2030-following-introduction-apple-pay [Accessed 1 April 2022]

Murthy G, Fernandez-Vidal M, Barreto R (2019) Fintechs and Financial Inclusion. [online] Cgap.org. Available at: https://www.cgap.org/sites/default/files/publications/2019_05_Focus_Note_Fintech_and_Financial_Inclusion_1_0.pdf [Accessed 23 August 2021]

Naderi N (2021) Utilizing Blockchain Technology in International Remittances for Poverty Reduction and Inclusive Growth. In: Taghizadeh-Hesary F, Panthamit N, Yoshino N (eds) *Poverty Reduction for Inclusive Sustainable Growth in Developing Asia. Economics, Law, and Institutions in Asia Pacific.* Springer, Singapore. doi:10.1007/978–981-16–1107-0_7

NST Business (2021). [online] Available at: https://www.nst.com.my/business/2021/04/678645/parlo-posts-wider-net-loss-q4-banks-workforce-related-services [Accessed 17 August 2021]

OECD (2019) Financial Literacy Needs of Migrants and their Families in the Commonwealth of Independent States, Paris. Available at: www.oecd.org/daf/fin/financial-education/financial-education.htm

Papadaki M, Karamitsos I (2021) Blockchain Technology in the Middle East and North Africa Region. *Inf Technol J* 27(3):617 634

Paracha Z (2021) *Dubai's Now Money Raises $7 Million to Expand Its Digital Banking Solution for Unbanked Workers Across GCC.* [online] MENAbytes. Available at: https://www.menabytes.com/now-money-7-million/ [Accessed 24 August 2022]

Pearce D (2011) Financial Inclusion in the Middle East and North Africa: Analysis and Roadmap Recommendations. The World Bank

Pew Research Center (2016) Middle East's Migrant Population More Than Doubles Since 2005. [online] Available at: https://www.pewresearch.org/global/2016/10/18/middle-easts-migrant-population-more-than-doubles-since-2005/ [Accessed 5 August 2021]

Ponti J (2021) Tech Empowers Indonesian Migrant Workers. [online] *OpenGov Asia.* Available at: https://opengovasia.com/tech-empowers-indonesian-migrant-workers/ [Accessed 9 August 2021]

Reinke J (2007) Remittances in the Balance of Payments Framework: Current Problems and Forthcoming Improvements. In *Presentation to Seminar on Remittance Statistics at the Center of Excellence in Finance, Ljubljana, Slovenia. imf.* org/external/np/sta/bop/pdf/rem. pdf

Ripple (2018) XRP, The Digital Asset of Payments. Available at: https://ripple.com/xrp/ [Accessed June 6, 2021]

Schilirò D (2013) Diversification and Development of the United Arab Emirates Economy. *J Appl Econ Sci* 13(2):228–239

Schilirò D (2021) Fintech in Dubai: Development and Ecosystem. [online] Academia.edu. Available at: https://www.academia.edu/59140866/Fintech_in_Dubai_Development_and_Ecosystem [Accessed 1 March 2022]

Schroeder D (2017) Iran in 2025: An Optimist's View. [online] *Afsa.org.* Available at: https://afsa.org/iran-2025-optimists-view [Accessed 1 April 2022]

Serrao MV, Sequeira AH, Varambally KVM (2013) Conceptual Framework to Investigate the Accessibility and Impact of Financial Inclusion. *Indian J Res* 2(9):47–49

Shankar A (2020) Parlo Bhd. [online] The Edge Markets. Available at: https://www.theedgemarkets.com/article/parlo-plans-rm258m-private-placement-fund-migrant-worker-biz-debt-repayment [Accessed 5 September 2021]

Soufaih A (2020) Revolutionizing International Remittance Payments Using Cryptocurrency and Blockchain-based Technology. https://repository.upenn.edu/cgi/viewcontent.cgi?article=1085&context=sire [Accessed 5 September 2021]

Tajudin M, Omar R, Smedlund A, Aziz RP (2020) Financing with Heart and Intelligence: Augmenting Intimacy and Sustainability through Islamic Fintech. *Int J Adv Sci Eng Inf Technol* 29(9):1638–1664

The Edge Markets (2020) From Tourism to Foreign Workforce Digitalisation. Available at: https://www.theedgemarkets.com/content/advertise/from-tourism-foreign-workforce-digitalisation [Accessed 24 August 2021]

The Fintech Times (2021) Fintech: Middle East & Africa 2021. The Fintech Landscape, Key Spotlight Markets and Future Trends Report. Available at: http://www.fintr.org/wp-content/uploads/2021/04/The-Fintech-Times_Fintech-Middle-East-Africa-2021-Report-2.pdf [Accessed June 6, 2021]

Varzaru AA, Bocean CG, Cazacu M (2021) Rethinking Tourism Industry in Pandemic COVID-19 Period. *Sustain* 13:6956. doi:10.3390/su13126956

Velasco K (2021) Fintech, Remittances and Migrants' Prosperity. [online] Discovery.ucl.ac.uk. Available at: https://discovery.ucl.ac.uk/id/eprint/10128014/7/Velasco_Fintech%20and%20remittances.pdf [Accessed 25 June 2021]

Ventura L (2021) Global Finance Magazine: World's Most Unbanked Countries 2021. [online] *Global Finance Magazine*. Available at: https://www.gfmag.com/global-data/economic-data/worlds-most-unbanked-countries [Accessed 3 July 2021]

Vickers E, Alexander C (2019) Why Migration Is Bigger and More Contentious Than Ever. *Bloomberg.com*. Available at: https://www.bloomberg.com/graphics/2019-how-migration-is-changing-our-world/ [Accessed September 7, 2021]

Walker M (2021) Country Reports | The Fintech Times. Retrieved 24 August 2022, from https://thefintechtimes.com/country-reports/

World Bank (2018) "Financial Inclusion" [online] Available at: https://www.worldbank.org/en/topic/financialinclusion/overview#1 [Accessed 10 February 2022]

World Bank (2020) International Migrant Stock (% of population) Available at: https://databank.worldbank.org/source/jobs/Series/SM.POP.TOTL.ZS. [Accessed 1 August 2021]

World Bank (2021a) Migrant Workers: Pandemic Realities for Asia-Pacific's 48 Million International Migrants. Available at: https://www.ilo.org/asia/media-centre/news/WCMS_793027/lang--en/index.htm [Accessed September 1, 2021]

World Bank (2021b) Remittance Prices Worldwide. Available at: https://remittanceprices.worldbank.org/en/about-remittance-prices-worldwide [Accessed September 1, 2021]

World Bank (2021c) An Analysis of Trends in Cost of Remittance Services; Remittance Prices Worldwide Quarterly. Issue 38. Available at: https://remittanceprices.worldbank.org/sites/default/files/rpw_main_report_and_annex_q221.pdf

Yayboke E (2020) Can I Stay or Can I Go Now? Longer-Term Impacts of COVID-19 on Global Migration. https://www.csis.org/analysis/can-i-stay-or-can-i-go-now-longer-term-impacts-covid-19-global-migration [Accessed September 1, 2021].

Zarrouk H, ElGhak T, Bakhouche A (2021) Exploring Economic and Technological Determinants of FinTech Startups' Success and Growth in the United Arab Emirates. *J Open Innov Technol Mark Complex* 7:50. doi:10.3390/ joitmc7010050

13 The impact of COVID-19 pandemic on innovative Fintech in India

M. Subramanian

1 Introduction

Fintech is an integrated term based on finance and technology that describes the 21st-century financial services sector. Earlier the term was used to describe the backbone of financial institutions; now, it is described as "any institution that fulfills the important role of channeling funds from those with surplus funds to others with shortages of funds," as compared to traditional institutions that do not use high-tech to accomplish this task (Cornett et al., 2015). To meet the financial needs of any institution, traditional ones are usually built without the use of financial technology.

According to Cornett et al. (2015), financial institutions allow financial services to move from money suppliers to fund demanders, comprising commercial banks, thrifts, insurance companies, securities firms, investment banks, finance businesses, mutual funds, and pension funds. Kashyap (2016) demonstrated that "financial institutions are at the nascent stage of digital disruption," which has a beneficial influence on early adopters of fintech services to meet customer needs and a negative impact on traditional institutions that have not attempted to implement fintech (Chishti and Barberis, 2016).

Currently, fintech includes anything technologically innovative in the financial industry. It has almost completely explained every aspect of financial matters. It has changed and disrupted the banking system, insurance firms, non-bank financial institutions, payment banks, stock exchanges, and investment advisory firms. Fintech companies use specialized software and algorithms to help businesses and consumers manage their financial and investment operations efficiently.

Innovative fintech began to grow after 1990, following the liberalization of banks in India. Gradually, pressure was applied on technologies such as magnetic ink character recognition (MICR), electronic transfers, and other e-payments. The adoption of technology, however, was slow, allowing innovative fintech startups to fill a gap. During the 2005–2013 period, many initiatives such as Oxigen, Mobikwik, Paytm, and Freecharge have come in to help move the economy into electronic payments. However, fintech's expertise was held in place due to regulatory uncertainties and savings strategies on the part of existing financial institutions and governments.

DOI: 10.4324/9781003220220-17

India's innovative fintech revolution began around 2015 with the development of startups in the public and private sectors and the availability of government policies and regulatory frameworks. However, India was still in the process of adapting to commercial technology through the economic ecosystem. Over the past five years, India has built a strong infrastructure to incubate and grow innovative fintech. Many banks have introduced mobile applications to facilitate digital transactions. Banks also work closely with fintech in areas such as insurance, Robo-advisory, other loans, customer experience solutions, and collaborative solutions. Digital financial services allow financial systems to perform their key functions of providing access to assets and risk management. They also help reduce transaction costs and deliver services to a place and time where they are most needed.

The fintech sector in India can be classified into four main categories, namely Wealthtech, Insuretech, Lending, and Payment. New technologies and business models are developed by emerging startups in the Wealthtech industry. Actions that propel a business forward include the increased acceptance of mobile platforms and the elimination of information asymmetry between small and major financial institutions and investors. The Indian fintech space has always been similar to digital payments.

The Reserve Bank of India (RBI) has granted fintechs licenses to establish payment banks that provide investment, remittance, and savings services. These payment banks are expected to use the benefits from their lower operating costs to reach more customers with better services. Such companies are also capable of managing risks and making good use of their assets. Maintaining the robustness and durability of such models requires updating data and technical capabilities to extract detailed information. The advent of technologies such as smartphones and the availability of skilled workers represent two of the challenges facing the sector.

Banks no longer view innovative fintech startups as disruptive entities. Innovative fintechs have been shown to act as banking and financial assistants. In investing in fintech firms and startups and collaborating with them on a variety of operational projects, banks use a variety of tactics to adopt innovative technologies. Banks and non-banks are collaborating to provide the Indian customer with a blend of trust and innovation (Das, 2020). They have expanded into new areas, including insurance, asset management, stock trading, and other businesses that use financial technology to boost sales and profits.

The impressive performance of the Indian fintech sector can be attributed to events including (i) powerful support from the government and promotion of fintech policies; (ii) Aadhar Database, digital infrastructure, and the India Stack initiative; (iii) residential regulators such as the Security and Exchange Board of India, the Insurance Regulatory and Development Authority, and the Reserve Bank of India that allow fintech to grow without adverse conditions; (iv) millennials switching to digital banking solutions leading to the growth of fintech; (v) the unscrupulous banking industry losing its share of the private sector and fintechs appearing to have seized the opportunity to provide better services.

Innovative fintech in India is no longer a futuristic technology. Fintech solutions are cost-effective, adaptable, and secure, and they have the ability to address important banking concerns such as boosting access to financial services, enhancing customer experience, avoiding fraud, and increasing improper lending without displacing physical banks. The two will be able to learn from each other as a result of their partnership, which will eventually lead to improved customer service. Innovative fintech firms have the potential to succeed in India because of its human resources; the country's young people are increasingly using new technologies, and a large number of banks will require out-of-the-box solutions to help people access financial services and benefit from digital integration programs. India's creative fintech story is meant to inspire others and transform the banking industry in ways that can reshape a sick industry into a strong one with competitive advantages (Gurung, 2018).

The fintech industry has thus supplied the country with much-needed infrastructure, government, and regulatory backing, allowing this sector to thrive in quite a short period of time. The fintech sector is predicted to grow as more projects arise to suit the demands of individuals who are increasingly pursuing digital integration as a result of low online prices that enable faster and broader access to online services.

The future of innovative fintech in India is bright. With developments taking place in key innovative fintech areas, it is predicted that India will make full use of this technology. In the future, innovative fintech is likely to incorporate many new technologies such as artificial intelligence (AI), blockchain, cloud computing, data analytics, and the Internet of things (IoT), and Python will enable firms to offer new solutions to consumers and investors. It is important to have an in-depth understanding of concepts such as trading algorithms, Robo-advisory, peer-to-peer lending, and Insuretech, which aim to bring efficiency and investment into processes, delivery, and access to the financial services sector. However, threats exist, such as cyber-attacks, which can be overcome with robust and effective security measures.

India has become one of the world's most rapidly growing economies. However, according to a survey by the Global Financial Literacy Excellence Center (GFLS, 2015), only 24% of Indian adults are financially literate. Compared to other major emerging economies, India has a very low level of financial literacy due to inequality between states and the lack of formal training and awareness. Nonetheless, there is still scope for further development.

Financial inclusion is crucial for India's economic progress. A huge portion of India's population is still unable to access official banking services. After the PRC, India is the world's second-largest country in terms of financial exclusion, with an estimated 190 million people without a bank account, according to the World Bank's Global Findex Data (GF, 2014). Half of those who have bank accounts are also inactive, meaning that most of their everyday transactions are still done in cash. Traditional banking and financial models leave gaps in financial inclusion, which can be bridged with the application of novel financial technology. Financial inclusion necessitates the development of alternative solutions such as fintech.

Furthermore, Indian innovative fintech is currently facing one of the biggest challenges to date, namely the Corona Virus Disease (COVID-19). Under the current COVID situation, however, fintech has made a significant contribution toward security and protection; as people are advised to avoid leaving their homes and preserve social distance protocols during the pandemic, they are using online payments and other digital-based financial services like e-wallets, credit/debit cards, and unified payments interface (UPI). Given these benefits, it is no surprise that innovative fintech holds the key to making financial inclusion safer and more secure in the post-COVIID-19 world.

Robust financial services will become the way for many people and enterprises in this new normal scenario, and companies that offer digital financial services will be better positioned to benefit from this circumstance. Fintech, like any other business, must be ready to meet this expanding demand and extend its corporate information technology infrastructure as it adapts to the new climate. COVID-19, like any other crisis, is compelling many firms to act. The pandemic also demonstrates the frailty of commercial IT infrastructures, as it arises under the weight of rising demand and dwindling IT service desk capacity.

This chapter seeks to explore the influence of COVID-19 on innovative fintech in India. The study focuses on the growth and development of innovative fintech, which includes three phases, namely pre-COVID-19, during COVID-19, and post-CovID-19. The research methodology adopted is primarily descriptive and includes a comprehensive literature review. This paper highlights some of the key areas from recent research trends and draws on the author's professional expertise in the field. Research recommendations regarding innovative fintech's future prospects provide policymakers, economists, researchers, and financial experts with better insights and a deeper understanding of the innovative fintech industry in India.

2 Literature review

Arora (2020) stated that the COVID-19 pandemic provides a unique opportunity for policymakers and other stakeholders to work toward achieving the dream of creating a real digital economy that closes the digital divide between urban and rural areas. Financial inclusion will be the most powerful pillar behind the agent network. Financial services can be delivered in a more orderly and systematic manner.

The impact of the COVID-19 pandemic on digital banking and fintech adoption was explored by Fu and Mishra (2022). Based on mobile app data from a globally representative sample, the spread of the COVID-19 pandemic and the lockdowns enforced by governments led to a large increase in the rate of finance app downloads. The elements that may have influenced this effect on the demand side and gained a better understanding of the winners from the supply side digital acceleration were also examined. According to the study findings, traditional incumbents grew their digital products the fastest in the beginning, but Bigtech businesses and newer fintech providers eventually outpaced them over time. The study also looked at the uptake of fintech apps for both personal and business use.

According to Vasenska et al. (2021), the concerns surrounding financial transactions with fintech are becoming increasingly obvious in the light of contemporary crises after the COVID-19 pandemic and expanding global economic uncertainties. As a result, utilizing fintech financial transactions leads to a risk-reduction strategy when interacting with others. Furthermore, fintech financial transactions can help customers save money. Therefore, fintech applications may be viewed as more competitive than traditional banking systems during times of crisis.

COVID-19 has a profound effect on our lives as a whole. The priority remains to protect employees, customers, and the wider community. In a way, fintech is better organized, with technology at its core and the robustness, flexibility, and remote performance that are already embedded in its DNA. At the same time, cash, financial security, and quick access to government programs will no doubt be high in mind. We believe that fintech and SME leaders should consider three key factors: respond, recover, and thrive (Deloitte, 2020).

The COVID-19 pandemic has engulfed the entire financial industry, and raising funding in the current market has been proven difficult. Fintech companies at the forefront can see a few rounds, as investors choose to double up on big, more mature winners. The year 2020 saw major transactions, with intermediate cycles increasing the share by 8% as space matured (CB Insights, 2020).

According to Horgan et al. (2020), countering the COVID-19 storm, the flashing lights gives powerful captions for data and digital technologies to protect and promote health and well-being as well as inspire hope for the future. Telemedicine has provided a new dimension in care, forcing governments and international organizations to acknowledge the significance of data in tracking and tracing outbreaks of infection.

Arunachalam and Crentsil (2020) concluded that fintech will disrupt and transform traditional banking and financial transactions in an unprecedented way. According to them, what we are seeing now is only the beginning, and much needs to be done if fintech will turn the game and move toward achieving 100% sustainable financial inclusion by 2030, in line with the United Nations Sustainable Development Goals (UNSDG # 1.3). We need fintech, now more than ever before in the era of COVID-19, but we also need an environment-friendly ecosystem with supporting infrastructure as well as allowed latitude.

The foundation of Indian fintech was laid over a decade ago in building critical resources. The current state of the Indian fintech industry is the result of a complex mix of technology providers, legal actions, business opportunities, and other specific aspects of the country. RBI has urged fintech companies to overcome digital divisions and promote active customer engagement across urban and rural areas as well as the various manufacturing and consumer sectors. As a payment system regulator, the RBI has taken a number of actions to increase productivity, continue access to safe, efficient, and affordable payment systems, and assist those who are still involved in payment systems. In this connection, RBI's Vision 2021 takes into account four scoring positions (4Cs): convenience, cost, confidence, and competitiveness (RBI Bulletin, 2020).

According to Suryono, Budi, and Purvandari (2020), the development of digital transformation is reflected in the emergence of fintech systems, one of the most significant financial developments. These initiatives are quickly expanding, owing to factors such as the sharing economy, legislation, and information technology. Fintech research, however, is still restricted. Fintechs provide a variety of services, including financial services, payment through electronic wallets, e-commerce, e-insurance, e-aggregators, as well as for cryptocurrencies like Bitcoin, providing an opportunity to delve deeper into the fintech research problems and trends.

Burragoni (2020) concludes that the current situation is more beneficial, as India has the advantage of human capital, technological advancement, and better access to the Internet and mobile technology. The most important demographic of the population is 850 million subscribers which is 4 times the number of people using the Internet (about 205 million). According to Vatsa (2020), the expected increase in the coming years is accentuated by the fact that 71% of consumers rely on digital social media for their purchasing decisions, while 78% of people are influenced by corporate social media posts about purchasing decisions. While making a purchasing decision, 93% of digital online users consider visual content as one of the most important factors.

Khan et al. (2020) indicated that trust was a strong determinant of the business community to adopt and use fintech in financial services in GCC countries during the pandemic. As a result, many entrepreneurs fear the safety and security of fintech financial services, which can be adjusted. Only then can they accept and expand their use of fintech financial services. In addition, the study showed that the simple use of visual energy had a weak influence on the intention of believing and using fintech financial services.

According to Olatunji (2020), fintech has made democratic and revolutionary changes in the financial services industry. Ordinary banks are just a handful of stakeholders in the financial and technology sector, as startups and new entrants are on the rise. Information technology (IT), e-commerce firms, crowdfunding, instant payments, online lending websites, and other programs have disrupted the financial services market. Fintech creates new financial, technical, and legal realities, severely disrupting existing regulatory frameworks and legal systems.

Makina (2019) pointed out that fintech is truly changing the nature of financial services. One of its key implications is the blurring of the boundaries between financial institutions, markets, and innovative non-financial service providers. In addition to improving the quality and range of financial services, fintech accelerates the investment agenda. While official financial institutions find rural areas less profitable in expanding branch networks, fintech services such as mobile phones and e-wallets provide affordable financial services in many remote parts of the country.

Ozili (2020) suggested a range of policy options to boost financial inclusion during the COVID-19 pandemic that includes (i) prioritizing digital payment services, (ii) building confidence in fintech, (iii) constructive regulation, (iv) continuous money distribution, (v) to do everything possible to get money to people as fast as possible, and (vi) to ensure that people always have enough money in times of crisis. It is now important for governments, financial institutions, and fintech firms to make the best decisions to help vulnerable people and families as soon as possible. The government's commitment to promoting financial inclusion at all costs would be put to the test during these probationary periods.

The Indian fintech sector was expected to grow to roughly US$2.4 billion by 2020, according to the National Association of Software and Service Companies (NASSCOM). The mainstream Indian economy has embraced the fintech possibility, owing to growth in e-commerce and high mobile phone usage. The transaction value of the fintech sector in India was predicted to be around US$33 billion in 2016, with a five-year CAGR of 22% expected to reach US$73 billion by 2020. In addition, the Indian government supports and encourages the fintech industry as well as the development of new fintech concepts and technologies (Vijay, 2019).

According to Krishna Priya and Anusha (2019), the Indian fintech market is growing with an estimated population of US$1.3 billion. India's vast population of unbanked and underbanked people make it a center of financial technology around the world. Fintech is regarded as a game-changer, with many creative technologies that can disrupt the conventional financial markets. Fintech has grown rapidly in India over the last five years and is expected to continue to grow steadily in the near future.

Parameshwar et al. (2019) asserted that traditional financial institutions have significant implications for savings and the number of financial accounts due to fintech activities, services such as mobile phone accounts, utility billing, mobile and Internet use to access a financial institution account, and digital payments. In line with this, supporters of fintech companies such as venture capitalists and private equity have positive advantages, while mergers and acquisitions have a negative influence on the GDP of Asian countries.

The fact that India's banking population has dropped from 577 million to 233 million, according to Sanmath (2018), speaks eloquently about the progress of financial inclusion efforts. Today, technology is a significant and quantifiable provider. Baiju and Radhakumari (2017) mentioned that the concepts of fintech firms and digital payments have become pillars of the economy. Their study highlights the review of existing literature to help identify research areas to assess the effectiveness and contribution of fintech to economic growth. Despite its rapid expansion over the last decade, fintech has yet to establish itself in India as a major financial services provider, according to Gurung (2018). As a result, combining fintech with traditional financial institutions and banks could provide support assistance to the Indian financial industry in taking it to a new course.

The analysis of Varga (2017) provides a complete overview of the core value concept behind fintechs, including the use of resource-based ideas, business models, human-centered design, and open-ended design. This document introduces how fintechs can function as a new strategic provider in the emerging financial sector and solve the issues of people at the bottom of the pyramid, which positively influences the triple bottom line. Sleeves (2016) stated that the global consortium brings fintech to the market, and consumers are closer to supporting new businesses and reducing reliance on the government for the continuation of any country including the so-called fintech services.

Muthukannan et al. (2020) explained that fintech ecosystems (FE) are characterized by a network of diverse, consistent, flexible, and complex agents that work together to provide a wide range of financial products and services so as to retain customers. With the growth in the number of compatible technologies, the complexity of fintech ecosystems is growing exponentially as new players emerge and new connections are built. According to Jose (2020), fintech presents prospects, notably in terms of financial stability and financial integration. Above all, financial technology innovation has the potential to level the playing field for all participants and empower unallocated and unconstrained populations.

Fintech also has the ability to fundamentally transform financial systems, provide customers with a wide selection of financial products at competitive prices, while also helping financial institutions operate more efficiently, according to Dhal (2020). In addition, Dhal argues that fintech's rapid and flexible transformation should be monitored and evaluated so that regulators and the public can keep up with changing technological and business trends.

Nicoletti (2017) indicated that fintech start-ups compete with established financial institutions by providing customer-centric services that provide faster speed and flexibility, and they are spreading like wildfire all across the world. Big data, blockchain, Robo-advisors, and the Internet of Everything (IOE) are all examples of fintech companies engaged in a process of "intermediation through innovation."

According to Oshodin et al. (2017), fintech is building a new ecosystem with incumbents, start-ups, and tech businesses forming partnerships, alliances, and investments. Future financial institutions will have to operate in a fundamentally different way than today's structures if they want to gain a competitive advantage by meeting the expectations of clients who are highly volatile as the world changes. These institutions must provide better performance and a better customer experience at a lesser cost (Margaris, 2016).

According to Anikina et al. (2016), under today's economic conditions, innovative activities take on greater importance and ensure that specific regions and the country as a whole become more competitive. A high degree of innovative activity allows for the creation of conditions for long-term economic growth and the most efficient utilization of present resources. The administration of the innovation sphere at the regional level plays a unique role at this stage of development.

To stay competitive, several financial institutions around the world are upgrading their technology. Koffi (2016) recently examined the disruptions of traditional financial institutions as well as the remedies they could provide in conjunction with the IT industry. The study thoroughly examined the process of redefining financial services such as remittance, asset management, and payments using an IT-based platform. In terms of raising client expectations and expanding business potential, electronic, digital, and fintech services have advanced.

Fintech landscape identified the following nine technologies that, individually or collectively, facilitate fintech's current and future innovations: (i) process and external operations, (ii) cloud technology, (iii) robotic process automation (RPA), (iv) digital transformation, (v) blockchain, (vi) advanced analytics, (vii) artificial intelligence (AI), (viii) smart contracts, and (ix) the Internet of Things. Fintech has already made a significant impact, and fintech entrepreneurs are disrupting the financial services industry in a variety of ways (Ernst and Young, 2016). Fintech has evolved dramatically, according to Desai (2015), from supplementary resources utilized by financial institutions to the complete portfolio industry, Robo-advisors, mobile planning as well as payment programs, crowdfunding, and online lending platforms.

The study of Muganyi et al. (2022) shows that fintech supports the development of the financial sector by improving access (credit), debt (deposit), and savings within financial institutions. Research also shows that the emergence of fintech in the area of financial management (management technology: Regtech) can significantly improve the results of financial development. Therefore, it is important for regulators to follow policies that measure growth in the fintech industry while minimizing related risks.

Based on the above review of literature, it is evident that innovative fintech disrupts and transforms India's traditional banking and financial systems in unprecedented ways. Furthermore, COVID-19 provides a unique opportunity for policymakers and other stakeholders to collaborate on realizing the dream of a real digital economy.

3 Pre-COVID-19 phase

India saw extraordinary growth in the innovative fintech adoption rate, investments, and startups during the period from 2015 to 2020. These five years were characterized by the fintech industry's slow and steady growth, reaching a stunning level when compared to the majority of fintechs around the world. The following are some of the distinguishing characteristic features of the Indian fintech industry during the pre-COVID-19 phase.

India has become a leading country in the world in fintech adoption. The fintech industry has met many of the digital needs that people face on a daily basis, resulting in an increase in fintech services. India has risen to the top of the list of the world's fastest-growing fintech markets. Along with China, India had the highest adoption rate of fintech (around 87%) among all emerging markets in the world at the start of the COVID-19 pandemic. The global adoption rate, however, was around 64% (PWC-FICCI, 2020).

According to Ernst and Young's (EY) Fintech Adoption Index 2017, India has the second highest fintech adoption rate (52%) among 20 global countries. This is true in all five service categories, with digitally active Indian consumers adopting services at rates that are 50% to 100% greater than global averages (EY Fintech Adoption Index). The Fintech Adoption Index for India is depicted in Figure 13.1.

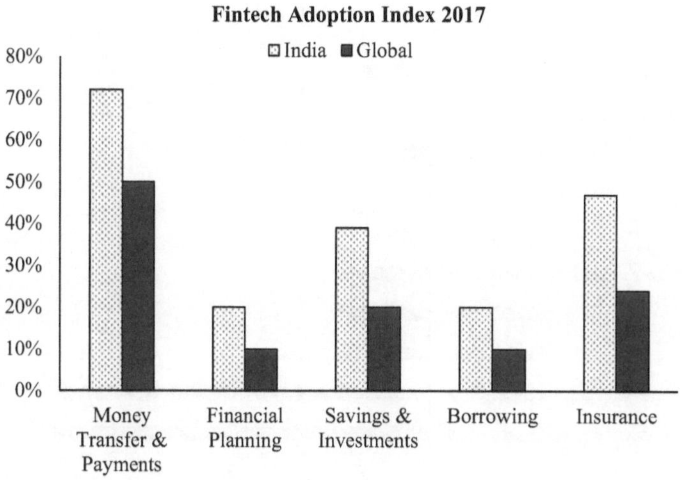

Figure 13.1 Fintech Adoption Index.
Source: Author Compilation; Data: Ernst and Young Fintech Adoption Index India (2017).

According to the EY Global Fintech Adoption Index 2019, India exceeded fintech's global adoption rate after various initiatives were undertaken by the government to promote financial transactions through technology. The global rate rose to 64% in 2019, while emerging markets like China and India were leading by 87%. Countries such as Russia and South Africa accounted for 82%, while developed markets such as the Netherlands accounted for 73%.

The increase in fintech penetration and adoption in all sectors during this phase has had a positive influence on the Indian economy. The growth of online digital transactions has enabled transparent, secure, fast, and cost-effective methods that are benefitting businesses, consumers, and the government alike.

In India, fintech has played a crucial role in the evolution of the financial sector. Fintech has quietly but steadily implemented big changes in traditional financial institutions, from providing online recharge services to providing basic savings bank deposit accounts with online payment banks. In 2016, India's fintech sector attracted a massive US$270 million in funding, demonstrating investor confidence in this promising area. With a return on investment in fintech ventures of 29%, India has outperformed the global average of 20%. In 2016, the fintech sector's transaction value was anticipated to be US$33 billion and, with a five-year annual growth rate of 22%, was expected to reach US$73 billion. Since then, the number has increased (Gurung, 2018).

India is emerging into a powerful ecosystem that offers fintech a start-up platform with the potential to become a billion-dollar unicorn. From taking on new parts to exploring foreign markets, the start of fintech in India is gearing up for further aspirations. The sector-wise fintech investments in India are shown in Figure 13.2.

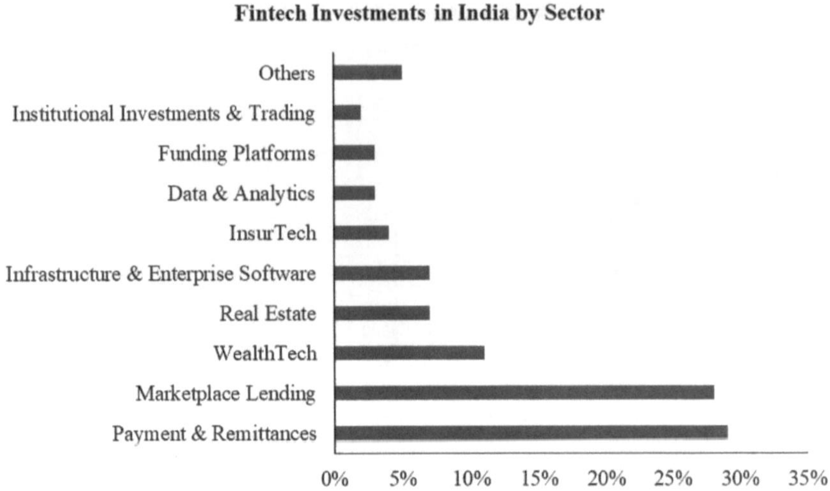

Figure 13.2 Fintech Investments in India.
Source: Author Compilation; Data: Fintech Global, Fintech Investments in India by Sector, 2017.

Fintech's steady growth was reflected in investors' perceptions. Prior to the COVID-19 pandemic, the Indian fintech ecosystem saw a positive trend in fintech's financial investments activity, with the US$ 2.6 billion invested in fintechs in 2019. Despite declining investment trends in fintech worldwide, the Indian fintech environmental initiative has experienced an upsurge in investments, garnering US$ 2.6 billion in funding during the start of 2019 (PWC and FICCI, 2020). The top 100 fintech firms in the world by business models during the years 2018 and 2019 are shown in Figure 13.3.

Fintechs have diversified into different areas. Traditional lending and payment firms have been replaced by insurance, wealth, brokerage, and multi-sectoral companies in the top 100 fintechs. India has seen the rapid growth of fintech companies over the past five years, as its market size was expected to grow from US$1.2 billion in 2014 to US$2.4 billion by 2020, and the number of deals increased from 103 in 2017 to 132 in 2018 (KPMG, 2019).

With a growing number of startups, the fintech industry in India has attracted larger investments. Government efforts to promote digitalization, demonetization, Jan Dhan Yojana, Aadhaar and the Unified Payment Interface (UPI), and other digital finance initiatives had a significant influence on the industry's growth and financial inclusion.

The fintech market in India has emerged as highly competitive and having strong growth potential. For new players entering the Indian fintech industry, however, robust control systems often serve as key entry barriers. India has begun to develop into a fintech startup hub, with international investors actively investing in fintech startups. According to the fintechs survey (CB Insights, 2020), India is now ranked third on the global list of the 250 most promising fintech firms, as shown in Figure 13.4.

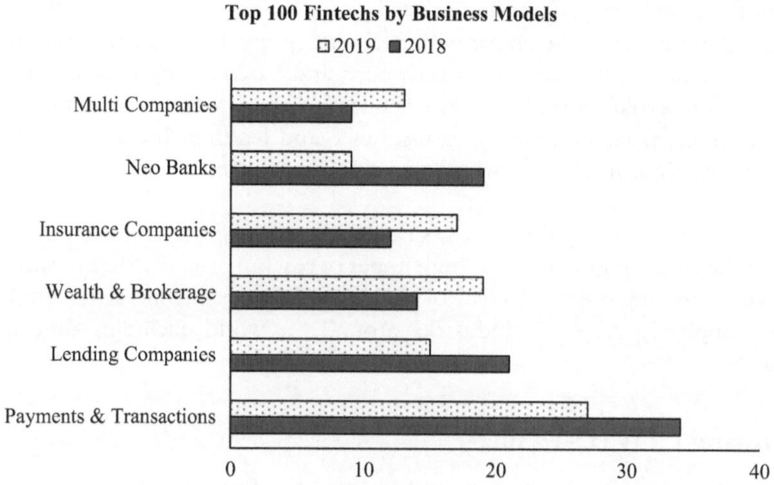

Figure 13.3 Top 100 Fintechs by Business Models.
Source: Author Compilation; Data: Fintech 100. KPMG and H2 Venture (2019), RBI (2020).

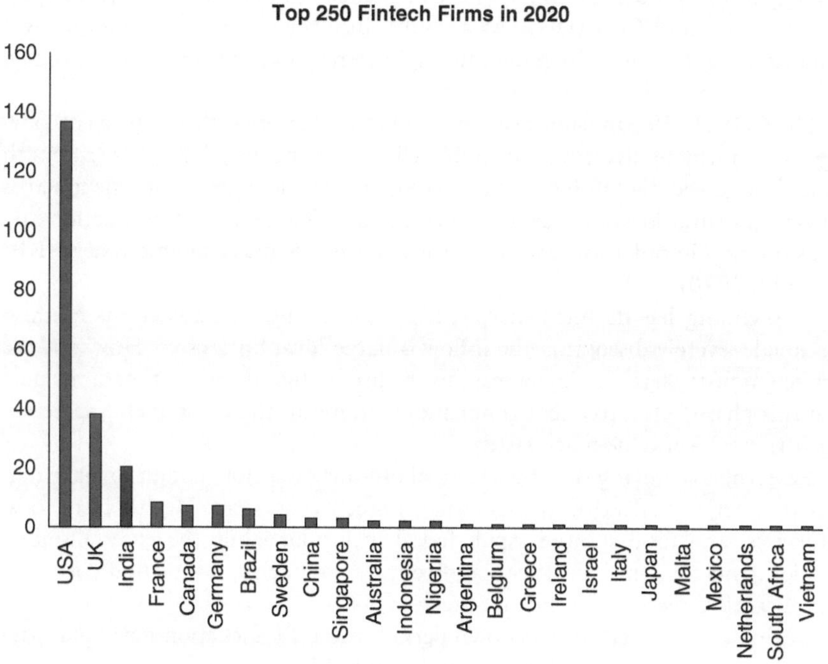

Figure 13.4 Top 250 Global Fintechs in 2020.
Source: Author Compilation; Data: Fintech 250 listing by CB Insights, March 2020.

According to Matrix India and McKinsey & Company, India has become one of the world's major fintech markets by combining finance and technology. India's growth may not be on par with its foreign peers, but it is well-positioned, thanks to a talented pipeline of lower-priced and hardworking people. Fintech services have revolutionized the way organizations and consumers perform routine activities, from fundraising to insurance and lending. India is becoming a more appealing market in the world, as these patterns become more widely adopted.

As mentioned, during the pre-COVID-19 phase, the fintech industry in India was on the verge of growth, with high hopes of reaching the pinnacle of success! However, the unpredictable crisis of the COVID-19 pandemic at the start of 2020 completely shook the industries around the world, including fintech in India.

4 During COVID-19 phase

During the COVID-19 phase, the Indian fintech industry faced one of its most significant obstacles. People relied on online payment and other digital payment methods, such as credit or debit cards, e-wallets, and UPI, to fulfill their financial obligations during the COVID-19 pandemic lockdown. These digital start-up systems enabled people to fulfill their financial obligations without leaving their homes, allowing them to adhere to the mandated social distance policies to prevent the spread of COVID-19. As a result, since the nationwide shutdown was announced in March 2020, numerous digital payment providers have noticed an increase in online payment transactions.

The COVID-19 pandemic also cast doubt on the notion that fintechs encourage investment by assisting vulnerable clients during or after a crisis. Fintech must bridge the digital divide and encourage fair customer involvement across urban and rural locations, as well as across multiple phases of production and consumption in order to create a healthy and sustainable economic system (RBI Bulletin, 2020).

As spending has declined sharply, the value of digital transactions has also declined, severely disrupting the inflow of large local businesses. However, the fintech industry has seen an increase in the use of digital payment methods during this phase. Also, payment companies working in the e-commerce space see their transaction value much faster.

Nevertheless, buying only the essential products was not enough to make digital transactions effective in the Indian fintech ecosystem. Health care, tolls, groceries, and food showed rapid digital inclusion, while the entertainment, fashion, and tourism industries stagnated, thus reducing transaction costs and significantly affecting the Indian fintech industry.

During the COVID-19 lockdown period, the UPI allocation for digital payments in terms of value and volume is shown in Figure 13.5.

Recognizing the uncertainty created by COVID-19, several fintech firms began to face pressure on many fronts. Fundraising has always been difficult, especially for early-stage businesses, and many investors focused on fintechs

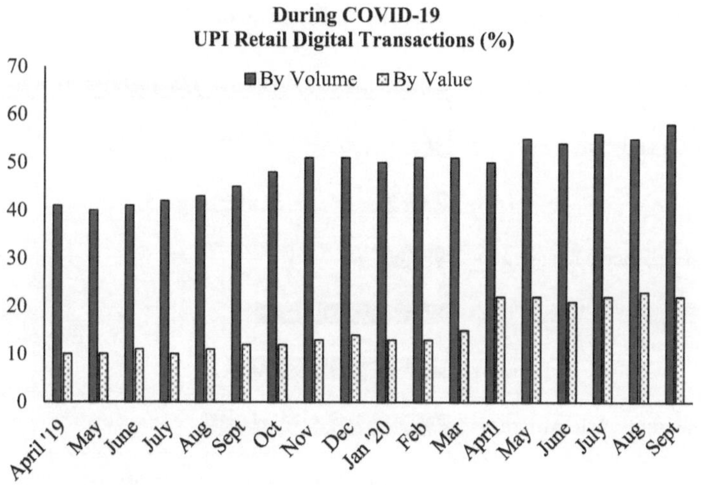

Figure 13.5 Retail Digital Transactions During COVID-19.
Source: Author Compilation; Data: Retail Payment Statistics, National Payments Corporation of India.

established with explicit business models. In addition, declining interest rates and a sharp decline have dramatically altered the thinking of many industries.

Although the fintech businesses among them reported extremely modest performance disruptions, a study of 250 Indian startups confirmed that the pandemic had a detrimental impact on the industry (FICCI-IAN, 2020). According to the MEDICI India Fintech Report, 2020, India's fintech investment grew not only in 2019, but also in the first half of 2020. From January to June 2020, investment in fintech reached US$ 1.47 billion, which is 60% over the same period in 2019. India's fintech start-up revenue doubled in the first half of 2020, which proposes a global downturn. The sector-wise status of fintech startups in India is shown in Figure 13.6.

During the COVID-19 phase, due to lockdown and the mandatory requirement of social distance, online transactions in India have grown by 80% compared to 2019. In terms of consumer credit, urban dwellers received fintech loan services to avoid heavy paperwork during the COVID-19 situation, and rural people benefitted from other forms of access to credit in order to distance themselves from other lenders.

While fintech's global corporate finances are low, some parts of the fintech ecosystem are actually standing for long-term benefits from the COVID-19. Mimicking other sectors, fintech's operations and investments have remained stagnant for the first five months of 2020. Also, while funding is low and some sectors are risky, others have received long-term benefits from the pandemic.

In response to this issue, many fintechs, like the rest of the financial system, have been overworked. Many businesses, such as Insuretech and Proptech, have secured

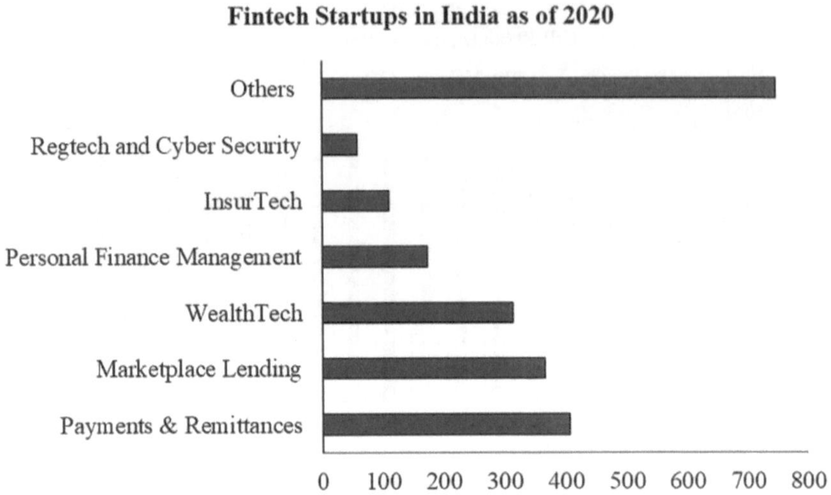

Figure 13.6 Fintech Startups in India as of 2020.
Source: Author Compilation, Data: Statista (2020).

loans and investments from investors and lenders themselves. Others have used better cost-effective methods, such as staff downsizing. Because most of the revenue is based on transaction volume, the most important strategy during the COVID-19 pandemic is to ensure the reduction of fixed and variable costs.

Maintaining stability in performance is obviously important. Customer requests for tolerance and freedom, as well as small business loans established by Coronavirus Aid, Relief, and the Economic Security Act's Payroll Protection Program (PPP), are flooding fintechs in the lending sector (CARES Act). Fintechs, which focus on payments and assets, improve infrastructure by adding capabilities or investing in new investments to withstand the burden of high transaction costs.

Given a large number of startups already in the market, Insuretechs had a tough time attracting investors. In addition, as insurers concentrated on urgent needs and cost control after COVID-19, attracting end-users could be difficult. Current market fluctuations and social trends have hampered the development of the Proptechs sector, forcing investors to stop working until it became clear that they would be able to sell their assets. To keep their clients afloat, some Proptechs offered discounts and competitive deals until the end. Aside from market leaders like Paytm, PolisBazaar, and Zerodha, only a few Indian fintechs have excelled in terms of performance and profitability.

This problem has been compounded by COVID-19. Fintechs' lending finance had a substantial influence on the withdrawal volume decrease of 80%–90%. The payment system has remained relatively unaffected. Despite the fact that transaction volume dropped by 20%–50% at the outset of the lockdown, payment startups saw an increase of more than 10% in average transaction size. Payment players are already seeing volume rebound as economic activity picks up.

Indian fintechs have lessened the influence of COVID-19 by changing their business models in response to the public health crisis and its positive recovery. This has resulted in consistent cost reductions of 15%–20%, performance conversion to semi/full remote, and product roadmap transformations such as closing sectors, delaying product introduction, or introducing new products.

COVID-19 has presented several opportunities for fintechs to partner with those in power to help them accelerate their transformation digitally, as Indian consumers move at an unprecedented rate to digital transactions. Overall, fintechs in India are positive and confident for the foreseeable future, with most of them anticipating a complete recovery by 2021–2022.

5 Post-COVID-19 phase

The COVID-19 pandemic, in general, has caused a lot of stress, but the fintech industry is likely to continue transforming financial services for the benefit of everyone. The post-COVID-19 stage can be seen as a transition or recovery phase from new normal to old normal. Fintech's growth trajectory is projected to continue as it embraces new COVID-19 prospects and leverages its unique assets and capabilities. However, as the COVID-19 pandemic has not entirely vanished and much uncertainty still exists, it is important to proceed with caution.

Fintech's growth rate in India in the pre-COVID-19, during COVID-19, and post-COVID-19 phases are shown in Figure 13.7.

The COVID-19 pandemic has transformed fintech in India. All indications are that fintech has been a prominent sector during the pandemic and beyond, both in business and investments. As the uncertainty of the COVID-19

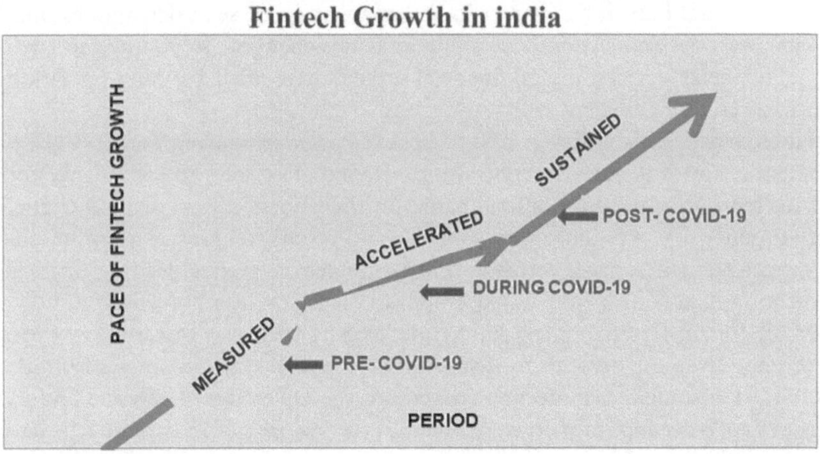

Figure 13.7 Fintech Growth Phase-wise.
Source: Author depiction.

pandemic continues, fintechs are under pressure in many sectors. However, as India's broader economy goes from the response to the recovery process, new opportunities are likely to open up for other fintechs. The key question is how they can use their unique assets and capabilities to take advantage of potential opportunities in the future. It can be a wonderful time to think and act boldly.

After the initial struggle to protect workers, customers, and local communities in India, the fintech sector is now enduring the COVID-19 crisis with relatively positive results. With the lockdowns set globally, large-scale digital payment systems have risen to popularity, and more efficient businesses are starting to use much needed fintechs. Some of the key expected outcomes that will build fintech in India are discussed below:

There are many bright spots in the fintech sector, considering the daunting outlook posited by the global economic downturn. The adoption of digital payments has accelerated, as it has the potential to bring new goods and services to customers and businesses. Fintechs, which distribute digital trading, have seen significant momentum as a result of the closure of several brick-and-mortar stores. The use of fintech applications such as Google Pay and Paytm has increased in India as a result of social distancing initiatives.

In India, during the COVID-19 phase, people and businesses used new digital platforms as needed. In the post-COVID-19 phase, the situation is expected to endure beyond the pandemic, as these Internet users discover new ways of behaving, new best practices, and adapt to a new normal in the digital age. This is particularly true in the case of senior fintech users regarding lockdown health, consumer basic food, online communication, education, and digital content.

Prior to pandemic, it was clear that fintech would play a key role in financial transactions going forward. COVID-19 has undoubtedly accelerated that process. In the post-COVID-19 environment, market models are being re-evaluated to implement new techniques and remote capabilities. During the COVID-19 process, several fintech companies in India saw an increase in demand, as operational practices and customer banking activities changed. In contrast to traditional financial services, digital financial services have made banking operations much faster, more efficient, and less expensive.

Fintech in India is doing its best to benefit customers during the COVID-19 pandemic, and it is likely to continue to expand after the pandemic. Investors are likely to place pressure on companies in their portfolios to reconsider their core product practices, customer support, and results. As long as they are able to monetize their services across common sources of revenue, leading financial institutions can benefit from a new emphasis on digital user knowledge.

Many Indian fintechs have a hard time keeping their way to cash flow open, as revenue levels are difficult to sustain when the real economy suffers from the COVID-19 pandemic. Fintechs may require the collection of revenue and expenses in partnerships or mergers. However, the majority of Indian fintechs have shown resilience, giving them hope of surviving under a crisis. Fintechs have been able to weather disruptions thanks to their high level of financial equity, agile performance, and readiness to accept remote operations. They have also taken steps to mitigate risk and cut costs, including reducing their employment. This indicates that the post-COVID-19 era will likely be more promising.

Although public and private funds have contracted during the COVID-19 phase, it is a threat to fintechs that has just begun. Investors need to replicate certain assets and prioritize profits. For post-COVID-19, however, there is a good investment opportunity and it is combined with prices and terms that suit the buyer. Strategic investors will be looking for new consumer categories or available product features.

Financial inclusion will be a primary emphasis for fintechs, as the international economy recovers from the COVID-19 pandemic. Per World Bank statistics, there are around 1.7 billion unbanked people worldwide, and fintechs will be at the forefront of attempts to bring these people into the global financial system. This will help mitigate the COVID-19 pandemic's economic and societal consequences. Fintechs will help make financial services more democratic by offering basic and transparent financial services to citizens facing economic hardship in conjunction with financial institutions, retailers, and government agencies across all sectors (Deloitte, 2020).

In other disciplines, digital finance is also on the rise. Physical payments have become less effective due to health concerns in the COVID-19 situation, opening the door for more digital payments and e-wallets. Despite the fact that currency was projected to drop everywhere, COVID-19 has expedited that decline because of fears that handling cash could result in virus transmission to humans. According to a Mastercard (2020) survey on the consequences of the COVID-19 pandemic, 82% of respondents worldwide considered contactless as a clean payment method, with 74% saying that they would continue to use it post-COVID-19.

With over 2,100 fintechs, India is considered to be the world's major fintech market, only trailing the United States, China, and the United Kingdom. Despite the significant disruptions caused by COVID-19, fintech companies remain confident about the industry's long-term future. The scenario after COVID-19 will differ from the situation before COVID-19. This world will be proud of a new system of things while helping a different process of people after the lockdown. The persistence of social distance codes will reflect this change and other clean-up lifestyle changes in all sectors that have become commonplace since the onset of the COVID-19 pandemic.

New fintech players who will come up with the right high-tech solutions to make a significant financial impact will be comparable to their peers in the post-COVID-19 market. In conjunction with the reduction of virtual communication space, fintech's digital-based services prevent users from participating in a cash currency exchange that could act as a COVID-19 holder. Given such benefits, it is not surprising that fintechs contain the key to unlocking an extremely secure future despite the pandemic.

India has more than 504 million Internet users, making it the second largest Internet market in the world after China, according to a recent study. Surprisingly, 2019 was a year when the digital divide was growing exponentially, with rural internet users surpassing urban Internet users by 10%, a figure that was expected to increase. As a result, new fintech players were ready to disrupt the rural environment, and the future would see them conquer this segment of the market after the first highly effective solutions designed for rural consumers.

After COVID-19, in addition to a single visual interface for Indian users in all geographies, the fintech environment will see the introduction of new features that will help complete financial services. The new user interface will allow service providers to collaborate and deliver their products so that different services can be delivered on the same platform.

In view of the above, the post-COVID-19 fintech in India is likely to be more closely linked to digital life. All of the above factors indicate that the fintech industry in India could grow stronger in this difficult time of the COVID-19 pandemic by re-focusing on innovation and better principles, which will create opportunities for strategic investors along the way, if they are able to respond quickly to demand.

6 Conclusion and policy recommendations

The goal of cutting-edge fintech innovation is to make existing and future banking services as accessible to as many people as possible. Fintech employs a variety of software, technology, and digital platforms to provide customers with various financial services. It can provide financial products and services to the financially excluded population in a more accountable and efficient manner and in the shortest possible time by modifying traditional financial service companies' business models.

Due to the prevalence of financial exclusion, India has been obliged to implement alternative financial inclusion techniques for decades. One popular initiative is the use of innovative fintech in financial services. Fintech must be fostered to encourage those who are now financially excluded to open bank accounts. Improved monitoring of existing business models, research into the prospects of catering to a bigger and more diverse portfolio, and, most importantly, leveraging the country's high mobile connectivity penetration are all significant aspects.

Offer the necessary motivation for fintech implementation and adoption requires regular public awareness and financial literacy activities for the general public and stakeholders. Furthermore, switching from cash to non-cash purchases may result in a variety of incentives such as rebates, discounts, and subsidies. Close collaboration between stakeholders, including banks, financial institutions, fintech firms, telecom operators, Internet service providers, regulators, and government agencies will be critical to achieving the goal of complete fintech adoption, as it will help to reinforce market forces on both the demand and supply sides of the economy.

The innovative fintech industry also faces financial implications from the nationwide lockdown. However, in the midst of all the challenges, there is an opportunity, and fintech players can use their unique assets and skills to build new opportunities. Digital payments and transactions have seen substantial growth as a result of a pattern of social distance and a zero-touch approach.

This is an opportunity for all to reconsider, innovate, and diversify their methods. Fintech innovations have the ability to transform and reorient the country's ailing financial market.

The COVID-19 pandemic poses opportunities for growth and change, especially at a time when digital financial services can help the prevention of pandemic disease spread. It is important to jointly strengthen the efforts to exchange knowledge and network, depending on other financial structures and the global magnitude of COVID-19. To foster Indian fintech adoption and innovation that will benefit all, policymakers must strengthen their communication, knowledge exchange, and coordination efforts.

In India, a large number of people are not only uneducated and impoverished, but they also lack access to smartphones and the technical skills needed to use such technological services. In comparison to what has happened in the past, India's fintech sector must establish suitable solutions for this target audience.

To combat the rise of digital fraud and cybercrime, the latest updated Know-Your-Customer (KYC) services are required. As the world's commercial and financial institutions become increasingly interconnected, cybersecurity will become progressively more critical in protecting data. Fintech security professionals in India should bear this in mind when developing their products.

New digital products can reduce payment problems during difficult times. Innovative fintech service providers can use the latest methods of physical contactless communication while also making themselves open to a wider audience. These include, among other items, dynamic QR codes, biometric authentication, and contactless card payment. The fintech industry in India must make concerted efforts to provide entrepreneurs with a solid foundation and access to investment so that they have the opportunity to enter and grow through these difficult times.

Increased access to financial services, improved customer experience, and the prevention of fraud and illegal lending in banks are all concerns that innovative fintech firms must address. Fintech and banks working together will allow them to learn from one another, resulting in improved customer service. Banks should be able to control the state of non-performing assets in India using fintech solutions.

The Indian fintech industry should promote advanced applications like artificial intelligence (AI), machine learning (ML), and gig data for better and customized delivery. New business models such as Neobanks should be promoted in the Indian fintech market. Blockchain technology has risen to prominence as a major IT solution for keeping transactions secure and transparent. To fully harness the potential of blockchain and distributed ledger technology (DLT), fintech should do extensive research and build joint ventures with stakeholders.

An innovative fintech is an important tool that can empower policymakers to lead India through the worst challenge it has ever faced, the COVID-19 pandemic. A concerted effort to grow and enhance the innovative fintech industry in India will significantly boost the sustainable development goal (SDG) indicators, including financial inclusion, and help create a stronger, more equitable, safer, and prosperous society, as demonstrated by the relationship between fintech and many of the SDGs.

References

Anikina ID, Gukova VA, Golodova AA, Chekalkina AA (2016) Methodological Aspects of Prioritization of Financial Tools for Stimulation of Innovative Activities. *Eur Res Stud J* 19(2):100–112

Arora R (2020) Can Financial Inclusion Help India Achieve SDGs in COVID Era? Available via: https://medium.com/@reema.arora1983/can-financial-inclusion-help-india-achieve-sdgs-in-covid-era-11cad73108da

Arunachalam RS, Crentsil GLK (2020) Financial Inclusion in the COVID-19 Era. Workshop Presentation Paper. Online Participative Conference. The Financial Inclusion Advocacy Centre

Baiju S, Radhakumari C (2017) Fintech Revolution: A Step towards Digitization of Payments-Review of Existing Literature. *Int J Res Adv Dev* 1(2):1–9

Burragoni VK (2020) Financial Innovations: A Deeper Literature Review with a Focus on India. Available via: https://ssrn.com/abstract=2894973

CB INSIGHTS Research Brief (2020) How COVID-19 is Impacting Fintech Financing'. Available via: https://www.cbinsights.com/research/coronavirus-Fintech-financing-impact/

Chishti S, Barberis J (2016) *The Fintech Book: The Financial Technology Handbook for Investors, Entrepreneurs and Visionaries* (1st Ed.). John Wiley & Sons, pp 51–232

Cornett MM, Adair TA, Nofsinger J (2015) *Finance: Application & Theory* (3rd Ed.). McGraw-Hill Education, New York, pp 197–198

Das S (2020) Banking Landscape in the 21st Century, Speech Delivered at the Mint Annual Banking Conclave

Deloitte (2020) Fintech and SME Navigating COVID19. Available via: https://www2.deloitte.com/content/dam/Deloitte/uk/Documents/financial-services/deloitte-uk-Fintech-and-sme-navigating-covid19.pdf

Desai F (2015) The Evolution of Fintech. Forbes. Available via: https://www.forbes.com/sites/falgunidesai/2015/12/13/the-evolution-of-Fintech/#51fd9a277175 (Accessed on May 24, 2022)

Dhal S (2020) Fintech: The Force of Creative Disruption. RBI Bulletin, Available via: https://www.researchgate.net/publication/345759113

Ernst and Young (2016) German Fintech Landscape: An Opportunity for Rhein-Main-Neckar

Ernst and Young LLP (2017) The Battle for the Indian Consumer. Ernst and Young LLP

FICCI and IAN (2020) Survey on the Impact of COVID-19 on Indian Start-ups

Fu J, Mishra M (2022) Fintech in the Time of COVID-19: Technological Adoption during Crises. *J Financ Intermediation* 50:e100945

GF (2014) Global Findex Data. Available via: http://www.worldbank.org/globalfindex (Accessed on May 24, 2022)

GFLS (2015) Global Financial Literacy Survey. Financial Literacy Around the World: Insights from the Standard & Poor's Rating Services. World Bank Development Research Group. World Bank, Washington DC

Gurung S (2018) Fintech: A Messiah of the Ailing Banking Industry in India. *J Emerg Technol Innov Res* 5(10):159–164

Horgan D, Hackett J, Westphalen CB, Kalra D, Richer E, Romao M, Andreu AL, Lal JA, Bernini C, Tumiene B, Boccia S (2020) Digitalization and COVID-19: The Perfect Storm. *Biomedicine Hub* 5(3):1–23

Jose KJ (2020) Revamping Finance via Fintech: Promises, Perils, and Practices in ASEAN. *Foreign Policy Review* 13:129–144. doi:10.47706/KKIFPR.2020.13.

Kashyap (2016) *The Fintech Book: The Financial Technology Handbook for Investors, Entrepreneurs and Visionaries* (1st Ed.). John Wiley & Sons, p 22

Khan MAI, Rashid MAA, Farooque MMJ (2020) Entrepreneurial Intention to Adopt and Use Fin-Tech Financial Services During the Pandemic: A Case Study of Entrepreneurs in the Gulf Cooperation Council. *Int J Innov Res Multidiscip Field* 6(12):286–293

Koffi HWS (2016) The Fintech Revolution: An Opportunity for the West African Financial Sector. *Open J Appl Sci* 6:771–782

KPMG and H2 Ventures (2019) Fintech100 Leading Global Fintech Innovators

Krishna Priya P, Anusha K (2019) Fintech Issues and Challenges in India. *Int J Recent Technol Eng* 8(3):904–908

Makina D (2019) *Extending Financial Inclusion in Africa.* Science Direct, Elsevier

Margaris S (2016) *The Fintech Supermarket–The Bank is Dead, Long Live the Bank! The Fintech Book: The Financial Technology.* Handbook for Investors, Entrepreneurs and Visionaries, pp 238–240

MasterCard (2020) Mastercard Survey Shows the Global Surge in Digital Payments. Available via: https://www.mobilepaymentstoday.com/news/mastercard-survey-show-global-surge-in-digital-payments/ (Accessed on May 24, 2022)

Muganyi T, Yan L. Yin Y, Sun H, Gong X, TaghizadehHesary F (2022) Fintech, Regtech, and Financial Development: Evidence from China. Financial Innovation. Springer Open. 8:29, pp 1–20

Muthukannan P, Tan B, Gozman D, Johnson L (2020) The Emergence of a Fintech Ecosystem: A Case Study of the Vizag Fintech Valley in India. *Info Manag* 57(8):e103385

Nicoletti B (2017) *The Future of Fintech: Integrating Finance and Technology in Financial Services.* Springer

Olatunji T (2020) Advancing the Cause of Fintech in Nigeria through Regulation. *The Gravitas Rev Bus Propert Law* 11(4):17–34

Oshodin O, Molla A, Karanasios S, Ong CE (2017) Is Fintech a Disruption or a New Eco-System? An Exploratory Investigation of Banker Response to Fintech in Australia. In Proceeding of Australasian Conference on Information Systems. pp 1–11

Ozili Peterson K (2020) Financial Inclusion and Fintech during COVID-19 Crisis: Policy Solutions. Available via: https://dx.doi.org/10.2139/ssrn.3585662, SSRN 3585662

Parameshwar HS, Shruthie A, Cisse M, Kumar MA, Misra S (2019) Fintech and Disruptions: An Impact Assessment. *J Crit Rev* 6(6):88–97

PWC and FICCI (2020) Redefining the Fintech Experience: Impact of COVID-19. Available via: https://www.pwc.in/assets/pdfs/services/crisis-management/COVID-19/redefining-the-Fintech-experience-impact-of-COVID-19.pdf (Accessed on May 24, 2022)

RBI Bulletin (2020) Reserve Bank of India. Fintech: The Force of Creative Disruption

Sanmath A (2018) Fintech Banking: The Revolutionized Digital Banking. *Int J Trend Res Dev* 2018:172–180

Sleeves (2016) *The Fintech Book: The Financial Technology Handbook for Investors, Entrepreneurs and Visionaries* (1st Ed.). John Wiley & Sons, pp 51–179

Statista (2020) Available via: https://www.statista.com/outlook/dmo/Fintech/india (Accessed on May 24, 2022)

Suryono RR, Budi I, Purvandari B (2020) Challenges and Trends of Financial Technology (Fintech): A Systematic Literature Review. Information, Switzerland, pp 1–20

Varga D (2017) Fintech, the New Era of Financial Services. *Vezetéstudomány / Budapest Manag Rev* 48(11):22–32

Vasenska I, Dimitrov P, Davidkova BK, Krastev V, Durana P, Poulaki I (2021) Financial Transactions Using Fintech during the Covid-19 Crisis in Bulgaria. *Risks* 9(48). doi:10.3390/risks9030048

Vatsa VR (2020) Growth of Digital Payments and the Emergence of Fintech in India. *Paripex Indian J Res.* 9(5):40–42

Vijay C (2019) FinTech in India: Opportunities and Challenges. *SAARJ J Bank Insurance Res* 8(1):42–54

14 Fintech approach to assessing innovative SMEs' credit risk

Roohallah Aboojafari and Mahdi Dehghani

1 Introduction

Innovation is vital to economic growth, but it is not easy to motivate innovation and turn it into economic productivity. Firms and entrepreneurs innovate in the context of the socio-economic system. In this context, a well-functioning national financing system is essential, one that affects economic growth through capital accumulation and technological innovation (Levine, 2005). Laeven et al. showed that technological innovation and economic growth depend on a financier's innovation. The financial system should provide a suitable mechanism to finance the innovative project, which is substantial for growth (Laeven et al., 2015).

Innovation process and output are risky, idiosyncratic, unpredictable, and involve a very high probability of failure (O'Sullivan, 2006). From the perspective of investment theory, funding innovative activity such as R&D will underinvest, because it leads to an intangible asset which does not lead to stable earnings; projects often take a long time between conception and commercialization (Hall and Lerner, 2010; Wellalage et al., 2021). Every financial system should innovate to deal with this problem. Financial institutions profit from successful innovative projects, but innovation risks conflict with funding such projects. This trade-off determines the degree of innovation in the financial system (Thakor, 2012). Therefore, financial innovation requires financial resources be provided to companies and innovative activities in sufficient amounts and at appropriate times with reasonable costs to make innovative activity feasible.

The risk with innovative activities and knowledge-based companies is higher than the risk with other companies. Therefore, the process of allocating credit to them requires proper risk management, which aims to reduce the potential for risk by mitigating the probability and impact of losses that may occur. They may be caused by political issues, economic situations, natural factors, or technological advances (Ferreira de Araújo Lima et al., 2020). Financial institutions need to innovate to deal with the problem of managing risk, especially for SMEs.

Many financial firms lack the knowledge, resources, and reliable tools to support the risk management process, particularly for SMEs (Brustbauer, 2016). Researchers usually design risk management models for large companies, and they are inapplicable for small companies. Moreover, their implementation

DOI: 10.4324/9781003220220-18

depend on their capability and affordability. As mentioned by many scholars, the literature has focused mainly on evaluating the risk of large companies, which leads to a gap in the empirical evidence addressing small companies (Kim and Vonortas, 2014). Despite the importance and relevance of SMEs in world economies, only a few researchers have discussed the theme of risk management in them (Ferreira de Araújo Lima et al., 2020; Rostami et al., 2015; Toulová et al., 2016).

Recent advances in financial information and the establishment of data banks and big data have made it possible to provide more appropriate models for risk management of small- and medium-sized enterprises. One-dimension of risk management in small- and medium-sized enterprises is financial risk. Some barriers to funding SMEs caused by the high risk and uncertainty inherent in investments in innovation complicate the situation for both investors and entrepreneurs. Limited information is also a barrier to innovation investment (Lee et al., 2015). Lack of adequate collateral (usually in the form of landed property) for SMEs and startups, which leads to higher interest rates on loans, is another barrier to funding innovative firms (Yoshino and Taghizadeh-Hesary, 2019a; 2019b). In recent years, the surge of financial technologies has opened new possibilities for expanding access to credit for SMEs (Huang et al., 2020). Nicoletti et al. (2017) defines fintech as the application of new technology or innovative business models that leverage data in the financial sector to provide better services.

The Basel Committee on Banking Supervision (BCBS) defines fintech as a company that provides innovative services, a business model, or a startup of new technologies in the financial sector (Giglio, 2021). Fintech is a vast field, and its landscape is changing rapidly. Researchers have categorized this field in different ways. Imerman and Fabozzi (2020) created their taxonomy of the fintech ecosystem. Other fintech financial services are divided into payments technology, digital banking, digital wealth management, capital market, fintech lending, equity crowdfunding, Insurtech, and Proptech (Imerman and Fabozzi, 2020). Fintech lending (Lendtech and so on) uses appropriative technology, algorithms, machine learning, and big data to identify potential borrowers, evaluate their risk, and then set the loan terms, including the loan rate.

Providing financial services to SMEs has been a common problem for policymakers globally because of high information asymmetry. Fintech may be able to mitigate this problem. It offers financial institutions and businesses solutions to control their operational costs and manage their credit risk. Financial institutions use fintech as a platform to run their business operations with minimum cost. Lendtech companies, as part of the fintech industry, provide some solutions for the process of lending and mitigating credit risk. Recent developments in Lendtech reflect advances in credit risk assessment by employing big data and machine learning models. The fintech approach for credit risk assessment is still a new but growing field of research. Developing conceptual models for credit risk assessment will create a good capacity for lendtechs. Therefore, the aim of this study is to examine the variables affecting the credit risk of knowledge-based companies, variables that are required in the evaluation by lendtech companies. Therefore, this research will address the questions of what factors will affect the probability of default of innovative SMEs, and how lendtech companies can use these factors in designing models to assist financial institutions allocate resources.

This chapter shows that the fintech approach of combining hard and soft data significantly improves the accuracy of loan default prediction compared with the traditional approach. Its main focus is the evaluation of the credit risk of knowledge-based companies with specific reference to the information side, mainly for banks. After a short overview of the risk management process, especially for SMEs, the main variables for assessing credit risk are presented in Section 2. The methodology and data are presented in Sections 3 and 4. Section 4 also contains the data set description, explains the analytical strategy, and discusses the empirical results. In Section 5, we summarize the main findings and draw conclusions on policy implications.

2 Financing innovative SMEs and credit risk

Innovative activities like developing a new product, conducting R&D projects, and commercialization include uncertainty and risk. Underinvestment in innovation leads to financing constraints for this activity in the firm. The greatest expense of innovative activities is salaries and wages for scientists and researchers. This human-related investment cannot be collateralized. However, the firm may not wish to offer sufficient signals about the advantages of their innovative projects to credit providers (Hall and Lerner, 2010).

The financial system prepares the capital supply necessary to invest in equipment, construction, and R&D, and it is people that bring new products and services to the market. The financial industry delivers the capital needed to establish a firm and turn ideas into new products, driving innovative economic development (Mastroeni, 2008; OECD, 2013). Previous research has analyzed different parts of the relationship between finance and innovation. Studies on the capital structure and sources of financing consider market failure in financing innovation, internal/personal finance constraints on growth, and the specific role of venture capital (VC) in building high growth firms (Fraser et al., 2015; Hall and Lerner, 2010; Lerner and Nanda, 2020).

Despite the Modigliani–Miller theorem which discusses a specific market situation named by an efficient market, the value of a firm is unaffected by how that firm is financed (Modigliani and Miller, 1958). Myers and Majluf (1984) and particularly Fazzari et al. (1988) laid the foundations for the construction of the pecking order, which brings into evidence the traditional hierarchy in firms' financing sources (Fazzari et al., 1988; Myers and Majluf, 1984). They showed that under an imperfect market for external financing, focusing only on the cost of the financing source does not suffice. Still, the heterogeneity of the firm and financial institution matters. It is noteworthy that the pecking order theory is based on the hypothesis that the role of information asymmetries leads to preferences for cheaper internal financing. Then companies pursue costlier external financing (debt then equity) if there are insufficient internal funds (Kwak, 2021; Myers and Majluf, 1984; Vanacker and Manigart, 2010).

The traditional hierarchy will approximate reality in the usual case, but it will fail to explain firm financing behaviors in some instances. The most critical issue is an innovative project. Goyal and Frank showed, among other things, that the pecking order theory cannot explain the financing of small companies with high information asymmetry (Frank and Goyal, 2003). Lemmon and Zender (2019) argued that high-growth companies will quickly reach their debt capacity and issue outside equity as a last resort (Lemmon and Zender, 2019). Capital structure choice based on asymmetric information and high-risk costs is examined to develop a new perspective on the standard pecking order. Suppose the challenges of financing SMEs and the notion of financial need are essential considerations in capital structure choice. In that case, the model suggests a new approach to empirical examinations of capital structure. This strand of literature leads to the extended pecking order theory (Cumming, 2005, 2012; Lemmon and Zender, 2019).

More specifically, in the financial growth cycle approach proposed by Berger and Udell (which shows different financial resources needed at each stage of a firm's growth), we have seen that for innovative firms compared to traditional firms, risk capital precedes debt capital in the pecking order (Berger and Udell, 1998). The venture capital industry has already played its role of information production to mitigate information asymmetry and reduce the degree of information opacity that the innovative firm can turn into bank credit. The extended or bridged pecking order theory (BPOT) assumes that SMEs move directly from self-funding (internal equity) to external equity (provided by private equity investors or venture capital) in preference to or instead of debt financing (Błach et al., 2020; SAU, 2007). Financing innovation systems based on this approach are more than a banking system and the stock market. Governments intervene because of market failure and the priority setting of their plan. Therefore, the financing innovation system includes the government budget, the banking system, and the stock market. In a way, financial institutions like banks, market mechanisms like rating agencies, and regulatory policies like the central bank are all put together to confront the information asymmetry issue. Banks usually use three methods to analyze and manage credit risk: *financial history*, *collateral assets*, and *soft information* (Huang et al., 2020). Lendtech will propose new services and business models to the financial industry to provide more productive financial services.

Early research on financing innovation at the firm level based on asymmetric-information-based theories helped motivate our study (Aghion et al., 2004; Hsu et al., 2014). These works study the financial system in two aspects: banking and the stock market. The financial system should allow for the possibility of numerous gambles on new opportunities, about which little is known *ex-ante*, but which can reasonably be expected to be, on average, "failures" (Dosi, 1990).

The conventional financial institution will fail to face innovative SME financing. Those more innovative projects will face a "funding gap" that arises when they limit internal and external financial sources for their innovative initiatives (Mazzucato and Penna, 2016). From the functional perspective of the financial system, they produce information *ex-ante* about possible financial needs, supervision of investment projects, and considering corporate governance. They also provide financing, facilitate the trading, diversification, and management of risk, mobilize and pool savings, and ease the exchange of goods and services by the payment solution. However, significant differences in how financial systems meet these functions still remain (Levine, 2005; Merton, 1995).

One reason risk management has received so much ongoing attention is that financial disasters seem to occur regularly to remind us of the perils of "not getting it right." Risk management problems have led to the collapse of financial institutions such as Barings and Kidder and corporations such as Enron and WorldCom. According to the literature, enterprises are exposed to risks categorized into the following four types: financial, hazard, operational, and strategic risks (Lam, 2008). Financial risks (FR) stem from market forces, financial assets, or liabilities. They occur in different forms, such as capital risk, investment risk, interest rate risk, credit risk, currency risk, and financial market risk (Ferreira de Araújo Lima et al., 2020).

Credit risk is known as default risk, which draws the attention of SMEs' credit providers. Intelligent and responsible credit risk management is the bank's most significant profit driver. Hence, credit risk management associated with SMEs lending is central to banks' consumer credit management process. According to Colquitt (2007), credit risk is the potential of a bank borrower/counterparty to fail in meeting the obligations on the agreed-upon terms. A borrower can always default on his commitments (moral hazard) for one or the other, resulting in the crystallization of credit risk to the bank. The inability of an SME to pay interest payments (or repay the principal) will result in a default that might lead to bankruptcy. The default risk increases with the size of the loan because of more constraints on the firm's cash flow as a result of interest payments. Default risk explains why banks credit ration SME loans by giving them small loans. Financial institutions use various credit risk management approaches when extending credit to SME clients, depending on the volume of transactions and facility or loan size.

The banking industry is currently changing in response to swiftly changing customer behavior as well as technological and regulatory realities. Thus, banks must keep pace with changes in technology, such as big data and artificial intelligence. For example, MYbank mainly offers online loans to micro-firms with no credit access. The loans are small, short-term, and used primarily for operational purposes. It gives loans to a firm based on its cash flow more than its assets, and the historical average nonperforming loan (NPL) ratio has been about 2%. MYbank loans are granted with a "contact-free feature." MYbank's lending business is fully digitalized, from customer acquisition to loan underwriting and restructuring. It operates on the so-called 3-1-0 model, which promises user registration and application within 3 minutes, money transferred to an Alipay account within 1 second, and 0 human intervention. The contactless feature has dramatically reduced operating costs and ensured business continuity during the COVID-19 pandemic (Huang et al., 2020). This service would not be possible without intelligent models for assessing credit risk.

To analyze the credit risk of innovation companies, different financial and non-financial dimensions must be considered. When many variables in this field are considered in evaluation models, the necessity of using complex models becomes obvious. For this reason, various studies have examined the variables affecting credit risk. Studies have shown that the different variables affecting the credit risk of innovation companies can be classified into four sections. Table 14.1 shows the categories, variables, and researchers who have referred to these variables.

First, profitability shows the flow of income, profit, and return of the company to the assets and activities. Second, leverage represents the ratio of the company's short-term and long-term debt to its equity and assets. Third, liquidity shows the amount of cash available to the company and the relevant flow. Fourth, activity determines sales and revenue flow, on the one hand, and operating and support costs, on the other. Research shows that in the case of innovative companies, non-financial variables are also influential, including variables such as payment behavior of borrowers, corporate governance, and industry.

Table 14.1 Variables Affecting Credit Risk

Category	*Variables*	*Cited by*
Profitability	EBIT/Sales	Altman and Sabato (2013)
	EBITDA/Total assets	Altman and Sabato (2013), Gupta et al. (2014), Fernando et al. (2019)
	ROA	Altman and Sabato (2013), Arslan and Karan (2009), Kosmidis and Stavropoulos (2014), Donato and Nieddu (2015), Ciampi (2015), Mohammaddoost et al. (2021)
	Retained earnings/ Total assets	Altman and Sabato (2013), Gupta et al. (2014), Donato and Nieddu (2015), Fernando et al. (2019)
	Net income/Sales	Altman and Sabato (2013), Arslan and Karan (2009), Ciampi (2015), Donato and Nieddu (2015), Mohammaddoost et al. (2021)
	Gross profit/Sales	Arslan and Karan (2009), Kosmidis and Stavropoulos (2014), Mohammaddoost et al. (2021)
	EBT/Sales	Kosmidis and Stavropoulos (2014)
	ROE	Kosmidis and Stavropoulos (2014), Donato and Nieddu (2015), Ciampi (2015), Mohammaddoost et al. (2021)
	Operating profit/Sales	Mohammaddoost et al. (2021)
	Net income/Working capital	Mohammaddoost et al. (2021)
	Net income/Fixed assets	Mohammaddoost et al. (2021)

Leverage	Short-term debt/Equity (book value)	Altman and Sabato (2013)
	Equity (book value)/Total liabilities	Altman and Sabato (2013), Kosmidis and Stavropoulos (2014), Ciampi (2015), Donato and Nieddu (2015)
	Total liabilities/Total assets	Altman and Sabato (2013), Arslan and Karan (2009), Kosmidis and Stavropoulos (2014), Ciampi (2015), Mohammaddoost et al. (2021)
	Total liabilities/Equity (book value)	Kosmidis and Stavropoulos (2014), Mohammaddoost et al. (2021)
	Fixed assets/Equity (book value)	Mohammaddoost et al. (2021)
	Long-term debts/Equity (book value)	Mohammaddoost et al. (2021)
	Current debts/Equity (book value)	Gupta et al. (2014), Mohammaddoost et al. (2021)
	Equity (market value)/Total debt (book value)	Fernando et al. (2019)
	Current assets/Current liabilities	Gupta et al. (2014)
Liquidity	Current ratio	Arslan and Karan (2009), Gupta et al. (2014), Kosmidis and Stavropoulos (2014), Ciampi (2015), Donato and Nieddu (2015), Mohammaddoost et al. (2021)
	Quick ratio	Gupta et al. (2014), Kosmidis and Stavropoulos (2014), Donato and Nieddu (2015), Mohammaddoost et al. (2021)
	Working capital/Total assets	Fernando et al. (2019)
	Fixed assets/Total assets	Arslan and Karan (2009), Kosmidis and Stavropoulos (2014)
	Inventory/Total assets	Arslan and Karan (2009)
	Cash/Total assets (market value)	Gupta et al. (2014), Fernando et al. (2019)
Activity	Sales/Total assets	Altman and Sabato (2013), Kosmidis and Stavropoulos (2014), Fernando et al. (2019), Mohammaddoost et al. (2021)
	Sales/Fixed assets	Kosmidis and Stavropoulos (2014), Mohammaddoost et al. (2021)
	Costs/Inventories	Kosmidis and Stavropoulos (2014), Mohammaddoost et al. (2021)
	Financial Expenses/Total assets	Arslan and Karan (2009)
Nonfinancial	payment behavior of borrowers	Sbârcea (2008), Ono et al. (2014)
	innovation capacity/innovation type	Zhang et al. (2013), Oudgou (2021)
	Corporate Governance like Ownership structure and influence	Fernando et al. (2019), Ciampi (2015)
	Industry	Li et al. (2021)

Source: Authors' compilation.

In this section, an efficient and comprehensive scheme for the credit rating of innovative SMEs is presented. Various financial ratios and non-financial variables that describe the characteristics of SMEs and enable banks to categorize their SME customers into different groups are examined.

3 Analysis of innovative SMEs credit risk

Lendtech needs modeling of innovative companies' financial and non-financial data to provide appropriate services to financial institutions. Variables that affect the credit risk of innovative companies were examined, and Table 14.2 shows the variable that can be calculated from the database based on the literature review. Four categorical variables were added from the database, which shows the non-financial behavior of the innovative firm.

For statistical analysis of the data of innovative companies, an Asian country is considered. A unique database of innovative firms with data from 2,831 companies was used for further analysis. In the first stage, the descriptive data of this research is shown based on the extracted variables in Table 14.2. Then, due to the high number of variables, principal component analysis was used to summarize the information into fewer variables. This technique reduces the number of variables to components. In the following, we will evaluate the impact of each component on the default of companies.

Table 14.2 Variables of Model

No.	*Indicator*	*Definition*	*Category*
1	ROA	Net income/total assets	Profitability
2	OPM	Operating profit/total revenues	
3	EBITM	EBIT/total revenues	
4	NPR	Net income/total revenues	
5	GrossM	Gross income/total revenues	
6	RETA	Retained earnings/total assets	
7	NPWC	Net income/working capital	
8	DR	Total debt/total assets	Leverage
9	DE	Total debt/total equities	
10	FAE	Total fixed assets/total equities	
11	TLLE	Total long-term debts/total equities	
12	TCLE	Total current debts/total equities	
13	LTS	Long-term debt/capital	
14	TLS	Total debt to capital	
15	CR	Current ration	Liquidity
16	QR	Quick ratio	
17	WCR	Working capital/total assets	Activity
18	RAR	Total revenues/total assets	
19	TechCat	Technology categories of the firms	Categorical
20	KBTYP	Type of knowledge-base	
21	firmTYP	Type of firms	
22	AgeScale	Age scale of the firms	

Source: Authors' compilation.

3.1 Data description

Loan default refers to a situation in which a company does not pay loan installments. Six months is the soonest that a loan can transition from past due to default, even if the borrower never makes a payment. This definition is based on the regulation of banks or regulatory bodies in each country. In this research, loan default was considered when the company did not repay the loan installment after six months. Financial health and credit behavior are essential for managing credit risk. For this default, the variable derived from our database is a combination of credit behavior and loan default payment named credit soundness. Table 14.3 shows the descriptive statistics of the predictor variables for firm credit quality.

To clear the data and according to the literature, data more than six standard deviations from its average in each section is known as outlier data and is removed from the database. After deleting the data, 1,651 companies remained, of which 163 have defaulted.

3.2 Principal component analysis

Today, large datasets are increasingly used to study different disciplines. Analysis of this data requires statistical methods that can adequately classify this data. One such method is PCA, one of the oldest and most widely used techniques. Its idea is simple—reduce the dimensionality of a dataset while preserving as much variability as possible (Jolliffe and Cadima, 2016). Principal component analysis can also be called the Karhunen–Loève transform (KLT), named after Kari Karhunen and Michel Loève. This method has the additional advantage of indicating what is similar and what is different about the various models created (Ho and Wu, 2009).

Through PCA, the 18 quantity variables listed in Table 14.3 were used to determine the minimum number of components that can account for the correlated variance among SMEs. The Kaiser-Meyer-Olkin (KMO) test and Bartlett's test of sphericity were performed to examine the suitability of the data for factor analysis. KMO is a sampling adequacy measure that indicates the common variance that underlying factors might cause. High KMO values (larger than 0.60) generally suggest that factor analysis may be helpful, which was the case in this study: KMO = 0.72. If the KMO value is less than 0.5, factor analysis would not be beneficial. Bartlett's test of sphericity indicates whether the correlation matrix is an identity matrix, meaning that variables are unrelated. A significance level less than 0.05 suggests that there are significant relationships among the variables, which was the case in this study: significance of Bartlett's test < 0.0000 (Table 14.4).

Next, the number of factors used in the analysis was determined. Table 14.5 reports the estimated factors and their eigenvalues. Only those factors accounting for more than 10% of the variance (eigenvalues > 1) were kept in the analysis. As a result, only the first five factors were finally retained (Table 14.5).

Table 14.3 Descriptive Analysis

Variable	*Mean*	*Median*	*Mode*	*Standard Deviation*	*Kurtosis*	*Skewness*	*Minimum*	*Maximum*
ROA	−3.40599	0.008816	0	56.35915	547.6509	−22.4182	−1640.45	17.05177
OPM	−21.3529	0.019815	0	806.5604	2376.265	−47.6423	−41004.3	73.03855
EBITM	−24.2387	0.002264	0	864.0293	1928.901	−42.7739	−41206.9	36.6663
NPR	−22.7565	0.012776	0	834.1749	2151.056	−45.1498	−41206.9	55.68415
GrossM	0.163656	0.18093	0	2.431745	1086.649	−31.5624	−85.7378	1.235627
RETA	−5.55922	0.006507	0	100.7518	1258.609	−32.4342	−4320.94	0.999669
NPWC	0.163573	0.066776	0	2.479876	106.5711	−1.47645	−46.2112	34.41266
DR	6.278758	0.89813	0.799788	98.08923	1213.056	31.83935	0.000273	4160.348
DE	20.46604	1.674596	3.994693	325.237	1201.141	26.68456	−5730.04	13842.84
FAE	13.1016	0.29969	0	171.6473	482.4588	19.36814	−1183.37	5336.259
TLLE	0.600111	0	0	13.5524	1580.133	37.62326	−35.8547	612.0733
TCLE	19.72932	1.421847	3.958667	319.1601	1280.287	28.81318	−5044.25	13842.84
LTS	451.589	0	0	13783.16	1426.993	37.51264	0	558544.2
TLS	1727.662	21.58169	0.5	16732.29	1079.799	31.09954	0.001239	616514.2
CR	4.728014	0.961686	0.677612	73.94652	2125.517	43.91709	0	3660.862
QR	2.994915	0.101318	0	68.52751	2215.365	45.29832	0	3425.712
WCR	−5.40718	−0.0333	−0.25552	97.32733	1243.271	−32.2271	−4159.35	0.999175
ROA	22.97693	0.820209	0.186928	334.8759	636.6652	23.5967	−49.155	11179.7

Source: Authors' calculations.

Table 14.4 KMO and Bartlett's Test

KMO and Bartlett's Test		
Kaiser-Meyer-Olkin Measure of Sampling Adequacy.		0.7264
Bartlett's Test of Sphericity	Approx. Chi-Square	32059.258
	Df	153
	Sig.	0.0000

Table 14.5 Total Variance Explained

Component	*Eigenvalue*	*% of Variance*	*Cumulative Variance %*
Z1	5.219181	28.99545	28.99545
Z2	2.593427	14.40793	43.40337
Z3	1.862431	10.34684	53.75021
Z4	1.382609	7.681161	61.43137
Z5	1.219198	6.773322	68.20469
Z6	0.97502	5.416778	73.62147
Z7	0.915076	5.083757	78.70523
Z8	0.886563	4.925352	83.63058
Z9	0.636875	3.538193	87.16877
Z10	0.595923	3.310686	90.47946
Z11	0.553043	3.072459	93.55192
Z12	0.441548	2.453045	96.00496
Z13	0.355172	1.973178	97.97814
Z14	0.135944	0.755247	98.73339
Z15	0.122042	0.67801	99.4114
Z16	0.088604	0.492243	99.90364
Z17	0.017224	0.095691	99.99933
Z18	0.00012	0.000667	100

Source: Authors' calculations.

Taken together, Z1 through Z5 explain 68.20% of the total variance of the financial ratios.

Like Yoshino and Taghizadeh-Hesary (2014), the direct oblimin rotation was used to run the principal component analysis. Direct oblimin is the standard method for obtaining a non-orthogonal (oblique) solution; that is, the factors are allowed to be correlated. The pattern matrix must then be studied to interpret the revealed principal component analysis information. Table 14.3 presents the pattern matrix of factor loadings using the direct oblimin rotation method. Variations with significant loadings and absolute values for a given factor are highlighted boldly (Yoshino and Taghizadeh-Hesary, 2015).

As shown in Table 14.6, the first component, Z1, has five variables with an absolute value (> 0.5): ROA, OPM, EBITM, NPR, and GrossMof. For Z1, the variables with significant loadings are mainly OPM, EBITM, and NPR. Hence, Z1 generally reflects the net income of an SME. Because this component indicates the most variance of the dataset, the financial health of SMEs is based on this component. Thus, net income will show the content of this variable. Z2 has four significant loading variables: (a) Retained earnings/total assets, which is positive but not high, shows that SMEs rely less on retained income; (b) Total debt/total assets is negative; (c) The current ratio is positive and means an SME can repay the liability; (d) Working capital/total assets is positive, and the most loading variable shows SMEs need working capital to operate. These four variables indicate an SME with small borrowing and sizeable working capital and retained earnings, and therefore, it has plenty of short-term assets. Z3 reflects the leverage of SMEs. This factor has four variables with significant loadings (total debt/total equities and total current debts/total equities). Z4 shows the most loading factor on long-term liabilities. The last factor, Z5, reflects total revenue. It has three variables with extensive loading: positive values, net income/working capital liabilities, and total revenues/total assets, indicating that total revenue is essential to SMEs.

Table 14.7 shows the correlation matrix of the components Z1, Z2, Z3, Z4, and Z5. None of the correlations are significant, suggesting that using a standard orthogonal rotation method to force an orthogonal rotation would have been applicable.

In this section, 18 financial variables extracted from the literature from our dataset changed to five components based on statistical analysis. According to the data extracted from innovative companies in this Asian country, the variables of Z1 (net-income), Z2 (short-term assets), Z3 (total equity), Z4 (long-term

Table 14.6 Factor Loadings of Financial Variables after Direct Oblimin Rotation

Variables (Financial Ratios)	*Component*				
	Z1	*Z2*	*Z3*	*Z4*	*Z5*
ROA	0.64	0.3	-0.01	-0.03	-0.15
OPM	0.93	0.02	-0.01	0.03	0.01
EBITM	0.96	-0.02	0.03	-0.02	0.04
NPR	0.96	0.01	0	0.01	0.01
GrossM	0.42	-0.18	-0.14	0.24	0.21
RETA	0.19	0.76	0.08	-0.03	-0.16
NPWC	-0.13	0.09	0	0.15	0.49
DR	-0.08	-0.89	-0.02	0.02	0.16
DE	-0.02	0.02	0.97	0.01	0.03
FAE	0.07	-0.08	0.76	0.04	-0.09
TLLE	0.02	0	0.18	0.76	0.03
TCLE	-0.02	0.02	0.97	-0.01	0.03
LTS	0	0.01	-0.11	0.8	-0.06
TLS	0.08	-0.29	0.06	-0.29	0.25
CR	-0.04	0.79	-0.09	0.07	0.29
QR	-0.03	0.5	-0.01	-0.07	0.57
WCR	0.04	0.91	0.02	0.04	0.03
RAR	0.15	-0.22	0	-0.09	0.7

Source: Authors' calculations.

Note: The extraction method was principal component analysis. The rotation method was direct oblimin with Kaiser normalization (Yoshino and Taghizadeh, 2014).

Table 14.7 Component Correlation Matrix

Component	*Z1*	*Z2*	*Z3*	*Z4*	*Z5*
Z1 (Net income)	1	0.41	0.12	0.02	-0.02
Z2 (Short-term assets)	0.41	1	0.04	0.1	0
Z3 (Total equities)	0.12	0.04	1	0.07	-0.11
Z4 (Long-term liabilities)	0.02	0.1	0.07	1	-0.06
Z5 (Total revenues)	-0.02	0	-0.11	-0.06	1

Note: The extraction method is principal component analysis. The rotation method is direct oblimin with Kaiser Normalization; Source: Authors' calculations.

liabilities), and Z5 (total revenue) were considered. These components affect the financial health of a company. We ran a regression analysis to show how these variables affect a company's default using these five components.

Regression analysis was used to examine the effect of these and some non-financial variables. In the next section, the role of these components on the financial health of firms from the perspective of credit risk will be examined.

3.3 Logistic regression

PCA analysis reduces 18 financial variables to five components. Each of them contains information on several variables (financial ratios), and in preparation for these factors, the unnecessary information is eliminated by statistical techniques. Studies have shown that non-financial variables are determinants of the credit behavior of an innovative firm. Logistic regression was applied to analyze how these factors and non-financial variables affect a firm's default probability. Using these variables, we ran a regression for an equation (Eq.1) in which the dependent variable is the default, which is a binary variable (0 or 1). The right-hand side of the equation is a constant (c), 5 components (Z1, Z2, Z3, Z4, Z5), 2 non-financial variables, and u the error term.

$$\Upsilon = c + \alpha_1 Z_1 + \alpha_2 Z_2 + \alpha_3 Z_3 + \alpha_4 Z_4 + \alpha_5 Z_5 + \alpha_6 KB0_6 + \alpha_7 KB1_6 + \alpha_8 Age0_7 + \alpha_9 Age1_7 + u \qquad \text{(Eq. 1)}$$

We used logistic regression to investigate the relationship between SME's corporate default and independent variables using the random over-sampling technique. Independent variables were taken from the calculations of PCA from the previous section, which is explained in Section 3.2. We defined non-financial variables as follows:

KB: Knowledge-Based Type:

0.Non-Startup
1.Startup

Table 14.8 Logistic Regression Results

Coefficients	*Estimate*	*Std. Error*	*z value*	*Pr(>|z|)*	
(Intercept)	−0.65548	0.15686	−4.179	2.93E-05	***
Z1 (Net income)	−0.06594	0.05013	−1.315	0.188365	
Z2 (Short-term assets)	−0.09873	0.05089	−1.94	0.052391	.
Z3 (Total equities)	−0.18297	0.0534	−3.426	0.000612	***
Z4 (Long-term liabilities)	−0.05295	0.04822	−1.098	0.27212	
Z5 (Total revenues)	−0.3565	0.04916	−7.252	4.11E-13	***
KB1	0.476	0.12773	3.727	0.000194	***
Age1	0.56725	0.15951	3.556	0.000376	***
Signif. codes:	0 '***'	0.001 '**'	0.01 '*'	'.' 0.05	0.1 ' '

Source: Authors' calculations.

Age: the age scale of the firm:

0.If < 5 years
1.If ≥ 5 years

As shown in Table 14.8, three (Z2, Z3, and Z5) of the five numerical variables were significant. In addition, all categorical variables had the most significant relationship with the default. As it turns out, Z1 (net income), Z2 (short-term assets) and Z4 (long-term liabilities) had no significant relationship with the default. However, Z3 (total equities) and Z5 (total revenues) had the most significant corporate default relationship. Therefore, an increase of one unit in Z3 (total equities) multiplies the odds of default by 0.83 ($= e^{-0.18297}$). Also, an increase of one unit in Z5 (total revenues) multiplies the odds of default by 0.70 ($= e^{-0.3565}$). As shown in the table above, startup firms have 1.6 ($= e^{0.476}$) times the odds of the non-startup firms to default. Finally, firms more than five years old have 1.76 ($= e^{0.56725}$) times the odds of firms less than five years old to default.

As mentioned in the literature, non-financial variables effectively determine the default of innovative companies. In this case, Lendtech uses the model to predict the default probability base of innovative company's data. Overall, our findings suggest that the default risk rises with total equities and total revenues. It shows that in this business environment, internal resource is essential.

4 Conclusion and policy recommendations

Innovation plays a vital role in contemporary economic development. The development of technology and innovation leads to new products and services, which further leads to the competitiveness of economies. The Schumpeterian creative destruction will ultimately reflect the difference in the development of countries. Nevertheless, innovation is not easily funded in conventional financial markets. Innovation activities have several challenging characteristics that cause underinvesting for them. Firms may be reluctant to provide financial resources for innovation activities if those investments produce nonrival knowledge, thus threatening the firm's ability to get the total returns on their investments. However, innovation outputs are intangible and entail risk, leading to financial friction that makes it difficult for firms to repay funds from external investors.

With the advent of ICT and new technologies, new opportunities to overcome these obstacles were born. It is not surprising that it has changed into a new industry, even in the financial sector. Fintech links the financial industry, information technology (IT), and innovation in a business model.

SMEs usually have severe difficulties with raising money. The difficulty of credit supply leads to liquidity constraints in SMEs. Financial institutions mainly prefer to provide financial facilities to the latter sector. The high cost of evaluating and monitoring SMEs in the absence of credible credit rating companies results in many financial institutions being less interested in lending to SMEs. The Lendtech company is promoting to change the operation in the financial institution to one that uses information. They provide new services, business models, and new data analysis to mitigate the operating costs of financial institutions.

This chapter examined how fintech companies like Lendtech approach credit risk for innovative companies when access to all financial ratios is not feasible. Using a sample of 2,831 innovative SMEs and applying statistical analysis techniques, our results show that by using financial variables in addition to non-financial ones, we can describe the soundness of SMEs.

The 18 financial variables were reduced to five factors in this analysis. This case shows that innovative SMEs rely on internal financings like equity and their activities that create income. Studies have shown that because of the lack of financial data for these kinds of SMEs, non-financial variables are important. We use two non-financial variables to run logistic regression to analyze. Based on our dataset, whether or not SMEs are startups and whether their age is less or more than five years were non-financial variables.

The model shows that Z3 (total equities) and Z5 (total revenues) are significant, and as the literature reflects, non-financial variables are also significant. Innovative companies face liquidity constraints, and if their business model produces cash flow, they can repay their interest. Even if net income does not significantly affect default loans, long-term liabilities and short-term assets have no significant effect.

The policy implication of this chapter is that banks and financial institutions can use Lendtech and their credit risk analysis approach like the one developed in this article. They will help banks and financial institutions recognize SMEs that have proper credit behavior. Expanding their lending to sound SMEs would also help manage credit risk more efficiently. Lendtech will help banks set specific services for different SMEs based on their creditworthiness. This process would reduce operating costs, i.e., lower interest rates for financially healthy SMEs. Ultimately, better services to innovative companies will facilitate economic development.

References

Aghion P, Bond S, Klemm A, Marinescu I (2004) Technology and financial structure: Are innovative firms different? *J Eur Econ Assoc* 2(2–3):277–288. doi:10.1162/154247604323067989

Altman EI, Sabato G (2013) Modeling credit risk for SMEs: Evidence from the US market. In: Roggi O, Altman EI (Eds.), *Managing and Measuring Risk: Emerging Global Standards and Regulations After the Financial Crisis*, pp 251–279. World Scientific Publishing: Singapore

Arslan Ö, Karan MB (2009) Credit risks and internationalization of SMEs. *J Bus Econ Manag* 10(4):361–368

Berger A, Udell G (1998) The economics of small business finance: The roles of private equity and debt markets in the financial growth cycle. *J Bank Financ* 22(6):613–673. doi:10.1016/S0378-4266(98)00038-7

Błach J, Wieczorek-Kosmala M, Trzęsiok J (2020) Innovation in SMEs and financing mix. *J Risk Financ Manag* 13(9):206. doi:10.3390/jrfm13090206

Brustbauer J (2016). Enterprise risk management in SMEs: Towards a structural model. *Int Small Bus J* 34(1):70–85

Ciampi F (2015) Corporate governance characteristics and default prediction modeling for small enterprises. An empirical analysis of Italian firms. *J Bus Res* 68(5):1012–1025

Colquitt J (2007) *Credit Risk Management: How to Avoid Lending Disasters and Maximize Earnings*. Retrieved from: https://books.google.com/books?id=GzzRnN0bFYkC

Cumming D (2012) *The Oxford Handbook of Venture Capital* (Cumming D, Ed.). doi:10.1093/oxfordhb/9780195391596.001.0001

Cumming DJ (2005) Capital structure in venture finance. *J Corp Finance* 11(3):550–585. doi:10.1016/j.jcorpfin.2004.02.004

Donato F, Nieddu L (2015) The effects of performance ratios in predicting corporate bankruptcy: The Italian case. *International Conference on Decision Support System Technology*. Springer, pp 61–72

Dosi G (1990) Finance, innovation and industrial change. *J Econ Behav Organ* 13(3):299–319. doi:10.1016/0167-2681(90)90003-V

Fazzari S, Hubbard RG, Petersen B (1988) Investment, financing decisions, and tax policy. *Am Econ Rev* 78(2):200–205

Fernando JMR, Li L, Hou Y (2019) Corporate governance and default prediction: A reality test. *Appl Econ* 51(24):2669–2686

Ferreira de Araújo Lima P, Crema M, Verbano C (2020) Risk management in SMEs: A systematic literature review and future directions. *Eur Manag J* 38(1):78–94. doi:10.1016/J.EMJ.2019.06.005

Frank MZ, Goyal VK (2003) Testing the pecking order theory of capital structure. *J Financ Econ* 67(2):217–248

Fraser S, Bhaumik SK, Wright M (2015) What do we know about entrepreneurial finance and its relationship with growth? *Int Small Bus J* 33(1):70–88

Giglio F (2021) Fintech: A literature review. *Eur Res Stud J* 24(2B):600–627

Gupta J, Wilson N, Gregoriou A, Healy J (2014) The effect of internationalisation on modelling credit risk for SMEs: Evidence from UK market. *J Int Financial Mark Inst Money* 31:397–413

Hall B, Lerner J (2010) *The Financing of R&D and Innovation* (Vol. 1, Issue Chapter 14, pp. 609–639). In: Hall BH, Rosenberg N (Eds.), Elsevier: Amsterdam

Ho CTB, Wu DD (2009) Online banking performance evaluation using data envelopment analysis and principal component analysis. *Comput Oper Res* 36(6):1835–1842

Hsu PH, Tian X, Xu Y (2014) Financial development and innovation: Cross-country evidence. *J Financ Econ* 112(1):116–135. doi:10.1016/J.JFINECO.2013.12.002

Huang Y, Zhang L, Li Z, Qiu H, Sun T, Wang X, Berger H (2020) Fintech credit risk assessment for SMEs: Evidence from China. In IMF Working Papers (Vol. 2020). doi:10.5089/9781513557618.001.A001

Imerman MB, Fabozzi FJ (2020). Cashing in on innovation: a taxonomy of FinTech. *J Asset Manag* 21(3): 167–177

Jolliffe IT, Cadima J (2016) Principal component analysis: A review and recent developments. *Philos Trans A Math Phys Eng Sci* 374(2065):e20150202

Kim Y, Vonortas NS (2014). Managing risk in the formative years: Evidence from young enterprises in Europe. *Technovation* 34(8): 454–465

Kosmidis K, Stavropoulos A (2014) Corporate failure diagnosis in SMEs: A longitudinal analysis based on alternative prediction models. *Int J Account Inf Manag* 22(1):49–67. doi:10.1108/IJAIM-01-2013-0001

Kwak G (2021) Financing decision of high-tech SMEs in Korea: A revisitation to pecking order theory. *Appl Econ Lett* 28(16):1400–1406. doi:10.1080/13504851.2020.1820437

Levine R (2005) Finance and growth: Theory and evidence. In: Aghion P, Durlauf S (Ed.), *Handbook of Economic Growth*, edition 1, volume 1, chapter 12, pp 865–934, Elsevier: Amsterdam

Lam J (2008) Overview of enterprise risk management. In: *Handbook of Finance*. doi:10.1002/9780470404324.hof003007

Lemmon ML, Zender JF (2019) Asymmetric information, debt capacity, and capital structure. *J J Financial Quant Anal* 54(1):31–59

Lee N, Sameen H, Cowling M (2015). Access to finance for innovative SMEs since the financial crisis. *Res Policy* 44(2): 370–380

Lerner J, Nanda R (2020). Venture capital's role in financing innovation: What we know and how much we still need to learn. *J Econ Perspect* 34(3): 237–261

Li B, Xiao B, Yang Y (2021) Strengthen credit scoring system of small and micro businesses with soft information: Analysis and comparison based on neural network models. *J Intell Fuzzy Syst* 40(3):4257–4274

Mastroeni M (2008). *How Small Economies Finance High-tech Industries: Seeking Variance in Innovation Commercialization*. University of Toronto: Toronto

Mazzucato M, Penna CCR (2016) Beyond market failures: The market creating and shaping roles of state investment banks. *J Econ Policy Reform* 19(4):305–326. doi:10.1080/17487870.2016.1216416

Merton RC (1995). A functional perspective of financial intermediation. *Financial Management*, 23–41

Modigliani F, Miller MH (1958) The cost of capital, corporation finance and the theory of investment. *Am Econ Rev* 48(3):261–297

Mohammaddoost A, Falah Shams Dialestani MF, Eshaghi Gordji M, Ebadian A (2021) Evaluating the factors affecting on credit ratings of accepted corporates in Tehran securities exchange by using factor analysis and AHP. *Adv Math Finanace Appl* 6(1):161–177

Myers SC, Majluf NS (1984) Corporate financing and investment decisions when firms have information that investors do not have. *J Financ Econ* 13(2):187–221

Nicoletti B (2017) Fintech innovation. In: *The Future of FinTech. Palgrave Studies in Financial Services Technology*. Palgrave Macmillan, Cham. https://doi.org/10.1007/978-3-319-51415-4_4

OECD (2013) New sources of growth: Knowledge-based capital. Key Analysis and Policy Conclusions. In *Synthesis Report*. Organisation for Economic Co-operation and Development: Paris

Ono A, Hasumi R, Hirata H (2014) Differentiated use of small business credit scoring by relationship lenders and transactional lenders: Evidence from firm–bank matched data in Japan. *J Bank Financ* 42:371–380

Oudgou M (2021) Financial and non-financial obstacles to innovation: Empirical evidence at the firm level in the MENA region. *J Open Innov: Technol Mark Complex* 7(1):28

O'Sullivan M (2006). Finance and innovation. In: Fagerberg J, Mowery DC (Eds.), *The Oxford Handbook of Innovation*. Oxford University Press: Oxford

Rostami A, Sommerville J, Wong IL, Lee C (2015) Risk management implementation in small and medium enterprises in the UK construction industry. *Eng Constr Archit Manag* 22(1): 91–107

Sbârcea IR (2008). Practical approach to the vision over credit risk at the level of a Commercial Bank in Romania. Identification of credit risk in a credit portfolio granted for agriculture. *Rom Econ Bus Rev* 6(3): 84–101

SAU L (2007) New Pecking Order Financing for Innovative Firms: An Overview. MPRA Paper, 3659

Thakor Av (2012) Incentives to innovate and financial crises. *J Financ Econ* 103(1): 130–148

Toulová M, Tuzová M, Veselá L (2016). Key risk factors in internationalisation of Czech engineering small and medium-sized firms. *Int J Bus Glob* 17(3): 404–422

Vanacker TR, Manigart S (2010) Pecking order and debt capacity considerations for high-growth companies seeking financing. *Small Bus Econ* 35(1):53–69

Wellalage NH, Hunjra AI, Manita R, Locke SM (2021) Information communication technology and financial inclusion of innovative entrepreneurs. *Technol Forecast Soc Change* 163:120416

Yoshino N, Taghizadeh-Hesary F (2014) Analytical framework on credit risks for financing SMEs in Asia. *Asia Pacific Development Journal* 21(2):1–21. doi:10.18356/cb961558-en

Yoshino N, Taghizadeh-Hesary F (2015) Analysis of credit risk for small and medium-sized enterprises: Evidence from Asia. *Asian Dev Rev* 32(2):18–37

Yoshino N, Taghizadeh-Hesar F (2019a) Optimal credit guarantee ratio for small and medium-sized enterprises' financing: Evidence from Asia. *Econ Anal Policy* 62. https://doi.org/10.1016/j.eap.2018.09.011

Yoshino N, Taghizadeh-Hesary F (2019b) Unlocking SME finance in Asia: Roles of credit rating and credit guarantee Schemes. In *Unlocking SME Finance in Asia: Roles of Credit Rating and Credit Guarantee Schemes*. Taylor and Francis. https://doi.org/10.4324/9780429401060

Zhang M, He Y, Zhou Z (2013) Study on the influence factors of high-tech enterprise credit risk: Empirical evidence from China's listed companies. *Procedia Comput Sci* 17:901–910

Index

Page numbers in *italics* refer to figures; those in **bold** indicate tables.